ROMAN IBERIA

Economy, Society and Culture

Benedict Lowe

Duckworth

First published in 2009 by
Gerald Duckworth & Co. Ltd.
90-93 Cowcross Street
London EC1M 6BF
Tel: 020 7490 7300
Fax: 020 7490 0080
info@duckworth-publishers.co.uk
www.ducknet.co.uk

A catalogue record for this book is available
from the British Library

ISBN 978 0 7156 3499 8

Typeset by Ray Davies
Printed and bound in Great Britain by the
MPG Books Group

Contents

Acknowledgements

This book is a distant descendant of a PhD that was completed at Edinburgh, and I would like to reiterate my thanks to my original advisors John Richardson, Glenys Davies and Robert Curtis whose support has continued to be instructive. I would like also to thank Deborah Blake and her colleagues at Duckworth for their patience in dealing with a recalcitrant writer. I would like to thank the interlibrary loan staff of the Hamersley Library at Western Oregon University – in particular Lori Davidson – for their strenuous efforts to track down often obscure publications on my behalf.

The expertise and supportiveness of colleagues in Spain is a constant source of delight. I would like to thank the following for answering questions, providing published materials as well as other queries: Rafael Carmona Avila, Maria Dolores Costa of the Institut d'Estudis Empordanesos, Josep Muntal Muns of the Museu de Granollers, Francesc Aicart, Jordi López of the Reial Societat Arqueològica Tarraconense, Engràcia Torrella Suñé, the Directora of the Museu d'Art de Sabadell, Miquel Martí i Llambrich, Director of the Museu de la Pesca, Pilar Maldonado of the Real Academia de Córdoba and Anna Fuentes Fernández, the Directora de Patrimonio Cultural of the Ajuntament de Lloret de Mar. I would like also to thank the following institutions for their assistance: the Museu Comarcal del Maresme in Mataró and the Centro de Ediciones, Diputación de Málaga. It goes without saying that they improved but did not shape this book and whatever errors remain are my own contribution.

I would like to thank my wife Christy for her comments on the text and for her corrections to my Latin and Greek. My parents have proven a constant source of support and have helped in every way. It is to them – and to my brother – that this book is dedicated, as albeit inadequate repayment for all that they have done over many years.

Abbreviations

CIL = Deutsche Akademie der Wissenschaften zu Berlin, *Corpus inscriptionum latinarum* (G. Reimer, 1862-).
FGH = F. Jacoby, *Die Fragmente der griechischen Historiker* (Weidmann, 1923-58).
IG = Deutsche Akademie der Wissenschaften zu Berlin, *Inscriptiones Graecae* (G. Reimer, 1873-).
RIT = G. Alföldy, *Die römischen Inschriften von Tarraco* (W. de Gruyter, 1975).

List of Illustrations

1

Romanization and the Ancient Economy

The goal of this book is to explore the economic consequences of Rome's conquest of the Iberian Peninsula. Previous studies have viewed the consequences in political and social terms. Where the economy is discussed, it is treated as a facet of a far larger study on cultural change and Romanization. The goal of this study, therefore, is to examine the economic underpinning of the process of Romanization – essentially to ask whether or not Rome's conquest was economically beneficial to the native communities of the Iberian Peninsula. How did the native communities respond to external influences? What impact did contact with Rome have upon the economy of the Peninsula? Did the demands of the Roman state cause changes in the organization and scale of production at a local level? This is not to say that the economy should be divorced from its social and political context, but that the economy can be used as a starting point for analyzing the natives' response to the Roman conquest.

'Romanization' is a descriptive term used to describe the process of transformation brought about by interaction with Rome. The term is a modern one, first coined by Theodore Mommsen.[1] The fifth volume of Mommsen's *Römische Geschichte*, published in 1885, deals with the provinces of the Empire. Mommsen chose to structure his discussion of the western provinces around certain Roman institutions that the provinces had in common. These institutions then became the yardstick against which the adoption of Roman lifestyles – Romanization – could be measured. The early studies of Romanization were shaped by the imperialist perspectives of the nineteenth century. Implicit was a belief in the superiority of Roman culture over that of the barbarous provinces. What one thinks of Romanization is very much dependent upon what one thinks of imperialism. Romanization is often used interchangeably with 'assimilation' and 'acculturation'; however, it does not specify the means by which this process was carried out.

Central to the definition of 'Romanization' is the question of what actually was 'Roman'. Barrett (1997, 51) has pointed out that Roman culture was neither homogeneous nor static. It really only came to be defined during the age of Augustus. Many facets of Roman culture were borrowed from the Hellenistic world, making it difficult to distinguish a specifically Roman culture from the broader Hellenistic milieu. Nor could the Italians be considered truly 'Roman': in many parts of Italy indigenous cultures persisted until the first century AD (Keay 2001, 129). Romanization is often identified by the incidence of material evidence, such as adoption of Roman urban models, urban and rural architecture, roads, imported ceramics, the use of Latin and the Roman epigraphic habit. There is a tendency to see Romanization as a process that affected the entirety of the Peninsula in one form or another. The geographer Strabo (1.4.9) distinguishes between a civilized society and a barbarian one on the basis of law, political life, education and rhetoric. According to Tacitus (*Agricola* 21) it was the appearance of Roman architecture (temples, *fora* and housing), urbanism, the use of Latin, Roman dress and the amenities to support an appropriate lifestyle (arcades, baths and banquets). If these features are found then they are attributed to a successful policy of Romanization. Conversely, their absence indicates a failed Romanization. Our whole conception of Roman expansion implies a diffusionist perspective in which the natives are reduced to recipients. The agents for this process are usually seen as the presence of Romans and Italians either through the presence of the army, veterans or their offspring, or the gradual influx of merchants and businessmen.

Various reasons have been given for the process of Romanization and are worth reiterating here, although all present varying problems. One holds that Romanization was a 'top-down' process whereby the Roman state imposed Roman culture. Rome's civilizing mission is outlined by Virgil (*Aeneid* 851-2) and the sense of the cultural superiority of Rome is evident from the passages of Strabo and Tacitus mentioned above. Polybius (1.63.9) suggests that Rome had a deliberate policy of expansion, and with it a deliberate policy of acculturation exemplified by the commonalties observed by Mommsen. Mary Downs (1996, 32) has argued that Romanization is valid only as a descriptive term and that 'integration' is a more appropriate analytical concept to explain the incorporation of native cultures into the Roman world. Downs has proposed five variables that need to be considered to determine the outcome of the interaction between Roman and native (1996, 70-1). First, the cultural development and history of the native communities – and thus their adaptability to the Roman model. Secondly, the physical geography and environment that dictated the location of settlements and trade routes. Thirdly, the date of the conquest – there was little settlement and consistent policies towards the provinces until the first century BC. Fourthly, the circumstances and motivation of the conquest. Finally, the natives' response to the Roman conquest.

Increasingly, however, scholars have argued that there was no deliberate strategy of expansion and that Roman conquest came about through a series of short-term responses to a variety of different situations. Mary Downs (1996, 42) has noted the difference between the establishment of a *provincia* in the sense of a sphere of command and the establishment of Roman control. The lack of a consistent strategy and the character of the Peninsula as a disturbed frontier zone delayed the establishment of Roman control prompting a 'laissez faire' attitude towards the organization of the provinces. A salutary example is offered by the *Tabula Contrebia*. This inscription records the adjudication of a dispute in 87 BC over the construction of a canal between the communities of the Salluienses (modern Zaragoza) and the Allavonenses (modern Alagon) by the senate of Contrebia Belaisca on behalf of the governor C. Valerius Flaccus. The inscription is significant on several counts: the decision of the governor to have the case adjudicated by the municipal senate of Contrebia Belaisca, and the use of Roman legal terminology despite the fact that the case is not subject to Roman law and is decided on the basis of local rights and customs (Richardson 1983, 36-8).[2] As well as the imposition of Roman culture by the Roman state, acculturation may also have been encouraged by the native elite who adopted the trappings of Roman culture to enhance their status in the eyes of Rome as well as in their own communities.

Classical scholarship from the end of the twentieth century has done much to try to view Romanization from alternative perspectives, as the result of both Roman initiative and native reaction (e.g. Garnsey *et al.* 1987, 186). A process of 'self-Romanization' has been suggested whereby the adoption of Roman culture was prompted by native rather than Roman concerns (Sherwin White 1973, 222). All these models share the assumption that Romanization was a one-way process with the natives adopting Roman practices. While this approach is in part justified by the nature of our sources – both the archaeological and literary records are created or shaped by Romans – it does little for the study of the impact of the Romans on the provinces.

Alternatively, Romanization can be seen as an interactive process between Roman and native in which both cultures are transformed, leading to a hybrid provincial culture. 'Romanization was not a goal to be achieved; it was a phenomenon brought about through the fusion of two cultures' (Curchin 2004, 14). In a textual tradition dominated by Greek and Latin sources, the role of the native has been largely ignored in favour of an overwhelmingly positivist and diffusionist view of the relationships between Rome and Italy and the provinces. Not only are our fullest literary sources rarely contemporary, but even when contemporary accounts can be transmitted they are transmitted indirectly or shaped by literary conventions or audiences that take precedence over 'factual' accuracy (Keay 2001, 120).

Faced by the problems inherent in the term Romanization it would be tempting to reject the term completely in favour of an alternative construct. To do so, however, seems excessive: properly defined the term still retains value. Romanization was a process of cultural change brought about through interaction with the Roman world. The form that this change took, however, was determined by a variety of internal and external factors at the local, provincial and imperial levels – meaning that there was the potential for striking variations from one area to another. Not only could the physical manifestation of Romanization vary but so too could perceptions and responses to the changes therein. Particular features could be perceived differently by the inhabitants of a Roman colony, for example, compared to those of a *municipium* or indigenous *oppidum*.

Characteristic of all of these approaches is the concentration on the social, cultural and political aspects of Romanization. What is missing is an analysis of the economic impact of contact with Rome, and which in turn financed many of the archetypes of a Roman lifestyle.

L.C. West's *Imperial Roman Spain: Objects of Trade* (Oxford, 1929) provides a list of literary references for exports from the Iberian Peninsula. The impression given is of a wide variety of commodities and a scale of economic activity that has been likened to the 'modern' economy. While the literary source may be noting a particular exchange because it is exceptional, these references reflect a wider exchange of goods that were not deemed of note. For the economy to remain solvent there has to be a balance of trade: for each export there is an import. Thus the movement of goods outlined by West in turn fosters trade in secondary cargoes and other goods that are not attested in the literary record. The stability brought by the establishment of the *pax romana* enabled the creation of an infrastructure to support large-scale exchange. The movement of goods entailed the appearance of professional artisans and merchants who in turn played an increasingly important role in their communities. The Elder Pliny (*Natural History* 36.160) refers to *lapis specularis* (modern selenite) from Segobriga, the profits from the sale of which Curchin suggests is evident in the monumental architecture of Segobriga and in the presence of senatorial and equestrian families (2004, 148).

West's approach is fallacious on several counts. The literary evidence tells us little about the scale or purpose of these exchanges, their profitability or economic significance. In reaction to the 'modernizing' view of the economy, Sir Moses Finley argued for a more 'primitive' model in which a conception of the economy was absent. Production was primarily agrarian and limited to the demands of self-sufficiency: the 'widespread prevalence of household self-sufficiency in necessities was enough to put a brake on extensive production for export' (1973, 138). The lack of technological advancement, the two-year fallow cycle and the high costs of land transport limited the volume of exports (Finley 1973, 108). Although urban centres existed they were economically parasitic, relying upon the resources of their agricultural hinterland rather than developing manufacturing industries of their own (Finley 1973, 135). The homogeneity of the Mediterranean environment meant that dietary staples such as cereals, wine and olive oil were found throughout, so that there was no demand for their exchange. Communities instead focused on self-sufficiency. Where larger-scale production did occur, for example the manufacture of *terra sigillata italica* at Arezzo, the individual operations remained small-scale and the individuals involved were peripheral to the Roman social hierarchy (Finley 1973, 116).

However, the validity of Finley's arguments has been overturned by the growing volume of archaeological discoveries in recent years not only of sites engaged in economic activities on a larger scale than mere self-sufficiency, but also of the distribution of product containers (amphorae) and shipwrecks carrying amphorae. The distribution of particular types of pottery could be extensive: as early as the eighth century BC Attic SOS amphorae were found in Crete, Cyprus, Sicily, Italy and Spain. Whittaker (1985, 58) has even argued that the ideology of self-sufficiency was so pervasive that wealthy landowners would transport their produce over long distances to serve their own needs. Reliance on ceramic containers such as amphorae leads to a bias in our perception of the ancient economy in favour of products that were carried in ceramic vessels. Pottery vessels are much more common in the archaeological record than other forms of container such as barrels or sacks. The evidence for the high cost of land transport comes principally from Diocletian's Edict on Maximum Prices which gives the maximum cost for transport, not the actual cost. On the contrary, land transport may have been preferable, being more reliable and free from the hazards of the climate (Morley 2007, 26-7). This is not to deny the importance of maritime trade (the distribution of imported pottery makes clear the importance of the sea and rivers) but rather to emphasize that the choice is more complicated than it is often portrayed.

Reliance on the archaeological record can present many of the problems inherent in a text-based approach. While archaeology can show that trade took place, it cannot tell us why or in many cases by whom. In order to fully understand the operation of the ancient economy it needs to be viewed within its broader cultural setting. The ancient economy was as much about displaying adherence to a set of cultural values as it was about profit and logistics. The value of a particular commodity is not restricted to its financial worth but may instead reflect one's social or political status and identity or one's acceptance or rejection of cultural or political values (Morley 2007, 13). Exchange does not have to be purely profit-driven and self-sufficiency should not be dismissed as unproductive (Morley 2007, 9). While Roman agricultural writers repeatedly offer advice to landowners on how to maximize the return from their estates they say little about the marketing of this surplus. The homogeneity of the Mediterranean has been overstated: as any reading of Strabo or the *Periplus Maris Erythraei* makes clear, the ancients were aware of regional variations in supply and demand. Variations in supply are inherent to agrarian societies and can be alleviated by the import of goods from areas in which supplies are more abundant. Technological innovations introduced by the Romans made it increasingly possible to escape these environmental constraints. The most obvious examples of the susceptibility of exchange to geographic constraints are the availability of mineral deposits – in particular copper, silver, gold and tin.

The nexus of this exchange was the markets created by towns. Even though the environment created conditions that encouraged exchange, exchange would not have taken place without sufficient demand. Merchants would seek to ensure that the potential profits would outweigh the risks of any commercial undertaking. Keith Hopkins has calculated that the city of Rome needed to import 200,000 metric tons of wheat, of which only 80,000 was supplied by the *annona*, the remainder by private exchange (1983, 88). This would have in turn fostered the movement of secondary cargoes. The elite of the Roman world was primarily urban, therefore it was in towns that there was sufficient capital to create a demand for goods. Towns functioned as opportunities for competition as the elite sought to display social, economic and political authority. However, unlike Finley's view of towns as 'parasitic', variations in supply meant that the resources of their hinterlands alone could rarely meet the demands of towns. The generation of a tradable surplus generated revenue that could then be invested in the growth of the town. Thus the creation of towns led to the growth of trade. Even where towns were small enough to be largely self-sufficient an infrastructure had to be created to ensure the supply of resources from the surrounding hinterland. While the risks of commercial activity ensured that many farmers remained self-sufficient, the opportunities for profit offered by new levels of demand could be exploited by the farmers and landowners with the resources to do so. Thus exchange was channeled into areas best suited for commercial exchange (possessing good communications, resources, demand, available capital) whereas other parts of the Peninsula seem to have been relatively untouched by the Mediterranean market economy. According to Mary Downs (1996, 97): 'it is natural to posit an increase in levels of production in areas that were engaged in production for export. But there is no reason to assume that these levels were attained in other areas or that there were major changes in practices or in the basic subsistence economy.'

Several possible models have been suggested for the mechanisms of exchange: reciprocity, gift exchange and prestige trade where the value of the trade is determined not by economics but by what it represents. The ability even to conduct trade was a symbol of status: during the Republic legally binding contracts were limited to Roman and Latin citizens and to those who had been granted the *ius commercii* (Ulpian *Tit.* 19.4; Morley 2007, 69). The appearance of Roman goods within the communities of the Iberian Peninsula reflects not merely the existence of exchange but the creation of an infrastructure within which exchange could take place: the creation of a demand and the ability to meet this demand. Individual finds tell us little about the frequency of this exchange or its profitability. The importance of a commodity may well rest in its rarity and what it says about the social status, aspirations and allegiance of both its owner and its audience. The elite would initially use access to imported goods as a symbol of identity, but these same goods would then be imitated by peripheral members of the elite and by the lower echelons of society. This in turn fostered a need for more imported goods as the elite sought to reinforce their status.

The presence of Roman administrators and soldiers provided a stimulus to production and a demand for imported goods.[3] As well as the Romans and Italians themselves, there was also a hybrid population born of the Roman and Italian soldiers and native women – 4,000 of whom made up the population of the *colonia civium Latinorum et libertinorum* at Carteia in 171 BC (Livy 43.3). However, we need to be aware of the ethnicity and location of the individuals involved. While merchants and soldiers would have consisted of primarily non-elite Romans and Italians, the administration would have included elite Romans – who would then interact with the native elite.

The presence of imports may be due not only to commerce, but also to other forms of exchange – prestige trade, gift exchange or as taxes or tribute to supply the Roman government, army or settlers. We need to also consider what meaning both the Romans and natives placed on this exchange. While Roman and Italian imports follow patterns of trade that existed in the Iberian and Orientalizing periods, the mechanisms of this trade were altered by the creation of new demographic and economic parameters and the agenda of Rome towards the provinces. One of the most important advances of recent years has been to view artifacts such as pottery not merely as footprints of the advancing Roman presence but as manifestations of social and cultural values and meanings.

The locations in which exchange could take place were not only shaped by geography but by social, cultural and ideological concerns. The distinction between the fertile south and the inhospitable interior may be more ideological than real – reflecting a Roman view of the civilized south and the barbarous and hostile interior (Downs 1996, 94). Appian (53) attributes the warlike temperament of the inhabitants of the Meseta to their lack of agricultural resources.[4] The south and east of the Peninsula – Valencia, Murcia and Almería – consist of wide coastal plains that are dry and almost desert-like. The Sierra Morena extends from southern Portugal to the Sierra de Segura and separates Andalucía from the interior. The mountains are rich in copper, iron and argentiferous lead that has been exploited since the Neolithic at Azuaga-Fuenteovejuna and Los Pedroches (Domergue 1990, 110-11). The Subbetic mountains separate the Guadalquivir valley from the southern coast. The Subbetic mountains are not impassable but are cut by tributaries, such as the Guadalhorce-Guadalteba-Turón, which provide access inland from the coastal plain. The valley of the Guadalquivir extends for 500 km from the Bay of Cádiz to the Sierra de Cazorla in the province of Jáen. The climate is Mediterranean with long hot summers and cool, wet winters. The alluvial *campiña* to the south of the river is rich in olive oil, wine and cereal crops (Strabo 3.2.4-6; Pliny *Natural History* 3.1.7) as well as providing access to the mineral resources of the surrounding mountains. The wealth of the region prompted tales of the kingdom of Tartessos. The rest of the Peninsula has a predominantly continental climate.

By examining the economic organization of the Iberian Peninsula within its demographic, cultural and physical environment, I believe I can demonstrate that the Peninsula shows a greater degree of continuity (and economic growth?) than has previously been recognized. This continuity can only be discerned by first examining the economic state of the Peninsula prior to the arrival of the Romans. In order to understand this process we need to be aware of the previous economic history that shapes this integration. The conventional view of the replacement of a 'redistributive' economy with a 'monetary' economy implies a more primitive economy for the pre-Roman period that can only be corrected by exploring the economy of the Peninsula prior to the Roman conquest (Downs 1996, 96). Archaeological artifacts are as much a consequence of their immediate environment as a product of a cultural milieu that evolved over the preceding millennia (a point made by Keay 2001, 120). With this in mind, therefore, and in contrast to other studies that have focused on a particular region or period, I shall begin with the eighth century BC and the impact of Phoenician trade on the Peninsula.[5]

2

Expanding Horizons

Phoenician colonization

The Phoenician colonization of the Iberian Peninsula has been the subject of considerable debate, thanks to the nature of the evidence and the perception of the Phoenicians in European scholarship. Although recent scholarship has done much to remedy the misconceptions surrounding the Phoenician settlement of the Western Mediterranean, areas of debate remain: the date at which the initial settlement took place, the reasons for the colonial venture, the function of the settlements themselves, and their relationship with the native communities.

These uncertainties derive in no small part from the nature of the archaeological record: until the discoveries of the 1960s, evidence of the Phoenicians was limited to scattered funerary remains that offered little information for the settlements themselves.[1] In addition to scattered finds from Cádiz, Vélez-Málaga and Almuñécar, the most important site was the necropolis of Villaricos (Almería), excavated by Louis and Henri Siret from 1890 to 1914. The impact of the discoveries at Villaricos was limited by the lack of extensive publications of the early excavations – what publications there were concentrated upon a typology of the tombs and of grave goods, offering little for the study of Phoenician settlement more generally. Further to this, Siret's dating of the burials at Villaricos – the earliest graves were dated to the sixth century BC and continue until the first century AD – means that they add little to our knowledge of the initial phases of the Phoenician settlements.

The problems facing the interpretation of the finds from Villaricos are symptomatic of Phoenician archaeology during the first half of the twentieth century. The lack of archaeological evidence led scholars to rely upon the literary sources for the initial phases of settlement. We need to be aware, however, of the context of these references. No Phoenician sources survive and we are limited to scattered references in later Greek and Latin writers. The fullest account of the initial Phoenician colonization comes from Posidonius and is preserved by Strabo (3.5.5).[2] Strabo's account is worth recounting in full:

> In telling the stories of the following sort about the founding of Gades, the Gaditanians recall a certain oracle, which was actually given, they say, to the Tyrians, ordering them to send a colony to the Pillars of Heracles: The men who were sent for the sake of spying out the region, so the story goes, believed, when they got near to the strait at Calpe [Gibraltar], that the two capes which formed the strait were the end of the inhabited world and of Heracles' expedition, and that the capes themselves were what the oracle called 'Pillars'; and they therefore landed at a place inside the narrows, namely, where the city of the Exitanians now is [Almuñécar]; and there they offered sacrifice, but since the sacrifices did not prove favourable they turned homeward again; but the men who were sent at a later period went on outside the strait, about fifteen hundred stadia, to an island

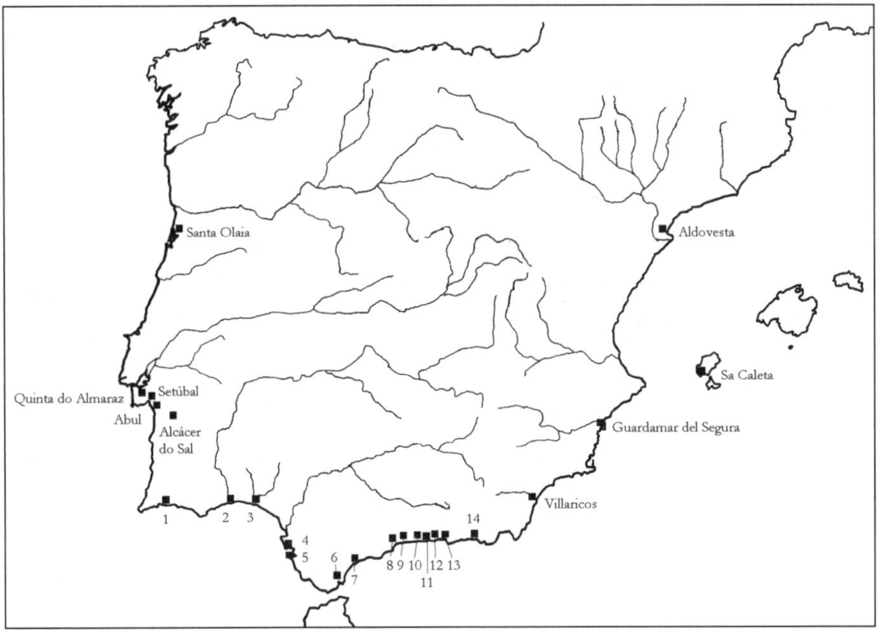

Map 1. Phoenician and native settlement during the Iron Age.

1. Cerro da Rocha Branca
2. Castro Marim
3. Huelva
4. Castillo de Doña Blanca
5. Cádiz
6. Cerro del Prado
7. Montilla
8. Cerro del Villar
9. Málaga
10. Toscanos
11. Morro de Mezquitilla
12. Chorreros
13. Almuñécar
14. Adra

> sacred to Heracles, situated near the city of Onoba [Huelva] in Iberia, and believing that this was where the Pillars were they offered sacrifice to the god, but since again the sacrifices did not prove favourable they went back home; but the men who arrived on the third expedition founded Gades [Cádiz], and placed the temple [of Melkart] on the eastern part of the island but the city in the western. (trans. H. Lloyd Jones, 1924)

According to Velleius Paterculus (1.2.1-3), the foundation of Cádiz took place eighty years after the fall of Troy, or *c.* 1103 BC.[3] It is difficult, however, to determine the reliablility of this date due to the lack of archaeological evidence from the city of Cádiz. The ancient settlement was spread over three islands: Erytheia, Kotinoussa, which housed the temple of Melqart, and Antípolis, perhaps the modern San Fernando (Aubet Semmler 1993, 223-30; Ponce 2000, 906-10). The exact location of the ancient settlement has been object of considerable debate. The earliest finds come from excavations on the Calle Concepción Arenal and Calle Botica in Santa María – the westernmost point of ancient Kotinoussa – and date from the mid-eighth century BC (Lavado Florido *et al.* 2000, 871; Muñoz Vicente *et al.* 2000, 882-3). A proto-Aeolian limestone column capital dating from the eighth to seventh century BC was recovered from the water on the south side of the island of San Sebastian and may have come from the temple of Melqart (Aubet Semmler 1993, 230).[4]

A second-millennium date for the foundation of the earliest Phoenician colonies has been contradicted by the discoveries of settlements along the Málaga coast that have taken place since the 1960s. The earliest occurred in March 1962 with the discovery and subsequent excavation of the necropolis of La Laurita on the Cerro de San Cristóbal that lies 800 m to the northwest of the castle at Almuñécar. Almuñécar – ancient Sexi – has already been mentioned as the first of the locations that Strabo says was settled by the Phoenicians prior to founding Cádiz. The ancient settlement lay on the rocky promontory of the Cerro del Castillo de S. Miguel between the hills of Cerro de San Cristóbal and Cerro de Velilla, overlooking the mouths of the Ríos Seco and Verde. Little excavation has been possible in the area of the settlement as it underlies the modern town. Finds of red slip plates in the Plaza de la Constitución and Calle Real date the urban centre to the mid-eighth century BC (Molina Fajardo 1991, 14).

Red slip plates are a particularly important tool in establishing the chronology of the early phases of the Phoenician colonies. Red slip pottery is typical of the Late Bronze Age in Phoenicia and Cyprus from the second millennium to the mid-first millennium BC (Maas-Lindemann 2000, 1596-7). Hermanfrid Schubart (1976) has proposed a chronology based on the diameter of the rim of the plate and the ratio of the width of the rim to the diameter of the plate. The rim size steadily increased with the passage of time. Schubart correlated the evolution of the red slip plates with the results of stratigraphic excavations on the Bay of Málaga – particularly those of Toscanos – to provide a chronology of the earliest settlements. The plates are divided into three groups: those from the earliest levels at Morro de Mezquitilla (Morro 1) have an average rim width of 1.8 cm; those from Chorreras (3.05 cm), Morro 2 (3.9 cm) and Toscanos I, I/II, II and III (4.2 cm, 3.75 cm, 4.25 cm and 4.5 cm respectively); and from Toscanos IV (4.9 cm), Morro 3 (6.0 cm) and Málaga (7.6 cm) (Barceló *et al.* 2000, 1460). The earliest examples from Morro de Mezquitilla date to the mid-eighth century BC, Toscanos III dates to *c.* 700 BC, and the final group to *c.* 600 BC. According to the chronology proposed by Schubart, the earliest red slip plates from La Laurita date to *c.* 700 BC (Pellicer Catalán 2002, 71).[5]

The most striking finds are 22 alabaster jars that were imported for use either as funerary urns (Pellicer Catalán 2002, 66) or as wine containers (Padró i Parcerisa 1986, 527). Four of the urns bear hieroglyphs recording the XXII Dynasty pharoahs Osorkon II (883-855 BC), Takelot II (860-835 BC) and Shoshenq III (835-783 BC). A marble vase of the XV Dynasty pharoah Apophis (*c.* 1585-1542 BC) had been found during the nineteenth century in unknown circumstances (Pellicer Catalán 2002, 67). The date at which these vases were deposited is uncertain; vases of this quality may have remained in circulation for a considerable period of time – witness that of Apophis. A date of the late eighth/early seventh century BC for Tomb 19B is given by two proto-Corinthian *kotylai* (Domínguez Monedero *et al.* 2001, 34). The finds from Almuñécar are important not only for their wealth and connections to Phoenicia and Egypt, but also because they directly contradict the dating of the settlement given by the literary sources.

The discrepancy between the date of the archaeological remains from Almuñécar and that given by the literary sources was reiterated in excavations carried out by the German Archaeological Institute in the Bay of Málaga. The site of Morro de Mezquitilla is situated on a low hill (32 m above sea level) on the east bank of the Río

Fig. 1. Tomb 1, Trayamar.

Algarrobo. The site was initially occupied in the Chalcolithic period during the second half of the third millennium BC (Phase A). Four phases of Phoenician occupation were identified (A/B1, B1-4) followed by Punic and Roman occupation (Phase C). C14 dates the earliest phase of Phoenician occupation to 820±90 BC (Martín Cordoba *et al.* 2002, 89), making Morro the earliest archaeologically attested Phoenician settlement in the Iberian Peninsula. The earliest buildings (Phase B1) contain red slip plates with diameters of less than 2.2 cm dating to the second third of the eighth century BC (Schubart 2002, 14-15). Also worthy of note are the finds of 'Fine Ware' – also known as 'Samarian Ware' from its initial discovery at Sarepta and Tyre (Maas-Lindemann 1997, 51). 'Fine Ware' is a high quality ware with a red slip that is widely distributed through the Near East and occurs in the West at Morro de Mezquitilla, Castillo de Doña Blanca and Huelva (Maas-Lindemann 1997, 54). Those from Morro de Mezquitilla match forms from Tyre dated to the mid- to late eighth century BC. These wares seem to have been brought to the West by the first Phoenician settlers, although it is interesting to note that 'Fine Ware' is absent from the Central Mediterranean (Maas-Lindemann 1997, 53-4).

Fig. 2. Río Vélez looking towards Cerro del Mar.

The strongly oriental character of the pottery assemblages from the initial phases at Morro de Mezquitilla is borne out by the cemetery associated with the settlement. As is typical of the Phoenician colonies, the necropolis for Morro de Mezquitilla was located across the Río Algarrobo at Trayamar. Five rock-cut chamber tombs were identified, of which only two were systematically studied and only one survives to the present (Tomb 1) (Schubart *et al.* 1976). The tombs and the accompanying grave goods are exclusively oriental in character. Tomb 1 was constructed at the beginning of the seventh century and remained in use until *c.* 600 BC (Martín Cordoba *et al.* 2002, 99; Schubart 2006, 139-40). Similar tombs have been excavated at Villaricos, Puente de Noy (Almuñécar) and Jardín (Aubet Semmler 1986). The re-use of these tombs, together with their wealth and oriental character, points to the existence of a hereditary elite of oriental origin.

The settlement of Toscanos lies at the foot of the Cerro del Peñón on the west bank of the Río Velez. The earliest excavations took place under the direction of Adolf Schulten between 1939 and 1941, with systematic excavations beginning under the auspices of the German Archaeological Institute in 1964. The earliest occupation on the site dates to 740-730 BC. Predating the colony at Toscanos is the neighbouring settlement of Chorreras. Located 800 m east of Morro de Mezquitilla, Chorreras was settled briefly between 750 and 700 BC; the population seems then to have moved to Toscanos which was enlarged at this time (Martín Cordoba *et al.* 2002, 92-4). The site has yielded red slip pottery with rims ranging between 1.9 and 4.7 cm in diameter (Martín Ruiz 1995, 83). The inhabitants of Chorreras seem to have utilized the necropolis of Lagos, which was contemporary with the settlement (Aubet Semmler *et al.* 1991). A short-lived colony was located at Montilla at the mouth of the Río Guadiaro, dating from the mid-eighth century to *c.* 700 BC (Martín Ruiz 1995, 62-3).

In order to resolve the wide discrepancy between the dates given by the literary sources for the first Phoenician settlers and the archaeological data from the sites themselves, the idea of a 'precolonial' phase has been suggested. This has been applied to the period *c.* 1100-825 BC and builds upon contacts that existed previously between Andalucía and the southeast of Iberia with Mycenaean Greece (Schubart *et al.* 1986, 501; García Martín 2003, 94). The precolonial period was marked not by the establishment of colonies but by more sporadic commercial contact in which Phoenician merchants would exchange goods with the natives without exercising any form of territorial control. The presence of these early voyages explains the scatter of second-millennium finds in the Western Mediterranean.[6] Unfortunately many of these finds are out of context, making their dating entirely subjective. Mycenaean LH III A2 or B pottery dated between 1400 and 1250 BC has been found at Llanete de los Moros (Montoro, Granada) (Martín de la Cruz 1990, 51-2). Sporadic contact of this type leaves little impression upon the archaeological record, and these scattered finds may be more appropriate to a later period than the initial contacts – one in which interaction became sufficiently stable and large-scale to leave traces in the archaeology (Millán León 1998, 21). The earliest reliably dated Phoenician colony was at Kition in Cyprus, dating to *c.* 820 BC, which gives a *terminus post quem* for the Phoenician colonization of the Western Mediterranean.[7]

Despite the lack of definite archaeological evidence for precolonial contact, it seems reasonable that the Phoenicians would not have founded Cádiz from scratch. They would have had some prior knowledge of available raw materials and the commercial potential of the site, as well as friendly relations with the natives guaranteeing security and access to the hinterland. Diodorus (5.20.1) implies that the foundation of Cádiz was preceded by Phoenician merchants undertaking trading voyages to the far west and that it was the success of these missions that prompted them to undertake the cost and risk of founding a permanent colony in the region.

Metallurgy in the Late Bronze Age

According to the literary sources, the Phoenicians were attracted by the wealth of mineral resources – particularly silver, gold and copper from Southern Spain. Diodorus (5.20.1-3) describes the Phoenicians becoming wealthy from trading silver with the native Iberians, while Strabo (3.2.11, 14) describes the wealth of silver that was possessed by the inhabitants of Tartessos.[8] Similarly when Herodotus (4.152) recounts that Kolaios of Samos was swept off course to land in Tartessos, he was able to pick up 60 talents of silver and make a handsome profit from the voyage. Strabo's description of the mineral wealth of the Sierra Morena (3.2.3) is probably pertinent to the colonial period also:

> On the north [of the Guadalquivir], there are some mountain ridges which extend parallel to the river, approaching it closely, sometimes more so, sometimes less, and they are full of mines. Silver, however, is most plentiful in the regions around Ilipa, and in those about Sisapo – I mean what is called the Old Sisapo as well as the New Sisapo; and at the place called Continae both copper and gold are mined at the same time … Beyond the Anas,

too, lie mountains that contain ores, and these mountains reach down to the Tagus River. (trans. H. Lloyd Jones)

Turdetania too was well-supplied with minerals (Strabo 3.2.8): 'up to the present moment, neither gold, nor silver, nor yet copper, nor iron, has been found anywhere in the world in a natural state, either in such quantity or of such good quality'. Tales of Iberia as a land of fabulous wealth may also explain the legendary King Arganthonios (whose name derives from the Greek *arguros*, Latin *argentum*, silver) and Claudius Iolaus' account of the foundation of Cádiz by the metallurgist Archelaus (*FGH* 788). The scale of this trade is most clear from the account of Diodorus (5.35.5) that not only describes the profitability of the Tartessian silver mines, but also places the impetus for their initial exploitation in the hands of the Phoenicians:

> Now the natives were ignorant of the use of the silver, and the Phoenicians, as they pursued their commercial enterprises and learned of what had taken place, purchased the silver in exchange for other wares of little if any worth. And this was the reason why the Phoenicians, as they transported this silver to Greece and Asia and to all other peoples, acquired great wealth. So far indeed did the merchants go in their greed that, in case their boats were fully laden and there still remained a great amount of silver, they would hammer the lead off the anchors and have the silver perform the service of the lead. And the result was that the Phoenicians, as in the course of many years they prospered greatly, thanks to commerce of this kind, sent forth many colonies, some to Sicily and its neigbouring islands, and others to Libya, Sardinia and Iberia. (trans. C.H. Oldfather, 1960)[9]

The importance of metal working to the communities of Southern Spain has long been recognized with domestic metallurgy first appearing in the El Argar and related cultures of the Early Bronze Age (1700-1400 BC). An area extending from Seville to the Atlantic coast has been estimated to contain one billion tons of ore (García García 1996, 276). The most important deposits lie in the Sierra Morena and the Sierra de Aracena in the vicinity of Río Tinto.

The geology of the Río Tinto is dominated by porphyry and pyrites that yield gold, silver and lesser quantities of copper, lead and iron. It has been estimated that between sixteen and twenty million tons of ancient slag remain on the site derived predominantly from the extraction of silver (Blanco Freijeiro *et al.* 1969, 124). The centre of the mining activity lay at Cerro Salomón, where occupation has been dated from the eighth to the seventh century BC (Blanco Freijeiro *et al.* 1969, 130). The scattering of slag throughout the site – rather than concentrated in industrial 'quarters' – points to the activities having been primarily domestic in scale – perhaps even seasonal, to judge by the poor quality and short occupation of the houses and the lack of luxury wheelmade wares (Ruiz Mata 1989, 222).[10] The inhabitants traded closely with the Phoenicians, and the lack of metal artifacts in spite of the evidence for metallurgy suggests that the products were shipped elsewhere. The basic technique for processing the silver seems to have been that of cupellation, whereby the crushed ore is combined with flux and heated to separate the slag from the lead and silver. The lead is then oxidized to leave pure silver. The use of cupellation indicates a high level of technical expertise and remained largely unchanged through the Late Bronze Age (twelfth to ninth centuries BC), Orientalizing and Roman periods (Rothenburg *et al.* 1981, 111-13).

The lack of archaeological evidence for the Late Bronze Age means that it is difficult to determine whether silver working was introduced by the Phoenicians or if the Phoenicians exploited a pre-existing indigenous metallurgy. During the second millennium BC the population was concentrated in areas with plentiful mineral or agricultural resources (Júdice Gamito 1988, 26) and the high level of technical expertise shown by the process of cupellation would support the latter hypothesis. Evidence of metallurgy at Chinflón predates the arrival of Phoenician wheel-made pottery and dates to the late ninth/early eighth century BC (Ruiz Mata 1989, 214; Rothenburg *et al.* 1981, 40).[11]

The earliest Phoenician contacts are difficult to date. A date in the first half of the eighth century BC is given by a mid-Geometric II Attic pyxis-box from Huelva (Domínguez Monedero *et al.* 2001, 10; Cabrera Bonet 2003, 62) previously identified as having come from a mid-Geometric *krater* (Shefton 1982, 342-3).[12] The lack of other painted Attic pottery west of the Adriatic at this date would suggest that the piece was brought by Phoenician merchants who had picked up the vessel in Cyprus or the Levant (Shefton 1982, 343).[13] Red slip plates from Huelva have a rim of less than 3.5 cm and are similar to examples from Toscanos I/II dating to the second half of the eighth century BC (Rufete Tomico 1999, 217). The concentration of Greek imports in western Andalucía in the eighth to sixth centuries BC suggests that the activities of the colonists were centred upon accessing the mineral resources of the southwest.[14] From the end of the eighth century BC Cerro Salomón was expanded to include the settlement at Quebrantahuesos. Although metallurgical activity is attested from the Late Bronze Age, the apogee of the settlement and of imported Phoenician pottery is in the seventh to sixth centuries BC (Pellicer Catalán 1983, 66; Ruiz Mata 1989, 219). The site is striking for the poor quality of the excavated structures and the lack of urban planning, suggesting seasonal occupation – a hypothesis that is re-inforced by the lack of luxury wheel-made wares.

Aznacóllar is located at the southeastern edge of the Iberian pyrite belt. Archaeological work carried out in 1992 revealed pre-Roman occupation at Cerro del Castillo and at Las Castrejones. Limited stratigraphic excavations at El Castillo have uncovered sixteen levels of occupation of which level II produced a sherd of hand-made pottery with stroke burnished decoration common in the final Bronze Age and early Iron Age. Quantities of slag from silver working, together with Phoenician pottery, were recovered from the surface of the site (Hunt Ortiz 1995, 449).

Excavations at Las Castrejones have produced abundant evidence of metalworking together with pottery of the eighth to sixth centuries BC. Forty-six kilograms of slag were recovered predominantly from the process of cupellation, although a piece of slag from copper working has been found on the acropolis. Two pieces of silver have been found, suggesting that the metal was refined on site: one is plain and the other decorated. The evidence of metalworking is scattered throughout the site together with 31 millstones, suggesting that metallurgical and agricultural activities took place indiscriminately without any specialization (Hunt Ortiz 1995, 450-2).

Once extracted, the ore could be taken down one of two routes: either down the Río Tinto to Huelva; or from the mines at Aznacóllar down the Guadalquivir to Cádiz through the native communities of Tejada la Vieja and San Bartolomé de Almonte. Excavations at Huelva have yielded evidence of metalworking as early as the eighth century BC (Fernández Jurado 2002, 246): quantities of silver slag and two smelting

Fig. 3. Castillo de Doña Blanca.

furnaces dated to the seventh century BC were excavated at Calle del Puerto n. 6; two furnaces at n. 8 and a further three furnaces with silver slag at Calle del Puerto n. 10. Evidence of smelting from Calle Méndez Núñez nos 4-6 dates between 725/700 and 540/530 BC (Gómez Ramos 1999, 126).[15]

The site of Tejada la Vieja covers an area of 6.5 ha overlooking the Río Corumbel. The earliest occupation dates from the Middle to Late Bronze Age and the site was fortified at some point before the arrival of the Phoenicians in the ninth/eighth century BC (Rothenburg *et al.* 1981, 245; Fernández Jurado, 1987, 103-4; García Sanz *et al.* 1995, 13; Gómez Toscano 1997, 93). The earliest imported red slip pottery dates to the second half of the seventh century BC (Fernández Jurado 1987, 147). Similar wares have been found at El Carambolo, Castillo de Doña Blanca and Cádiz, dated to the second half of the eighth century BC (Rufete Tomico 1999, 222). Although evidence of metalworking has been found, no furnaces have yet been discovered and it seems that whatever metalworking took place was small-scale (Rothenburg *et al.* 1981, 270-1; Fernández Jurado 1987, 113, 130; 2002, 250).[16]

Metallurgical activity at San Bartolomé was devoted to reworking silver with numerous finds of slag and nozzles (Gómez Ramos 1999, 124).[17] The lack of planning and flimsy character of the houses suggests that activities were seasonal and centred upon family groups (Ruiz Mata 1981, 154-6). The earliest evidence of metallurgy is contemporaneous with the earliest phases at San Pedro and has yielded pottery typical of the Late Bronze Age, *c.* 800 BC, predating the arrival of imported wheel-made Phoenician wares, *c.* 750-700 BC (Gómez Ramos 1999, 124).

From San Bartolomé metals were transported to Castillo de Doña Blanca. The site of Castillo de Doña Blanca lies at the foot of the Sierra de San Cristóbal at what was once the shoreline of the Bay of Cádiz. Blessed with an excellent natural harbour and easy access to the interior via the Guadalete and Guadalquivir, the site was settled by Phoenician merchants in the first half of the eighth century BC.[18] Fabric analysis of the pottery shows that the inhabitants of San Bartolomé imported red slip pottery from Castillo de Doña Blanca (Ruiz Mata 1986, 541). Red slip plates from Castillo de Doña Blanca were reaching El Carambolo (Seville) by the end of the eighth century BC (Ruiz Mata 1986, 549-50). Analysis of the slag from San Bartolomé and Castillo de Doña Blanca reveals similar proportions of lead and copper, though it would have been mined at Aznacóllar rather than Río Tinto where the slag contained a higher proportion of copper (Ruiz Mata 1986, 540). The presence of litharge at Castillo de Doña Blanca, in contrast to San Bartolomé, Tejada la Vieja or Aznacóllar, may suggest that the metal was brought here to be worked (Hunt Ortiz 1995, 454).

The nexus of these routes was the colony at Cádiz. The Phoenician merchants were able to access the mineral resources from Huelva, Seville and the Sierra Morena through a string of commercial centres – San Bartolomé, Tejada la Vieja and Castillo de Doña Blanca, culminating at Cádiz which served as the entrepot for the silver trade until the end of the seventh century BC. The fact that the Phoenicians did not initiate the trade in metals is suggested by the evidence of metallurgy prior to the first Phoenician imported goods – the potential profits attracting a permanent Phoenician presence and bearing out the literary descriptions of the initial exploration of the region. The arrival of the Phoenicians does, however, coincide with the intensification of mining activity – perhaps with the introduction of shaft and gallery mining.

The colonies along the Málaga coast have also produced evidence of metallurgy. Iron slag has been found in the earliest phase of Phoenician occupation at Morro de Mezquitilla (Phase A/B1) together with Chalcolithic and Phoenician pottery from the initial occupation of the colony (Schubart 1999, 246). A blacksmith's workshop consisting of two pairs of kilns (the identification of 'kilns' 5 and 6 is less certain) together with tools and slag from forging iron have been found in Corte 21, dated to the succeeding Phase B1a (Schubart 1999, 242-5; 2002, 7-9; 2006, 87-90; Gómez Ramos 1999, 121). Traces of copper or bronze are also present (Schubart 1999, 250; Mansel 2000, 1601-2). A larger and better preserved kiln was excavated in Corte 23, contemporaneous or slightly later than the kilns in 21 (Schubart 1999, 248; 2006, 92-4). Schubart suggests that this was not a primary smelting area – that the limited facilities and scarcity of slag meant that the ore was worked elsewhere, being brought to Morro de Mezquitilla for its final processing (Schubart 1999, 249; 2002, 9-10). Large quantities of iron and copper slag have been reported at Cerro del Mar (Gómez Ramos 1999, 122). A small furnace 1 m in diameter has been excavated at Chorreras, which was used for working iron (Martín Cordoba *et al.* 2002, 95).[19]

Larger-scale metalworking may have taken place at Toscanos. Excavations on the eastern slope of the Cerro del Peñón have revealed a small iron-working furnace 30 cm in diameter (Keesmann *et al.* 1989, 100), although the quantities of iron slag from elsewhere on the site suggests that other furnaces await discovery. Red slip plates (7.1 to 8 cm in diameter) date the furnace to the second half of the seventh century BC (Keesman *et al.* 1989, 101). Excavations in the Cortijo de Toscanos have revealed slag and nozzles dating to the mid-eighth century BC (Gómez Ramos 1999, 121).

The colony of Adra lies on the Cerro de Montecristo overlooking the mouth of the Río Grande, 15 km downstream from the iron resources of the Baja Alpujarra.

Excavations on the eastern slope of the Cerro de Montecristo have revealed pottery dating from *c.* 750 BC through the seventh century: handmade pottery of the Late Bronze Age and wheel-made wares including red slip plates with rims of 2-3 cm (López Castro *et al.* 1991, 984; Suárez Marquez *et al.* 1987, 17).[20] Iron slag has been found, suggesting metallurgical activities (Suárez Marquez *et al.* 1987, 17; López Castro *et al.* 1991, 987; Gómez Ramos 1999, 121).

The settlements were concentrated in the vicinity of Málaga (the Ríos Guadalhorce-Guadalmedina), the mouths of the Ríos Vélez and Algarrobo, and the confluence of the Ríos Guadalhorce-Guadalteba-Turón that provided access to the interior (Recio Ruiz 1993, 134). From the coast, Phoenician goods reached as far inland as Castulo where a number of orientalizing burials were located. In 1962 a wealthy burial was discovered at Estacar de Robarinas, containing a silver bowl, gold ring, iron weapons, bronze vessels, a Cerdeño 1 bronze belt and three bronze figures of the goddess Hathor that originally came from a *thymiaterion* (Blázquez Martínez *et al.* 1982, 415). The dating of the burial is problematic as the grave goods range in date from the eighth to the sixth century BC (Blanco Freijeiro 1963, 60-1). This may be due to the presence of two burials or reflect the circulation of prestige goods for a considerable period of time prior to their being placed in the tomb (Torres Ortiz 1999, 99-100). Further orientalizing tumuli are located at Los Higuerones, one of which (tumulus A) has been excavated containing a bronze *thymiaterion* decorated with animal figures and dated to the seventh century BC (Blázquez Martínez *et al.* 1982, 416-18; Torres Ortiz 1999, 100). A possible tumulus delimited by a perimeter of stones similar to tumuli A and B at Setefilla has been excavated at Cerrillo Blanco (Porcuna, Jaén). The tumulus overlies 24 inhumation graves dated to the seventh century BC on the basis of grave goods: Bencarron and double-spring *fibulae*, belt buckles and a decorated ivory comb similar to that from Acebuchal (González Navarrete *et al.* 1980, 189-91, 194-5; Torres Ortiz 1999, 98-9).

Tartessos

The impact that this contact with the Phoenicians had upon the native communities is an intrinsic component of the debates surrounding the kingdom of Tartessos. The earliest reference to Tartessos is that of Stesichorus of Himera (632/629-556/553 BC), cited by Strabo (3.2.11): 'It appears that the ancients knew the Guadalquivir under the name of the Tartessus, and Gades with the neighbouring islands under that of Erythia; and it is thought that we should understand in this sense the words of Stesichorus concerning the pastoral poet Geryon, that he was born "almost opposite to the renowned Erythia, in a rocky cave near to the abundant springs of the silver-bedded river Tartessus." They say that on the land enclosed between the two outlets of this river there formerly stood a city named, like the river, Tartessus, and that the district was called Tartessis, which the Turduli now inhabit' (trans. H.C. Hamilton and W. Falconer, 1903). The location of Tartessos is confused, having been equated with the Río Guadalquivir, a city at its mouth or even the region as a whole. That Tartessos was rich in silver is repeated by Anacreon (Strabo 3.2.14) whose allusion to ruling Tartessos for 150 years refers to the legendary king Arganthonios (Herodotus 1.163.1) – the same Arganthonios whose wealth attracted Kolaios of Samos. According to Ephorus, however, Tartessos was not synonymous with Cádiz but lay 250 stades distant (Ps.-Scymnos 162-8). Tartessos is portrayed as a developed society with a strong hereditary monarchy made wealthy through its trade in silver (Justin *Epitome* 44.4-16; Avienus *Ora Maritima* 423). The fullest description of Tartessos comes from the fourth-century AD *Ora Maritima* written by Rufius Festus Avienus.[21] As Javier de Hoz (1989) has noted, however, Avienus' narrative is hopelessly garbled, variously identifying Tartessos with the city of Cádiz (269-70, 851), a people (254-5), a mountain (308-9), an estuary (265-7), a river (225-6, 283-5) and a sea (54).[22] Unfortunately the literary sources are confused about those aspects which interest us most in respect to the relationship of Tartessos to the Phoenicians: the extent of interaction, the means by which this interaction took place and the date at which these developments took place – in other words whether or not the economic development of southwestern Spain pre- or post-dates the arrival of the Phoenicians in the mid-eighth century BC.

Evidence for Phoenician contact comes from the spread of orientalizing 'princely' tombs that are characterized by monumental architecture or tumuli and by wealthy grave goods (Martín Ruiz 2000, 1835): tumuli A, B and H at Setefilla, tumulus G at El Acebuchal, tumulus 1 at Las Cumbres, tombs 5, 9, 17 and 18 at La Joya, Estacar de Robarinas, tumulus A at Los Higuerones and Cerrillo Blanco.

The necropolis at Setefilla was originally excavated by G. Bonsor and R. Thouvenot but two tumuli (A & B) were re-excavated by Aubet in the 1970s (Torres Ortiz 1999, 86-95). Forty-five cremation burials dated to the Orientalizing I period (825-700 BC) were discovered underlying tumulus A (Aubet Semmler 1975, 65; Torres Ortiz 1999, 90-1). The cinerary urns are of poor quality and are typical of Tartessian settlements in the lower Guadalquivir during the eighth and ninth centuries BC and preceding the earliest Phoenician imports (Aubet Semmler 1975, 135-7; Maluquer de Motes *et al.* 1981, 134-8).[23] Similar vessels with a coarse ovoid body and a burnished neck continue to be common until the sixth century BC.

The most widespread form of pottery in tumulus A is carenated cups or plates with reticular burnished decoration – again characteristic of the communities of the lower Guadalquivir and most closely paralleling those from the seventh to sixth centuries BC (Maluquer de Motes *et al.* 1981, 137). Red slip pottery predominates among the imported Phoenician wares. The dating of these wares is a matter of some debate, as Tartessian sites may have continued to use archaic forms long after their replacement in the Phoenician colonies. Mariano Torres Ortiz, however, has dated the examples from tumuli A and B to the middle of the eighth century BC on the basis of Schubart's typology from Toscanos (Torres Ortiz 1996, 152).[24] The homogeneity of the fabric and its dissimilarity to that found in the Phoenician settlements at Málaga suggests an origin in a single workshop on the Bay of Cádiz (Aubet Semmler 1975, 142; Maluquer de Motes *et al.* 1981, 142-3).[25] Bronze *fibulae* and belt buckles are also present, dating to the eighth century BC (Torres Ortiz 1996, 152-4 *contra* Aubet Semmler 1975, 146-50; Maluquer de Motes *et al.* 1981, 143).[26]

Over the cremations a tumulus (A) was constructed measuring 29 m in diameter and containing a central chamber 10 x 5.50 m. The chamber contained an inhumation burial of which nothing remains (Maluquer de Motes *et al.* 1981, 66-7). Tumulus B is smaller, 16.70 m in diameter, rising to only 1.30 m, and overlies 33 cremation graves (Maluquer de Motes *et al.* 1981, 164-5, Torres Ortiz 1999, 92-3). No central chamber was found, and the tumulus was erected directly over the earlier cremations

(Maluquer de Motes *et al.* 1981, 167). The cremations echo those of tumulus A and would appear to be contemporaneous (Maluquer de Motes *et al.* 1981, 219). Tumulus H was excavated by Bonsor and Thouvenot in 1926 and seems to have been similar to Tumulus A as well as Tumulus G at El Acebuchal (Ruiz Delgado 1989, 253). Many of the grave goods recovered during the excavations of 1926-7 were lost during the civil war; however, in 1973 Maria Aubet published the surviving finds that had been deposited by Bonsor in the castle at Mairena de Alcor. Tumulus H produced the wealthiest orientalizing grave goods, including ivories and jewellery similar to that from Aliseda, Sines and Ebora (Aubet Semmler 1973, 13; Torres Ortiz 1999, 93-4).

The similarity of the grave goods from the tumuli to those from the underlying cremation burials points to cultural and demographic continuity. The change that occurred was one of growing wealth and access to imported goods among the upper strata of society (Maluquer de Motes *et al.* 1981, 154-5). The continuity in the type of grave goods further suggests that this change took place in a relatively short space of time at the end of the eighth century BC (Torres Ortiz 1996, *contra* Maluquer de Motes *et al.* 1981, 153-5).[27] Aubet's analysis of the skeletal remains further reinforces the impression of continuity with the survival of kinship groups from the Bronze Age: wealthy central burials were male with wealthy female and infant burials grouped around the periphery of the central grave (Aubet Semmler 1995, 404; Ruiz Mata 2001, 63).[28] The presence of men, women and children suggests that the tumuli represent kinship groups whose status was hereditary – hence the inclusion of children.

The social hierarchy represented by these 'princely' tombs is repeated elsewhere. The necropolis of Las Cumbres lies to the north of Castillo de Doña Blanca. Approximately 100 tombs have been identified in an area of 100 ha; however, only tumulus 1 has been excavated. The tumulus is 22 m in diameter and rises to a height of 1.80 m (Ruiz Mata *et al.* 1989, 288; Córdoba *et al.* 2000, 760; Ruiz Mata 2001, 140). It overlies 63 extant cremations as well as others destroyed during the construction of the tumulus. The centre of the tumulus overlies an *ustrinum* in which the corpse was cremated (Córdoba *et al.* 2000, 760; Ruiz Mata *et al.* 1989, 288). The cinerary urns echo those of Setefilla: biconical urns, vessels with a coarse ovoid body and burnished neck (Ruiz Mata *et al.* 1989, 291; Ruiz Mata 1991, 212). Some later burials use wheel-made Cruz del Negro type urns with a cylindrical neck and globular body decorated with a wide band of red slip and black lines (Ruiz Mata *et al.* 1989, 291). The poverty and lack of differentiation in the wealth of the grave goods are in marked contrast to the wealth of metalwork and imported Phoenician wares found in the thirteen burials in the adjoining secondary tumulus. Burial 24 is particularly wealthy, containing gold and silver necklaces, pendants, a Cerdeño type 1 bronze belt buckle, red slip and Cruz del Negro pottery, *alabastra* and *unguentaria* for perfumes and oil (Córdoba *et al.* 2000, 761; Ruiz Mata *et al.* 1989, 291-2). The burials are important in showing not only the social stratification that has occurred but also the rapid infiltration of Phoenician goods. The two tumuli seem to have been in use throughout the eighth century BC – the earliest burials in biconical urns and lacking Phoenician imports date to the first half of the century, with the other burials dating to the second half. As was the case at Setefilla, the cremation burials displaying a consistent level of wealth were replaced by the wealthier graves of the secondary tumulus grouped around an elite burial.

Twelve tumuli have been discovered at El Acebuchal to the southwest of Carmona.

The largest of these is tumulus G, measuring 30 m in diameter and 7 m in height. Like tumulus A at Setefilla the tumulus covers a central stone burial chamber containing two inhumations. The burial contained a variety of wealthy grave-goods including an ostrich egg, *fibulae* and belt buckles of Cerdeño type 1 dating to the eighth century BC (Torres Ortiz 1999, 74-6). A monumental inhumation burial has been excavated beneath tumulus B at Huerta del Cabello (del Arco Aguilar 1991, 99-101).[29] Similarly at Castilleja de Guzmán a tumulus containing a tomb chamber with three inhumations has been excavated (Torres Ortiz 2000, 361).[30]

The wealth of the Tartessian elite is particularly evident in the tombs at La Joya (Huelva). Nineteen tombs have been found which have yielded a variety of imported luxuries. Shefton has dated the Rhodian jar in tomb 5 to the end of the seventh century BC (Shefton 1982, 350). The tomb also contained a fragment of silver plate, a fragment of iron possibly pertaining to a belt buckle, a gold ring with a rectangular stamp depicting a griffin, a fragment of an ivory depicting a lotus flower, necklaces made of amber and seashell as well as hand and wheel-made pottery (Torres Ortiz 1999, 61).

The wealthiest of the burials was tomb 17, containing a single adult. The grave goods included a carriage decorated in bronze and horse trappings together with a bronze quiver, a bronze mirror, a Cerdeño type 3 belt buckle, two iron knives, an ivory box and two *alabastra* as well as a variety of ceramic and metal vessels including two Vuillemont R1 amphorae and a piriform bronze jug. A bronze *thymiaterion* has also been recovered from tomb 17, dated to 675/650 BC and perhaps originating in Cyprus (Almagro Gorbea 1974, 55), although a local origin in the Phoenician colonies has also been suggested (Aldana Nacher 1981, 131-4). The presence of *thymiateria* in both funerary and religious contexts suggests the association of Tartessian political and sacred authority and the adoption of Phoenician funerary ritual (Torres Ortiz 2000, 188). The red slip wares in tomb 1 date to the first half of the seventh century (Torres Ortiz 1996, 149). Tomb 9 contained a double burial: an inhumation together with hoplite weapons and a cremation together with gold jewellery placed at the feet of the inhumation (Garrido Roiz *et al.* 2000, 1806). This arrangement is similar to that of tomb 1 at Salamis, where it has been interpreted as the burial of a married couple of royal status. A scarab from tomb 9 bears an inscription of Psammetichus II (595-589 BC). Tomb 18 seems also to have been wealthy, containing bronze and iron weapons and vessels, a gold and amber pendant, and silver and ivory fragments; it may also have contained a carriage, to judge by the remains of bronze decoration found in the tomb.[31] The tombs from La Joya are important in the marked social stratification that they reveal. The wealthiest burials contain high quality imported grave-goods and echo the elite tombs of Etruria in their wealth and use of prestige symbols, while the poorest graves consist of multiple burials containing no grave goods at all.

The transition to a hierarchical society characterized by its willingness to receive oriental goods and by its adoption of Phoenician funerary practices seems to have taken place in a relatively short period in the eighth century BC. Tumuli A and H at Setefilla, tumulus G at El Acebuchal and tumulus 1 at Las Cumbres are contemporaneous with the Phoenician colonies of the eighth century BC, suggesting that the Phoenician settlers rapidly established relations with the native elites or that these ties preceded the establishment of permanent colonies.[32] Particularly significant is the *dromos* tomb at Roça do Casal do Meio in Portuguese Estremadura, which is dated to the ninth/tenth century BC although the chronology of the site is confused and it may be a re-used megalithic tomb (Spindler *et al.* 1973, 125-8; Torres Ortiz 1999, 114). The establishment of early contacts with the local elite will have facilitated the siting and survival of the earliest Phoenician settlements.[33]

The profits that accrued through contact with the Phoenicians in turn encouraged the Tartessian elite to exploit the resources of their hinterland. Cunliffe (1995, 16) has noted that elite orientalizing burials were concentrated in two areas: the first in the vicinity of Huelva and Carmona representing the core of the Tartessian realm; and the second along the valley of the Guadiana linking the Tartessian core with the mining regions of the northwest. The redistribution of luxury goods enabled the Tartessian elite to control access to raw materials in areas beyond their own direct control. Unfortunately the mechanics of this exchange are difficult to determine in view of the comparative lack of archaeological evidence from peripheral areas such as Extremadura (Celestino Pérez 1995, 67).

The most important of the sites in Extremadura is the necropolis of Medellín. The necropolis lies on an outcrop overlooking the fertile valley of the Guadiana and straddling the silver route that linked the northwest with the Bay of Cádiz. Although lacking the wealth of the 'princely' tombs found further south, the burials have yielded a variety of orientalizing goods: red slip plates, Cruz del Negro urns, double-spring and ring-shaped *fibulae*, scarabs – one with the name of Tuthmosis III, belt buckles, ivory combs, cosmetic palettes and decorated plaques, rings and two silver pendants – one decorated with cosmological imagery similar to examples from Trayamar, and a mid/late Corinthian *aryballos* (Almagro Gorbea 1991, 162). The most famous discovery was of an Attic black-figure *kylix* attributed to the potter Eucheiros and dated *c.* 560-550 BC (Almagro Gorbea 1971, 176-7). The most abundant pottery from Medellín is grey ware characteristic of orientalizing sites from the start of the seventh century BC. Although the site lacks the indications of a wealthy stratified society seen further south, the graves at Medellín are prosperous and in contact with the Tartessian and Phoenician communities of Andalucía and southern Portugal between *c.* 630 and 450 BC (Almagro Gorbea 1991, 163).[34]

The picture presented by Medellín is echoed in the limited excavations that were possible at the junction of the Río Aljucen and Río Guadiana in 1987. Although the state of the site meant that there was no stratigraphy or reliable dates, the pottery recovered from the cremation burials was characteristic of the orientalizing necropoleis of the Guadalquivir valley, Huelva and southern Portugal – as well as specifically Alcacer do Sal and the seventh-century burials at Medellín (Enríquez Navascués *et al.* 1991, 47-50).

Four groups of orientalizing cremation burials (Pajares I, II, III and El Cardenillo) have been found at Villanueva de la Vera dated from the end of the sixth century to the beginning of the fourth century BC (Celestino Pérez 1999, 85; González Cordero *et al.* 1993, 260; Rodríguez Díaz *et al.* 2001, 171).[35] The burials were placed in natural tumuli echoing the tumuli of the Guadalquivir valley and the unexcavated tumulus at Tudal. The close proximity of the cemeteries may reflect their use by individual familial or kinship groups within the same community (Celestino Pérez 1999, 86).[36]

Excavations of Pajares II in 1992-3 revealed 23 burials in addition to four that were already known. The most striking feature of the burials were five bronze cinerary urns that are distinguished from those further south by their having been beaten rather than moulded into shape (Celestino Pérez 1999, 76). A range of orientalizing jewellery has been found, consisting of two gold pendants or sheets with granular decoration of cosmological images, a piece of a gold diadem, a fragment of gold sheet depicting a face and a gold plaque depicting a lion or griffin (Celestino Pérez 1999, 112-18; González Cordero *et al.* 1993, 250-7). The items were locally produced pieces of feminine jewellery similar to the burial of a wealthy woman and child from Belvís de la Jara dating to the mid-eighth or early seventh century BC (Pereira Sieso *et al.* 1986; Torres Ortiz 1999, 111-12). The hoard discovered at Talavera la Vieja consists of gold and silver jewellery and orientalizing bronzework together with one or more cremation burials. Five of the seven pieces of pottery found were carenated grey ware (Celestino Pérez *et al.* 2002, 50).

In 1920 an orientalizing hoard of metalwork was discovered at Aliseda. The hoard consists of a variety of gold, silver and bronze pieces, not only locally produced but also imported pieces from the Eastern Mediterranean dated to the end of the seventh century BC (Torres Ortiz 1999, 109). The hoard is clearly princely in status and strongly oriental in character with parallels in Andalucía and Etruria. The hoard of bronzes from Cabezo de Araya may have been deposited in a similar fashion to those found in 1923 at Huelva dating from *c.* 850 BC, from where they may have originated (Enríquez Navascues 1990, 72).

A primary goal of this exchange of luxuries was to acquire access to raw materials, especially tin and silver. Pliny (*Natural History* 4.115; 33.6) also refers to the gold-bearing sands of the Tagus, and iron was found in small quantities in the vicinity of Caceres (Rodríguez Diaz *et al.* 2001, 26-7).[37] The necropolis at Medellín has yielded evidence of metalworking in the form of a smelting crucible, however it is not known what metal was being worked (Almagro Gorbea 1971, 196). The most important discoveries have been those of the mining community of Cerro de San Cristóbal in Logrosán, where mining recovered materials of the Late Neolithic and Bronze Age together with moulds and slag dated to the Bronze Age (Sos Baynat 1997, 276).[38] Agricultural resources may also have provided an attraction with orientalizing hoards like that of Talavera la Vieja, situated in proximity to the fertile lands of the Tagus valley (Celestino Pérez 1999, 90). One of the vessels from Talavera la Vieja contained 50 g of carbonized naked wheat (Rodríguez Díaz *et al.* 2001, 173).

Phoenician colonization elsewhere in the Peninsula

One of the important contributions that archaeology has made in recent years has been the realization that Phoenician colonization was far more widespread than was previously assumed, with settlements extending along the Atlantic coast in the west and as far north as Cataluña in the east. One such 'peripheral' area consisted of southern and central Portugal. Phoenician goods are found along the Algarve and the Atlantic coast, concentrating around the estuaries that provided access to the interior (Arruda 1999, 257). Unfortunately the lack of suitable sites for study renders any conclusions about the Phoenician impact tentative, although the pattern suggests a similar relationship to other peripheral areas of Tartessos.

The most intense contact with the Mediterranean is found in the Algarve, where a number of sites have yielded evidence of oriental contact as early as the beginning of the first millennium BC. The site of Castro Marim lies near the mouth of the Río Guadiana. Excavations have revealed little of the Bronze Age and early Iron Age occupation although there is orientalizing pottery of the second half of the seventh century BC: red slip pottery, grey ware, tripods, a *pithos* with painted red and black decoration, and Mañá A 1 or Vuillemont R1 (Ramón T. 10.1.2.1) amphorae (Arruda 1996, 97; 1999, 43-8). From Castro Marim imports travelled north along the Río Guadiana to the mineral resources of the Baixo Alentejo – Attic pottery has been found at Mértola, Azougada, Moura and Castelo de Serpa (Arruda *et al.* 1998, 126, 146-7; Arruda 1999, 53). Like Castro Marim, Cerro da Rocha Branca was a fortified site controlling access inland – in this case the Río Arade – and receiving imported pottery from the eighth century BC (Gomes *et al.* 1986, 78; Cardoso 2000, 319).[39]

Further north along the Atlantic coast, a Phoenician settlement was established at Abul, lying on a promontory at the mouth of the Río Sado – which like the Guadiana penetrates the interior as far as the Baixo Alentejo.[40] Excavations have revealed two phases of construction dating to the seventh to sixth centuries BC (Mayet *et al.* 1992, 318-20; 1993, 133-4; 2000, 850). A square building arranged around a central patio was built in the first phase and remodelled in the second half of the seventh century BC by the addition of a corridor around the patio and an altar in the centre (Mayet *et al.* 2000, 851-2; 2001, 176-7). The pottery recovered is of a strongly orientalizing character: red slip plates dated to the second half of the seventh century, carenated bowls, grey ware plates and bowls, Cruz del Negro urns, Vuillemont R1 amphorae (Ramón T. 10.1.1.1) produced in the Phoenician colonies from the second quarter of the eighth century to the first half of the seventh century BC, and Ramón T. 10.1.2.1 amphorae dated between 675/650 and 575/550 BC (Mayet *et al.* 2000, 850-1; 2001, 181-2; Ramón Torres 1995, 229-31; Arruda 1999, 88-90). Unfortunately the purpose of the structure is unclear, although the oriental architecture and lack of preceding Bronze Age levels supports the contention that it is a Phoenician settlement perhaps functioning as an *emporion* (Mayet *et al.* 1992, 323; 2000, 853). The building recalls that of Cancho Roano and may have served a similar function (Arruda 1999, 91).

Abul interacted closely with the neighbouring native sites of Alcácer do Sal and Setúbal, which saw an influx of orientalizing pottery in the seventh to sixth centuries BC (Mayet *et al.* 1993, 138). The rapid decline of indigenous hand-made pottery is particularly striking: three phases of Iron Age occupation have been identified at Setúbal – hand-made wares predominate (84.4%) in the earliest level dated to the seventh century BC, dropping to 23.9% in the succeeding phase, and 18% in Phase III, dated to the end of the fifth and beginning of the fourth century BC (Arruda 1999, 92-5). Similarly wheel-made pottery accounts for 91.3% of the total found in the earliest Iron Age level at Alcácer do Sal, replacing the exclusively hand-made wares found in the preceding Bronze Age level II (Arruda 1999, 67).

In 1972 a Bronze Age *tholos* tomb was excavated at Roça do Casal do Meio near Sesimbra on the coast west of Setubal at the mouth of the Río Sado. The tomb consists of a circular structure surrounding a funerary chamber 3.3 m in diameter and preserved to a height of 1 m that was entered through a 4.20 m long entrance passage. The perimeter of the tomb was defined by 30 stones rising to a height of 1.5 m (Spindler *et al.* 1973, 103-9). Two inhumations were uncovered in the central chamber with a limited repetoire of grave goods: an ivory comb, bronze tweezers, a nail, a bronze *fibula* and a bronze belt buckle together with a biconical urn and a high sided bowl and other fragments (Spindler *et al.* 1973, 118-25). The tomb has been dated to the tenth/ninth centuries BC on the basis of the *fibula* and the ivory (Spindler *et al.* 1973, 125-8). The importance of the tomb stems from its monumental Mediterranean character clearly marking the burial of two high status individuals.[41]

The necropolis of Senhor dos Mártires lies 1 km west of Alcácer do Sal and contains cremations dating from the mid-seventh century to the beginning of the fourth century BC (Arruda 1999, 80). Unfortunately the association of finds with specific tombs is difficult; however, the necropolis has yielded a variety of orientalizing grave goods: grey ware, Cruz del Negro urns, weapons, items of adornment: belt buckles, *fibulae* (double-spring, ring-shaped, Acebuchal type), a scarab bearing the name of Psammetichus I (664-610 BC). In 1968, Antonio Cavaleiro Paixão excavated 27 burials from the earliest phases of the site, of which he has published tomb 22/80 (1983, 277). The grave goods contained an Egyptianizing scarab depicting two anthropomorphic figures, a bronze ring and iron weapons (Cavaleiro Paixão 1983, 282-3). Seventeen tombs have been excavated at Monte A-Do-Mealha-Nova (Alves Dias *et al.* 1970, 176). The most substantial tomb (tomb 1) includes a silver ring containing a scarab of the XXIII Dynasty pharoah Pedubast (818-793 BC) (Alves Dias *et al.* 1970, 181-2).

The sixth-century BC rectangular cist tomb at Herdade do Gaio (Sines, Baixo Alentejo) has yielded a spectacular hoard of orientalizing goods consisting of gold jewellery: a pair of earrings, necklaces; amber, glass and cornelian beads and pendants, glass *unguentaria*, the base of an *alabastron* and a scarab bearing the name of the pharoah Tuthmosis III (1479-1424 BC) (da Costa 1966, 530-1; Arruda 1999, 96-7). The wealth of the orientalizing treasure is comparable to the hoards from Andalucía and clearly marks the occupant of the tomb as a powerful high status individual in contact with the Phoenician settlers to the south.

A similar orientalizing presence is found at the mouth of the Tagus at Quinta do Almaraz, Cova da Piedade, Quinta do Facho, S.Paulo, Lisboa, Outorela I and II, Moinhos da Atalaia, Santa Eufémia and Freiria during the seventh to fifth centuries BC (Arruda 1999, 102-37), as well as around the Mondego estuary at Santa Olaia, Crasto de Tavarede, Chões, Fonte de Cabanas and Pardinheiros (Arruda 1999, 227-45). Unfortunately, the archaeological evidence from these sites tells us little about their structure; however, evidence from several necropoleis supports the existence of a hierarchical society along the lines of that of southern Spain.

The desire to gain access to mineral resources was an important goal of the Phoenicians in fostering these ties with the native elite. Between 1992 and 1993, Isabel Pereira excavated a metal workshop at Santa Olaia on the mouth of the Río Mondego. A series of kilns was uncovered extending over an area of 960 m^2 and dated between the seventh and fifth centuries BC (Arruda 1999, 238; Pereira 1996, 62-3). Earlier excavations revealed three Iron Age phases in the construction of rectangular structures with no preceding Bronze Age occupation (Arruda 1999, 229). Large quantities of Phoenician and orientalizing pottery were found dating from the first half of the seventh century BC, particularly notable being the find of perfume burners similar to those from Trayamar and Jardín (Arruda 1999, 230-7). The location of the site on what was originally an island at the mouth of the river, the quantity and diversity of oriental and orientalizing pottery and the oriental architecture not only stress the importance of the site to the Phoenicians but also that the settlers were Phoenician in origin. Unfortunately it is not clear what metal was being worked, although the lack of mineral resources in the vicinity means that it must have been brought from further inland along the Mondego where there were supplies of tin and gold.

Arruda (1999, 251-2, 254) has suggested that the ores originated in the vicinity of Conímbriga. Although the extent of the Roman remains has prevented a complete understanding of the earlier periods of the site, excavations have revealed occupation of the Late Bronze and Iron Age (Arruda 1999, 246-7). The pottery includes locally produced grey ware – although some may have been imported from Santa Olaia and southern Spain, red slip plates and bowls, polichrome wares, Ramón T. 10.1.2.1 amphorae produced at Málaga (Arruda 1999, 247-9). Among the other finds a decorated ivory dated *c.* 600-450 BC is particularly worthy of note (Arruda 1999, 250-1). From Conímbriga goods travelled down the Mondego valley to Crasto de Talaverde before reaching Santa Olaia (Arruda 1999, 242). By the seventh century BC the Phoenicians were also travelling north of the Río Mondego (Millán León 1998, 74): merchants from Cádiz were trading as far as the Oestymnides (Avienus *Ora Maritima* 113-16) and the Cassiterides (Strabo 3.5.11) – either Galicia, Brittany or Britain. Orientalizing jewellery has been found along the coast at Baião, Malhada and Paços de Ferreira (González Ruibal 2004, 293-4).

In addition to the Phoenician settlements along the Atlantic coast, recent years have also seen the discovery of Phoenician colonies along the Mediterranean coast of the Peninsula. The first Phoenician imports appear along the southeast coast in the eighth century BC.[42] In 1985 a Phoenician settlement was discovered at La Fonteta (Guardamar del Segura) at the mouth of the Río Segura. The presence of imported East Greek and proto-Corinthian pottery dates the Iron Age occupation on the site to the period 750-545 BC (González Prats 1999, 38; González Prats *et al.* 2002, 117-18). These remains underlie an elaborate defensive wall constructed in the third quarter of the seventh century BC (González Prats 1999, 13; cf. also Azuar *et al.* 1998, 117).[43]

The site has produced evidence of metalworking from the earliest levels in the eighth century BC. Three small furnaces have been found in the earliest phase as well as slag and other remains dated 720-670 BC (Phase II) (González Prats 1999, 26-8). Phase III has produced the most evidence of metalworking with the discovery of two workshops: one from trench 7 with *tuyères*, melting pots, sandstone moulds, metal cakes and slag from copper and iron working; a second in trench 14 was devoted to the production of copper or bronze. Pottery – red slip plates, lamps (one with the Phoenician graffito MLQRT YSP) and *oinochoes* date these workshops to the first half of the seventh century BC (González Prats *et al.* 1997, 355-6). The kiln found in Phase VII (560-550 BC) contained a piece of litharge or lead oxide that is a by-product of the process of cupellation (González Prats *et al.* 1999, 268-9). The volume of evidence suggests that metalworking played a central role in the economy of the settlement throughout the Iron Age occupation of the site.The Phoenician settlement seems to have interacted closely with the neighbouring site of Cabezo Pequeño del Estaño, located 2,000 m inland overlooking the mouths of the Segura and Vinalopó. The site was occupied for a comparatively short period from the end of the eighth century to the mid- to late seventh century BC (García Menárguez 1994, 279). In addition to orientalizing pottery and elaborate fortifications, the site has also produced evidence of metalworking including a cake of lead perhaps used in cupellation (González Prats *et al.* 2000, 1531).

The Iberian settlement of El Oral (San Fulgencio) is situated on the slopes of the

Sierra de El Molar on the northern edge of the marshes at the mouth of the Ríos Segura and Vinalopó. Excavations in 1981-4 revealed a fortified settlement dated to the end of the sixth and first half of the fifth century BC (Abad Casal *et al.* 1993, 189). Iron slag has been found at various locations through the site, and house IVD has been identified as a metal workshop containing a hearth and quantities of iron and iron slag (Abad Casal *et al.* 1993, 193-5). A piece of litharge indicates that the production of silver through cupellation also took place, while iron can also be used to extract silver from jarosite (Abad Casal *et al.* 1993, 198-9).[44] The lack of evidence for furnaces, the distribution of slag throughout the settlement and the absence of mineral resources in the vicinity suggest that metalworking was secondary – minerals perhaps being brought from the Sierra de Orihuela or Callosa de Segura (Doménech Morante 1993, 202-3). The abundance of amphorae: Mañá-Pascual A4, Iberian, Massiliot and Corinthian Koehler B; together with Attic black glaze and an Etruscan bronze *olpe* suggest that the inhabitants enjoyed close relations with Cádiz and Empúries (Abad Casal *et al.* 1993, 200).

The goal of the Phoenicians was to gain access to the resources of copper and silver that were to be found in the Sierra de Crevillente (González Prats 1992, 244).[45] Phoenician imports – ivories, faience, *fibulae* – first reached the native settlement of Peña Negra in the second half of the ninth century BC, predating the foundation of the colony at La Fonteta (González Prats 1992, 253). Excavations at Peña Negra have revealed four phases of occupation dating from 900/850 to 550/530 BC (González Prats 1986, 280; 1992, 248-9). The site was located to exploit the mineral resources of the vicinity, and a metal workshop that produced weapons and other implements similar to those from Huelva and the Atlantic has been excavated, dated between 780 and 750 BC (González Prats 1992, 246-9).[46] The volume of imports increased from *c.* 700 BC with the profits from this trade allowing the restructuring of the settlement on a larger scale (covering an area of 34 ha) and the construction of fortifications. Fabric analysis of the pottery has shown not only that was it imported from the Phoenician settlements along the Málaga coast and on Ibiza, but that Phoenician forms were also produced in Peña Negra itself (González Prats 1986, 292-4; González Prats *et al.* 1983, 121, 124).[47]

The attribution of these forms to Peña Negra Phase II A at the beginning of the seventh century BC shows that Phoenician artisans were resident in the native settlement relatively quickly after the foundation of the Phoenician colony at the mouth of the Segura. A Phoenician graffito reading BD'ŠMN has been found on the base of a locally produced red slip plate and locally produced Vuillemont R1 amphorae bear incised potters' marks – an oriental practice that is also found at Morro de Mezquitilla (González Prats 1982, 328-31, 364, 384; 1986, 294-7, 301). In addition to pottery the Phoenician artisans also produced orientalizing jewellery similar to that from Etruria (González Prats 1993, 185). The burial of one of these oriental artisans has been found at Camí de Catral (González Prats 1991, 113).

Peña Negra was not alone in the intensity of its relations with the Phoenician settlers. An orientalizing community has been excavated at El Castellar de Librilla overlooking the valley of the Río Guadalentín. Five phases of occupation have been excavated, dating between the middle of the eighth century and the fourth century BC (Ros Sala 1993, 80; Gómez Ramos 1999, 120). Two iron-working furnaces have been excavated, the earliest (N) belonging to Phases II and III from the Late Bronze and Early Iron Ages (Ros Sala 1993, 82-4). The second, furnace E, is associated with

Phases IV and V. The lack of iron artifacts from the settlement itself led the excavator to suggest that the metallurgical activity on the site was geared primarily towards export (Ros Sala 1993, 91).

As well as having access to metals, the valleys of the Segura and Vinalopó link the Mediterranean coast with the Meseta and the upper Guadalquivir. The importance of this route is reflected in Avienus' inclusion of the region within Tartessos (*OM* 462) and the distribution of Phoenician and orientalizing goods during the seventh century and first half of the sixth century BC. El Monastil (Elda) on the middle Vinalopó received not only imports from La Fonteta but also Phoenician pottery produced at Peña Negra (Poveda Navarro 1994, 489-92; 2000, 1864-5). Surface collection from the Sierra de Camara 5 km west of El Monastil has revealed not only pottery imported from Peña Negra but also locally produced pottery bearing graffiti suggesting the presence of Phoenician artisans (Poveda Navarro 2000, 1865). The Phoenician settlers may have been attracted to the site by the quantities of iron ore to be found in the vicinity which would have gone to supply the needs of Peña Negra and the Phoenician settlements at the mouth of the Segura (Poveda Navarro 2000, 1866).

Oriental goods are found sporadically along the coast of Alicante and Valencia to the north of the Segura.[48] In 2000, twenty-five cremation burials were excavated at Les Casetes (Villajoyosa) and yielded a variety of orientalizing grave-goods: red slip and grey ware pottery; weapons; a faience canteen decorated with hieroglyphic inscriptions; steatite and glass amulets decorated with Egyptian deities and motifs; decorated ostrich eggs; gold, silver and bronze jewellery (García Gandía 2003, 219-20). The most elaborate of the tombs was chamber tomb 17, echoing tombs from Andalucía (Trayamar, Setefilla, Villaricos). Although partially destroyed, it yielded a belt buckle of a type widely found in Tartessian necropoleis in Sevilla, Huelva and southern Portugal, and a *thymiaterion* similar to those of wealthy burials elsewhere, for example tomb 17 at La Joya (García Gandía 2003, 225-6).[49]

Small quantities of Phoenician goods are found further north, for example at Vinarragell and Torrelló del Boverot d'Almassora – where fabric analysis has established parallels with the pottery from Peña Negra (Clausell Cantavella 2000, 1773). The goal of the Phoenicians may have been to obtain the mineral resources of the Ebro valley (Santos Retolaza 2003, 91-2). A number of sites have yielded evidence of Phoenician trade associated with metal working in the seventh century BC: Torrasa de la Vall de Uxó and Els Castellets de La Jana as well as the vicinity of Rosell (Oliver Foix 1991, 1097). Excavations in 1986-7 revealed a small Phoenician enclave at Aldovesta overlooking the Río Ebro (Mascort *et al.* 1991, 1078). The site was occupied from *c.* 650 to the first quarter of the sixth century BC. The largest structure (Building A) was a granary or storehouse containing Vuillemont R1 and Ebusitanian Mañá A1 amphorae. A mould for casting bronze or lead ingots was found in building E (Mascort *et al.* 1991, 1074-6; Sanmartí Grego 1991, 122).

Ibiza seems to have played a central role in this exchange. According to Diodorus Siculus, Carthaginians settled on the island in 654 BC (Diod. 5.16). Excavations at Puig des Molins revealed cremation burials dated to the mid-seventh century BC (Ramón Torres 1994, Costas Ribas *et al.* 1991, 783). The Phoenician settlement of Sa Caleta lies in the southwest of the island and was a substantial community extending to 4 ha in size (Ramón Torres 2002, 131). The site has yielded a variety of orientalizing pottery: amphorae, red slip, grey ware, bichrome and polichrome painted vessels, giving a date of the later seventh century BC. A number of Egyptian scarabs dating to the seventh/sixth centuries BC are preserved, including an example with a hieroglyphic inscription perhaps referring to the pharoah Psammetichus I (595-589 BC) (Ramón Torres 1994, 342). The site has also produced evidence of metalworking: nodules of argentiferous lead sulfide and an oven for working iron (Ramón Torres 2002, 134). The settlement of Sa Caleta is significant in that it is contemporaneous with the appearance of imports along the northeastern coast of the Peninsula. It is possible that the inhabitants of Sa Caleta acted as intermediaries, exchanging minerals for amphora-borne products (Ramón Torres 2002, 148).

The role of agriculture in the Phoenician economy

Discoveries of Phoenician settlers and merchants over a far larger area throw into question their reliance on the trade in metals. The abundance of colonies along the coast of Málaga together with quantities of Phoenician goods in the Guadalquivir valley has led to the suggestion that the goal of the Phoenicians was access to agricultural land rather than commercial activities relating to the trade in minerals (Alvar *et al.* 1988, 169-70). Carlos Wagner and Jaime Alvar (1989, 65-77) suggested that the Phoenician exodus was caused by a variety of demographic and economic factors arising from over-population and exhaustion of agricultural resources exacerbated by the Assyrian conquest of the Phoenician cities.[50] The importance of agriculture to the Phoenicians was first discussed by Whittaker (1974, 62-3) but it is only since the work of Wagner and Alvar that it has been widely recognized. Phoenician colonies were established at the mouths of fertile river valleys in areas which the lack of native inhabitants enabled the Phoenicians to exploit the agricultural resources of the vicinity (Wagner *et al.* 1989, 89-91). The abundance of Phoenician goods in the Tartessian necropoleis (eg. Cruz del Negro, Frigiliana, Setefilla and Medellín) points to the presence of Phoenician settlers in the agricultural communities of the lower Guadalquivir (Alvar *et al.* 1988, 180-1; Wagner *et al.* 1989, 98-9) – areas that are distinct from those containing mineral resources.

The model of 'agricultural colonization' proposed by Wagner and Alvar has been subjected to criticism on a number of counts, most importantly the tendency to attribute the incidence of Phoenician goods in the Guadalquivir valley to Phoenician settlers rather than to the profound acculturation that was taking place among the Tartessian communities. However, it is important to recognize the role that agriculture played in the economy of the Phoenician settlements.

The growing volume of fieldwork in southern Spain and Portugal has revealed a hierarchy of smaller agricultural communities located in the hinterland of the Phoenician colonies. During the seventh century BC there was an enormous increase in the number of agricultural villages in the hinterland of the colonies: in the valley of the Guadalhorce, Ronda and the valley of the Río Guadalteba (García Alfonso 2000, 1802).

The site of Cerro del Villar lies on what was originally an island at the mouth of the Río Guadalhorce (Aubet Semmler 1991, 102; Aubet Semmler *et al.* 1999, 29; Carmona González 2003, 19). The site was settled by the Phoenicians at the end of the eighth century and abandoned *c.* 570-560 BC in favour of Málaga. The valley of the Guadalhorce provided the colonists with access to the communities of Tartessos.

The route ran via Antequera where the site of Castillejos de Teba has yielded a red slip plate echoing those of Phase I at Morro de Mezquitilla, dated to the first half of the eighth century BC (García Alfonso 1993, 62, 67).[51]

The valley also provided fertile agricultural land suitable for the cultivation of wheat, barley and vines that were shipped in amphorae manufactured in Cerro del Villar. A ceramic workshop producing amphorae has been excavated in sector 3/4, dated to the final phase of the site in the early sixth century BC (Aubet Semmler 1995, 140; Aubet Semmler *et al.* 1999, 151-6; Barceló *et al.* 1995, 149-50; Curià *et al.* 2000, 1475-6).[52] The scale of the operation is clear from the quantities of amphorae found: 1,351 examples, as well as the typological uniformity of the amphorae produced: almost all were sack-shaped Vuillemont R1 vessels (Ramón T. 10.1.2.1) (Aubet Semmler *et al.* 1999, 176-81; Barceló *et al.* 1995, 158).[53] This type of amphora dates between 675/650 and 575/550 BC (Ramón Torres 1995, 231).

The specialized production of amphorae on this scale implies large-scale exploitation of the available resources, both agricultural and marine: wine, oil, grain and fish. Faunal remains reveal a predominance of cereals (21.12%) followed by vegetables (6%) and grapes (5.28%) from the second half of the eighth century and beginning of the sixth century (Cortes 5 and 7) (Aubet Semmler *et al.* 1999, 308). The large number of weeds extracted during threshing (62%) indicates that threshing took place within the colony – an hypothesis borne out by the presence of stone querns (Aubet Semmler 1993, 266; 2002, 91-2).[54] Aubet has suggested that the agricultural potential so far exceeded the requirements of the Phoenician colony that the economic focus of the colony was the export of surplus cereal production (2002, 93-4). As well as cereal crops the colony also produced significant quantities of grapes: 21.66% of the faunal remains from the late seventh century BC levels in Cortes 2, 2B, 2E, 6A and 6B are grapes, followed by cereals which account for 14.82% (Aubet Semmler *et al.* 1999, 309).[55]

The importance of agricultural production in the economy of the colony is reinforced by the appearance of smaller agricultural villages in the hinterland of the colony in the second half of the seventh century BC (Aubet Semmler *et al.* 2003, 70). Upland settlements like Llano del Virgen and Cerro de la Peluca were abandoned in favour of sites better situated to exploit the agricultural resources of the valley (Aubet Semmler *et al.* 1999, 57).

Unfortunately few of these secondary sites have been excavated. The site of Loma del Aeropuerto lies 2 km north of Cerro del Villar on what was the ancient shoreline. The limited excavations carried out in 1986 revealed pottery dating to the sixth century BC (Aubet Semmler *et al.* 1999, 59-64). The site seems to have been a native one related to the agricultural activities of the Phoenician colony (Aubet Semmler 1995, 140). Seventh-century levels have also been identified at a number of other sites: Cártama, Cerro de las Torres, Aratispi and Campamento Benítez (Aubet Semmler *et al.* 1999, 55-6). Located on the Río Cauche, Aratispi controlled land well suited for agriculture and livestock as well as routes inland to Granada and the Río Genil. These sites are characterized by the preponderance of locally produced amphorae: 80% of the finds from Cortijo de Nina consist of hand-made pottery – predominantly amphorae from Cerro del Villar (Aubet Semmler *et al.* 2003, 70). An important concentration of settlements lay at the confluence of the Ríos Guadalhorce, Guadalteba and Turón providing access to agricultural and mineral resources as well as to Cádiz and Granada (Aubet Semmler 1995, 142).

Fig. 4. Warehouse (Building C), Toscanos.

A similar pattern of agricultural exploitation seems to have existed elsewhere. The colony at Toscanos seems to have undergone a transformation *c.* 700 BC – the density of population increased in stratum II and by the mid-seventh century the city wall was extended to include the neighbouring Cerro de Alarcón and Cerro del Peñón – an area of 12-15 ha, although the density of the population in this area is unclear (Niemeyer 2002, 40). Toscanos IV was the most prosperous period of the site with workshops devoted to copper and iron working on the eastern slope of Cerro del Peñón dated to the seventh to sixth centuries BC (Martín Córdoba *et al.* 2002, 74).

The growing size and importance of the colony may be reflected in the construction of harbour installations in the second half of the seventh century BC (Arteaga *et al.* 1997, 117). The urban layout of the colony was restructured with the construction of a large warehouse (Building C; 11 x 15 m) and dependent houses (Buildings E, F and G) *c.* 700 BC (Niemeyer 2002, 35).[56] The commercial function of this building is clear from the quantity of amphorae found (Niemeyer 1995, 69; Sánchez Fernández 2003, 64-67): 72% of the pottery from level IVc consists of storage vessels (Martín Ruiz 1995, 73).[57]

The construction of a substantial warehouse building within the colony suggests the increased exploitation of the agricultural resources in the vicinity at the end of the eighth century BC. Osteological evidence supports the existence of intensive agriculture in the valley of the Río Vélez (Aubet Semmler 2002, 90-1). Cattle predominate, accounting for 49% of domesticated animals in levels dated to the late eighth century

BC, increasing to 62% *c.* 700 BC and reaching 63-80% in strata IV-V, dated to the seventh century. The increase in the number of cattle is in contrast to the declining numbers of sheep and goats (from 42% in stratum I to 18-31% in strata IV-V) and the scarcity of pigs during all phases of occupation. In addition to being consumed, the cattle were probably also used as traction. Pigs damage cultivated soils and their absence supports the existence of intensive agriculture in the hinterland of the colony.

Smaller agricultural villages have been found at Benajarafe, Los Algarrobeños and Cerca Niebla. Finds from Benajarafe indicate two periods of occupation, in the seventh to sixth centuries and third to second centuries BC. The agricultural role of the site is indicated by the abundance of amphorae during the initial period of occupation (Martín Córdoba *et al.* 2002, 86-7). Surplus production was shipped in Mañá A and ovoid amphorae from the kiln at Los Algarrobeños (Martín Córdoba *et al.* 1993).[58] The site of Cerca Niebla lies 2,000 m to the north of Toscanos. Excavations revealed the remains of houses and a hearth confined to a single phase of occupation dating to the seventh century BC (Gran Aymerich 1972, 414, 422). The similarity of the pottery to that of Toscanos suggests that the site enjoyed close relations with the colonists, and to judge by the extant housing and handmade wares was of secondary importance.

A similar agricultural settlement may have existed at Los Pinares near Morro de Mezquitilla at the mouth of the Río Algarrobo. Rescue excavations in 1987 revealed remains of rectangular housing dated to the second half of the seventh century BC (Martín Córdoba *et al.* 2002, 95-6; Aubet Semmler 1995, 145).

Several smaller sites have been identified in the hinterland of Lisboa at the mouth of the Tagus. Excavations have uncovered two small sites at Outorela (Outorela I and II) dated to the end of the sixth or the fifth century BC (Arruda 1999, 130-1). The site of Moinhos da Atalaia lies to the north of Outorela and was occupied during the Chalcolithic, Bronze and Iron Ages. Iron Age occupation was contemporaneous with Outorela and has yielded a similar range of pottery: grey ware, amphorae and pithoi (Arruda 1999, 131-3). Excavations at Quinta do Almaraz have revealed quantities of grapes, although there is no evidence of wine production (Arruda 1999, 109).

Environmental analysis from Castillo de Doña Blanca reveals a change in the focus of agricultural activities in the settlement during the later sixth century BC. During Phases I-III (675-550 BC) barley, wheat and canary grass are most common; however, while these species remain important there is a dramatic increase in the importance of vine cultivation: with grapes accounting for 32.8% of the sample from Phase IV (550-500 BC) compared to 6.25% during Phase III (Roselló *et al.* 1994, 25-7).[59] The faunal evidence, together with the evidence from Cerro del Villar and Toscanos for the production and storage of amphorae, points to a shift in the focus of the colonies during the sixth century BC with the development of viticulture.

Two wine-presses (houses IX and XIV) dating from the end of the fourth century BC have been excavated at Las Cumbres (Ruiz Mata *et al.* 1999, 125-6; Niveau de Villedary y Mariñas *et al.* 2000, 895). The first consists of three basins lined with *opus caementicium*, in the upper two of which the grapes were pressed, releasing must that drained into the basin below. Two circular structures found at Las Cumbres may have been used to heat must (Ruiz Mata *et al.* 1999, 126; 1998, 390; Niveau de Villedary y Mariñas *et al.* 2000, 896).[60] A store of amphorae was excavated from house X, consisting of forms derived from Mañá-Pascual A4, Muñoz A5 that may have been produced in the kilns at Torre Alta, quantities of 'Iberopunic' forms (Ramón T.

4.2.2.5; Florido XI, Muñoz C1 and 2, Pellicer D), and Greco-Italic and Punic forms from the central Mediterranean (Ruiz Mata *et al.* 1999, 127; Niveau de Villedary y Mariñas 1999, 133-5; Niveau de Villedary y Mariñas *et al.* 2000, 896-7). The presence of Mañá-Pascual A4 and Muñoz A5 suggests close ties with the Bay of Cádiz – a connection supported by the presence of black glaze pottery from Kouass. A similar press has been excavated from third-century BC levels at Castillo de Doña Blanca.

The earliest evidence for wine making comes from the indigenous settlement of L'Alt de Benimaquía (Denia).[61] Excavations have revealed a fortified orientalizing community dated between 625 and 550 BC (Gómez Bellard *et al.* 1993, 20-1). Excavations between 1989 and 1991 uncovered an area of 150 m^2 south of the city wall containing a substantial winery. Four rooms have been found to contain basins and pressing floors (Gómez Bellard *et al.* 1993, 21; 1993, 382-8; 1994, 14-16).

The layout of the winery conforms to the descriptions of later Roman agricultural writers: Varro (*De Re Rustica* 1.54), Columella (*De Re Rustica* 12.18) and Cato the Elder (*De Agricultura* 23-6). When the grapes were brought in from the vineyards they were separated out for various uses – either to be eaten or to be processed. The grapes were treaded and the must was drained off into *dolia* or vats lined with pitch to ferment. The grapes were pressed again to remove any remaining must, which was then allowed to ferment for 30 days. Rooms 4 and 5 contain platforms and basins similar to those described by Palladius (*De Agricultura* 1.18). The acidity of the wine could be reduced by adding chalk or marble dust. It was important for the wine to be kept at a cool temperature in order to prevent spoilage. Burying the *dolia* could regulate the temperature, and Cato the Elder says that the containers should be wiped off twice a day to keep them cool. Pliny suggests that the containers should be placed under windows facing northeast or east to allow the circulation of cool air (*Natural History* 133-5). Palladius (*De Agricultura* 1.18) adds that they should be away from stables, dung heaps or standing water as the smell might adversely affect the wine. The wine would then be racked and placed in amphorae for aging or transportation. The amphorae used were local imitations of Phoenician Vuillemont R1 vessels (Gómez Bellard *et al.* 1993, 20; 1994, 17). Particularly significant are the 7,000 grape pips found on the floor of room 2. The grapes are of the cultivated variety introduced by the Phoenicians and not the wild grapes used previously (Gómez Bellard *et al.* 1993, 25). The use of cultivated grapes together with the Vuillemont R1 amphorae clearly associates the production of wine at L'Alt de Benimaquía with the Phoenician settlements to the south.

This exploitation of agricultural resources has been borne out by the early appearance of locally produced amphorae. Although no kilns have been discovered, the distribution of Vuillemont R1 (Ramón T. 10.1.1.1) amphorae suggests that they were manufactured along the Straits of Gibraltar *c.* 750 BC (Ramón Torres 1995, 229-30). Significant quantities have been found in the Phoenician settlements at Castillo de Doña Blanca and along the Málaga coast (at Cerro del Villar, Chorreras, Morro de Mezquitilla, Toscanos, Cerro de Alarcón and Alumuñécar), as well as in the Tartessian settlements (Huelva, El Carambolo, San Bartolomé de Almonte, Carmona). Further afield they are found at orientalizing sites along the east coast (Aldovesta, Vinarragell, La Torrassa, Los Villares, Peña Negra, El Castellar de Librilla) as well as occasionally further east (at Sulcis, Ischia and Carthage). Unfortunately there is little evidence for the contents of these vessels although their presence in the winery at L'Alt de Benimaquía suggests that they were used to carry wine. This exchange of agricultural produce underwent a dramatic increase from *c.* 675-650 BC with the widespread distribution of Ramón T. 10.1.2.1 amphorae extending from Alcacer do Sal to Cataluña (Ramón Torres 1995, 230-1).

Fabric analysis has been carried out on 29 sherds of Vuillemont R1 amphorae recovered from orientalizing levels at Ronda la Vieja dated from 820 ± 80 BC and contemporary with the earliest Phoenician imports. Analysis revealed that 23 of the sherds were locally produced (Padial *et al.* 2000, 1843-4). This early date for the first indigenous amphora production is also found at Cerro de los Infantes (Pinos Puente, Granada) where a kiln producing Vuillemont R1 amphorae has been excavated in level XI. The kiln dates to the second half of the seventh century or beginning of the sixth century BC (Contreras *et al.* 1983, 534). Analysis of amphorae dated to the end of the sixth century BC from Cerro Macareno indicates that the clay was extracted in the vicinity of the settlement (González Vilches *et al.* 1982, 391; Belén Deamos 2000, 36-9).[62] Four kilns dated between the middle of the fifth century (H I and II) and the fourth century (G) were excavated in 1974 together with quantities of sack-shaped amphorae from a pit in front of kiln G (Belén Deamos 2000, 39-42; Ruiz Mata *et al.* 1999, 95-6). A similar kiln has been excavated at Pajar de Artillo producing Ramón T. 8.1.1.2 and Muñoz A5 (T. 8.2.1.1), dating to the fourth century (Belén Deamos 2000, 42-5).[63]

Fabric analysis carried out on sixteen sherds suggests a local origin for Mañá-Pascual A4 amphorae found during excavations in the Palace of the Marqués de Saltillo in Carmona (Belén Deamos *et al.* 1997, 328; Belén Deamos 2000, 45). The rims conform to the earliest examples of this type of amphora dating to the end of the sixth and the fifth century BC (Belén Deamos *et al.* 1997, 85). Eight kilns were excavated to the north of the city with quantities of Muñoz A5 amphorae (Rodríguez Rodríguez 2001, 311-13).

Further evidence of wine production is to be found in the vicinity of Requena-Utiel: four kilns have been excavated at Las Casillas del Cura (Venta del Moro, Valencia) dated to the end of the sixth century or early fifth century BC (Martínez Valle *et al.* 2000, 227; Duarte Martínez *et al.* 2000, 231-5). Excavations in 1997 uncovered a poorly preserved kiln containing amphorae similar to the Phoenician forms produced at Los Villares de Caudete de las Fuentes, where grape seeds have also been found together with wine presses at La Solana de las Piletas (Martínez Valle *et al.* 2000, 227).[64]

There may also have been an expansion of agricultural activities in the vicinity of Cádiz. Pedro Carretero Poblete has suggested that several rural sites in the hinterland of Cádiz originate at the end of the fifth century BC: La Calerilla (Jerez de la Frontera), Esperilla (Espera), Cerro de la Monjas (Trebujena) and Cerro del Berrueco (Medina Sidonia). Only limited excavations have taken place and the identification of these sites is based on the presence of Ramón T. 8.1.1.2 and Muñoz A5 (T. 8.2.1.1) amphorae that were produced in the vicinity of Cádiz from the end of the fifth century BC to the third century BC (Carretero Poblete 2004, 2; Ramón Torres 1995, 222, 225-6).

The exploitation of marine resources

As well as exploiting the agricultural resources of their hinterland, the colonies seem also to have made use of the available marine resources. Strabo praises the coasts of Andalucía for their wealth of marine life (3.2.7) and Ps.-Aristotle mentions that the voyages of Gaditanian fishermen lasted for as long as four days (*De Mirabilibus Auscultationibus* 136). Analysis of fish bones from Cerro del Villar indicates the presence of both coastal and pelagic species with *Clupeidae* and *Sparidae* being the most numerous. The former predominates, with the sardine accounting for more than 40% of the total while of the *Sparidae* the bream (*Boops boops*) is most common (Aubet Semmler *et al.* 1999, 322-3). *Sparidae* are widespread on sites in southern Spain and are the most common family at Castillo de Doña Blanca, reaching 47.5% of the total fish (Roselló *et al.* 1994, 108). The concentration of tunny in levels dated to the second half of the seventh century BC is also worthy of note. In contrast to the typical discovery of the more durable vertebrae, the tunny are represented by bones of the median fins. The excavators have suggested that the tunny was not locally caught, but that the meat from the fish was traded to the site from elsewhere (Roselló *et al.* 1994, 118-19).[65] A fragment of an unidentified amphora was found with fish scales adhering to the inner surface during excavations at Plaza de las Monjas 12/Calle de Méndez Núñez 7-13 in Huelva (González de Canales Cerisola *et al.* 2004, 176).[66]

Storage and trading of fish would have required preservation either as salt fish – the Latin *salsamentum* – or as fish sauce, as fish spoil quickly after their removal from water. Several Attic comedians of the fourth and fifth centuries BC refer to the existence of Spanish fish sauce, and Ps.-Aristotle records that Gades sent salted tunny to Carthage (*De Mirabilibus Auscultationibus* 136).[67] Unfortunately contemporary descriptions of the production techniques do not survive; however, several sources from the Roman period record the techniques involved, which do not seem to have changed from the earlier Phoenician practices.

According to the Roman agricultural writer Columella, writing in the first century AD, the process of salting fish was similar to that of salting pork (*De Re Rustica* 12.55.1-4). Columella describes a process of brining whereby the meat is interspersed with alternating layers of salt which is then compressed through the application of weight to ensure that the meat would become fully immersed in salt. The high level of salinity – 70% (Curtis 1991, 19) – will have ensured the preservation of the fish. Cato the Elder describes a process of mild curing in which the meat was immersed in salt for seventeen days, although larger amounts could be used to hasten the process after which the meat would be smoked (*De Agricultura* 162). Hard curing entails the use of higher quantities of salt and results in very salty meat with better preservative qualities.

Several sources describe the production of fish sauce (Curtis 1991, 6-15; 2001, 404-6). Pliny does no more than list the ingredients, namely the fleshy parts of fish combined with salt (*Natural History* 31.43.93). A fuller description is to be found in Manilius' poem, *Astronomica* (5.565-81). Although giving only a scanty account of the processing itself Manilius describes the catching of the tunny and the cutting up of the fish along the shore.

A number of later texts preserve two recipes for processing fish sauce. A recipe for producing fish sauce is appended to a ninth- or tenth-century manuscript of the third-century AD *De Medicamentis* of Ps.-Gargilius Martialis. The text describes a process of dry salting similar to that described by Cato the Elder whereby layers of herbs, spices, fish and salt are placed in a container which is then left in the sun to ferment for 27 days, being stirred regularly (*De Medicamentis* 62). The sauce was then drained and bottled. A second process of brining is preserved in a single manuscript of the *Breviarium Rerum Gestarum Populi Romani* of Rufius Festus. The mixture of salt and fish is cooked in a bronze pot until it reduced by two-thirds, at which point the sauce is strained and bottled (Curtis 1991, 192-3).[68]

The fullest description, however, comes from the tenth-century AD Greek agricultural manual, the *Geoponica*. In a chapter entitled 'On the preparation of *gara*', the author gives two methods of producing fish sauce (20.46.1-6). In the first, the fish are placed in a salt solution and allowed to ferment in the sun for a period of up to three months, at which time the mixture is drained. The second method involves placing the fish in brine that is boiled until the mixture begins to reduce before straining the resulting fish sauce. The primary concern seems to have been the maintenance of a sufficient level of salinity. Cato the Elder tells us that to salt hams, one *modius* of salt should be added to each ham (*De Agricultura* 162).[69] According to the *Geoponica* the brine had to be salty enough to float an egg (20.46.3) – a mixture of one *modius* of fish to two *sextarii* of salt, or a salt to fish ratio of 1:8 (Curtis 1991, 13).

It seems reasonable to suppose that, in view of the time-span of these recipes, the processes of salting and producing fish sauce remained unchanged throughout antiquity and are equally applicable to the Phoenician salting installations. The process of dry salting in vats is most suitable for the processing of large quantities of fish and would have been the norm in salting installations. Brining would have been less appropriate for the salting of large quantities of fish, though it may have been employed as a supplement to other processing.

Over the last twenty years excavations in the city of Cádiz have uncovered several fish salting installations dating perhaps as early as the eighth century BC. Excavations carried out on the Calle Cánovas de Castillo in 2002 uncovered occupation dated to the eighth century BC associated with remains of marine molluscs and fish, in particular tunny (Niveau de Villedary 2007, 428). The earliest phases of occupation at Teatro de Andalucía, dating between the eighth and fifth centuries BC, included evidence of the consumption of fish (Cobos Rodríguez *et al.* 1995, 117; Niveau de Villedary 2007, 428; Cobos Rodríguez 1999, 20).

From the sixth to fifth centuries BC onwards the evidence becomes more plentiful. The most extensively excavated of the factories is that of Las Redes which lies on the beach at Fuentebravía (Puerto de Santa Maria). The factory functioned from 430 to 200 BC, although the apogee of industrial activities was during Phase I (430-325 BC) (Muñoz Vicente *et al.* 1987, 491-2; Vallejo Sánchez *et al.* 1997, 109; Ruiz Gil 1991, 1211). The excavations at Las Redes have enabled a more complete picture of the organization of the factory to be gained. The complex consists of five rooms and extends over an area of 10.70 x 10.60 m. The first room appears to have been used for the preparation and dissection of the fish as the soil has been darkened by the decomposition of the organic remains. The floor of the second room consists of pebbles mixed with ground pottery and lime. The floor slopes towards the shore to facilitate cleaning and the room was probably used for washing the fish. The third room seems to have been the principal entrance to the factory. Room four contained various fishing implements: hooks, net weights and needles and seems to have been used as a storage area. The salting itself took place in room five which contained two vats used to macerate the fish in salt (Muñoz Vicente *et al.* 1987, 492; 1999, 202). The presence of vats recalls the process of dry salting described by Ps.-Gargilius Martialis and the author of the *Geoponica*. No heating facilities have been found.

An important fish saltery was uncovered in 1984 and 1985 in the Plaza de Asdrúbal (Muñoz Vicente *et al.* 1987, 488; 1999, 202-3).[70] The earliest phase of the factory dates to the end of the sixth century BC and fifth century BC and consists of a series of pits filled with pottery (amphorae, red slip plates, attic imports), fishing implements and the bones of tunny fish (Muñoz Vicente *et al.* 2004, 136; Vallejo Sánchez *et al.* 1997, 108; Ramón Torres 1995, 85). The majority of the amphorae are Mañá-Pascual A4a, although Corinthian A and B and vessels derived from Mañá A1 are also present (Muñoz Vicente *et al.* 1987, 488). The nearby factory in the Avenida de Andalucía seems to have been similar in date, operating from the fifth to the second century BC (Muñoz Vicente *et al.* 1987, 489-90; Muñoz Vicente *et al.* 1999, 203).

A possible fifth-century BC fish factory was found in the vicinity of the Teatro de Andalucía in 1994-5 on the basis of finds of fish bones and A4a and A4c amphorae (Muñoz Vicente *et al.* 1999, 204; 2004, 139-40).[71] The salting vat discovered on the corner of Avdas. García de Sola and de Portugal is tentatively dated to the fourth century BC (Muñoz Vicente *et al.* 1987, 490; 2004, 139; Vallejo Sánchez *et al.* 1997, 109).[72] In 1987 excavations between Calles Ferrocarril and Brunete uncovered four salting vats, one of which seems to have been in use during the fourth century BC.[73] An adjoining necropolis dates from the fourth century BC to the first century AD (Perdigones Moreno *et al.* 1989, 93-4).

A similar factory to that of Las Redes has been recently excavated at El Pinar Hondo. The factory seems to have been at its most active in the fifth to fourth centuries BC although it remained in use until a point at the end of the third century or during the second century BC (Gutiérrez López 2003, 246-7). A storage area for fishing implements and Mañá-Pascual A4 amphorae has been found together with two vats for salting (Gutiérrez López 2003, 244-5). The presence of a furnace suggests that dry salting may have been supplemented by the quicker recipes found in Rufius Festus and the *Geoponica*. Recent excavations have uncovered a similar factory at Puerto 19 near the mouth of the Río Guadalete, dating from the fifth century BC (Sáez Romero *et al.* 2007, 466).

Excavations in Camposoto revealed a complex of seven kilns associated with a possible fish saltery. The kilns are organized in three groups: kilns 2a, b and 3, 1 and 5, 4, 6 and 7. Two phases of activity have been identified beginning in the first half of the sixth century BC (Gago Vidal *et al.* 2000, 47). From the second half of the sixth century BC ceramic production became increasingly focused on Mañá-Pascual A4a amphorae (Gago Vidal *et al.* 2000, 49). Fifty-four intact examples of this type of amphora containing fish bones were found in front of kilns 2 and 3 (Gago Vidal *et al.* 2000, 42-3). Five species of fish were identified: the most numerous was the tunny (*Thunnus thynnus*) which accounts for 59.04% of the sample, followed by monkfish (*Lophius piscatorius*) (13.52%) and hake (*Merluccis merluccius*) (7.95%) (Ramón Torres *et al.* 2007, 306).[74] The finds of fish suggest that there were salting vats in the vicinity, though excavations have yet to find the installations themselves.[75] The kilns may also have produced small quantities of Ionian and Corinthian amphorae (Ramón Torres *et al.* 2007, 94-6).[76] The excavators have suggested that these were used to carry wine and are related to the imitation of Attic wine cups and *skyphoi* (Ramón Torres *et al.* 2007, 118). Carbonized grape seeds (*Vitis vinifera*) have been found in the fill of kiln 3 (Ramón Torres *et al.* 2007, 19-20).

Evidence for the exportation of Gaditanian fish sauce comes from the so-called

'Punic Amphora Room' in Corinth where Mañá-Pascual A4 amphorae have been found together with filleted fish and dated to *c.* 460-440 BC (Maniatis *et al.* 1984, 205). Sea bream was most common, together with tunny (Williams 1979, 117). Fabric analysis of the amphorae indicates that the amphorae originated around the Straits of Gibraltar without any further precision, although parallels were noted with the fabric of southern Spanish fish sauce amphorae (Maniatis *et al.* 1984, 216). The return trade explains the presence of Corinthian A and B amphorae at fisheries around the Bay of Cádiz. Two Mañá-Pascual A4 amphorae have been found at Olympia in contexts dated to 450-430 BC (López Castro 1995, 65).

The organization of this industry has been the subject of considerable debate, with hypotheses ranging from small-scale installations operating at a familial level to governmental and religious control (Gutiérrez López 2004, 242; Gago Vidal *et al.* 2000, 52; Muñoz Vicente *et al.* 1999, 209-11). While the individual installations do not seem to have been large, the marked concentration of fisheries around the Bay of Cádiz together with the large-scale production of amphorae to support the salting industry and the evidence of trade with the city of Corinth indicate that from the beginning of the fifth century BC Cádiz was the scene of large-scale industrial exploitation of marine resources.[77]

The Phoenician colonists were also engaged in the production of purple dye. The discovery of purple was attributed to the Phoenicians – the name derives from the Greek *phoenix*, meaning 'purple'.[78] According to mythology Melqart made the discovery as he walked along the shore with his dog and the nymph Tyros. The dog chewed on a murex shell, producing the purple that Melqart then used to dye a gown for his consort (Pollux *Onomasticon* 1.45-8). Tyrian purple was particularly noted (Strabo 16.2.23). Pliny could comment that the fame of Tyre rested on its shellfish and purple dye (*Natural History* 5.17.46): 'nunc omnis eius nobilitas conchylio atque purpura constat'.

The fullest description of the techniques of producing purple dye also comes from Pliny (*Natural History* 9.62.133). The dye is extracted primarily from three species of mollusc – *Murex trunculus*, *Murex brandaris* and *Purpura haemastoma*.[79] The dye-bearing glands are removed from the shells and then macerated in salt for three days. The glands are then placed in water and heated for nine days at which time the mixture is strained and the dye tested by dipping a washed fleece.[80] In view of the large quantities of molluscs required – 8,000 snails are needed to produce just one gram of dye (Reece 1980, 90) – the most common archaeological evidence of dyeing consists of broken shells.

Quantities of crushed molluscs have been found in Late Bronze contexts at Ugarit, Sarepta and Tel Akko (Brody 2002, 74). The residue of purple dye has been found on the interior of a thirteenth-century BC vessel at Sarepta associated with *Murex trunculus* (McGovern *et al.* 1988, 81). Phoenician colonists transplanted the industry to the west and quantities of murex shells have been found at a number of colonies. Murex shells are found at Almuñécar, Toscanos and Morro de Mezquitilla (Schubart *et al.* 1969, 149; Aubet Semmler 1993, 264).

Although the growing volume of archaeological studies will no doubt further refine this picture, the economic complexity of the Phoenician colonies is now becoming evident. The initial importance of metallurgy seems clear thanks to the early appearance of Phoenician goods in the Sierra de Aracena, the Sierra Morena and the Sierra de Crevillente as well as the presence of metal workshops in the earliest levels of Phoenician colonies on the coast of Málaga and the Segura valley. However the colonies seem to have experienced a gradual transformation through the seventh and early sixth centuries BC. The period is characterized by growing diversification of the economies of the colonies – particularly notably in respect of wine and salted fish from the end of the sixth century BC – and the appearance of locally produced amphorae. The culmination of this process lies in the so-called sixth-century 'crisis'.

The 'sixth-century crisis'

Archaeologists commonly speak of a profound 'crisis' or 'transformation' that affected the Phoenician colonies and their Tartessian neighbours in the sixth century BC. The abandonment of the colonies at Toscanos and Cerro del Villar *c.* 570-550 BC is often taken as symptomactic of this 'crisis'. The 'crisis' has been attributed to a variety of factors both internally and externally relating to the fall of Tyre to the Babylonians in 573 BC and the exhaustion of the resources of Tartessos leading to the exploitation of peripheral areas. Competition from these peripheral polities proved too much for the Tartessian kingdom and led to the growth of powerful Iberian states elsewhere (Júdice Gamito 1988, 138). These states are treated as separate entities in their own right by the classical sources – the Turdetani, Oretani, Carpetani, Vaccei, Vettones, Lusitani and Celts (Strabo 3.3.4-5).

The evidence from Toscanos and Cerro del Villar does not bear out the occurrence of a widespread crisis among the Phoenician colonies. The reasons for the abandonment of Toscanos are unclear.[81] That the Phoenician inhabitants remained in the vicinity, however, is indicated by the continued use of the Jardín necropolis. In 1967 the necropolis of Jardín was discovered lying 500 m north of Toscanos. The subsequent excavations have uncovered more than 100 burials ranging in date from the second half of the sixth century to the fourth century BC (Schubart *et al.* 1995, 59). The earliest phase of the necropolis coincides with the final period of occupation at Toscanos. Later burials relate to occupation at Cerro del Mar. Oswaldo Arteaga has suggested that the inhabitants of Toscanos relocated to the opposite bank of the Río Vélez, where excavations have revealed a sequence of occupation from the fifth to the second centuries BC (Arteaga 1981, 295; 1997, 166). Seventh-century BC burials have also been excavated on the southern slope of Cerro del Mar (Arteaga 1997, 163). Only tomb 14 has been published, but it is similar to sixth-century BC burials from Jardín containing fragments of alabaster, red slip pottery and a proto-Corinthian *kotyle* of the early seventh century BC (Domínguez Monedero *et al.* 2001, 33; Martín Córdoba *et al.* 2002, 84).

The silting-up of the estuary of the Río Guadalhorce prompted the abandonment of Cerro del Villar. Deforestation brought about by intensive agriculture hastened the process of alluvial deposition throughout the seventh century BC. By 600 BC the lower slopes of the colony had been abandoned as a result of flooding (Aubet Semmler 1991, 624; Aubet Semmler *et al.* 2003, 63). The population relocated to Málaga, where occupation began during the first half of the sixth century BC (Gran Aymerich 1985, 137). Málaga offered the settlers excellent harbour facilities accessing Tartessos and the upper Guadalquivir (Avienus *Ora Maritima* 178-82). The economic importance of Málaga is clear from the quantities of amphorae discovered in the earliest phases of the town (accounting for 66% of the total finds) (Gran Aymerich 1985, 137).

The arrival of the Greeks

This transformation is reflected in the distribution of Greek pottery. After a short hiatus at the end of the sixth century BC there was a dramatic resurgence in the quantity of Greek imports – particularly Athenian wares – from the middle of the fifth century BC (Cabrera Bonet 1998, 200). Whereas earlier Greek imports had been brought by Phoenician merchants to the vicinity of Huelva (Shefton 1982, 342; García Martín 2003, 94) the distribution of Greek pottery is now concentrated along the east coast. The reasons for this change are unclear. They may have been external to the Peninsula: Phoenician trade being curtailed by the fall of Tyre, and East Greek goods disappearing after the fall of Phocaea to the Persians – although Athenian trade to the east coast remained unaffected (Shefton 1982, 364-5).

The reason for this shift was long thought to have been the exclusion of Greek merchants from Andalucía by the Carthaginians following the battle of Alalia (535 BC) and the subsequent treaty of 509 BC (Shefton 1982, 366-7). Arteaga has envisaged the creation of a 'Gaditanian League' which restricted access to the markets of the Straits of Gibraltar (Arteaga 2001, 260-2). Excavations in Huelva have, however, revealed that Attic pottery continued to arrive in considerable quantities: Castulo cups, Saint Valentin *kantharoi*, garlanded and owl *skyphoi* and red-figure cups (Fernández Jurado 1989, 151). Excavations in the Roman theatre and the Convent of S. Agustín in Málaga reveal a preponderance of East Greek wares in the first half of the sixth century BC (71%) which disappear by the end of the century. At this point Greek imports are exclusively Athenian (Gran Aymerich 1988, 211, 213; 1989, 171-3). The peak of Attic imports in Málaga dates between 430 and 370 BC (Gran Aymerich 1988, 173). Taken over the Peninsula as a whole, the increase in Greek wares during this period is dramatic: whereas 6.9% of Greek pottery dates to 450-425 BC, 13.6% dates to 425-400 increasing to 26.8% in 400-375 BC and 39.5% between 375 and 350 BC (Rouillard 1991, 110).

The impetus for the revival of Attic imports from *c.* 430 BC was the Phocaean colony at Empúries where there is a marked concentration of Attic imports: black-glaze type C stemmed cups, black-figure cup-*skyphoi* and red-figure vessels – particularly those of the Marlay painter (Rouillard 1991, 117; Shefton 1995, 129).[82] The earliest of these are the type C stemmed cups which date from the end of the sixth century to the early fifth century BC (Shefton 1995, 128). According to Strabo (3.4.8) the colony was founded by Phocaeans from Massilia (see also Ps.-Scymnos 5.203-4). The Greeks first settled on a small island on the southern shore of the Gulf of Rosas – the modern village of San Martí d'Empuries, before moving on to the mainland (Ruiz de Arbulo 1992, 60; Rouillard 1991, 247-51). The foundation of the Palaiapolis took place shortly after the foundation of Massilia, *c.* 600 BC, with the foundation of the Neapolis occurring *c.* 550 BC (Almagro Basch 1964, 76-86; Sanmartí Grego *et al.* 1988, 7).

In contrast to Massilia, Empúries enjoyed a dramatic increase in the quantity of imported Greek pottery from *c.* 500 BC, which extended to the Iberian communities of the hinterland *c.* 425 BC (Rouillard 1991, 107, 112; Picazo 1977, 133). This increase in Greek commerce prompted a restructuring of the native settlements towards an intensification of agricultural production (Pons i Brun 1993, 106). The defences of the settlement at Mas Castellar de Pontós were demolished at the end of the fifth century or beginning of the fourth century BC to make way for an expansion of the settlement and more intensive agriculture associated with large quantities of imported Attic pottery (Pons i Brun 1993, 108; Martín Ortega *et al.* 2001, 45). The quantity of Attic imports suggests that the impetus came from the demand for cereals from Athens (Sanmartí Grego 1996, 31).[83]

Evidence for cereal production comes in the form of silos that have been excavated at a number of native settlements situated along the edge of the coastal plain of the Alt Empordà (Martín Ortega *et al.* 2001, 41-2).[84] According to Varro (*De Re Rustica* 1.57), the use of silos to store grain was a feature of eastern Iberia.[85] The silos were lined with hay to protect the grain from air and humidity, thus preventing bacterial growth and enabling the storage of cereals for considerable periods (Cuesta *et al.* 1985, 240; Curtis 2001, 325-6).

As many as 2,500-3,000 silos have been discovered at Mas Castellar de Pontós (Bouso García *et al.* 2000, 119). Located 20 km inland of Empúries and Rhode on a low hill overlooking the course of the Alguema, the site possessed easy access to Empúries and the coast via the Río Fluvià 2 km to the south (Adroher *et al.* 1993, 32; Pons i Brun *et al.* 2001, 146). Two phases of occupation have been identified: the first consists of a fortified *oppidum* (fifth to fourth centuries BC) and succeeding agricultural community focused on the production and trade of cereal crops (Bouso García *et al.* 2000, 117-18; Pons i Brun 1993, 108; Pons i Brun *et al.* 2001, 148). The fill of the silos contained pottery of the seventh to fourth centuries BC as well as *thymiateria* of Tanit-Demeter similar to examples from Empúries dated to 250-200 BC (Pujol Puigvehí 1989, vol. 2, 31-4). A Greek presence is reinforced by the identification of a possible sanctuary to Demeter-Persephone (Building 1) dated to the fourth to second centuries BC (Adroher *et al.* 1993, 41-53).

The most striking feature of the settlement is the storage capacity of the silos: increasing from 545 litres before 400 BC to an average of 3,348 litres between 300 and 175 BC, a total capacity of over 283 tonnes of cereal (Bouso García *et al.* 2000, 119-20). Of the faunal remains cereals predominate (52,107 remains = 71%): millet is most common, accounting for 44% of the sample, followed by wheat and barley (Canal i Barcala 2000, 127). Vegetables are also present as well as increasing quantities of grapes during the final phases of the site (Canal i Barcala 2000, 129-30). Storage on this scale required Mas Castellar to be the centre of a surrounding agricultural hinterland consisting of smaller farms and silos – several of which have been identified.[86]

Fourteen silos have been excavated at La Qüestió d'en Solà (Ermedàs) together with Attic imports and other pottery of the fourth to second centuries BC (Pujol Puigvehí 1989 vol. 2, 52-5; Pons i Brun *et al.* 2001, 153).[87] Eleven silos have been excavated at Olivet d'en Requesens (Creixell) dated to the second half of the fifth and the fourth century BC (Pons i Brun *et al.* 2001, 153; Pujol Puigvehí 1989 vol. 2, 51-2). Silos have been found further afield at Puig Sorrer, Camp del Pla and Vilafant (Pons i Brun *et al.* 2001, 153-4).

The silos are concentrated along the periphery of the marshy coastal plain and the lack of any substantial settlements between Empúries and Mas Castellar points to the latter having served a central role in supplying the Greeks. Surplus production would be gathered at Mas Castellar from where it was transported to the colony at Empúries, receiving in return Attic wares which account for 25% of the pottery from the fifth and fourth centuries BC (Bouso García *et al.* 2000, 122). The presence of the Greek sanctuary at Mas Castellar served as guarantor and facilitator of this exchange.

The valley of the Daró provided fertile agricultural land suitable for the cultivation of cereal crops. Empúries seems to have enjoyed particularly close relations with the native settlements in the vicinity of Ullastret: the *oppida* of Puig de Sant Andreu and Illa d'en Reixac.[88] The earliest occupation dates to the end of the seventh century and seems quickly to have come into contact with the Greeks during the first half of the sixth century BC, importing Ionian B2 cups dated to *c.* 575 BC together with locally produced grey ware imitations (Domínguez Monedero *et al.* 2001, 73-6; Pujol Puigvehí 1989, vol. 1, 280). More than 200 silos have been excavated, reflecting the expanding agricultural importance of the settlement in the fourth and third centuries BC (Plana i Mallart *et al.* 2001, 165; Martín Ortega 1978, 15). Plant remains from Illa d'en Reixac reveal a decline in trees in favour of an intensification of cereal cultivation during this period (Martín Ortega *et al.* 1999, 325; Plana i Mallart *et al.* 2001, 173). Surveys of the hinterland have uncovered smaller agricultural settlements characterized by a predominance of coarse wares and amphorae dated predominately to the fourth and third centuries BC (Plana i Mallart *et al.* 2001, 165-72). The impetus for this expansion came from Empúries, coinciding with an increase in the volume and ubiquity of Attic pottery at Puig de Sant Andreu which reaches its apogee in the first half of the fourth century BC (Picazo 1977, 126).[89]

The economy of Empúries was not, however, confined to the trade in cereals. According to Strabo (3.4.9) the inhabitants of Empúries were particularly noted for their skill in working flax. Flax (*Linum usitassimum*), thrives in a moist temperate climate, the highest quality fibre being produced in coastal areas (Kampp 1939, 165). The stalk fibres of the plant were extracted to produce linen (Pliny *Natural History* 19.16-18).[90]

The region was also noted for its mineral resources.[91] The most important was the alluvial silver that attracted Phoenician and Massiliot merchants to the southern Pyrenees (Diodorus 5.35; Ps.-Aristotle *De Mirabilibus Auscultationibus* 87). Copper, argentiferous lead, iron and gold were found inland from Empúries in the valleys of the Ter and Fresser and along the coast to the south at Gavarres and Begur (Ruiz de Arbulo 1984, 125; Carme Rovira 1993, 72, 128-30).[92] Iron, lead, silver and sulphur were mined at La Mena (San Feliu de Buixalleu) until the beginning of the twentieth century. Three native settlements were located in the proximity of the mines: Torre de la Mora, Castell de Montsoriu and Turó de Buixalleu, which received Attic imports in the fifth century BC (Martín Ortega *et al.* 2001, 48).

The earliest evidence of bronzeworking from Illa d'en Reixac dates to the final quarter of the sixth century BC (Martín Ortega *et al.* 1999, 225). A partially preserved furnace (FR-80) dates to the end of the fifth century BC (Martín Ortega *et al.* 1999, 235-6; 2000, 250; Carme Rovira 1993, 99). Iron slag is also found throughout the site: the earliest evidence dates to the second quarter of the sixth century BC, but the greatest quantities of slag are found between 400 and 350 BC (Martín Ortega *et al.* 1999, 245; 2000, 249). An iron workshop has been excavated at Puig de Sant Andreu, dated to the final quarter of the third century and beginning of the second century BC (Martín Ortega *et al.* 2000, 250).[93] The cupellation of lead also took place: tubes similar to those from the workshop at Empúries have been found at Illa d'en Reixac, dated between 380 and 325 BC (Martín Ortega *et al.* 1999, 232-4).[94]

The role of Empúries as an entrepot in the exchange of metals is clear from the abundant evidence of metallurgical activity in the Neapolis (Ruiz de Arbulo 1989, 317).[95] Excavations in the northwest of the Neapolis in 1919 uncovered a small silver workshop dated to the fifth and fourth centuries BC containing a small furnace used in the cupellation of lead (Ruiz de Arbulo 1984, 127; 1989, 318-19; Carme Rovira 1993, 95; Gómez Ramos 1999, 144).[96] Excavations in the parking area to the south of the Neapolis revealed two furnaces and evidence of cupellation, dated from the end of the second century to the mid-first century BC (Sanmartí Grego *et al.* 1983, 129).

The market for these goods seems to have been twofold: Athens and the Greek colonies of Southern Italy, and the Phoenician settlements of Southern Spain via Ebusus, rather than Marseilles.[97] Connections with Athens are shown by the distribution of Castulo cups. These are a particularly important form that was produced in Athens *c.* 475 BC, perhaps for specifically 'barbarian' markets (Shefton 1995, 136-7). They are found in considerable quantities in Southern Italy and Sicily but are most common in Iberia (Sánchez Fernández 1992, 329; 2003, 134-5; Shefton 1995, 137). Although sporadic examples have been found from the first half of the fifth century, the volume of imports increases dramatically in the second half of the fifth century BC (Shefton 1995, 143).[98] Castulo cups were ubiquitous from the middle of the fifth century to the second quarter of the fourth century BC, reaching 82 of the 140 sites listed by Rouillard as receiving Attic imports during the fifth century BC (Rouillard 1991, 122). Three hundred and sixty Castulo cups have been found at Cancho Roano dated between 450 and 375 BC (Buxeda i Garrigós *et al.* 1999, 159).

The existence of ties with Southern Italy is reinforced by the presence of ovoid amphorae characteristic of Southern Italy within the pottery store excavated to the north of the Asclepeion in 1988, dated to the fourth century BC. The excavators suggest an origin at Locri Epizephyri where similar amphorae have been found associated with kilns (Sanmartí Grego 1995, 33-4).[99] Magna Graecia may also have provided a source for the Etruscan amphorae and bronzes that are found at Empúries (Castellanos Roca 1996, 84-5, 89-93; Sanmartí Grego 1990, 167-8; Ramón Torres 1995, 37). Punic amphorae from the central Mediterranean have been found throughout the Neapolis: Ramón T. 4.2.1.1 produced in western Sicily or North Africa at the end of the fifth and early fourth centuries BC; type 4.2.1.5 produced during the fourth century; 5.2.3.1 and 2 that were produced in Carthage and its environs during the last quarter of the third century BC and first quarter of the second century (Ramón Torres 1995, 36-8).[100]

That these goods were carried by Punic rather than Greek merchants is suggested by the discovery of a wreck dated between 360 and 340 BC at El Sec in the Bay of Palma de Majorca (Parker 1992, 392-4; Ramón Torres 1991, 61-2; 1995, 61-2; Rouillard 1991, 178-9). The wreck carried a disparate cargo including bronze vessels produced in Etruria or Southern Italy, Greek amphorae from a variety of different sources, vines, millstones (including two Pompeian rotary mills), copper ingots and substantial quantities of Attic red-figure pottery including Black Thyrsus kraters, *skyphoi* by the Fat Boy Painter and Vienna 116 cups – bearing Greek and Phoenician graffiti (Arribas *et al.* 1987, 607-9). The ship would have sailed from a Greek port to a Phoenician harbour in the Central Mediterranean before continuing to Majorca (Parker 1992, 393). One of the millstones came from Mulargia in Sardinia and the ship may have put in there before reaching Ibiza where it took on board local PE 14 and

PE 22 amphorae – perhaps carrying wine. The vessel may have also put in at Illeta dels Banyets (Campello) where similar graffiti have been found on Attic pottery (García Martín 2003, 119-20). Its eventual destination may have been Empúries, as the pottery assemblage from the wreck closely echoes the types found in the storeroom excavated north of the Asclepeion (Sanmartí Grego *et al.* 1995, 38).

From Empúries, the Greek imports were redistributed south along the Levantine coast to the Phoenician settlements of Andalucía and Huelva, as well as to Ebusus. From the second half of the fifth century Attic imports began to reach the communities of the east coast in increasing quantities, peaking between 375 and 350 BC (39.5% of Greek imports date to this period) (Rouillard 1991, 110). Greek pottery is ubiquitous throughout the coastal hinterland and along routes to the interior via the low-lying valleys that penetrate the coastal mountains of the Baetic Cordillera, extending as far inland as the central Meseta and the upper reaches of the Tagus valley (Rouillard 1991, 124-5). Brian Shefton (1994, 71) has suggested that the importance of Empúries lay as a staging-post for Greek vessels heading south to Andalucía. These connections are reflected in the presence of Attic and Corinthian wares in Southern Spain and Gaditanian amphorae at Empúries (Cabrera Bonet 1994, 97).

A cargo of Mañá-Pascual A4 amphorae dated *c.* 400 BC from the Togomago I wreck has been found off Cap Roig on the northeastern coast of Ibiza (Ramón Torres 1985, 378, 385-6; 1995, 72). The cargo originated in the Straits of the Gibraltar, and fabric analysis of it matches that of Vuillemont R1 amphorae produced on the Bay of Cádiz (Ramón Torres 1985, 380).[101] The eventual destination of the vessel may have been Empúries, where Mañá-Pascual A4 amphorae have been found to the northeast of the temple of Serapis in levels dated to the last quarter of the fifth century BC (Sanmartí Grego *et al.* 1990, 177). 68% of the amphorae from Empúries were of Ibero-Punic or Gaditanian origin (Cabrera Bonet 1994, 95; Sanmartí Grego *et al.* 1990, 170).

The role of Ibiza as an intermediary in this exchange is reflected in the wreck that lies off Cala Binisafuller on the southeast shore of Menorca. The wreck dates to *c.* 300 BC and carried a substantial cargo of Mañá B3 amphorae (150 vessels) (Ramón Torres 1995, 59; Parker 1992, 73-4; Guerrero Ayuso *et al.* 1989, 117). Mañá B3 amphorae may have originated in Cataluña where kilns have been identified at Can Badell and Santa Cecília. A deformed example has been found at Santa Creu d'Olorde (Miró i Canals 1983, 172-3). The Catalan origin of the ship is reinforced by attribution of the ballast of the ship to the vicinity of Las Gavarres (Guerrero Ayuso 2000, 170). The amphorae may also have originated at Illeta dels Banyets (García Martín 2003, 30-1). The cargo also included Ebusitanian PE 14 and PE 15 amphorae that may have carried wine.[102]

The heterogeneous nature of the cargo implies 'indirect trade' with small coastal vessels plying between a multitude of smaller harbours en route between Empúries, Cadíz, Ibiza and Southern Italy. Cargoes would be gathered and exchanged at multiple locations along the route of the vessel. This short-haul coastal shipping prompted the spread of imported wares throughout the coastal hinterland. No homogeneous cargo of Ebusitanian amphorae has yet been excavated. Despite important local production, particularly of PE 14 and PE 22, their appearance in wreck sites is almost exclusively secondary, being found in heterogeneous cargoes trading from the communities of eastern Spain and Empúries. The importance of Ibiza lay not in providing a market or a primary harbour and destination for long-distance trade, but as an intermediary through which goods would pass en route from the Central Mediterranean to Spain and Southern France.

According to Strabo (3.4.6), three Greek colonies were located to the south of the Río Sucro: Hemeroskopeion, Alonis and Akra Leuke. Unfortunately these have yet to be securely identified. Hemeroskopeion is generally located at Dianium (modern Denia) from Strabo's description of the temple of Ephesian Artemis here (3.4.6), and it is generally accepted that it is from this that the Latin Dianium is derived.[103] Alonis is conventionally located at Benidorm, although Pierre Rouillard has suggested Santa Pola (Rouillard 1991, 304).[104] Akra Leuke lay in the vicinity of the modern Alicante – perhaps at Tossal de Manises, the Roman Lucentum (Rouillard 1991, 286-8). The archaeological evidence for these colonies remains inconclusive and no definite Greek settlements have yet been found. The abundance of Attic imports has suggested an alternative model for Greek trade through smaller harbours that functioned as 'ports of trade' or 'emporia': Grau Vell (Sagunto), La Illeta dels Banyets (Campello), La Albufereta, Santa Pola, Los Nietos. Neither model is, however, entirely appropriate to the relationship of the Greeks to the native communities and the connotations of the Greek concept of an 'emporion' (Aranegui Gascó 2004, 68-9).

The site of Grau Vell lies on the coast 6 km southeast of the town of Sagunto, near the mouth of the Río Palància. The earliest phase of occupation is dated by the presence of imported Attic black glaze dated to 420-325 BC (Aranegui Gascó 1982, 90-2).[105] The existence of commercial ties with Empúries is confirmed by the discovery of a lead inscription from the Neapolis dated to the end of the sixth century BC (Sanmartí Grego *et al.* 1987; 1988, 100-2). The letter records a shipment of wine from Saiganthe that was purchased from an Iberian merchant by the name of Besped[... . In 2002 a lead inscription was discovered inscribed in Iberian and dated between the fifth century and the beginning of the fourth century BC (Aranegui Gascó 2004, 78). The proximity of the harbour at Grau Vell to the settlement at Sagunto makes it unlikely that it functioned as an independent 'port of trade' – rather it was part of a hierarchy of settlements based around the centre on El Tossal del Castell de Sagunt.

The earliest occupation is dated to the sixth century BC thanks to the presence of Phoenician amphorae and Ionian 132 cups (Aranegui Gascó 2004, 33-5). Excavations carried out by Pierre Rouillard in the area of Tres Pouets in 1976-7 enabled the fortifications to be dated to the second quarter of the fourth century BC (Martí Bonafé 1998, 105). Excavations conducted by González Simancas between the Plaza de San Fernando and Plaza de Estudiantes in 1921 revealed a layer of ash, burnt bones and cinerary urns that were identified as having come from a necropolis disturbed by later Roman construction (Martí Bonafé 1998, 79-82; Gil-Mascarell *et al.* 1977, 209-10).[106] The extant grave goods probably date to the third to second centuries BC (Aranegui Gascó 2004, 37). Although the literary sources refer to the existence of temples of Aphrodite (Polybius 3.97.6-8) and Artemis (Pliny *Natural History* 16.216), no traces of these structures survive (Aranegui Gascó 2004, 98).[107] A possible sacred area dated to the fourth century BC has been found in the Plaza de la Conejera where excavations in 1993-4 revealed quantities of ash, animal bones, loom weights, ostraka and an Attic black glaze cup (Aranegui Gascó 2004, 37-9).

El Tossal del Castell de Sagunt controlled an area 250 km^2 over the lower valley of the Río Palància extending from the Sierra de Espadán in the north to the Albufera of Valencia in the south. Twenty-four sites have been identified within this area, ranging in size from 5 ha to individual towers like that at Segart or sanctuaries like that of Liber Pater at La Muntanya Frontera (Aranegui Gascó 2004, 45). The smaller sites of less than 2,500 m^2 in size served specific functions – to control roads, as territorial boundaries, or related to the exploitation of agricultural resources. A pottery kiln dated between 425 and 350 BC has been located in the course of agricultural work at Pla de Piquer. Proximity to the Río Palància suggests a specialized function located away from settlement and located close to the communication route offered by the river (Aranegui Gascó *et al.* 1995, 133). The kiln produced predominantly fine storage jars with bichrome geometric decoration (Aranegui Gascó *et al.* 1995, 133-44; Martí Bonafé 1998, 152-63; Aranegui Gascó 2004, 47-4). Examples of the pottery produced at Pla de Piquer were found in the excavations at Tres Pouets from where it was redistributed through the lower Palància, Túria and the coast (Aranegui Gascó *et al.* 1995, 146). A second kiln may have been located nearby at Riera where quantities of ceramic waste have been found together with millstones (Martí Bonafé 1998, 164).

Quantities of amphorae (including a Ramón T. 8.2.1.1) and storage vessels together with ceramic waste were found during the digging of a ditch at Ponera near Molí de les Pintes (Martí Bonafé 1998, 194-6).[108] Amphorae together with Iberian wares and ceramic waste have been found at La Muntanyeta (Albalat dels Tarongers), and a kiln has been reported at El Planet (Gil-Mascarell *et al.* 1977, 197; Martí Bonafé 1998, 141-5; Aranegui Gascó 2004, 50; Llobregat Conesa 1972, 70-1; Munzó Nogués 1946, 64-7). Munzó Nogués refers to ten kilns that were found at Montíber together with Iberian and Roman pottery. As well as pottery, Munzó Nogués (1946, 62-3) also reports the discovery of loom weights and evidence of iron working. Two kilns were recorded on the northern slope of the Lloma de Matoses (Gil-Mascarell *et al.* 1977, 201-2).[109] Interpretation of these sites is difficult as none have been subject to extensive excavation; however, they suggest the existence of a hierarchy of settlements in the hinterland of El Tossal del Castell de Sagunt engaged in the production of pottery. Ribera Lacomba identified his form I 8 amphora as having been produced in the vicinity of Sagunto during the third to first centuries BC (Ribera Lacomba 1982, 107).

In addition to ceramic production, loom weights have been found at a number of sites in the hinterland of Sagunto: at La Caixa, Cerro del Calvario, Cabeçol de Molvedre, Palmosa, and more than 100 at El Planet (Gil-Mascarell *et al.* 1977, 197-202; Llobregat 1972, 64-72). Munzó Nogués reports the presence of iron slag at Calvario (1946, 68).

Characteristic of the smaller fortified sites is that of Punta dels Llops which guarded the approaches to the oppidum of Sant Miquel de Lliria. The site was located on an outcrop of the Sierra Calderona rising to a height of 427 m above sea level and overlooking Olocau and the gully of the Carraixet. Two distinct phases of occupation have been identified: one dated to the Bronze Age and the other to the Iberian period. The beginning of the Iberian phase is dated to the end of the fifth century BC thanks to the presence of Attic black glaze pottery in the fill of the floor of rooms 1 and 2 (Bonet Rosado *et al.* 2002, 147).

The site was engaged in a variety of economic activities both agricultural and metallurgical. Both manual and fixed millstones have been found at various locations: a hand mill has been found in situ in room 2 and a second example has been found in room 13. A complete fixed mill was found in a fragmentary state in room 4 and the *meta* of a second was found in the disturbed remains of room 5 (Bonet Rosado *et al.* 2002, 118-20).[110] The presence of the fixed mill in room 4 (65 cm in diameter) together with the discovery of four further fragments of a mill from the same room suggest that the structure served a specialist function, milling flour on a scale sufficient to supply the needs of the entire community (Bonet Rosado *et al.* 2002, 187). Clothed barley is characteristic of the area, followed by lesser quantities of naked wheat, millet and spelt-wheat, of which barley and spelt-wheat are better suited to the poor soils around Punta dels Llops. The poor quality of the soils may also explain the exploitation of fruit trees well suited to this type of terrain. Grape seeds have been found in a bowl in room 1, acorns in rooms 2 and 4 and in the street in front of room 6, and pomegranates from an amphora in room 1 and the street in front of room 6. To these can be added the hazelnuts and walnuts revealed by faunal analysis (Bonet Rosado *et al.* 2002, 172). The inhabitants also exploited the banks of the surrounding streams, harvesting poplars, alders, hackberries and ash (Bonet Rosado *et al.* 2002, 174).

As well as agricultural activities, the site has yielded abundant evidence of metalworking. In 1978 a furnace was excavated in room 2 used in the cupellation of lead to extract silver. Quantities of litharge have been found in room 5, together with lead sheets in rooms 2, 3, 5 and 6 (Bonet Rosado *et al.* 2002, 198-204). Seven iron ingots have also been found, although there is no evidence of ironworking having taken place, suggesting that the iron could be shipped raw for preparation elsewhere – perhaps at Sant Miquel de Lliria where ingots have also been found (Bonet Rosado *et al.* 2002, 201-2). The use of specific buildings for specific functions led the excavators to suggest that activities were not organized along familial lines (Bonet Rosado *et al.* 2002, 37-8). Imports were concentrated in room 1, identified as a public or religious building (Bonet Rosado *et al.* 2002, 38-42; Almagro Gorbea *et al.* 1999, 69; Moneo 2003, 179). Although Attic red figure pottery is present in small quantities together with greater numbers of Attic black glaze dated to the fourth century BC (accounting for 13.2% of the imported pottery, Bonet Rosado *et al.* 2002, 147-8), Italian imports predominate: early Campanian A accounts for 35% of the imported wares (Bonet Rosado *et al.* 2002, 151). The preponderance of Italic imports dates to the final phase of the site, *c.* 200-190/180 BC (Bonet Rosado *et al.* 2002, 207). Punic imports are represented by only four pieces, two of which came from Ibiza (Bonet Rosado *et al.* 2002, 151). In contrast to the absence of imported amphorae, the inhabitants received amphorae produced in the vicinity of Sagunto (Bonet Rosado *et al.* 2004, 128-9). The excavators suggest that imported goods were decanted into locally produced Iberian amphorae at coastal sites were imported wares are more abundant (Bonet Rosado *et al.* 2002, 207).

The abundance of Attic imports at La Illeta dels Banyets is particularly striking – yielding 375 pieces (García Martín 2003, 90). The site lies on a small promontory at El Campello on the coast of Alicante. Excavations began in 1931 and have uncovered an area of 2,000 m^2 with occupation dating to the Bronze Age, Iberian and Roman periods (Figueras Pachero 1934, 12-15; Olcina Doménech *et al.* 1997, 25-9; García Martín 2003, 23-4). The presence of Attic black-figure imports dates the Iberian settlement to the middle of the fifth century BC (García Martín 2003, 42). The commonest imports are Attic black glaze (representing 90.93% of the total imports) of which the most numerous are Castulo cups dated to 450-375 BC (García Martín 1997, 184; 2003, 57-61). The apogee of imported wares dates between 400 and 350

Fig. 5. View of the site of Illeta dels Banyets (El Campello).

BC, accounting for 86.67% of the total imports (García Martín 2003, 101). The last imported wares date the abandonment of the site to the beginning of the third century (García Martín 2003, 31). In addition to imported Attic wares the storehouse associated with temple A also yielded imported amphorae: Ebusitanian PE 14 as well as lesser quantities of Mañá-Pascual A4, Muñoz A5 – both of which originated in the Phoenician settlements of Andalucía and carried salt fish products – and Greco-Italic and Corinthian Koehler A vessels (Álvarez García 1997, 145-50).

Six kilns have been excavated, dated to the fourth to third centuries BC (López Segui 1997, 249; 2000, 243).[111] 95% of the pottery recovered from the kilns consisted of Ribera I 3/Mañá B 3 amphorae (García Martín 2003, 31). The Mañá B 3 amphora found at Binisafuller may have been produced here (López Segui 2000, 247; Guerrero Ayuso *et al.* 1997, 170). Nuria Álvarez has suggested that the amphorae carried salted fish, as fish vats dated to the Roman period located at the southeastern end of the site may have been in use during the Iberian period (Álvarez García 1997, 165).[112]

In addition to the produce of the sea the settlement acted as a central location for the redistribution of the agricultural resources. Excavations in 1982-3 revealed a storehouse (Álvarez García 1997, 25) along the southern façade of the principal street running east-west, dated between the beginning of the fourth century and the beginning of the third century BC (Álvarez García 1997, 135, 161). Álvarez has suggested parallels with granaries at La Moleta del Remei (Alcanar-Montsià), El Amarejo (Bonete-Albacete) and El Monastil (Elda) (Álvarez García 1997, 138-9). From Illeta dels Banyets Attic imports were restributed inland to L'Alcoià and El Comtat, where the range of imports mirrors that of the coastal site (García Martín 2003, 108-9).

Particularly notable is the abundance of graffiti found on Attic pottery of the fourth century BC, although two examples (7 and 14) are dated to the end of the fifth century. García Martín (2003, 111-22) has published 36 examples primarily written in Greco-Iberian – a local adaption of Ionian that is found only in isolated examples from a small number of sites in the vicinity: Benilloba, Els Baradells and El Puig de Alcoi (García Martín 2003, 112).[113] Javier de Hoz (1994, 248) has suggested that the use of this script was to facilitate transactions between Iberians and Phocaean merchants. Three (nos 21, 22 and 25) are written in Punic (García Martín 2003, 117-18).

E.A. Llobregat has suggested that Illeta dels Banyets functioned as a 'port of trade' (Llobregat Conesa 1997, 15-20) – a neutral location devoted to commerce under the protection of a sanctuary. Two possible temples have been identified: temples A and B.[114] In 1982 temple A was uncovered, consisting of a rectangular tripartite building with colonnaded frontage similar to examples from Greece and Etruria (Llobregat Conesa 1983, 250-1; 1985, 281; 1985, 298). Excavations in 1983 revealed a square *temenos* (temple B) occupied in two phases during the fourth century BC and dedicated to a fertility deity of oriental origin (Llobregat Conesa 1985, 282-3; 1985, 301-2).[115] In the same year excavations uncovered a rectangular storehouse (Ib 25) associated with temple A (Álvarez García 1997, 135-6).

Between 1984 and 1986 excavations uncovered a square building 150 m^2 in size adjoining the rectangular storehouse and temple B – the so-called 'Casa del Cura'. The building enjoyed two phases of occupation: the first dating to the first half of the fourth century BC and the second to the second half of the fourth century and the beginning of the third century BC (Pastor Mira 1999, 448). During the first phase the building was divided into three ranges of rooms: rooms 27, 30, 31 and 29A; rooms 32, 33, 34 and 35; and room 29B. The first of these seems to have been a wealthy residence with wall and floor decoration and large quantities of imported fine wares (Llobregat Conesa 1993, 103). Room 34 contains a rectangular basin 1.50 m wide and 0.30 m in depth constructed of adobe lined with plaster. A drain runs east from the base of the basin to a cistern lined with plaster. Although initially identified as a

Fig. 6. Temple A, Illeta dels Banyets.

catchment for rain this has been reinterpreted as a winepress similar to those from L'Alt de Benimaquía. The grapes were pressed in the basin and the must drained off into the adjoining cistern (Pastor Mira 1999, 446-7). The juxtaposition of temples, stores, kilns, winery, possible fishery and harbour accords well with a commercial function, while the lack of fortifications and presence of an oriental population supports the excavator's contention that this was neutral location functioning as a 'port of trade'.

Three phases of occupation have been identified at La Loma del Escorial (Los Nietos), beginning in the fifth century and followed by evidence of reconstruction in the mid-fourth century BC. The fourth-century reconstruction is associated with the construction of fortifications in the eastern sector of the site (García Cano *et al.* 1995, 129-30; García Cano 2001, 186).[116] Excavations have revealed substantial evidence of metalworking: in 1993 a large furnace 2.80 m in diameter was excavated outside the fortifications, and a further five furnaces containing slag have been found to the southwest in sector III. The furnaces were used to produce silver through cupellation (García Cano 2001, 192, 195). The larger furnace is cut through layers dating to the first half of the fourth century BC and contains two rim pieces from Ebusitanian PE 16 amphorae dated to the second half of the third century and a fragment of Campanian A (García Cano *et al.* 1995, 135; García Cano 2001, 188-9, 195). Raw materials may have come from the mines at Atamaría and Llano del Beal via the Carrasquilla (García Cano *et al.* 1995, 147).

From the coast Greek goods could travel inland via the valleys of the Vinalopó, Segura and the Jucar to the upper Guadalquivir and the mineral resources of Castulo (Linares). The Sierra Morena was an important source of minerals – in particular silver that was intensively mined during the Roman period (Gutiérrez Soler *et al.* 2000, 260-2); as well as being an area rich in agricultural potential – cereals, vines and olives (Strabo 3.4.8). Excavations at Castulo have yielded evidence of silver and copper working (Gómez Ramos 1999, 123).[117] The earliest Attic imports reach Castulo in the final quarter of the fifth century and in increasing quantities from the beginning of the fourth century BC (Sánchez Fernández 1989, 161-2). From Castulo imports were redistributed out to peripheral settlements (Sánchez Fernández 1989, 164), reaching Castellones de Ceal at the middle of the fourth century BC (Chapa *et al.* 1984, 232-3).[118] The number and variety of imports reaching these peripheral locations remained less than in the central settlement (Sánchez Fernández 1989, 163). Unlike their ubiquity at Castulo, Attic imports are confined to particularly wealthy burials – tombs 43 and 176 at Baza and cremation 1 at Castellones de Ceal.

The transformations of the third and fourth centuries BC

The influx of Attic imports and the intensification of agriculture enabled an increase in the number and size of hilltop *oppida* that controlled the resources of the surrounding valleys and fostered agricultural exploitation to feed the growing population and produce surpluses for trade. In order to enhance their control, the elite manipulated the distribution of prestige imports and displayed their status through their monumental burials. The fortified *oppida* consisted of proto-urban centres housing industrial activities geared towards the transformation of the resources of the hinterland for commercial purposes.

Fig. 7. The fortified *oppidum* of Sant Antoni de Calaceite (photograph courtesy of Jim and Chris Lowe)

The diversification of the economy is part of a broader transition that took place from the middle of the sixth century BC and saw the replacement of the chiefdom with a class-based state structure (Santos Velasco 1989, 224). By the third century BC this process had culminated in the growth of regional polities (Grau Mira 2003, 273; Ruiz Rodríguez *et al.* 1998, 259-60). The appearance of a hierarchy of settlements enabled a deliberate exploitation of agricultural resources. States could regulate territory, agricultural exploitation and trade networks, leading to the replacement of tribal chiefs with aristocracies whose power was based on the control of land. While artisans played an increasingly important role, society was still fundamentally agrarian with the aristocracy basing their status not only the reception and redistribution of imported luxuries but through their control of agricultural production. The stimuli provided by the Phoenicians and Greeks enabled the native communities who controlled the agricultural resources to grow wealthy and gradually develop the infrastructure to better exploit these resources. The intensity of this development is reflected in Strabo's statement that Turdetania contained two hundred cities (3.2.1) – a figure that probably dates to this period.

The evolution of these polities is unclear because of the lack of archaeological evidence for the third and fourth centuries BC. The disappearance of Attic imports and the collapse of trade with the Mediterranean, which only recovers with the onset of Romanization, mark this 'crisis'. Attic imports at Empúries drop from 364 pieces in the first half of the third century BC (24.5% of the total imports) to five in the third quarter (1.2%) (Rouillard 1991, 129). Elsewhere the volume of Attic imports falls from 39.5% (375-350 BC) to 5.9% between 350 and 325 BC (Rouillard 1991, 110). The lack of Attic imports is compounded by the lack of stratified deposits dated to the second half of the fourth century (García Martín 2003, 103).

The economy of Cadíz seems to have suffered a period of dislocation with a number of sites being abandoned or in recession at this time. The fishery at Plaza de Asdrúbal has yielded only sporadic finds and no structural remains between the end of the fourth century and the final third of the third century BC (Niveau de Villedary y Mariñas 2007, 424). Fourth-century BC levels are absent from the fishery at Avenida de Andalucía (Muñoz Vicente *et al.* 1987, 490).

When the archaeological and historical record recovers at the end of the third century BC, Iberian society is structured along markedly different lines. The Barcid conquest seems to have resulted in an intensification of agricultural and industrial activity fuelled by the demands of the Carthaginian government after the First Punic War. José Luis López Castro has suggested that from the fifth century BC onwards, the Carthaginians encouraged an intensification of agricultural exploitation (López Castro 1992, 53-4). Carthaginian settlers – the Liby-Phoenicians or Blastophoenicians – are referred to by literary sources from Herodotus (fr. 5) in the fifth century BC to Ephorus, *c.* 350-334 BC (López Castro 1991, 57). Livy (21.45.5) records that Hannibal promised his soldiers land in Italy, Africa or Spain prior to the battle at Ticinus in 218 BC Appian (*Iberike* 235) under 155 BC refers to the Lusitanians besieging the Blastophoenicians who were Libyans settled in Spain by Hannibal.[119] López Castro has suggested that the use of Punic legends and images on coins issued by the Phoenician cities on the south coast during the second to first centuries BC reflects the presence of these settlers, although he does not offer a connection with rural settlement (López Castro 1992, 58-61).

The presence of black glaze pottery may reflect the expansion of Carthaginian economic interests during the First and Second Punic Wars. Black glaze pottery was produced in North Africa from the beginning of the third century BC imitating earlier Attic pottery (Byrsa 401 and Byrsa 661 forms) and is most widely distributed during the second half of the third century (López Castro 1995, 78). As Adolfo Domínguez Monedero (1995, 231-2) has noted previously, the presence of commercial ties with Carthage does not necessarily indicate Carthaginian colonization but instead reflects the commercial importance of Cádiz.

Several rural sites have been identified in the hinterland of Cádiz and on the coast of Almería. The most important of these is the site of Cerro Naranja (Jerez de la Frontera) which lies on a small hill overlooking the Llanos de Caulina. Excavations in 1985 uncovered a small farm dating to the end of the fourth century and beginning of the third century BC. The farm may have been devoted to olive cultivation and the base of a possible press or *trapetum* was found in the central courtyard (Ruiz Mata *et al.* 1998, 393). Two cisterns were found which the excavators identified as having held olive oil on the basis of ethnographic parallels. Ramón T. 8.1.1.2 and Muñoz A5 (T. 8.2.1.1) amphorae were particularly abundant (Carretero Poblete 2004, 3). In addition Carretero Poblete (2004) has identified a number of possible rural farms in the hinterland of Cádiz on the basis of finds of amphorae: Regajo, La Calerilla, Guadalcacín (Jerez de la Frontera); Cerro del Berrueco (Medina Sidonia); Esperilla (Espero); Cerro de las Monjas (Trebujena). This intensification of agricultural production in turn fueled the growth of the ceramic industry in Cádiz to produce the amphorae needed to transport surplus production.

Excavations on the island of San Fernando (Cádiz) have revealed an increase in the number of ceramic kilns from the middle of the third century BC. Excavations that have taken place at Torre Alta since December 1987 have uncovered seven kilns. Five phases of occupation have been identified, the earliest of which (kilns H 3 and H 4) dates from the middle of the third century BC. Pottery production seems to have increased during the Second Punic War with the construction of further kilns: H 1, H 2 and H 5. The bulk of production consisted of Muñoz A5 (T. 8.2.1.1) amphorae with smaller quantities of Mañá-Pascual A4 (T. 12.1.1.1/2) also present (Sáez Romero 2004, 708-10; Muñoz Vicente *et al.* 2004, 145-8; Sáez Romero *et al.* 2004, 205-6; García Vargas 1998, 156-8).

Contemporaneous with Torre Alta is the kiln excavated in 2002-3 at La Milagrosa, producing Muñoz A5 (T. 8.2.1.1) amphorae (Bernal Casasola *et al.* 2004, 611). Similar amphorae to those from Torre Alta have been found in ceramic waste from Cerro de la Batería. Production began in the late third century BC with Muñoz A5 (T. 8.2.1.1), Mañá-Pascual A4 (T. 12.1.1.1/2) and local imitations of Greco-Italic amphorae as well as Carthaginian T. 5.2.3.1 and Turdetanian T. 8.1.1.2 (Montero Fernández *et al.* 2004, 418). Muñoz A5 (T. 8.2.1.1), Mañá-Pascual A4 (T. 12.1.1.1/2) and Greco-Italic amphorae were also produced in the vicinity of Centro Atlántida (Montero Fernández *et al.* 2004, 420).

Further kilns have been excavated on the Avenida Pery Junquera. Excavations directed by Beatriz González Torraya in 1997 identified eleven kilns together with remains of a possible fish saltery (González Torraya *et al.* 2000, 176-7; Carretero Poblete 2004, 427; Muñoz Vicente *et al.* 2004, 148; Ramón Torres 2004, 72-3; Sáez Romero *et al.* 2004, 205). 16.1% of the amphorae recovered from the kiln consist of Mañá-Pascual A4a and b amphorae dating from the end of the sixth century BC to the beginning of the fourth century BC. Mañá-Pascual A4f from the later third century BC are also present together with small quantities of Muñoz A5 (2.1%, four examples) (González Torraya *et al.* 2000, 183).

As well as an increase in the production of amphorae, the region also saw a revival in the production of salted fish. After a period of decline characterized by a lack of small finds, the fishery at Plaza de Asdrúbal was remodelled in the final quarter of the third century and remained in operation until the second century or first half of the first century BC (Niveau de Villedary y Mariñas 2007, 419). There was a resurgence of activity at Avenida de Andalucía with the construction of a circular structure during the final third of the third century BC (Muñoz Vicente *et al.* 1987, 490).

3

The Republican Period

Roman and Italian immigration

Despite their importance, the first and second centuries BC remain one of the least understood periods of Roman Spain. Until recently, archaeology has focused upon individual sites or monumental remains that reflect Roman influence, neglecting both the external relationship of the individual site to other components of the broader landscape and the internal organization of the site. Native elements have been neglected in favour of more readily recognizable Roman features, encouraging an impression of the steady disappearance of native occupation in favour of Roman dwellings. Many of the sites are known only from finds of Republican or Iberian pottery underlying later levels of occupation. The dating of these sites relies upon imported pottery (Campanian A and B wares, Greco-Italic and Dr 1 amphorae) while our knowledge of native wares and the sites upon which it is found remains problematic.

In the absence of definitive excavations, Roman settlement has typically been seen in terms of the presence of certain archetypes of Roman influence: the use of Roman building techniques (*tegulae*, *imbrices* and *opus signinum*) and decoration (mosaics, stucco, marble statuary). From the end of the second century BC we begin to see rural sites that display these attributes. Conventionally these sites have been identified as Romanized rural houses or villas.

The use of the term 'villa' presents a number of problems. The definition of what actually constitutes a 'villa' – and thus its relationship to other forms of rural settlement – remains the subject of considerable debate. These difficulties stem in no small part from the Romans' own indiscriminate use of the term to describe anything from a luxurious country house to a simple farmhouse (Percival 1976, 13-15; Fernández Castro 1982, 23; Villanueva Acuña 1991, 320). A villa was a rural dwelling that formed the centre of a *fundus* or estate, distinguished from other rural dwellings that were described more generally as *aedificia* ('buildings'), *tuguriae* ('huts') or *casae* ('houses'). The villa serves a variety of functions: residential (the *pars urbana*), agricultural (the *pars rustica*) and storage (the *pars fructuaria*). Essentially the villa represents the appearance not only of rural housing constructed according to Roman or Italian models, but also the implantation of Roman agricultural practice and land use. The Roman agricultural writers stress the need for fertile soils, a healthy climate and a range of resources. The villa should have access to communication routes (either by road or sea) and to urban centres – as a source of labour and as a market for surplus produce. As few sites have been fully excavated and the term 'villa' has been used indiscriminately to describe even sites that have subsequently turned out to be towns, the term 'villa' will be used here only to describe sites that have yielded evidence of the *pars urbana*. The term 'farm' will be used for sites where only agricultural facilities have been discovered.

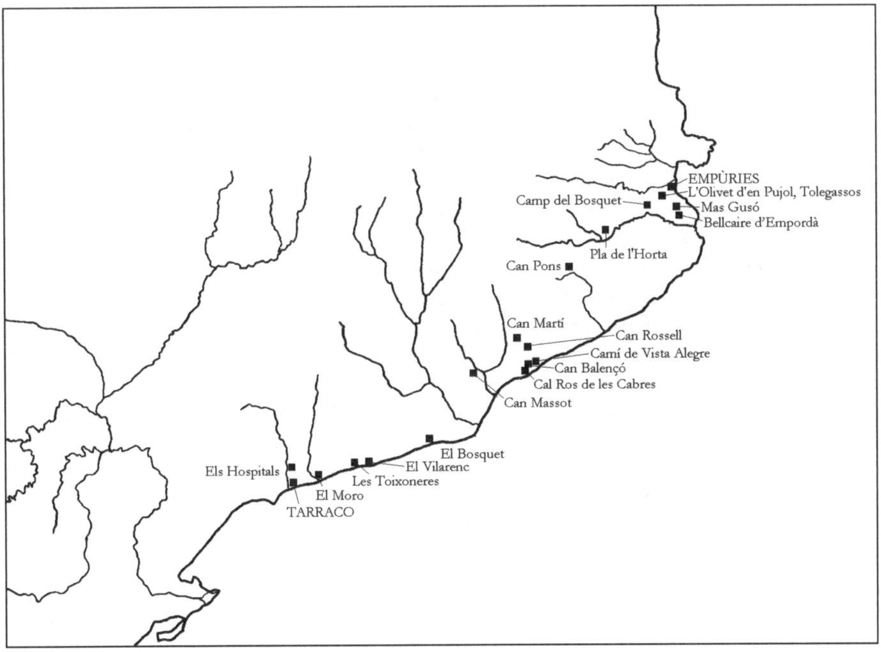

Map 2. Roman villas in Cataluña during the first century BC.

The earliest examples of Roman villas are found in Cataluña, dating to the end of the second century BC. The villa of Can Martí (Samalús, Vàlles Oriental) was discovered in 1957 lying 435 m above sea level on the southern slope of Montseny. An area of 10 x 7.50 m has been uncovered of the *pars urbana* of the villa, consisting of four rooms decorated in *opus incertum* and mosaics of *opus signinum* – two of which may have been the *atrium* (room 4) and *tablinum* (room 1) (Aquilué i Abadías *et al.* 1990, 91-3; Jàrrega Domínguez 2000, 284). The pavement of *opus tessellatum* that decorates room 1 is typical of Italian houses dating to the end of the second century BC (Aquilué i Abadías *et al.* 1990, 95). Room 3 has been identified as a possible *ala* containing traces of Pompeian first style painting dated to *c.*150-80 BC. The floor consists of *opus signinum* decorated with white *tesserae* dating to the end of the second century/beginning of the first century BC (Aquilué i Abadías *et al.* 1990, 95-6).[1]

The villa of El Moro (Torredembarra) lies 700 m from the shore on the bank of the Subanyoles. Excavations in 1984 revealed remains of a Republican villa constructed at the end of the second century/beginning of the first century BC and decorated with mosaics of *opus signinum* of similar date to those from Can Martí. The villa was expanded during the Augustan period with the construction of baths (Terré 1993, 266; Jàrrega Domínguez 2000, 290-1). Excavations at Can Massot (Montmeló) have uncovered remains of a Republican villa decorated with paintings and pavements of *opus signinum* and a possible *impluvium* (Cantarell *et al.* 1998, 138-9; Jàrrega Domínguez 2000, 285-6).

Five silos have been excavated approximately 200 m to the southeast of the villa at El Secà de l'Advocada. Dr 1 B amphorae were recovered from silo 4 with one bearing the stamp SEX(ti) STATI (Cantarell *et al.* 1998, 140-1; Jàrrega Domínguez 2000, 286). Excavations since 1971 have uncovered remains of a substantial villa more than 3,500 m^2 in size at Can Terrés (La Garriga, Vallès Oriental), occupied from *c.* 50 BC (Pardo 1984, 10; Orri i Rovira *et al.* 1990, 20).[2] Iberian and Campanian pottery has been found at Camí del Cementeri (Cabrils) together with *opus signinum*, suggesting the existence of a farm dated to the Republican period (Prevosti i Monclús 1981, 151). Mariano Ribas reported a villa and hippocaust at Can Carbonell (Cabrera de Mar) on the right bank of the riera d'Agell (Prevosti i Monclús 1981, 197).

From the middle of the second century BC there is a dramatic increase in rural settlement in the coastal areas of Cataluña. The spread of rural settlement in areas of high agricultural potential is often associated with the economic stimulus offered by the Roman presence. A number of factors may explain this increase. According to Keith Hopkins (1980, 101-2) Rome's imposition of taxes led to an increase in the volume of trade as the provinces had to produce an exportable surplus of goods in order to generate the revenue necessary to meet the demands of the Roman treasury. Farmers were forced to produce and sell a surplus in order to pay taxes. The gradual creation of urban centres stimulated demand for surplus agricultural produce leading to an intensification of agricultural exploitation.

The appearance of Roman agricultural practices is often connected with the spread of Roman towns. Unfortunately our knowledge of urbanism during the Republic is limited. The scholarly consensus has long been that – at least in southern Spain – the impact of the Roman conquest was extensive: Strabo (3.2.15) commented that the adoption of Roman culture was so pervasive that the Turdetani even forgot their own language! The presence of a substantial Roman garrison throughout the period of the Republic acted as an agent of Romanization as well as providing a source of immigrants. As well as Roman and Italian soldiers, native Spaniards also served: for example, 40,000 natives fought on the Roman side at Numantia (Appian *Iberike* 92.403, 97.419). Literary sources refer to a limited number of urban foundations carried out by governors during the Republic. The earliest Roman settlement was founded at Itálica (Santiponce) in the Guadalquivir valley in 206 BC. The town was established by Scipio Africanus to house wounded veterans of his Spanish campaigns (Appian *Iberike* 38). Two towns were attributed to Tiberius Sempronius Gracchus: Gracchuris in the Ebro valley was founded in 178 BC (Livy *Periochae* 41; Festus 86) and Iliturgis lay in the Guadalquivir valley. Corduba was established by M. Claudius Marcellus in 169/8 or 152/1 BC (Strabo 3.2.1). In *c.* 138 BC D. Iunius Brutus settled former soldiers of Viriathus at Brutobriga (Appian *Iberike* 86), and Valentia was founded at this time (Livy *Periochae* 55).[3]

Unfortunately, even where a settlement is known the status and character of the community is a matter of debate: according to Velleius Paterculus (1.15.4) the earliest overseas Roman colony was established by Caius Gracchus at Carthage in 123-122 BC. If Velleius is correct, then none of these communities was recognized by the Roman state and they seem to have consisted of mixed native-immigrant communities.[4] Strabo is explicit that Marcellus' foundation of Corduba was composed of 'picked Romans and natives' (3.2.1).[5] The only community granted Roman status was the Latin *colonia libertinorum* ('colony of freedmen') that was established at Carteia

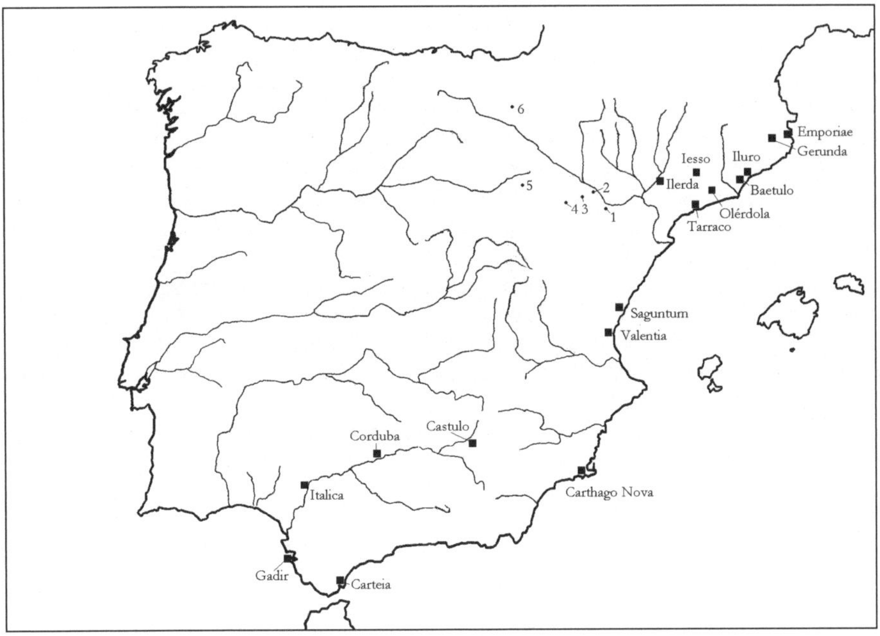

Map 3. Roman settlement during the Republic.

1. Cabezo de Alcalá	4. Duron de Belmonte
2. La Cabañeta	5. La Caridad de Caminreal
3. Contrebia Belaisca	6. Andelos

in 171 BC (Livy 43.3.1-4). The grant was made in response to an appeal by 4,000 men who were the offspring of Roman soldiers and Spanish women. Most of these communities have yielded few structural remains that support a substantial Roman or Italian presence prior to the first century BC. This absence has led to the suggestion that Romans and Italians did not settle in the Peninsula in sufficient numbers to justify the creation of Latin or Roman colonies (Marín Díaz 1988, 88-93).[6]

Recent excavations, however, suggest the presence of Roman and Italian immigrants. Archaeological excavations have confirmed the foundation of Valentia in *c.* 138 BC and revealed the Italian character of the town with a grid layout, baths, a *horreum* and shops (Keay 2003, 157-8).[7] A *capitolium* was constructed at Saguntum during the second century BC (Aranegui Gascó 1994, 72-3). A bath complex and a temple decorated with Pompeian First Style paintings were constructed at Cabezo de Alcalá (Azaila) at the beginning of the first century BC (Beltrán Lloris 2002, 436). The podium of a small temple (measuring 7.80 x 5.20 m) has been excavated at Huesca, dating to the first half of the first century BC (Beltrán Lloris 2002, 449).[8] An inscription on a mosaic floor from La Cabañeta (Burgo de Ebro) gives the names of two Latin *magistri*, suggesting the presence of a *conventus civium romanorum*, or informal group of Roman citizens (Keay 2003, 160).

The arrival of immigrants would have been encouraged by the establishment of Narbo Martius in 118 BC and the establishment of the Via Domitia in place of the Via

Heraclea (Casas i Genover *et al.* 2003, 290). In 1880 a milestone was found at Can Vendrell, erected by Manius Sergius the proconsul of Hispania Citerior in 120-110 BC (Miró i Canals *et al.* 1998, 383). The road network extended inland along the Ebro valley where milestones of the governor Q. Fabius Labeo have been found dating between 118 and 110 BC (Beltrán Lloris 2002, 452).

While Roman and Italian immigrants were not yet present in sufficient numbers to justify the creation of Roman or Italian communities, sufficient numbers appear to have been present in the coastal communities of the Peninsula to create a demand for Italian imports. Campanian A black glaze pottery produced on the Bay of Naples begins to reach the coastal areas in large quantities from the beginning of the second century BC. At Riells-La Clota it is particularly abundant *c.* 150 BC (Nieto Prieto *et al.* 1985, 147). The influx of Italian trade into Grau Vell during the third and second centuries BC prompted the expansion of the harbour with the construction of a quay 130 m long (de Juan Fuertes 2002, 124).

From 218 BC onwards Greco-Italic amphorae appear in many sites – those in coastal sites like Empúries and Cartagena can be attributed to the presence of Italians; however, in native communities their presence reflects demand among the natives. Jaime Molina Vidal has noted that the percentages of Greco-Italic amphorae are similar between sites with a substantial immigrant population (El Molinete, Cartagena 54.6%) and those without (El Tossal de Manises 48.2%, El Monastil 60.9% and Sagunto 47.1%) (Molina Vidal 1997, 184-6).

Recent work in the Ebro valley has suggested that settlement patterns were reorganized in the late second century BC. Several native sites in the Ebro valley and along the coast of Cataluña were remodelled as Roman communities: Iluro (Mataró), Baetulo (Badalona), Iesso (Guissona), Aeso (Isona) and Olérdola (Keay 2003, 159; Guitart i Duran 1994, 205-10). The process may have been gradual, as the population dispersed to the low-lying rural sites that were better suited for agricultural and commercial activities. The *oppidum* at Cadira del Bisbe (Premià de Dalt) was fortified at the end of the third century BC and shows signs of Romanization: the presence of Campanian A pottery, the use of *tegulae* and *imbrices* and a wine press. However, the scarcity of B-oïde wares and the absence of any finds of the first century BC suggest that the site was abandoned prior to this, although the precise date of abandonment cannot be determined (Olesti i Vilà 1995, 417-18).

While the *oppidum* of La Serreta was abandoned, several smaller sites survived: El Castellar de Perputxent, El Xarpolar, El Castellar de Cocentaina, El Pitxòcol, El Castellar and El Castell de Penàguila. As well as the smaller *oppida*, several small rural sites appear at this time suggesting that the population remained but relocated to lower-lying sites with better access to agricultural land (Grau Mira 2003, 62).

The development of viticulture

Oriol Olesti i Vilà associated the intensification of rural settlement with a shift from an economy centred upon cereal cultivation to viticulture (Olesti i Vilà 1995, 165, 192; 1998, 247). The abandonment of silos at several sites coincides with the beginning of amphora production. The final phase of the silos at Alella Autopista coincides with the earliest appearance of local imitations of Dr 1 amphorae, similarly at Pont de Premià and Can Notxa with Tarraconense 1 amphorae. The storeroom at

L'Olivet d'en Pujol overlies three silos, two of which date to the second half of the fourth century BC (Casas i Genover 1989, 39; 1993, 25).[9] Silo SJ 101 at Mas Castellar dates from 200-175 BC. The silo contained a variety of bronze and iron implements, a painted *kalathos* and eight complete Greco-Italic amphorae. Three of the amphorae carry marks: one in Greek interpreted as an H; one in Latin inscribed before firing on the shoulder reading MAR.RVLIO; and the other on both handles with a name in Greek (García Sánchez 1997, 258). A silo underlying room 29 of the villa at Els Hospitals was filled in between 100 and 50 BC (Macias Solé *et al.* 2007, 72).

Symptomatic of the transition from cereal cultivation to viticulture is the site of El Bosquet, discovered in 1979 and excavated between February and March 1984. Two phases of occupation have been identified. The first dates from between the middle of the second century and the end of the first century BC and seems to have been devoted to cereal cultivation with the excavation of nine silos (fosses 1-9). At the end of the first century BC the focus of activities shifted to viticulture. Four basins lined with *opus signinum* were constructed together with a rectangular area measuring 12 x 4 m containing cavities for *dolia* (Bosch *et al.* 1987, 229-30; 1993, 135; Nolla i Brufau *et al.* 1984, 94-101). The site is perhaps related to the possible villa lying 200 m to the east at Lluena from which, although it has not been excavated, the reported finds date from the first century BC (Nolla i Brufau *et al.* 1984, 101). According to the excavators the storage capacity of the *dolia* was 21,600 litres of wine per annum of which the local consumption was 1,834 litres leaving 19,766 litres available for export (Bosch *et al.* 1987, 231).[10]

Rescue excavations carried out at Camí Vell del Llor (Sant Boi de Llobregat) in 1983 revealed a small farm occupied from the end of the fourth century BC to the beginning of the first century AD. The first phase consisted of two silos containing Punic and Massiliot amphorae and a Protocampanian *krater* dated *c.* 345 BC (Molist i Capella 1998, 395). The site was remodelled *c.* 175 BC after which it underwent rapid Romanization characterized by a steady increase in the volume of Italian imports (Campanian A and B, Italian coarse wares and amphorae) and building materials (*tegulae* and *imbrices*), with a decrease in the quantities of local pottery (Molist i Capella 1998, 396-9). According to the excavators, the large quantity of local amphorae indicates that the site was engaged in wine production (Molist i Capella 1998, 400).[11]

A villa has been located at Santa Margarida de Montbui (Igualada, Anoía). Since 1978 excavations have revealed pavements of *opus testaceum*, *dolia*, *tegulae* and a hypocaust indicating the presence of both *pars rustica* and *pars urbana*. The villa was occupied from the second century BC to the third century AD (Berni Millet *et al.* 2005, 176-7). It is located in good farmland and the abundance of *dolia* suggests that it was engaged in wine production. Surprisingly the villa has not yielded evidence of Tarraconensian amphorae – this may be due to the distance of the villa from the coast. The wine may have been carried not in amphorae that were suited to marine transport, but in containers like barrels that were more suitable for land transport (Berni Millet *et al.* 2005, 177).

Two phases of Republican occupation have been uncovered at Ca l'Estrada (Canovelles): the first (Phase IIIa) was devoted to cereal cultivation dating to the end of the second century BC. The site was remodelled *c.* 75 BC with the construction of a large rectangular building (600-650 m^2) (Phase IIIb) arranged around a courtyard.

Although no specific installations have been found, the quantity of amphorae and *dolia* found in areas 7 and 8 suggests that the complex was devoted to viticulture. Occupation ceased in the middle of the first century BC (Fortó Garcia *et al.* 2005, 10-12).

In 1981 the site of L'Olivet d'en Pujol (Viladamat) was discovered at the base of the eastern slope of Palau Borrell, 5 km to the southwest of Empúries. Excavations revealed a rectangular structure containing 75 *dolia* (Casas i Genover 1989, 21-3; 1993, 25; Brun 2004, 265). The earliest phase of occupation (level V) has produced Punic Mañá C amphorae, Italian Dr 1 A amphorae, Emporitanian grey ware, Campanian A and B vessels and Iberian pottery dating to the end of the second century/first half of the first century BC (Casas i Genover 1989, 24-5). The foundations of the walls contain Campanian B wares (Lamboglia 5/7 and 2) dated to 110 and 100 BC respectively (Casas i Genover 1989, 32).

The villa of Tolegassos lies 500 m from L'Olivet d'en Pujol. Seven phases of occupation have been excavated dating from the end of the second century BC to the fourth century AD (Casas i Genover 1993, 24; 1995, 278).[12] Remains dating to the end of the second century BC have been found in the fill of silos 2088, 2404 and 2416. The first contained Italian imported pottery including Campanian A and B, Dr 1 A-B and Greco-Italic amphorae, as well as Iberian painted pottery, grey ware from Empúries and white glaze ware typical of the second half of the second century/first half of the first century BC (Casas i Genover *et al.* 1996, 70-3; 2003, 16-17). The presence of Campanian A and b-oïde vessels, Emporitanian grey ware, white glaze and painted wares and Dr 1 A amphorae dates silo 2404 to the end of the second century/beginning of the first century BC (Casas i Genover *et al.* 1996, 80-1; Casas i Genover *et al.* 2003, 18-22). Silo 2416 has yielded Emporitanian grey ware, white glaze pottery, Campanian ware and Dr 1 and Lamboglia 2 amphorae dating between 110 and 70 BC (Casas i Genover *et al.* 1996, 83-4; 2003, 25-8). A waste tip of Dr 1 A and B amphorae were found together with Campanian A and B (Casas i Genover *et al.* 2003, 29). The remains come from a native farm that was destroyed to make way for the construction of a small Italic villa at the end of the second century BC (Casas i Genover 1995, 278; Casas i Genover *et al.* 1996, 67-8; 2003, 49). Remains pertaining to this first villa are scarce: a pavement of *opus signinum* containing Dr 1 and Campanian B pottery was found in silo 2404 (Casas i Genover *et al.* 1996, 76; 2003, 18). Column fragments from silo 2060 may also have come from the early villa (Casas i Genover *et al.* 2003, 49). Remodelling during the Augustan period and the construction of a larger villa *c.* 40-50 AD destroyed the remains of the earlier phases.

A possible storeroom containing *dolia* and amphorae has also been found at Can Balençó in the town of Argentona (El Maresme). Although it was initially reported in 1989, subsequent excavations have uncovered an area of 1,022 m^2 occupied in two phases from the middle of the second century to the end of the first century BC, at which point it was destroyed by fire. Two pits have been excavated to the west of rooms B and C. The pits contain quantities of ceramic rubbish including Campanian A and B, Greco-Italic amphorae, Italian Dr 1 B and locally produced Tarraconense 1 amphorae dating from the middle of the second century to the middle of the first century BC (Carreres Vidal *et al.* 1992, 163-9).[13]

Construction work in 1989 allowed the excavation of an area of 300 m^2 at Can Rossell (Llinars del Vallès) revealing a series of rooms laid out around a courtyard.

The complex dates from the first to the final quarters of the first century BC; the site was abandoned shortly prior to 20 BC. Although only parts of the site have been excavated, the presence of *dolia* and amphorae in the courtyard suggests that the site was devoted to storage – probably of wine (Barrasetas i Dunjó *et al.* 1997, 10-12).[14] A basin/*lacus* (4.25 x 4.25 m) has been found at Can Xacó (Cabrera de Mar) dating from the first century BC to the second century AD. Mariano Ribas says this was part of a villa, but there are no other structural remains (Prevosti i Monclús 1981, 197-201).

Wineries have also been found in urban contexts. The site of Segeda I lay on the Poyo de Mara overlooking the Río Perejiles, a tributary of the Río Jalón. Excavations since 1998 have uncovered remains of the city that was destroyed by Fulvius Nobilior in 153 BC (Appian *Iberike* 44-7) prompting the settlement to move to the site of Durón de Belmonte de Gracián. Excavations in area 2 on the eastern slope of the town have revealed a quadrangular two-storey house (sector 1) extending over an area of 90 m^2. The largest room (space 5) contains a plaster-lined basin with traces of wine deposits. The structure has been identified as a winepress with remains of cultivated vines (*Vitis vinifera*) and jars lined with resin. The capacity to produce 2,000 litres of wine far exceeds the requirements for domestic use (Burillo Mozota *et al.* 2006, 3-4). A winery has been uncovered to the northwest of the town of Contrebia Belaisca, modern Botorrita, consisting of six rooms containing basins lined with plaster. A storage area has also been found containing ten *dolia* (Beltrán Lloris 2002, 457).[15] Analysis of one of the *dolia* has revealed traces of a red colouring that may be the residue of wine. This *dolium* has a graffito engraved prior to firing with SYRBUY, which may be the name of the potter similar to the 'Reducenos aukia' found on a *dolium* from Albalate de Arzobispo (Beltrán Lloris 2002, 461).

Several smaller sites have been excavated which served specific functions related to agriculture. Excavations in the centre of the town of Bellcaire d'Empordà in January-February 2000 uncovered remains of a small winery.[16] Four distinct areas were identified, with the press located in area 1. The room is floored with *opus signinum* with recesses for the piers and a pressing area 1.5 m in diameter. The resulting must drained into a cistern to the west (area 3) with a capacity of 2,500 litres (Codina 2004, 8-12). Areas 2 and 4 appear to have been used for storage with area 2 also housing the drum or screw of the adjoining press (Codina 2004, 17-18). Later agricultural activities have disturbed much of the stratigraphy, but the pottery suggests a phase of Iberian occupation dating from the third to the end of the second century/beginning of the first century BC. The press was abandoned during the reign of Augustus (Codina 2004, 14). Although only a limited area has been excavated, the absence of any imported fine ware pottery prompted Ferran Codina to suggest that the site was purely utilitarian with no residential component (Codina 2004, 17).

In 1979 a winepress was discovered at Sant Miquel de Vinebre (Ribera d'Ebre, Tarragona) dating to the end of the second century/middle of the first century BC. Finds of black glaze pottery date between 100 and 50 BC (Genera 1987, 233-6). Two basins lined with *opus signinum* are reported at Mercadell (Lledó) (Nolla i Brufau *et al.* 1984, 85). A basin lined with *opus signinum* and dated to the end of the second century BC has been found underlying the villa at Cal Ros de les Cabres (Ocata-El Masnou) (Olesti i Vilà 1998, 247).

In 1992 excavations uncovered the remains of a farm at Casa del Racó. The site lies on the northern slope of the hill of Sant Julià, 100 m from the Rìo Ter. Three phases have been identified. The first consists of three small structures constructed in dry stone walling and a silo that was replaced by a larger structure (1,000 m^2 in size) arranged along the north and east sides of a courtyard (Burch *et al.* 1994, 124-5). The paucity of finds means that the dating of the phases is difficult: the initial phase of occupation dates to the first quarter of the first century BC. The earliest pottery is Campanian B, dated to the end of the second century/beginning of the first century BC (Burch *et al.* 1994, 128). The lack of residential quarters together with finds of *dolia* and a rectangular deposit to the north (Burch *et al.* 1994, 132) suggest that the complex was primarily agricultural.

Construction of a football pitch at Can Pons in September 1993 uncovered remains of a farm dated to the second half of the second century/first quarter of the first century BC (Font Valentí *et al.* 1996, 101; 1996, 58, 61; 2000, 254). The farm consists of a rectangular building (170 m^2) divided into six rooms. The farm seems to have been devoted to wine production with a small basin and *dolium* in room IV.[17] Room V may have been devoted to textile working containing forty loom weights. The structure is grouped around room II, which together with Room I appears to have been residential in use (Font Valentí *et al.* 1996, 96; 1996, 60; 2000, 255-6).[18]

Victor Revilla Calvo (2004, 189) has noted a number of difficulties with a shift from cereal cultivation to viticulture. It is impossible to determine how widespread the use of *dolia* would have been. The initial appearance of locally produced amphorae has not been reliably dated – many are known only from the second half of the first century BC. No clear relationship has been established between kilns and agricultural activities.[19] Finally he has questioned the suitability of proposing a widespread change upon the ancient economy. On the contrary there seems to have been a gradual shift towards viticulture during the first century BC that culminates in the age of Augustus (Revilla Calvo 2004, 189).

Evidence from the villa of Tolegassos supports the contention that this shift was more gradual. Remains from fill 2106, dated to the second half of the second century BC, revealed 241 grape seeds and 597 cereal grains, above all barley (*Hordeum vulgare*) and also wheat (*Triticum aestivum-durum*). The grapes were probably consumed as fruit in view of the volume of imported Italian wine (Casas i Genover *et al.* 2003, 255). Despite the appearance of viticulture, cereals continued to predominate in Augustan levels and especially level 2117 (186 examples) – principally barley but also some wheat (Casas i Genover *et al.* 2003, 256). The presence of more than 100 fragments of hand mills has suggested that much of the cereal crop was for local consumption (Casas i Genover *et al.* 2003, 257). The base of a large fixed mill has also been found. The *dolia* on the site could have held 40,000 kg of grain – the yield of 20/25 ha at 2,000 kg per ha, or fifty ha at 750-1,000 kg per ha. Allowing for the cultivation of other crops, the villa would have controlled an area of three hundred *iugera*. This would have been a far larger estate than the average of 100 *iugera* that has been suggested for the villas of the Maresme (Casas i Genover *et al.* 2003, 257).

Faunal remains from Augustan and Imperial levels of silo 2060 reveal a high percentage of cattle during the Augustan period (85% from level 2068 and 44% from level 2062) compared to 44% and 3% sheep and goats from these respective levels (Casas i Genover *et al.* 2003, 257-8). Silo 2060 has also yielded evidence of marine molluscs – the most numerous of which is *Glycymeris violacescens*, a type of mussel found in shallow or sandy water (Casas i Genover *et al.* 2003, 259). Although fishhooks have been found in various rooms, the excavators believe that the villa was too far from the sea for the inhabitants to have been engaged in sea fishing. Instead, fish was obtained from local merchants or caught in nearby rivers or lakes (Casas i Genover *et al.* 2003, 260).

But were these villas and farms built by Italian immigrants or by natives? The appearance of Italianate architecture has been used to suggest that there was an influx of Italian settlers at this time and the establishment of the 'villa system'. The beginning of wine production in Cataluña in the second half of the second century BC coincides with a restructuring of native society with the abandonment of some *oppida* and the appearance of a dispersed rural population. Although these rural farms adopt aspects of Roman construction (*tegulae, imbrices*) they are not villas in the Italian sense. Indications of Italian settlement in the region are rare and few literary sources refer to immigration: Caesar (*Bellum Civile* 1. 86-7) describes the Pompeian army at Ilerda containing soldiers 'qui habeant domicilium aut possessionem in Hispania'. Isabel Arrayás Morales (2005, 175) has suggested that the initiative came not from Italian or Roman settlers but from Romanized natives.

Oriel Olesti i Vilà (1997, 81-2) has argued that these sites are characterized by what she has called an Iberian materiel culture: despite Roman architectural elements (*tegulae, dolia, opus signinum*, plastered walls, etc.) and imports (Campanian A and B pottery, Italian Dr 1 amphorae etc.), Iberian pottery predominates.[20] The predominance of indigenous pottery at Can Pons is particularly striking, accounting for 88.9% of the ceramics found (Font Valentí *et al.* 1996, 61; 1996, 98). 61.07% of the pottery from Casa del Racò was locally produced (Burch *et al.* 1994, 128). Only at five sites can we find luxurious rural dwellings with Italian features that can be characterized as 'Roman': Mas Gusó, Can Martí, El Moro, Can Massot and Can Terres. Even here the ethnicity of the occupants is unclear and while the inhabitants seem to have been wealthy, they were not necessarily Italian.

Excavations at Caridad de Caminreal (Teruel) have uncovered an Italianate town house constructed around a peristyle courtyard and covering an area of 915 m^2. The house was constructed at the end of the second century BC and destroyed *c.* 75-72 BC – perhaps during the Sertorian War (Vicente *et al.* 1993, 749). An Iberian inscription on the *opus signinum* mosaic in the *oecus* reading 'l.i.ki.n.e.te e.ki.a.r. u.s.e.ke.r.te.ku' identifies the owner as the native Likine (the '-te' being a suffix of uncertain meaning) of Osicerda near Alcañiz (Vicente *et al.* 1993, 750-7).[21] Likine is also named in an Iberian inscription that was discovered in 1990 at Andelos (Muruzábal de Andión). The inscription consists of white *tesserae* on an *opus signinum* pavement and reads 'LIKINE ABULORAUNE EKIEN BILBILIARS'. 'Abuloraune' may be a name and 'Bilbiliars' perhaps refers to Bilbilis. 'Ekien' and 'ekiar' may be a form of greeting similar to the Latin 'salve' (Mezquíriz Irujo 1991, 365-6). A mosaic has been excavated from the *tablinum* of a house from Ilici (La Alcudia de Elche, Alicante). In contrast to the use of *opus signinum* that characterizes Roman settlement in the Western Mediterranean, the mosaic is constructed with pebbles along Hellenistic lines. The mosaic depicts a star surrounded by a chequer-board pattern and border of vegetation. Below the centrepiece and to the left indigenous names written in Latin letters are inserted into the mosaic. The legend on the left reads ACOS, while the three lines below read: L.SAILACOS /]ELSADINI.COR / SCRAD… O. Comparison with mosaics from Delos gives a date at the end of the second century or beginning of the first century BC (Abad Casal 1986, 98-104; 2006, 119).

Excavations in 1988-9 on Calle Don Juan de Aragón (n. 9) in Zaragoza uncovered a winter *triclinium* and adjoining *oecus* dating to the first third of the first century BC (Galve Izquierdo 1996, 54). The rooms contain a pavement of *opus signinum* decorated with white tesserae: that of the *oecus* consists of a circular design 3.5 m in diameter with borders of swastikas and waves around a star (2.05 m in diameter). The corners are decorated with depictions of dolphins. The decoration of the *triclinium* consists of rectangular niches for the dining couches arranged around a circular motif (Galve Izquierdo 1996, 37-43). Traces of wall painting survive in the corner of the room to the left of the entrance (Galve Izquierdo 1996, 52-3). The owner was perhaps Iberian: the name 'e i ke_bi' is found on amphorae from the site (Galve Izquierdo 1996, 95-9).

In these cases it would appear that while the houses display Roman elements, the occupants were natives who adopted the trappings of a Roman lifestyle. This demographic continuity is reflected in the siting of villas in the proximity of earlier Iberian settlements. The villa at El Roser (Calella) has yielded evidence of occupation from the Iberian period continuing through the first and second centuries BC with finds of Iberian pottery, Campanian A and B wares and Dr 1 amphorae (López Mullor 1985). Finds of Campanian A and B and Dr 1B amphorae at Mas Carbotí suggest that the site was occupied prior to the establishment of the villa in the Augustan period (López Mullor *et al.* 1985, 38-43; Burch *et al.* 1998, 23). The farm at Can Feu (Sant Quirze del Vallès), constructed at the end of the first century BC, was preceded by an Iberian settlement abandoned in the first half of the century (Carbonell *et al.* 1998, 289).

Prior to the construction of the earliest villa at Vilarenc (Calafell) in the middle of the first century BC the site appears to have been occupied by an Iberian farm. A small pottery kiln has been found dating to the end of the second century/beginning of the first century BC, together with an iron-working area and a grain silo. The pottery found dates the site to the fourth century BC onwards (Revilla Calvo 2003, 287). In 1989 a villa was discovered underlying the church of Santa Maria in Castelldefels. The villa was constructed at the end of the first century BC overlying Iberian occupation dating from the third century BC until it was replaced by the construction of the villa (López Mullor 1993, 97-8).

The *pars urbana* and baths of a villa have been found at La Quintana (Cervià de Ter). The villa was constructed in the middle of the first century BC. Two silos have been excavated underlying the baths that were filled in at the end of the second century BC (Tremoleda i Trilla *et al.* 1993, 145). The villa at Ametllers (Tossa de Mar) was preceded by a period of Iberian occupation dating at least to the second/first centuries BC. *Terra sigillata* from the site continued to carry Iberian graffiti in the mid-first century AD (López Mullor 1993, 212-13). After the Iberian settlement at Darró (Vilanova i la Geltru) was abandoned at the end of the third century BC, a villa was constructed on the site *c.* 40/30 BC (Olesti i Vilà 1998, 246; López Mullor *et al.* 1995, 302). Olesti i Vilà (1998, 247) suggests that the establishment of the villa at Llafranc marks the transfer of the population from the neighbouring Iberian settlement of St Sebastià down onto the plain. Residual Iberian pottery has been found in the villa (Barti Català *et al.* 1989, 244). A *tegula* from the villa bears an Iberian stamp, although Revilla Calvo (1995, 281) considers it illegible.

3. The Republican Period

Several later villas were preceded by occupation during the Iberian and Republican periods. A wealthy villa was excavated at Pla de l'Horta (Sarrìa de Ter, Gironès) by Miquel Oliva in 1970-2. The villa lies on the fertile alluvial plain of the Río Ter, 5 km from Gerunda and 200 m from the Via Augusta. Excavations have revealed parts of the residential wing of the villa decorated with polichrome and geometric mosaics (rooms A, B, C, D and D 1) (Nolla i Brufau 1982, 114-15; Nolla i Brufau *et al.* 1984, 181-7).[22] Almost nothing is known of the first phase of occupation which has been dated by pottery to the end of the second century/beginning of the first century BC. The only structural remains dated to this period are two walls found underneath the mosaics in room A (level 4) (Nolla i Brufau 1982, 119-20). The villa may have engaged in olive oil or vine cultivation. A possible press has been excavated in room G. A basin lined with *opus signinum* is situated in the northwest corner of the room and the base for a *dolium* has been found against the southern wall (Palahí Grimal *et al.* 1994, 162-3).

The villa at Mas Gusó (Bellcaire d'Empordà) lies 3,500 m to the southeast of the villa at Tolegassos on the edge of the lake at Bellcaire. The villa itself dates from the first half of the first century to the second half of the third century AD, but the presence of Attic pottery, Iberian *kalathoi* and painted ware, and Emporitanian grey ware indicates an earlier phase of occupation dating from the third century BC. The only structure remaining from this phase is a wall built of stone and mortar (E. 1007) (Casas i Genover 1988, 10-11). The small Iberian settlement at Les Toixoneres was destroyed in the third quarter of the second century BC and a small Italian style villa was constructed over the southeast corner of the Iberian remains (Jàrrega Domínguez 2000, 289).

Sector II of the Augustan villa at Mas d'Aragó has yielded evidence of Iberian occupation. Several finds date from the fifth century BC onwards: a fragment of an inset lip *kylix* dating to the third quarter of the fifth century BC, an Attic black glaze cup dating to the beginning of the fourth century BC, and an Attic black glaze *skyphos* dating to the first half of the fourth century BC (Borras i Querol 1987, 386-7). Iberian pottery of the third and fourth centuries BC was also found together with two small fragments of Campanian B (Borras i Querol 1987, 387). The kilns at El Roser (Calella) continued to produce Iberian forms of pottery alongside Roman types. Types derived from Iberian *kalathoi*, biconical jars and hemispherical bowls continued to be produced alongside Tarraconense 1, Pascual 1 and Dr 2-4 until the Flavian period (López Mullor *et al.* 1985, 177-8).

In addition to material culture, several of these sites are characterized by Iberian construction techniques – dry stone walls and beaten earth floors. Unfortunately the paucity of the archaeological remains of these initial phases means that we do not know much about the extent and function of these sites. It does, however, seem that there was an increase in the number of rural settlements during the second half of the second century BC, with several wineries dating to this period: L'Olivet d'en Pujol, Can Balençó, Bellcaire d'Empordà, Sant Miquel de Vinebre and Can Pons.

Together with the increased production of wine, the region also sees the beginnings of the local imitation of Italian amphorae that were used in the long-distance shipment of wine and olive oil. The earliest production consisted of locally produced imitations of Dr 1 amphorae. Although typologically similar to Italian Dr 1 amphorae, their fabric is identical to that of amphorae that were later produced in Tarraconensis (Pascual 1 and Dr 2-4), specifically in the region of Laietania (Comas i Solà *et al.* 1998, 153; Miró i Canals 1988, 60-1).

At Riera de St. Simó (Mataró) production of Dr 1 amphorae replaced earlier Iberian flat-bottomed Mañá B 3 amphorae (Miró i Canals 1988, 40). Three kilns have been excavated dating from the end of the third century/beginning of the second century to the first century BC (Ribas i Beltrán 1982; Pons Mellado 1982, 185-91; García i Roselló *et al.* 1996, 411-12). The amphorae may also have been produced at Torrent de Sistres (Alella, Maresme) where a kiln has been found together with imitated Dr 1 and Pascual 1 amphorae (Miró i Canals 1988, 36). Excavations at Alella Autopista (La Plana, Cal Petxo) have revealed quantities of misfired Dr 1 imitations together with remains of late Republican occupation: *tegulae*, Campanian B, Iberian painted and coarse wares (Olesti i Vilà 1995, 410-11; Miró i Canals 1988, 35-6).[23]

Rescue excavations carried out at Carrer Nou 54, Mataró are particularly important not only for the discovery of locally produced Dr 1 amphorae but also for the presence of seven locally produced Lamboglia 2 in levels dated to 75-50 BC.[24] The fabric is typical of other amphorae produced in the region (García i Rosselló *et al.* 1996, 399-402). The amphorae seem to have been produced in the middle years of the first century BC. Examples have been found together with Tarraconense 1, Pascual 1 and Dr 2-4 amphorae at La Salut (Sabadell) (Revilla Calvo 1995, 210). Examples from Burriac date between 80 and 70 BC, while examples from Carrer Sant Josep and Carrer de Rosés in Baetulo, and from Montpalau, date to 40-30 BC (Comas i Solà *et al.* 1998, 156). Examples have been found together with Tarraconense 1 and Dr 1B amphorae dated 60/50 BC from the harbour area of Baetulo (Comas i Solà 1998, 221). Production of Dr 1 seems to have ceased *c.* 40-30 BC when the form was replaced by Tarraconense 1 and Pascual 1 amphorae (Comas i Solà *et al.* 1998, 156).[25]

The discovery of these vessels at the anchorages of Les Sorres and Vilassar de Mar as well as at Bordeaux suggests that the form was exported (Comas i Solà 1998, 225). Unfortunately the amphorae are too scarce to offer any information regarding the market or ethnicity of the producers. The forms are contemporaneous with the establishment of Italian villas in the area – although it has not been possible to associate the production of these vessels with any specific villas.

Amphora production becomes more widespread around the middle of the first century BC with the appearance of a new form derived from Dr 1: Laietana 1/Tarraconense 1.[26] Laietana 1 amphorae were first identified in 1985 at Baetulo by M. Comas, and simultaneously by J. Ma. Nolla as Tarraconense 1 at Empúries (Comas i Solà 1987, 163-4; Nolla i Brufau *et al.* 1984, 109-11; Nolla i Brufau 1987, 217).[27]

Typologically the vessels are similar to Dr 1 amphorae: they vary between 70 and 85 cm in height and have an ovoid body and conical neck with a vertical lip measuring between 3 and 6 cm in height. Handles are short and robust and extend from below the lip to the middle of the shoulder of the amphora. They are distinguished from the Italian vessels by their fabric which is typical of later forms produced in Cataluña (Nolla i Brufau *et al.* 1984, 112).

According to Comas i Solà, production began during the second half of the first century BC: examples from level III of the excavations on Carrer Sant Josep and Rosés in Baetulo date to *c.* 40-30 BC (Comas i Solà *et al.* 1998, 156). In 1976 excavations on Carrer Pujol uncovered a silo containing Tarraconense 1 amphorae dating between 50/40 and 30 BC (Comas i Solà 1985, 17-19). An example excavated in 1987 at Calle Don Juan n. 9, Zaragoza, dates from *c.* 50-40 BC (level c2) (Aguarod Otal 1992, 109).

Production continued until the beginning of the first century AD: examples have been found alongside Dr 1 B, Pascual 1 and Dr 16 amphorae in the cargo of the Cap Béar 3 wreck dated to *c.* 50-25 BC (Parker 1992, 97-8; Liou *et al.* 1985, 547-51; Colls 1986, 205). Tarraconense 1 amphorae were found with Pascual 1 amphorae in the excavations carried out in the curia and basilica of the forum of Empúries in 1982, bearing the stamp L.VENVLEI. Tarraconense 1 vessels are also found alongside Pascual 1 and Dr 28 amphorae from the Muralla Rubert excavations at Empúries (Nolla i Brufau *et al.* 1984, 137). Examples have been found alongside Pascual 1 and Dr 2-4 amphorae at Castell de la Fosca (Palamós) (Nolla i Brufau *et al.* 1984, 138). An example was found with a cargo of Dr 2-4 in the Dramont B wreck dating to the early first century AD, though the vessel probably formed part of the ship's stores, not the cargo (Parker 1998, 166-7; Nolla i Brufau *et al.* 1984, 133). The amphora probably carried wine, and examples from Palamós contained a resin lining used to line amphorae that contained wine or salted fish (Miró i Canals 1988, 69).

Several kilns may have produced Tarraconense 1 amphorae. Excavations at El Sot del Camp (Sant Vicenç de Montalt) have unearthed a villa dating from the first half of the first century BC to the end of the first century AD.[28] Three rooms have been uncovered: two paved with *opus signinum* as well as a ceramic workshop consisting of a kiln and ceramic dump. Tarraconense 1, Oberaden 74, Pascual 1 and Dr 2-4 were produced here. Several stamps have been found: PHIL and PHILOD (Philodamus) have been found on Pascual 1 and Oberaden 74 respectively. REO and ...TE have been found on Pascual 1 vessels. The most common stamp, however, is L VOLTEIL, of which there are 30 examples on Tarraconense 1, Pascual 1 and Dr 2-4 amphorae (Olesti i Vilà 1995, 481-2; Miró i Canals 1988, 41-3; Prevosti i Monclús 1981, 517-22).

Excavations at La Salut (Sabadell) have revealed a wealthy villa dating from the end of the first century BC to the third century AD. The villa seems to have been engaged in wine production, containing a store of 68 *dolia*, a basin and a possible press (Revilla Calvo 1995, 210; Miró i Canals 1988, 28-9; Gorges 1979, 214). Four kilns have been excavated that produced local Dr 1 amphorae, Tarraconense 1, Pascual 1 and Dr 2-4 amphorae. One of the Tarraconense 1 amphorae bears the mark M.COS (Revilla Calvo 1995, 211; García i Roselló *et al.* 1996, 413). A kiln producing Tarraconense 1 amphorae dated to the middle of the first century BC has been excavated at Les Casetes (Mataró) (Olesti i Vilà 1995, 473). A kiln producing Tarraconense 1 and Pascual 1 amphorae has been excavated at Horta Nova (Arenys de Mar) (Olesti i Vilà 1995, 491). The kiln at Can Notxa (Argentona) may have produced Tarraconense 1 amphorae (Olesti i Vilà 1995, 446). The earliest phase of occupation at Can Majoral (Mataró) dates from the middle of the second century BC and a kiln producing Tarraconense 1 has been dated to the succeeding phase (IIb) (Olesti i Vilà 1995, 459-60).

Unfortunately the evidence for much of this production comes from ceramic waste and not from the kilns themselves. Many of the sites are known only from surface finds or partial excavations and many have subsequently been destroyed. We know very little, therefore, of the function and scale of these kilns.

An important source of evidence about the identity of the subject comes from their choice of nomenclature. Unfortunately, the use of a Latin name does not necessarily indicate a Roman or Italian immigrant. Natives might adopt a Roman name not only to express their *amicitia* with a Roman patron, but as an expression of their *Romanitas* and as a means to set themselves apart from their neighbours and to encourage the impression of their closeness to Rome. It is clear from the *Turma Salluitana* inscription that natives adopted Roman nomenclature prior to their receipt of citizenship (*CIL* 1, 709; Knapp 1978, 190-2). The identities of the producers of the earliest Dr 1 amphorae are unclear as stamps are rare, however, both Latin and native *nomina* have been found. The name Q. FABI is found on examples from Can Portell and Can Balençó (Carreres Vidal *et al.* 1992, 171). Particularly interesting are two Iberian stamps that were found on the handles of Dr 1B amphorae found in the hinterland of Tarraco. The stamps read 'nio' and 'nio ..' and have been dated to the second half of the first century BC (Arrayás Morales 2005, 188; Pérez Suñé *et al.* 1997, 362). Two stamps have been found on a single Dr 1A amphora from Can Vendrell: one Latin reading Q.E. and the second Iberian reading 'ke' or 'ko' (Olesti i Vilà 1998, 249).

Stamps on Tarraconense 1 amphorae are more common and are overwhelmingly Latin. Pena and Barreda (1997, 71-2) contend that they give the names of Italians who settled in the Peninsula between 50 and 45 BC. Monserrat Comas i Solà has suggested that the producers are related to the colony established by Caesar at Narbo Martius in 45 BC (Comas i Solà 1998, 226). The stamp L. VENULEI appears on Tarraconense 1 amphorae from Empúries, as well as in lesser quantities at Cabo de Creus, Vieille-Toulouse and Agen. According to Pena and Barreda (1997, 55-66) the Venulei were an equestrian family, perhaps of Campanian origin, who suffered during the Sullan proscriptions in 82 BC. Partisans of Caesar, they were elevated to the senate between 49-45 BC and a Venuleius is found as a legate of C. Calvisius Sabinus in Africa in 43 BC (Cicero *Ad Familiares* 12, 30, 7). Lucius Venuleius appears on a tombstone from Valencia (*CIL* 2.3769).

The stamp L. VOLTEIL is found on Tarraconense 1 amphorae from Baetulo. Examples have been found on the wrecks of Illes Formigues (Palamós), Cap Béar A, at Port-la-Nautique and Fos-sur-Mer. L. Volteilius was a potter working at El Sot del Camp (Sant Vincenç de Montalt) where the stamp occurs more than 30 times, not only on Tarraconense 1 but also on Pascual 1 and Dr 2-4 amphorae (Comas i Solá 1997, 16; Miró i Canals 1988, 42; Pascual Guash 1980, 276-8; Tchernia 1971, 47; Pascual Guash 1991, 81-4; Bergé 1990, 158-60; Bouscaras 1984, 122-3). The name was Italian in origin – the *gens* was perhaps Samnite. Miró connects the name with Etruria (Miró i Canals 1988, 213-14; 1988, 246).[29] Ricardo Pascual Guash (1980, 278; Foerster *et al.* 1987, 88) suggests that Volteilius is derived from Volteius referred to by Cicero (*In Verrem* 3, 48) and is a freedman of the latter *gens*. Pena and Barreda have suggested that the potter was related to the L. Volteilius Severus and L. Volteilius Suavis attested at Narbo Martius (*CIL* 12.5256) (Pena *et al.* 1997, 66-70).

Five examples of the stamp Q. MEVI have been found on Tarraconense 1 amphorae from Baetulo (Comas i Solà 1997, 17-18; 1985, 130). The stamp has also been found at Empúries and Castell de la Fosca (Palamós) (Pascual Guash 1991, 124) as well as alongside Pascual 1 amphorae at Can Peixau (Padrós 1998, 187). Quintus Mevius was perhaps related to the P.MEVI who is also found on a Tarraconense 1 amphora from Cap Béar 3 (Colls 1986, 205). MEVI also appears on Pascual 1 amphorae at Baetulo and Port-la-Nautique (Comas i Solà 1997, 28; 1985, 132; Pascual Guash 1991, 89; Bergé 1990, 161). The name is Italian in origin, the *nomen* Mevius being common among the Volscii (Vilà i Bota 1996, 297; Miró i Canals 1988, 243).

The stamp C.MVCI has also been found among the Tarraconense 1 amphorae at Baetulo as well as at Vinyoles d'Orís (Comas i Solà 1997, 15). Jordi Miró i Canals (1988, 212; 1988, 245) has suggested that the stamp is from a member of the family of the Muci Scaevolae. The family was of Italian origin and one member of it, the senator P. Mucius Scaevola, was patron of city of Tarraco in the middle of the first century BC.

SEX.STA has been found on Tarraconense 1 amphorae from Baetulo and Empúries (Comas i Solà 1997, 18; Nolla i Brufau *et al.* 1984, 118). Stabilius is attested at Barcelona and Empúries, Statorius from Empúries and Statius from Tarragona (Pascual Guash 1991, 139). The name is Oscan and is common in Campania, Umbria and Picenum. Miró i Canals suggests that it refers to a Statius of Samnite origin who was elevated to the senate after 87 BC and was among those proscribed by the Second Triumvirate in 43 BC. Alternatively it may refer to the merchant Sextus Statius, governor of Cilicia in 51 BC (1988, 212; 1988, 245). The excavators have suggested that the stamp of SEX STATI found in a silo at El Secà de l'Advocada was produced near Cosa (Cantarell *et al.* 1998, 140-1; Jàrrega Domínguez 2000, 286).

C.IVN appears on a Tarraconense 1 amphora found off the coast between Mataró Llavaneres (Pascual Guash 1981, 240-4; Nolla i Brufau *et al.* 1984, 134). The Iunii were of Oscan origin and are found in Empúries, Sigarra, Pacs and Tarraco where eleven members of the *gens* are recorded – one of whom held the office of *sevir* (Miró i Canals 1988, 210-11; 1988, 244).

A single example of the stamp of C.SERVILI has been found on the rim of a Tarraconense 1 amphora at Baetulo (Comas i Solà 1997, 16). The stamp may be related to the Servilii Caepiones: Q. Servilius Caepio (*cos.* 140) was proconsul of Ulterior in 140-139 BC and Q. Servilius Caepio (*pr.* 109) governed Ulterior between 109 and 107 BC.

Iberian stamps are rare: an example from Calle Don Juan de Aragón (n. 9) (Zaragoza) has an Iberian stamp that reads 'e i ke_bi'. The meaning of the stamp is uncertain: recording either the name of a location or estate; or of an Iberian landowner named eikebilos, eikebin, eikebir or eikebuir (Aguardo Otal 1992, 113-14; Galve Izquierdo 1996, 95-9). Other Iberian stamps have been found. One was found on the handle of an Iberian amphora from a silo excavated by Pere Giró i Romeu in 1944 at La Bassa (Santa Margarida i els Monjos, Alt Penedès). The stamp was recovered from silo II and dates to the first century BC. The stamp reads 'u.r'.ce.bo.r' – perhaps a name (Ros Mateos 2005, 187-9; Pérez Suñé *et al.* 1997, 362). A second stamp from La Alcudia (Elche) dates between the final third of the third century and the middle of the first century BC. The reading of the stamp is problematic and perhaps reads 'cu.n.ca.e' in Turdetanian characters (Pérez Suñé *et al.* 1997, 362; Ribera Lacomba 1982, 84). 'ba.n' has been found on an Iberian amphora from La Serreta (Alcoy) dating to the third to mid-second century BC (Pérez Suñé *et al.* 1997, 362; Ribera Lacomba 1982, 53). An Iberian amphora found on the surface at El Moluengo (Villagordo de Cabriel) bears the inscription 'e. (..) ke' (Pérez Suñé *et al.* 1997, 362; Ribera Lacomba 1982, 129). A stamp written in Iberian has been found on a fragment of a *dolium* from the fill of a silo at Jardí Park (Premià de Dalt). The inscription reads 'l.a.u.r'.ko.': 'l.a.u.r'' is an anthroponym and 'ko.' may be an abbreviation of a longer name (Olesti i Vilà 1995, 75-6).

The incidence of stamps on Laietanian Dr 1 amphorae is too rare to enable us to reach any conclusions regarding the identity of the individuals responsible for the production of these vessels, although both Iberian and Latin names have been found. The earliest Dr 1 amphorae at Burriac dated *c.* 80-70 BC fit well with the settlement of Empúries *c.* 125-75 BC, suggesting that the instigation came from the Italian settlers established there. While some individuals attested on Tarraconense 1 amphorae may be connected with members of the local or Roman elite, for example Caius Mucius and Caius Iunius, many of the names that appear are Italian rather than Roman in origin – Venuleius, Volteilius, Statius and Mevius. It is particularly worthy of note that these names are largely absent from the epigraphy of the Peninsula. While it is hazardous to link these stamps with specific individuals, in the absence of *tria nomina* I would suggest that these stamps were issued by non-citizen Italian settlers. Vines take seven to ten years to produce a harvest, so the estates that produced wine carried in Tarraconense 1 amphorae *c.* 40 BC would have been established *c.* 50 BC. Particularly interesting are the Iberian stamps that appear on Tarraconense 1 vessels. While stamps are found on Phoenician vessels and copied by native potters these are pictographic; epigraphic stamps appear only at the middle of the first century BC as Iberian landowners imitated the practice of their Italian neighbours on both Dr 1 and Tarraconense 1 amphorae.

Recent work has thrown light upon the distribution of Tarraconense 1 amphorae. The form has been found at a number of locations in Cataluña: in Empúries, Palamós, Lloret de Mar, Baetulo, Barcelona and Tarragona (Nolla i Brufau 1987, 218-19; Miró i Canals 1988, 120-2). A wreck was discovered in 1958 at Palamós lying 100 m northwest of the lighthouse on the Illes Formigues (Gerona). The cargo consists of 30 Tarraconense 1 amphorae – one of which bears the stamp L.VOLTEIL (Foerster *et al.* 1987, 86-7; Parker 1998, 299; Nolla i Brufau *et al.* 1984, 121). Pascual has reported the find of fragments of Tarraconense 1 vessels on the coast of Llavaneres and Mataró (Pascual Guash 1981, 240-2). Outside the Peninsula the form has been identified at a number of sites in France: Vieille-Toulouse, Agen, Vienne/St Romain en Gal (Miró i Canals 1988, 122-3), Lyon (Nolla i Brufau *et al.* 1984-5, 133) and Agde, as well as in Italy at La Longarina (Ostia) (Hesnard 1980, 147-8; Buxó Capdevila *et al.* 2002, 180).

In 1982 a wreck – Cap Béar 3 – was discovered 500 m to the south of Port Vendres. The cargo consists of amphorae from a variety of sources: there are at least 160 Italian Dr 1B, as well as Baetican Dr 12 (sixteen examples), and Catalan Pascual 1 and Tarraconense 1 vessels (Colls 1986, 203; Parker 1992, 97). The stamp P.MEVI is perhaps related to those of Quintus Mevius found at Baetulo (Comas i Solà 1997, 17-18) and BL is reported by Ribas at Torre Llauder (Miró i Canals 1988, 38). Limited as the sample is, the distribution of Tarraconense 1 echoes that of the succeeding Pascual 1 vessels and represents the increasing export of wine from the region.

Italian immigration and the mines of the Cartagena and the Sierra Morena

Italian immigrants may also have been attracted to the southeast of the Peninsula, where an important component of the imperialist view of a deliberate policy of Romanization is that Rome sought to control the mineral resources of the Peninsula. Diodorus (5.36.3) says that there was an early influx of immigrants to exploit the mineral resources of Cartagena.[30] According to Polybius the silver mines in the Sierra of Cartagena extended over an area of 400 stadia, employed 40,000 workmen and provided the Roman treasury with a daily revenue of 25,000 drachmae (Strabo 3.2.10). The appearance of silver denarii from the middle of the second century BC may indicate an increase in silver mining at that time. According to Livy (34.21.7) in 195 BC after pacifying the province, Cato instituted the payment of *vectigal* or rent for the exploitation of salt sources and of iron and silver mines in Hispania Citerior: 'pacata provincia vectigalia magna instituit ex ferrariis argentariisque, quibus tum institutis locupletior in dies provincia fuit'.

Roman interest in the mines is reflected in the early appearance of coins in the mining areas – for example at Cabezo Agudo (La Union), as well as the large number of sites that have yielded Campanian A pottery. The foci of mining activities lay in the Sierra de Cartagena and at Mazarrón. The Sierra de Cartagena extends from the east of Cartagena for 28 km towards Cabo de Palos. The most abundant minerals are lead, silver, copper, iron and zinc. The most important mines were located in the vicinity of La Unión where 31 sites have been identified dating from the end of the third century to the middle of the first century BC (Berrocal Caparrós 1997, 112-14). The majority of these sites date from the middle of the second century. Substantial mine workings have been found at Cabezo Rajao, consisting of an opencast trench 450 m long and 15-30 m wide. The ore was extracted through shafts, the largest of which was the Pozo de Reyes, 133 m deep, from which galleries extend for a further 180 m (Ramallo Asensio *et al.* 1994, 100).

The mining town of Cabezo Agudo lies on a small hill rising to a height of 180 m above sea level to the northeast of Cabezo Rajao. Lead slag containing silver and copper has been found together with litharge. Occupation dates from the second half of the second century to the middle of the first century BC. A variety of pottery has been found: Campanian A, B and C wares, Greco-Italic amphorae, Dr 1, Mañá C and D amphorae, Iberian *kalathoi*, Italian Mayet III and Vegas 13 vessels and a piece of Gaulish *terra sigillata* (Fernández de Avilés 1942, 138-9; Ruiz Valderas 1995, 155). A small villa has been excavated at Los Ruices, two rooms of which were decorated with pavements of *opus signinum*. The villa dates from the end of the second or beginning of the first century BC and seems to have been associated with the activities of the nearby mines, to judge by the quantities of slag that have been found (Ramallo Asensio *et al.* 1994, 102). Two rooms have been excavated at Mina Balsa decorated in *opus signinum* with marble and white *tesserae* dating from the end of the third century to the beginning of the first century BC (Ramallo Asensio *et al.* 1994, 102; Ruiz Valderas 1995, 158).[31]

The ore could have travelled south via the Boltada or los Chorrillos to the Bahía de Portman where a wealthy villa has been excavated at Huerta del Paturro. Excavations have revealed two large basins lined with *opus signinum* (7.50 x 15.25 x 1.15 m and 6.25 x 14.50 x 1.30 m) of uncertain function: perhaps used either for the washing of ore or the preparation of fish sauces or esparto grass. Republican levels have been found in Sector A of the villa dated to the first half of the second century BC by finds of Campanian A pottery (Ruiz Valderas 1995, 160). The basins were filled in during the second century AD and replaced with the *pars urbana* which survived until the first third of the third century AD (Berrocal Caparrós 1997, 113; Ramallo Asensio *et al.* 1994, 96-7). Three basins lined with *opus signinum* have been found at the villa of La

Paloma (Barranco de los Chorillos). Occupation dates from the second century BC to the first century AD. Among the finds are Dr 1 A amphorae (Ramallo Asensio *et al.* 1994, 97; Ruiz Valderas 1995, 157). Ore could also travel north to the Mar Menor along the Rambla del Estrecho to Los Nietos or towards Cabo de Palos where the site of Castillet has yielded abundant *dolia*, amphorae and slag (Ramallo Asensio *et al.* 1994, 98-9).

To the west of Cartagena several mines have been located in the vicinity of Mazarrón where silver, lead, copper, iron and zinc were extracted. The mine of Coto Fortuna lies 8 km west of Mazarrón on the slopes of the Sierra de las Moreras. The silver mines here were the largest in the region yielding 2.5 kg of silver per metric ton of lead (Ramallo Asensio *et al.* 1985, 53). The mines at San Cristóbal and Los Perules to the northwest of Mazarrón were worked from the second century BC: Campanian A from Loma de Sánchez dates from the first half of the second century BC (Ramallo Asensio *et al.* 1985, 61). Dr 1 amphorae, Campanian A and B pottery and pavements of *opus signinum* dating to the first century BC have been recovered from the mine at Esperanza on the Cerro de San Cristóbal (Ramallo Asensio *et al.* 1985, 57-8). Opencast mining took place at Pedreras Viejas located 4 km to the west of Mazarrón. Mining seems to have begun in the first century BC and continued until the first century AD (Ramallo Asensio *et al.* 1985, 61-2; 1994, 110). Several mines have produced evidence of metalworking taking place in the immediate vicinity. Slag, together with large numbers of amphorae, *terra sigillata* and *tegulae* dating from the first century BC to the first century AD have been found at El Escorial at the foot of the Cabezo de San Cristóbal (Ramallo Asensio *et al.* 1985, 63).

From the mines at San Cristóbal and Los Perules the ore could be transported to the coast where several sites have produced evidence of metalworking: in 1980 a smelting furnace was discovered during agricultural work at Loma de Herrerías. Three basins used in the washing of the ore were also found, containing large quantities of slag rich in iron and lead (Arana Castillo 1983, 940; Ramallo Asensio 1983, 926-7).[32] The workshop dates from the first half of the second century BC with increasing quantities of imported pottery through the first century BC (Ramallo Asensio 1983, 929; Ramallo Asensio *et al.* 1994, 113-14).

A metal workshop has been found on the coast at El Mojón, dated to the second half of the second century and the first century BC thanks to the presence of Campanian A and B wares, Dr 1 and Dr 18 amphorae. As well as quantities of slag, three small basins have been found along the shore with furnaces 200 m inland. The furnaces were used to produce silver through cupellation as litharge has been found together with lead ingots – one of which bears a stamp that reads PICAE (Ramallo Asensio *et al.* 1985, 62-3).[33] A metalworking furnace has been found in the final phase of La Gacha, dated to the first quarter of the first century BC (Agüera Martínez *et al.* 1993, 528). Roman housing together with slag has been found beside the beach at El Caraleño to the west of Bolnuevo. The site was in use from the second half of the first century BC to the second half of the first century AD (Ramallo Asensio *et al.* 1985, 63).

The presence of Italian immigrants working in the mines is suggested by the abundance of imported Italian pottery: Campanian A and B fine wares, Greco-Italic and Dr 1 amphorae. The increased volume of Campanian A pottery reaching Cartagena during the final decade of the third and the first quarter of the second century BC is particularly striking, reaching 72.7% of the pottery found (Ruiz Valderas

2004, 95).[34] Levels dated to the second half of the second century BC have yielded 81.92% of Campanian A pottery, reflecting what Elena Ruiz Valderas believes is the increasingly Romanized and Italian character of the population (2004, 97).

It is at this time that the city of Cartagena is remodelled, particularly the port. An inscription was discovered in the Castillo de la Concepción in the eighteenth century. Dated to the end of the second or the first quarter of the first century BC, this inscription refers to construction work of 'pilae III et fundament(a) ex caement(o)' unfortunately not located, although perhaps related to harbour work (Abascal and Ramallo 1997, 73-4; Noguera Celdrán 2004, 70-1).[35]

An Italianate temple dedicated to the Syrian goddess Atargatis was constructed on the Cerro de Molinete (Ramallo and Ruiz 1994). An altar dated to the first century BC and dedicated by Sex. Numisius, the slave of Lucius, was found at the end of the nineteenth century at Rambla de la Boltada. It may have been erected by a slave of one of the families responsible for working the mines at Cartagena (Ruiz Valderas 1995, 157; Ramallo Asensio *et al.* 1994, 96). In 1993 a shrine or *sacellum* to Iuppiter Stator was discovered at Cabezo Gallufo. Finds of Dr 1A, Lamboglia 2 and Mañá C2b amphorae and Campanian A pottery date the shrine to the end of the second or beginning of the first century BC. The dedicatory inscription in the *opus signinum* pavement records the dedicator as the freedman Marcus Aquinius Andro: M(arcus) AQVINI M(arci) L(ibertus) ANDRO/ IOVI STATOR D(e) S(ua) P(ecunia)/ L(ibens) M(erito) (Ruiz Valderas 2004, 98; Martín Camino *et al.* 1996, 29-35; Noguera Celdrán 2004, 72; Abascal Palazón *et al.* 1997, 441-3; Orejas *et al.* 2002, 583).

A tombstone discovered in 1887 at Coto Fortuna was erected for one Alexandra by her son L. Rubellius Philodamus. Philodamus is also found on a tombstone from Lorca erected for his father L. Rubellius Philostratus. The Rubellii were a family of Italian origin known above all from the Augustan and Julio-Claudian periods. The Greek *cognomina* suggest that these were freedmen of oriental origin (Belda Navarro 1975, 270-1; Ramallo Asensio *et al.* 1985, 55; 1994, 106-7; González Blanco 1996, 144). A Greek freedman also appears on an inscription from Los Escoriales that reads L.Argentari.Nicander / Salve (Ramallo Asensio *et al.* 1994, 106). An inscription from La Cañada (Los Beatos) reads:]AVONIUS /]RUFUS /]OUF(entina tribu). The inscription dates to the second half of the first century BC. The tribe originated in Latium (Antolinos Marín 1999, 110).

The most useful tools for exploring the individuals involved in mining, however, are the inscriptions found on lead ingots. According to Claude Domergue the names reflect the influx of Italians and Campanians: C. Messius, C. Fiduius, P. Nona, L. Planius from Campania; M. Raius and C. Utius from Southern Italy (1966, 64). Forty-nine ingots have been recovered from a wreck off the Cabo de Palos. The following stamps have been found: M.AQVINI.C.F, C.MESSI.L.F, C.VTIVS.C.F, M.SEX.CALVI.M.F. and L.PLANI.L.F.RVSSINI (Mas García 1985, 162-3; Parker 1992, 65-6). The inscription C(ai).MESSI(i).L(ucii).F(ilii) refers to an Oscan *gens* found in Campania and among the Volsci. A Caius Messius is attested on Delos during the second century BC (Belda 1975, 81). A Marcus Messius Samalcio (or Samalo), a *faber lapidarius*, is known from Cartagena (Domergue 1966, 49-50).

Fourteen ingots stamped C.VTIVS.C.F have also been found within a cargo of Dr 1B amphorae from a wreck at Punta dell'Arco dated to the first half of the first century BC (Parker 1992, 351). A second wreck at Punta Falcone off the northwest coast of

Sardinia carried sixteen lead ingots with the same stamp (Parker 1992, 353). Caius Utius is perhaps related to the individual named on two ingots from Mazarrón which read C(aii) Uti(i) C(aii) F(ilii), Menen(ia tribu). The *gens* is perhaps Samnite in origin, while the Menenian tribe was located in Latium and Campania (Domergue 1966, 52-4; Ramallo Asensio *et al.* 1985, 64-5).

The Aquini were involved in mining from the middle of the second century BC: Caius and Marcus Aquinius are found on ingots from Cartagena (Domergue 1966, 44-6, 54-7). They are perhaps connected with the freedman M. Aquinius Andro, recorded in the dedication to Iuppiter Stator from Cabezo Gallufo. They may also be connected with the *duovir quinquennalis* Caius Aquinius Mela, found on late Republican coins from the city. The *gens* was Oscan in origin – perhaps originating among the Volsci (Domergue 1966, 44-6).

Several members of the *gens* of the Pontilieni that originated in Picenum were involved in mining: C. Pontilienus M.f. Fab., C. Pontilienus M.f. and M. (et) C. Pontilieni M.f. have been found on lead ingots from various mines in the region, and a Pil(emo) Pontili(enorum) M. (et) C. s(ervus) is attested on an inscription from Cabo de Palos (Abascal Palazón *et al.* 1997, 235-7).

In 1878 an ingot reading P.NON.AE.P.F.NVC was dragged from the harbour at Cartagena. The inscription reads P(ublii) Nonae P(ublii) f(ilii) Nuc(erini). The suffix -a on Nonae is Etruscan corresponding to the Latin Nonius. The *cognomen* Nucerinus refers to the town of Nuceria in Campania (Domergue 1966, 46-8). Also from the harbour at Cartagena is an ingot with an inscription reading: C(aii).FIDUI(i).C(aii).F(ilii) // S(purii).L[uc]RETI(I).S(purii).F(ilii) – Fiduius/Fidubius is Oscan in origin while the Lucretii are widely attested throughout Italy (Domergue 1966, 50-2). A further ingot reads M(arci).RAI(i).RUFI // FER(ocis ?) – the *gens* Raius is found in Samnium, Campania and Apulia (Domergue 1966, 58-9).

In 1878 another ingot reading L.PLANI.L.F was found in the harbour at Cartagena. This individual is related to the L. Planius Russinus who is found on stamps from a number of locations (Domergue 1965, 10-14). Examples have been found on ingots from the Agde J wreck dated to the late second century or early first century BC (Parker 1992, 45). The same individual appears on an ingot from a wreck at Cala Cartoe off the eastern coast of Sardinia (Boninu 1985, 451). Ten examples have been found on a wreck at Mahdia dating to the beginning of the first century BC. The wreck was discovered in 1907 lying three miles to the northeast of Ras Mahedia (Parker 1992, 252). An ingot reading M. Plani. L. f. / Russini has been published by Zucca (1985, 150) from a wreck off the coast of the island of Mal di Ventre. M. Planius Russinus also appears on ingots from Ripatransone (Ascoli) and Mahdia (Domergue 1965, 14). The *gens* is found in Narbonne, Rome, Southern Latium and Campania. Cicero (*ad Familiares* 9.13) refers to a M. Planius Heres, however, the connection between him and the individuals named on the ingots is unclear (Domergue 1965, 21-3).

The Atellii are one of the most common *gentes* found in Cartagena. Several members are attested on lead ingots from the first half of the first century BC onwards: the earliest is Cn. Atellius T.f. whose *tribus Menenia* suggests that he received citizenship at the end of the Social War (Domergue 1990, 321).[36] The same individual is found on ingots from the Mahdia wreck (Domergue 1965, 18). Several members appear as moneyers on coins of the city from the middle of the first century BC onwards, and Cn. Atellius Flaccus was *duovir quinquennalis* in AD 37-38 (Abascal Palazón *et al.* 1997, 249).

Fifteen ingots have been recovered from a wreck at Niedo Ciervo (Aguilas). The bulk of the cargo consists of Dr 1C amphorae, dating the wreck to the late Republic. Thirteen of the ingots were inscribed Q SEI.P.F.MEN POSTVMI. The *gens* originated in Southern Italy, which accords with Q. Seius Postumus' membership of the Menenian tribe. Claude Domergue has suggested that this is the same individual as the *eques* of that name who Cicero tells us was poisoned by P. Clodius Pulcher in 58/57 BC in order to acquire his house on the Palatine (Cicero, *De Domo Sua* 115; Domergue *et al.* 1983, 905-7).

Unfortunately these inscriptions do not tell us the manner in which these individuals exploited the mines. If we are to follow the argument that Rome pursued a deliberate policy of exploiting the mineral resources of the Peninsula then we would expect to see evidence of *societates publicanorum* operating the mines on behalf of the Roman state. According to Peter Brunt (1962, 105) and Ernst Badian (1972, 32), the Spanish silver mines were exploited by *societates publicanorum* from the time of Cato the Elder's governorship in 195 BC. The regulations from the copper and silver mine at Vipasca in the province of Lusitania are important in showing Imperial involvement. They date to the reign of Hadrian and record that the rights to work a particular mine were leased from the *procurator metallorum* in return for payment of half the ore mined or a monetary equivalent.

Cicero (*De Lege Agraria* 1,2,5; 2,19,51) makes it clear that there was *ager publicus* in the vicinity of Cartagena – the only *ager publicus* attested in the Peninsula – and it seems reasonable to equate this with the silver mines in the area. Several *societates* are recorded on ingots: lead ingots from Agde J bear stamps of the SOC GARGILI T F ET M LAETILI ML and SOC.M.C.PONTILIOENORVM.M.F. (Parker 1992, 45). This *societas* also appears on ingots from a wreck at Mal di Ventre off the coast of Sardinia. Most of the cargo of *c.* 1,000 ingots are marked SOC M C PONTILIENORVM or M C PONTILIENORVM M F as well as a smaller number of CARVLIVS HISPALLIS or CARVLIVS HISPALIVS (Parker 1992, 255-6). SOC appeared on a no longer extant ingot from a wreck at Gavetti in the Strait of Bonifacio (Parker 1992, 188). Several stamps refer to *societates* by geographical location: the mines at Coto Fortuna were operated by the *societas argentariarum fodinarum montis Ilurconensis* or *societas montis argentarii Ilurco(nensis)*.[37] Blázquez Martínez (1986, 48) has suggested that the S.C. found at El Centenillo refers to the *societas Castulonensis* that worked silver mines in the Sierra Morena from the first century BC until the reign of Claudius. According to Pliny, the cinnabar and mercury mines at Sisapo (La Bienvenida) in the Sierra Morena were worked by a *societas* (*Natural History* 33.18). This *societas* may appear on an inscription from Capua (*CIL* 10.3964) which refers to a *villicus sociorum Sisaponensium ex Provinciae Ulteriore*.

By the time of Strabo at the end of the first century BC the situation had changed with mines now being owned by private individuals (3.2.10). John Richardson (1976, 142) has noted that neither Diodorus nor Polybius refer to *societates* and likens the descriptions to 'a nineteenth-century gold-rush' rather than the operations of large-scale financiers. Richardson suggests that the lessees were private individuals rather than *societates* (1976, 146). The number and size of individual mines in the region seem to reflect smaller-scale operations and the figures given by Polybius for the size of the operations are those of the entire mining region and not of an individual lessee (Richardson 1976, 143). While *societates* do appear on lead ingots from Cartagena, the majority of inscriptions refer to individuals – probably the lessees of the mines (Domergue 1965, 20).

Claude Domergue (1966, 64) has shown that the families attested on ingots appear among the municipal elite of Carthago Nova from the end of the Republic onwards. The *duoviri quinquennales* C. Aquinius Mela, C. Laetilius Apalus, P. Turullius and Q. Varius Hiberus were members of families attested on ingots. Q. Varius Hiberus served as *duovir quinquennalis* on three occasions during the reign of Augustus and an ingot reading Q. VARI HIBERI was found in the harbour at Cherchel in Algeria in 1847 (Parker 1992, 139). The number of individuals attested in this manner makes clear the wealth and importance that accrued from the mining industry in the area.

Several small houses have been discovered on the hill above the metalworkshop at Loma de Herrerías. Although not systematically excavated, in the 1970s a pavement of *opus signinum* was discovered decorated with black and white *tesserae* and an inscription that reads [...]VM.FAC.//HEISCE.MAG.CVR.SELE [...]//CAELI (Ramallo Asensio *et al.* 1994, 114-15; Gorges 1979, 318), which Sebastian Ramallo Asensio suggests refers to the *curales* or *curatores* of a *collegium argentarii* that erected a building in the vicinity. The Seleucus referred to in the inscription is perhaps the same individual as the T. Cassius Seleucus who is attested on an inscription from Cartagena (*CIL* 2.3458) (Ramallo Asensio 1983, 928). Similar *collegia* may be recorded at Cabo de Palos and Cartagena. The first was found at Cerro del Mosquito (El Castillet) and dates to *c.* 100 BC. The inscription gives the names of several individuals of varying status – free men, freedmen and slaves with Italian *nomina*: C. Poplicius, L. Cervius, L. Talepius, Cn. Tongilius, L. Paquius, Q. Veratius, Pilemus Pontillimus and Q. Claudius Postumius (*CIL* 2.3433). The second inscription from Castillo de la Concepción lists the *magistri* of the *collegium* responsible for the construction of harbour work: the freedmen Marcus Puupius, Sextus Luucius (?), Sextus Gaep[, Marcus Prosius, Numerius Titius and Caius Vereius; the slaves Antiochus, Eleuter, Philemo, Alexander and Acerdo. Juan Abascal and Sebastián Ramallo have noted that this form of inscription parallels those of the *magistri* of Capua dating between 112/11 and 71 BC (Abascal Palazón *et al.* 1997, 71-7). Both inscriptions refer to *collegia* administered by *magistri* and composed of individuals of varying status, although there are significant numbers of freedmen and slaves (Ramallo Asensio *et al.* 1994, 116-17). Cristóbal Belda Navarro (1975, 157-8) has noted the use of archaic language (*coriarunt*, *heisce*) and forms (the nominative ending in *-i* that is derived from Italian dialects).

Mining declined in the region from the second half of the first century BC perhaps as the wealth accrued through investment in mines was transferred to the land holdings of the municipal elite. Strabo (3.2.10) contrasts the situation at the time of Polybius with that of his own day; however, elsewhere he makes clear that the mines were still active (3.4.6). Although the bulk of the ingots discussed by Domergue date to the late second century and mid-first century BC some are later – for example, the stamp COLON.AVGVSTI.FERM that was recovered from the harbour at Cartagena in 1878 must post-date the foundation of the colony under Augustus. Archaeological evidence shows that mining activity continued at least until the first quarter of the first century AD (Orejas *et al.* 2002, 586). Occupation of the metalworkshop at Los Beatos ceased during the second half of the first century AD (Antolinos Marín 1999, 110). According to González Simancas a coin of Trajan has been recovered from the mine at San Antonio de Padua (Ramallo Asensio *et al.* 1985, 59).

As Almudena Orejas and Javier Sánchez-Palencia (2002) have pointed out, the importance of mining in the region has led to a tendency to underestimate other economic activities. A number of sites have produced evidence of fishing, farming and commerce and at several sites mining or metallurgy took place together with agricultural activities. As mining declined, there seems to have been a move of population to areas better suited for agriculture – for example, the Alto Guadalentín, where more than 45 large or medium-sized rural sites have been located (Orejas *et al.* 2002, 587). This expansion may be due to the elevation of Carthago Nova to the status of a colony late in the first century BC.

Cartagena was particularly noted for the production of *garum*. In 1875 an inscription was discovered at Las Puertas de Murcia. The inscription dates from *c.* AD 10-14 and records a dedication to the *duovir* C. Laetilius by the guild of *piscatores et propolae* (*CIL* 2.5929). Fish tanks dated to the first century BC have been found near milestone 442 in Puerto de Mazarrón (Mas García 2004, 57).

Declining mining activity at Cartagena may have prompted the villas at Las Mateas and Paturro (Portmán) to focus on fishing activities from the Augustan period (Ruiz Valderas 1995, 154). The villa of Las Mateas was excavated in 1958, followed by a small rescue excavation in 1988. The earlier Republican farm was replaced in the second half of the first century BC by a fish factory. The apogee of the factory, however, appears to date to the Julio-Claudian period with the site being abandoned in the middle of the second century AD (Ruiz Valderas 1995, 172-4). The existence of Republican occupation underlying the first-century AD fishery at Castillicos is indicated by the presence of Campanian A and B pottery (Ruiz Valderas 1995, 174). Excavations in 1985 revealed a fish factory to the east of the villa at Portmán that was abandoned at the end of the second century AD (Ruiz Valderas 1995, 174-6). Rescue excavations at the mouth of La Rambla uncovered three basins lined with *opus signinum* dating to the first century BC or Augustan period that were perhaps associated with the villa at Huerto del Francés (Ramallo Asensio *et al.* 1994, 96).

Several villas have been excavated on the coastal plain between the Sierra Minera and the Mar Menor. Excavations at Los Ruices in 1979 uncovered a villa dated from the first century BC to the mid-late second century AD. Fragments of *opus signinum* together with Campanian A and B have been found at Lo Rizo (Ruiz Valderas 1995, 162). Excavations at Tiro de Pichón revealed pavements of *opus signinum* and pottery dating from the second century BC: Campanian A and B, Greco-Italic, Dr 1 and Dr 2-4 amphorae, Arretine and Gaulish *terra sigillata* and *terra sigillata africana clara A* (Ruiz Valderas 1995, 163). Millstones and an oil press have been found at Cabezo Ventura together with Campanian A and B pottery, Greco-Italic and Dr 1 amphorae (Ruiz Valderas 1995, 163). The site of La Atalaya seems to have been engaged in both metallurgical and agricultural activities with finds of litharge and lead, as well as millstones and amphorae. The earliest occupation dates to the second century BC and continued until the middle of the second century AD, although the site is at its most prosperous during the second and first centuries BC (Ruiz Valderas 1995, 163).

The villa of El Castillet (Cabo de Palos) lies on a hill overlooking the harbour of

Cala Reona. As well as the *pars urbana* decorated with *opus signinum* and *opus scutulatum* floors, painted stucco and moulded cornices, excavations have revealed storerooms containing *dolia* and amphorae imported from Apulia and Southern Italy. Ruiz Valderas (1995, 169-71) suggests that these amphorae will have come from the harbour at Cala Reona for redistribution to the neighbouring mining communities.

Cartagena was also famed for its cultivation of esparto grass that was used for basketry and rope making. Pliny (*Natural History* 19.26) describes the *Campo Espartario* extending over an area of 6,500 km^2.[38] The volume of Roman remains at Los Ceniceros including pottery and *opus signinum* has led Belda Navarro (1975, 180-2) to suggest that at least ten villas were situated in the vicinity dating from the third and second centuries BC onwards. The volume of Dr 1 B amphorae recovered from Cabezo Vulcano on the left of the road from Mazarrón to Aguilas has led to the suggestion that Italian wine was stored here (Ramallo Asensio *et al.* 1985, 60). Basins lined with *opus signinum* have been reported at La Paloma and Eugenia and were used to macerate either *garum* or esparto grass. Quantities of slag were also found (Berrocal Caparrós 1997, 112).

Important mines located in the Sierra Morena were intensively exploited from the first century BC. The Republican mines in the area were not fundamentally different from those of the pre-Roman period (Blanco Freijero *et al.* 1981, 173). According to Pliny, the most important mines were the silver mines located in the area of Castulo (*Natural History* 10, 38,7). One of the largest mines is located at El Centenillo, 15 km to the northwest of La Carolina. The largest vein – Mirador – extends for at least 870 m at a depth of 225 m. Three furnaces have been found: at La Tejeruela, La Fabriquilla and Cerro del Plomo, together with quantities of litharge left over from cupellation, and various lead pieces – some stamped with S.C. Operations began in the second or first centuries BC (Domergue 1987, 265-71).

Important silver mines were located at La Loba (Fuenteovejuna, Córdoba) and Diógenes (Ciudad Real). A single phase of operation has been identified dating from the end of the second century and first half of the first century BC. The most abundant pottery were Dr 1B amphorae, although Greco-Italic and vessels similar to Dr 2 are also present as well as small quantities of Campanian A and B (Blázquez Martínez 1982, 35-6).

The nexus of these mines was the site of Valderrepisa (Fuencaliente) where abundant lead and slag have been recovered. The settlement was an extensive one, extending over as much as 4 ha. Although the limited scale of excavations means that the layout of the site is unclear, excavations of sector A in 1990-1 revealed a street with a central terracotta water pipe (Fernández Rodríguez *et al.* 1993, 25-6). The excavators have noted that the construction types are analogous to those of El Centenillo, La Loba, El Cerro del Plomo, Villasviejas del Tamuja and Mina Diógenes (Fernández Rodríguez *et al.* 1993, 30). Evidence of metalworking has also come from La Dehesa (Fuencaliente) 4 km from Velderrepisa (Domergue 1988, 77). Important copper mines were situated to the north of Andújar.

Smaller mines may also have existed: quantities of red ochre found at Las Viñas located on the right bank of the Río Salado in southeastern Córdoba may have come from nearby workings (Leiva Briones *et al.* 1992, 248).[39] Copper and iron slag has been found at Los López (Carcabuey) together with evidence of olive oil processing. The site appears to have been occupied from the end of the Republic to the second century AD (Carrillo Díaz-Pines 1995, 69-70). Rescue excavations have uncovered a settlement at Horno del Castillo (Guarromán) dating from the middle of the first century BC to the fourth century AD. From the beginning of the first century AD the site seems to have been devoted to the processing of ore. During the final phase the settlement appears to have moved down the slope of the Cerro Castillejo where a well-preserved smelting furnace has been excavated. A store of *dolia* has also been excavated from the final phase, suggesting that during this period the site was also engaged in agricultural activities (Haley 2003, 30).

Mines could be leased by the state to *societates publicanorum*, smaller *societates* and individuals or worked privately. Several *societates publicanorum* are known – the most famous is the *societas Sisaponensis* which worked the cinnabar and mercury mines at Sisapo (La Bienvenida) near Almadén (Haley 2003, 27). The mines in the vicinity of Castulo were administered by the *societas C(astulonensis)* attested at El Centenillo. A lead ingot from Castulo bears the mark T.IVENTI-M.LV ... – the first part refers to T. Iuventius; the second is uncertain, perhaps referring to M. Lucretius (Contreras 1996, 84-7; Domergue 1990, 256). Pliny (*Natural History* 34.165) refers to two mines: the *metallum Antonianum* and *metallum Samariense* which Haley (2003, 27) has suggested originated as private workings during the Republic.

The large number of Italians attested in the mines around Carthago Nova is in stark contrast to elsewhere in the Peninsula where natives are involved. Posidonius, writing at the end of the second or beginning of the first century BC, says that the Iberians worked copper and silver mines in Turdetania (Diodorus 5.36.1-3). Haley (2003, 28-9) has suggested that the urban layout of Valderrepisa points to the presence of Italians.

The mines of Lusitania may also have begun to operate during the late Republic. The presence of Republican pottery and coins at several sites suggests that the exploitation of the mines in Lusitania began prior to the reign of Augustus. A lamp dating to the first half of the first century BC has been found at Plasenzuela. Coin hoards dating to the end of the second or early first century BC have been found at Penhagarica, Idanha-a-Velha, Idanha-a-Nova, Atalaia and Monforte da Beira (Edmondson 1987, 42-4).

Republican villas elsewhere in the Peninsula

Evidence for Republican villas elsewhere in the Peninsula is scarce. Iberian and Roman pottery has been found together with a kiln at El Planet (Albalat dels Tarongers). The site is located on the right-bank of the barranc de Segart, 300 m from the Río Palància. It was originally identified as a Roman villa: Roman and Iberian pottery together with a kiln were excavated by Monzó Nogués (1946, 35 n. 1, 65-6, 151; Martí Bonafé 1998, 141-3).

The earliest villas in the Guadalquivir valley may date to the end of the Republic. The villa of El Coronil may have been preceded by Iberian occupation. Large quantities of pottery have been recovered from the site of El Bollo III on the slopes of the Torre de El Bollo, 10 km from Montellano. The earliest pottery, Punic amphorae and Iberian wares date to the third and fourth centuries BC. Four fragments of Campanian A ware has been found, one of which may be a local imitation. The finds from the site come from the surface, but parts of a pavement of *opus spicatum* have also been found (Oria Segura *et al.* 1990, 50-4). Finds of Iberian pottery and

Campanian ware suggest that the possible villa at Ruchenilla may have been occupied from the first century BC (Oria Segura *et al.* 1990, 100).

Rescue excavations carried out in 1990 at Arbollón (Carmo) uncovered a substantial ceramic workshop. Seven of the kilns date to the first phase of activity on the site during the second century BC and the remaining kiln dates to the second phase during the first century AD. The workshop was abandoned at the end of the first or beginning of the second century AD. The kilns produced Muñoz A5 and Pellicer B-C amphorae as well as coarse ware pottery (Chic García *et al.* 2004, 289).

The spread of Campanian pottery and Dr 1 amphorae in the Guadalquivir valley shows that the area was already open to material Romanization during the first century BC. Pedro Lacort Navarro has suggested that the focus of the farms in the lower Guadalquivr valley was cereal cultivation. In 1981 at least ten silos were uncovered at Caserío del Gramalejo (Castro del Río). The capacity of each silo was approximately 35 m^3 (Lacort Navarro 1985, 365-6). Ten large silos have been found at Cortijo Nuevo de la Silera, each with a capacity of 68 m^3 (Lacort Navarro 1985, 368-70). The ten silos at Caserío del Gramalejo had a capacity of 274,680 kg of grain; however, if there were as many as 40 silos the capacity would have reached 1,098,720 kg, or 160,000 *modii*. The ten silos at Cortijo Nuevo de la Silera contained 533,664 kg of grain (Lacort Navarro 1985, 372-3). Storage on this scale would have enabled grain to be stockpiled against the risk of poor harvests, or to meet not only the needs of the local community but also the demands of the Roman state (Haley 2003, 24-5).

The fishing industry

As we have seen, Cádiz enjoyed an economic resurgence during the second half of the third century BC, fuelled by the demands of Carthage's wars with Rome. López Castro (1995) has suggested that it was the desire to maintain this privileged economic position that prompted the Gaditanians to sign a bilateral treaty with Rome – the *foedus Gaditanum* – in 206 BC. The treaty not only preserved the economic independence of Cádiz but also opened the markets of Italy to Gaditanian merchants. Recent work has thrown light on the state of the economy during the second century BC, stressing continuity from the preceding period and the lack of Roman interference.

Although there are signs of dislocation caused by the Second Punic War, disruption seems to have been limited.[40] The fishing industry seems to have enjoyed a period of expansion. Several earlier factories continued to function, for example, at Avenida de Andalucía and Calle Ferrocarril. Plaza de Asdrúbal continued until the second century or first half of the first century BC (Niveau de Villedary y Mariñas 2007, 419).

In addition, several new factories were established. A small factory has been excavated at Calle Campos Elíseos dating from the second half of the second century to the end of the first century BC (Lagóstena Barrios 2001, 108). Excavations on Calle Luis Milena have uncovered a pair of salting vats as well as pavements lined with *opus signinum* that may be part of a larger fish saltery dating from the third century to the first century BC (Sáez Romero *et al.* 2007, 468-9).

Particularly notable is the appearance of larger factories, which Lazaro Lagóstena Barrios (2001, 112) has likened to the large factories along the Straits of Gibraltar and at Tróia. Excavations carried out in 1994-5 following the demolition of the Teatro Andalucía revealed a necropolis dating to the first and second centuries BC and a fish factory of the first to fifth centuries AD.[41] The excavated area of the factory extends over 330 m^2 and consists of 26 vats arranged around a courtyard paved with *opus signinum* (Cobos Rodríguez 1999, 28-30). In 1997-8 a fishery was excavated in the Plaza de Asdrúbal/Paseo Marítimo. The factory extends over an area of 500 m^2 and operated from the end of the third century/beginning of the second century BC until the middle of the first century AD (Niveau de Villedary y Mariñas 2007, 429).

A possible fish factory has been discovered on Calle Gregorio Marañón. Rescue excavations have revealed two pavements of *opus signinum* together with a basin lined with *opus signinum* on the eastern edge of the site (Blanco Jimenez 1991, 78-9).[42] Two phases of occupation have been identified: the first dates to the first century BC, and the site was remodelled in the Augustan period. Dr 1C and Mañá C2b have been found together with Dr 9 vessels from the second phase (Blanco Jimenez 1991, 79-81).[43]

Not only do the smaller fisheries outside the city continue to function – in some cases until the first century AD – there is also an increase in the number of large-scale fish-salting installations located within the city. The growing economic importance of Cádiz is reflected in the growth of the city during the first century BC and the building progamme carried out by L. Cornelius Balbus.

Although second-century BC levels at many fisheries are obscured by later construction, several fisheries along the Straits of Gibraltar may have been in use at this time. The most important of these is Baelo Claudia, modern Bolonia. The existence of fish factories on the site was first reported in 1870. Since that time six fish factories have been excavated at the junction of the town and the beach to the south. Several

Fig. 8. Factory VI, Baelo Claudia.

Fig. 9. Fish saltery north of the *decumanus*, Baelo Claudia.

locations in the southwest of the town have revealed evidence of Republican occupation. In 1966 two fish salting vats were excavated containing Dr 1A, B and C and Dr 21-22 amphorae together with Campanian A and B pottery. The pottery dates the vats to the end of the second century or beginning of the first century BC. Two further vats were dated to the second half of the first century BC (Arévalo González *et al.* 2007, 80; 2007, 74; Alarcón Castellano 2007, 227; Sillières 1995, 52). In 1979 excavations of a saltery to the north of the *decumanus maximus* carried out by Jean-Nöel Bonneville uncovered levels dating to the middle of the first century BC. These levels contained bones and scales of tunny together with the remains of a salting vat (Dardaine *et al.* 1980, 403-7; Arévalo González *et al.* 2007, 78).

Excavations conducted in 2001 dated the construction of the *opus signinum* pavement of 'Conjunto Industrial VI' to the second quarter of the first century BC. Late black-slip pottery, Dr 1 A and Dr 7-11 amphorae were recovered (Arévalo González *et al.* 2007, 82; 2002, 27). Underlying the pavement, part of a storage area was uncovered. Several amphorae were found: Mañá C2b, Dr 1 A and late Greco-Italic amphorae dating to the final third of the second century BC. While the imported amphorae were empty or contained traces of wine, a Punic Mañá C2b and the locally produced Greco-Italic and Dr 1 A amphorae contained the residue of fish sauce made from mackerel and tunny (Arévalo González *et al.* 2007, 82-3; 2002, 28; Bernal Casasola *et al.* 2003, 305-11; 2007, 251-7; 2007, 357-62, 365-74).[44] The discovery of locally produced late Greco-Italic or early Dr 1 A amphorae containing fish bones suggests that fish sauces were produced locally by the end of the second century BC.

Contemporaneous with the Republican phases at Baelo Claudia is the small fish factory at Punta Camarinal-El Anclón. The bases of two basins lined with *opus signinum* have been found. The installations seem to have been in use from *c.* 140/130 BC until at least the first quarter of the first century BC (Arévalo González *et al.* 2007, 86-7; Bernal Casasola *et al.* 2007, 299-305). A large deposit of marine molluscs and fish bones has also been found, including 683 vertebrae from tunny, suggesting that the fish were deposited intact (Arévalo González *et al.* 2007, 87-8). The fishery may have been abandoned as a consequence of the intensification of fish salting at Baelo Claudia.

Several other fisheries have been identified from the Republican period. Three salting vats have been discovered underlying the first-century AD fishery at Carteia (sector 3). The vats are associated with Iberian pottery and Campanian ware giving a date in the first century BC (Lagóstena Barrios 2001, 134; Woods *et al.* 1967, 8-28). In 1982 a salting vat was uncovered in Corte 11 at Cerro del Mar associated with Mañá C2 amphorae, late Campanian A and Campanian B pottery dating to the second half of the second century BC (Arteaga 1985, 212-13). Mañá C2 amphorae have also been found at several fisheries dated to the imperial period: Benalmadena-Costa (Rodríguez Oliva 1982, 47), Puente Carranque (López Malax 1971, 57-8) and Calle Carretería (Málaga) (Mora Serrano *et al.* 1997, 30).

As well as an increase in the number of fisheries, the second half of the second century BC also saw an increase in the production of amphorae. During the final third of the second century BC there was also a shift away from traditional amphorae types and the introduction of new forms, Mañá C2b and local imitations of Italian Dr 1A amphorae. Lázaro Lagóstena Barrios' (1996) survey has identified several possible kilns in the area of El Puerto de Santa María. Building work carried out on Calle Javier de Burgos uncovered a dump of amphorae consisting principally of Mañá C2b and Dr 1 B and C vessels (Lagóstena Barrios 1996, 32).[45] Mañá C2 vessels have been found associated with Dr 7 amphorae at Los Sauces and at Hijuela del Tío Prieto (Lagóstena Barrios 1996, 35-41).

Excavations in 1993 and 1994 revealed a ceramic workshop at Buena Vista to the north of the Sierra de San Cristóbal. The workshop dates from the second half of the second century BC to the middle of the first century AD. Mañá C2b, Dr 1C and Dr 7/11 amphorae were found (Lagóstena Barrios *et al.* 2004, 62; 1996, 59). A possible ceramic workshop has been found at La Florida were a cistern has been found associated with quantities of amphorae (Lagóstena Barrios *et al.* 2004, 63). Two phases of ceramic production have been identified at Vaina dating to between the second half of the second century/beginning of the first century and the second half of the first century AD. Dr 1 B and C, Mañá C2b and Dr 7/11 amphorae have been found. Mañá C2b and Dr 7/11 have also been found a short distance to the north at Venta Alta (Lagóstena Barrios *et al.* 2004, 66).

Ceramic production continued at Torre Alta with three kilns (H 1, H 2 and H 5) continuing to function through Phase 4 although with an increase in the volume of Muñoz E2, Mañá-Pascual A4 and Greco-Italic amphorae. In about 180-170 BC the kilns were replaced by two kilns located 20 m to the south on the Avenida Al-Andalus. Production seems to have been uninterrupted with the continued production of Muñoz E2 and Greco-Italic amphorae until *c.* 160-150 BC (Sáez Romero 2004, 709-10). The presence of late Campanian A pottery dating from *c.* 100 BC suggests that occupation may have continued until the first century BC (Niveau de Villedary y Mariñas 2004, 680).

Production also continued at Cerro de la Batería until the first century BC, to judge from the presence of Campanian A, B and B-oïde pottery. Muñoz E2, Mañá-Pascual A4 amphorae were produced during the first half of the second century BC and the final Muñoz A5 and Greco-Italic variants may have been produced at this time. From the final third of the second century BC production shifted to Mañá C2b amphorae although Italian Dr 1 A vessels may have also been imitated locally (Montero Fernández *et al.* 2004, 418-20). Mañá-Pascual A4 and Muñoz E2 were also produced at Campo del Gayro where two kilns were uncovered in 1998. Muñoz E2 and Mañá C2b were produced at Centro Atlántida (Montero Fernández *et al.* 2004, 420).

A single kiln (C 14) dated to the Republican period has been excavated on the Avenida Pery Junquera (González Torraya *et al.* 2000, 177), from which 186 identifiable fragments of amphorae have been recovered. The majority consist of Mañá C2b (36.5%) and Muñoz E2 (36.5%) (González Torraya *et al.* 2000, 181-3). Lesser quantities of Greco-Italic amphorae (principally Will types C and D) may also have been produced (Bustamente Álvarez *et al.* 2004, 442-5).[46] Production of Mañá C2b, Muñoz E2 and Dr 1A amphorae has been identified at El Canal (Sáez Romero 2004, 710). Mañá C2b amphorae were also produced on the Avenida de Portugal where a fragment of a kiln dated *c.* 120-110 BC was discovered in 2000-1 associated with quantities of ceramic waste (Bernal Casasola *et al.* 2004, 621).

Two kilns were partially excavated at Cerro de los Mártires in 1970, producing coarse wares together with Beltrán IA and IB and Mañá C2 amphorae. The amphorae together with the presence of black glaze pottery and *terra sigillata* date the operation of the kilns from the second century BC (Lagóstena Barrios 1996, 114-15). Recent excavations on Calle Asteroides have uncovered a ceramic workshop dating from the second half of the second century to the beginning of the first century BC (Lagóstena Barrios *et al.* 2004, 75).

The site of El Rinconcillo (Algeciras) is one of the best known kilns in Baetica since its excavation by M. Sotomayor in August 1966. The excavations revealed two circular kilns (1 and 2) both 4.43 m in diameter (Sotomayor 1969-70, 54-5). The kilns principally produced amphorae as well as *tegulae*, tiles and coarse ware pottery (Bernal Casasola *et al.* 2004, 591). The site is most important, however, for the discovery during the 1991 excavations of locally produced imitations of Italian Dr 1 A, Dr 1 B/C and Dr 1 C amphorae. Of these, Dr 1 B/C predominate, accounting for 78% of the amphorae from the initial phase of activity on the site (Phase II) increasing to 88% during the succeeding phase (III). Dr 1 B/C forms remain numerous throughout the occupation of the site: accounting for 49% of the amphorae during Phase IV compared to 37% Dr 7-13, 14% Dr 21-22. Only during Phase V do Dr 7-13 vessels predominate with 54% compared to 31% Dr 1 B/C and 14% Dr 21-22 (Fernández Cacho 1995, 183-4).[47]

The initial period of activity on the site (Phase II) has been dated to the second third of the first century BC (Fernández Cacho 1995, 70; 1995, 181). Darío Bernal Casasola and R. Jiménez-Camino Álvarez (2004, 600-1) have suggested, however, that the date for the appearance of local imitations of Dr 1 amphorae be moved back to the beginning of the first century or end of the second century BC. Examples of Dr 1 C amphorae dating between the end of the second century and 80 BC have been found at the site of La Loba. As well as Italian examples the site also received local imitations – similar to those from the kilns at El Rinconcillo (Algerciras) (Bernal Casasola *et al.* 2004, 600).[48]

As well as the appearance of imitations of Italian amphorae, Italian influence is also reflected in the appearance of rectangular kilns constructed along Italian lines replacing the oval kilns with central pillar that are characteristic of Punic production during the third century BC. In addition to the two kilns excavated at El Rinconcillo in 1966, two further kilns were found in 1991 and in 2000. The first is a small oval kiln (1.50 x 1.20 m) that may have produced coarse ware pottery, in view of the quantities of lids that were found. Rescue excavations carried out to the west in 2000 uncovered a further kiln (0.30 x 0.90 m), angular in shape with a central corridor and parallel walls (Lagóstena Barrios *et al.* 2004, 49; Bernal Casasola *et al.* 2004, 591-2). Darío Bernal Casasola and R. Jiménez-Camino Álvarez (2004, 597-600) have suggested that use of circular kilns with a central pillar may be a survival of the oval kilns with a central pillar that are characteristic of kilns dating to the Late Punic period of the third century BC. However, the rectangular kiln excavated at El Rinconcillo follows Italian models. The only parallel is the workshop at Mesas de Asta (Jerez de la Frontera) which was abandoned at the end of the first century BC (Bernal Casasola *et al.* 2004, 599). The dating of the kiln at El Rinconcillo is problematic, though it is conventionally dated to the end of the first century BC and first half of the first century AD (Bernal Casasola *et al.* 2004, 599).

The kilns may also have supplied the fisheries at Baelo Claudia which were operated by Italians such as the Sextii from Cosa who then produced locally the Dr 1 amphorae that they had manufactured in Italy. Local imitations of Dr 1 C were first discovered in 1966 during excavations at Baelo Claudia, when 30 examples were found in levels dated to the second half of the first century BC. Several stamps were found: OP.L.CAE[…], OP.M.LV[…], […]M.LVCR, S.C.C. and S.C.G. with the latter being associated with other stamps: OP.M.LVCR, OP.M.LV[…], OP.L.CAE[…], OP.L.C[…] and […] T. The Dr 1 C amphorae are contemporaneous with Dr 21-22 vessels with similar fabric and marks: S.C.G., […]M.LVCR, [.]P.M.LV[…] and OP.C.AVIENI (Étienne *et al.* 1994, 132). The abundance of both forms, similarities in fabric and epigraphy led the excavators to suggest that both were locally produced. OP[reads either Optatus or 'opus' signifying that the amphorae were produced by M. Lucretius, L. Cae(sius) and C.Avienius (Étienne *et al.* 1994, 133). S.C.G. was also found at El Rinconcillo together with S.CET. Robert Etienne and Françoise Mayet (1995, 134-5) have suggested that these both refer to a *Societas Cetariorum Gaditanorum* or *Socii Cetarii Gaditani* and perhaps relate to the stamps SOC, SOCI and CL. SOC from Puente Melchor (Millán León *et al.* 2000, 217).

The supplying of empty amphorae to the fisheries of the region as well as in North Africa may suggest the continued operation of the industrial *societates* of the 'Círculo del Estrecho' (Bernal Casasola *et al.* 2004, 602). The distribution of these stamps points to the Mediterranean as the market for goods from El Rinconcillo: examples of the stamp S.C.G. have been found at Baelo Claudia, Rome, Tharros and Delos. S.CET on the other hand is found only locally at El Rinconcillo and Carteia. The presence of Italian graffiti reading S C(?) and M on the amphorae underlying Conjunto Industrial VI has prompted Dario Bernal Casasola and others to suggest that the vessels were manufactured by Italian artisans, perhaps the family of the Sextii who traded fish sauce from Cosa (Bernal Casasola *et al.* 2003, 311-12). The presence of Italian potters may be related to the foundation of the *colonia latina libertinorum* at Carteia in 171 BC.

Although Italian *nomina* predominate, some Punic potters may have continued to operate. Several stamps have been found from the dump on Calle Gregorio Marañón:

the Punic stamp bdl'Hbt and the Latin AMIS.E, BAR.T, BALT and TAT have been found dating to the first century BC levels, and PHILO from the Augustan period (Lagóstena Barrios *et al.* 2004, 54; García Vargas 1998, 159-62). The stamp GVRA has been found on a locally produced Mañá C2b from La Florida. *Pondera* from the same site bear the graffito VINICIUS (Lagóstena Barrios *et al.* 2004, 63).

Italian immigration seems to have been concentrated in Cataluña, the mining areas in the vicinity of Cartagena and along the south coast. Evidence for immigration prior to the end of the second century BC is largely absent and even then appears to have been largely private and entrepreneurial. More significant than the number of immigrants was the opening up of the coastal areas of the Peninsula to the wider Mediterranean economy channeled through a limited number of Roman communities along the coast. This in turn created a demand that prompted a restructuring of rural settlement and the intensification of rural settlement. There is, however, no evidence of large-scale estates along the lines of the *latifundia* that were such an important feature of the Italian landscape.

The early villas or farms that were constructed in the northwest appear to have been constructed by Romanized natives. Several houses contain inscriptions indicating their owner was Iberian, at La Caridad de Caminreal, Andelos, La Alcudia de Elche and on Calle Don Juan de Aragón in Zaragoza. This hypothesis is supported by the evidence of Iberian phases of occupation underlying several later villas. Iberian stamps have been found on Dr 1 amphorae from Tarraco and Can Vendrell, and on Tarraconense 1 from Zaragoza, La Bassa, La Alcudia, La Serreta, El Moluengo and Jardí Park. Increasingly, however, Iberian names are replaced by Latin *nomina* and do not appear from the end of the first century BC.

The distribution of exported amphorae is limited but reflects an intensification of agriculture and the introduction of viticulture that would come to fruition at the end of the first century BC. Several farms devoted to wine production have been excavated in Cataluña: at Can Balençó, Ca l'Estrada, Santa Margarida de Montbui, El Bosquet, L'Olivet d'en Pujol, Bellcaire d'Emporda, Sant Miquel de Vinebre, Can Pons, Casa del Racó.

The situation in Cartagena is somewhat different as the archaeological evidence appears to support Diodorus' description of an influx of Italians to exploit the mineral resources of the region. Here the individuals appear to have been lower-class entrepreneurs who were able to use their profits from mining to enter the municipal elite by the end of the first century BC and as a consequence transferred their wealth from investing in mining into land.

Cádiz seems to have escaped any long-term detrimental effects caused by the Roman conquest. After a period for which we have little or no evidence, the picture we have is of not only continuity but also economic growth. The cordial relations between Cádiz and Rome enabled the former to take advantage of the commercial opportunities afforded by access to the wider Mediterranean. The appearance of amphorae imitating Italian Dr 1 vessels is significant, reflecting either the presence of Italian immigrants or the desire of the Spaniards to compete in a Mediterranean market. The success of Cádiz is reflected in the expansion enjoyed by the city in the later years of the first century BC.

4

Augustan Expansion

The spread of viticulture

The late first century BC is a crucial period in the economic development of the Iberian Peninsula. Roman involvement in the region dramatically increased during the Civil Wars of 49-45 BC. According to Suetonius (*Caesar* 42.1) Caesar settled 80,000 Roman citizens in colonies in Italy and the West, many of who would have been settled in the peninsula. Augustus' final pacification of the peninsula and the establishment of the *annona* would have had important consequences, enabling an increase in agricultural production and rural settlement.

The establishment of *coloniae* and *municipia* by Caesar and Augustus carried with it a restructuring of the rural landscape that is reflected in the spread of Roman rural settlement. Particular concentrations were located in Cataluña and the Guadalquivir valley. The spread of Roman land use and agriculture led in turn to increased evidence of viticulture and olive oil production and an increase in the volume of exports from the peninsula.

According to Pliny (*Natural History* 14.71), wine from Laietania was notable for its quantity and those of Lauro or Tarraco were known for their quality. According to Martial, on the other hand, the wines of the region were mediocre in quality (1.26): he advises Sextilianus to get 'faex Laietana' – 'Laietanian dregs' – from a tavern-keeper. Elsewhere, however, Martial likens wine from Tarraco to Tuscan wines and says that it is second only to the wines of Campania.

In contrast to the preceding period there is a dramatic increase in the number of villas devoted to viticulture. Excavations since 1971 have uncovered remains of a substantial villa at Can Terrés (La Garriga, Vallès Oriental). The villa is more than 3,500 m^2 in size and was occupied from the second half of the first century BC until the fifth century AD (Pardo 1984, 2; Orri i Rovira *et al.* 1990, 20). The villa was expanded during the third century AD with an increase in the size of facilities devoted to agricultural production – either wine or olive oil – and an expansion of the baths originally constructed during the preceding phase (Pardo 1984, 10). Traces of painted stucco survive on the north and west corners of the baths (Garriga Casteblanque 1996, 10).

A substantial winery was discovered at El Morè (Sant Pol del Mar) in 1930 and was excavated in 1995. The site is arranged over four terraces that extend over an area of 2,200 m^2. The northernmost terrace consists of a rectangular tower, to the south of which is the winery itself, consisting of fifteen rooms arranged around a courtyard. The rooms to the north and west of the courtyard provided accommodation for the workers while the eastern wing housed the rooms devoted to the preparation of the wine. Room VI functioned as the pressing room with the base of a press lying against the north wall.[1] Room VII to the south contained two square pits that have been identified as cellars for storage, and room VIII, paved with *opus signinum*, functioned as a press. Room XIV to the south of the courtyard, together with terraces three and four, contained *dolia*: there may have originally been as many as 140 *dolia*. Quantities of defective amphorae indicate that Pascual 1 and Dr 2-4 were produced in the vicinity. The winery was constructed between 10 BC and AD 20 and occupation continued until the fifth or sixth century AD (Brun 2004, 270-1).

Remains of polichrome mosaics, *opus signinum*, Roman pottery, *tegulae*, amphorae, *dolia* and stucco were reported at Camp d'Aviació dels Monjos in 1939. Three column bases have been found together with two rectangular basins that were identified as having been part of a bath suite attached to a wealthy villa dating to the first century BC or the early Imperial period. In 1990 eight or nine amphorae were reported to have been found on the site, suggesting that agricultural activities also took place here (Ros Mateos 2005, 189).

A substantial villa was discovered in 1899 lying 200 m from the shore at Cal Ros de les Cabres (Ocata-El Masnou). The villa dates from the late Republic to the late Imperial period (Prevosti i Monclús 1981, 59-60). Parts of the *pars rustica* were excavated in 1988-9, revealing five rooms arranged around a courtyard which, although only partially excavated, contained six *dolia* as well as two basins lined with *opus signinum* (Burés i Vilaseca *et al.* 1991, 115-16). The villa seems to have been engaged in wine production during the Augustan period, as excavations in 1984 yielded quantities of Pascual 1 amphorae (Jàrrega Domínguez 1987, 246).

Remains of a winery have been excavated 1 km south of Tossa de Mar at Ses Alzines. Excavations have uncovered an area of 22 x 11 m enclosing a suite of rooms around a porticoed courtyard (area 3). Area 2A was floored with *opus signinum* and preserves the circular base of a winepress (Burch *et al.* 1998, 25-6). Unfortunately the lack of stratigraphy means that the site is difficult to date, although its final abandonment seems to have taken place at the end of the first century AD (Burch *et al.* 1998, 29). The complex seems to have been purely utilitarian.

The site is similar in date and function to that of Mas Carbotí (Tossa, La Selva) where excavations in 1984 uncovered remains of a farm devoted to wine production. An area of 8 x 14 m was excavated, revealing the *pars rustica* of an unidentified farm or villa. The farm is dated to between the middle of the first century BC and AD 70-80, thanks to the presence of Campanian A and B pottery and Dr 1 B amphorae and the absence of *terra sigillata clara*. The building was of a similar construction to that at Ses Alzines with dry-stone walls. Apart from *tegulae*, Roman features were absent – which together with the scarcity of fine wares prompted the excavators to suggest that the building provided accommodation for farm workers (Burch *et al.* 1998, 23; López Mullor *et al.* 1985, 42-3).

A similar site to that of Mas Carbotí has been excavated at Mas Font, dating from the late Republic (Burch *et al.* 1998, 23). A substantial villa dating from the end of the Augustan period has been discovered beside the Playa Artigues at Pla de Palol (Fenals). Excavations since 1963 have uncovered a bath complex as well as the *pars rustica* of a villa together with a basin lined with *opus signinum* (Tremoleda i Trilla 2000, 18-19; Nolla i Brufau *et al.* 1984, 123-7).

A substantial villa has been found at Can Rafart (Mataró) with *opus sectile*, *opus tessellatum*, marble sculptural decoration and stucco. The *pars rustica* of the villa was devoted to the production of wine with two basins lined with *opus signinum* and a rectangular kiln. The presence of late Campanian A and B pottery dates the earliest phase of the villa to the first century BC (Prevosti i Monclús 1981, 337-57).

The villa of Ametllers lies on the eastern slope of the hill of Can Magí. The *pars rustica* occupies the lower slope of the site and consists of five rooms (PR1-PR4). To the west of the *pars rustica* at the base of the slope below the *pars urbana* were a number of basins lined with *opus signinum* and a press which were excavated by Ignasi Melé i Farré in the early twentieth century (López Mullor *et al.* 2001, 11-13; Gorges 1979, 260). The most recent excavations between 1985 and 1992 have yielded material from sondages (PU 1 and PU 3) that have dated the establishment of the villa to the end of the first century BC or first decade of the first century AD (López Mullor *et al.* 2001, 19).

The villa of Santa Maria de Sales (Viladecans) lies at the base of the hill of Sant Ramon. The villa was constructed at the end of the second or beginning of the first century BC. The apogee of the villa dates to the first century AD when the *pars rustica* was constructed, containing a wine press and basins lined with *opus signinum*. A store of *dolia* has been excavated to the southeast of the cemetery of Viladecans (Menéndez *et al.* 1993, 85; Solias i Arís 1985, 113-16).

A possible farm dating from the end of the first century BC to the third century AD has been found at the hermitage of La Mare de Déu del Bon Viatge in Sant Joan Despí (Cuesta *et al.* 1993, 91). Abundant pottery, together with a basin and quantities of *dolia*, has been found, suggesting that the site was engaged in wine production. Wine production may have taken place at Vall de Maria (Arenys de Mar) where a basin and pavement of *opus reticulatum* were discovered, identified in 1931 as a press or *torcularum* (Palou i Miquel 1993, 160).

Alongside the expansion in the number of villas and the spread of viticulture, the Augustan period also saw the appearance of a new amphora type – Pascual 1. First identified by Ricardo Pascual (1960), the form copies Dr 1 B wine amphorae that were produced in Campania, Latium and Etruria from the first quarter to the last decade of the first century BC (Peacock *et al.* 1986, 90). The form has an ovoid body, a short cylindrical neck and a pronounced rim in the form of a collar between 78 and 12 cm high. Handles are rounded and vertical with a vertical groove. The body tapers to a high point. The form is characteristic of Tarraconensian amphorae during the Augustan period and was widely produced throughout Cataluña (Pascual Guash 1977). The form was also produced in Southern France at Montans, Corneilham and Aspiran, where a stamp reading either LAETI or ATEPO has been found on the lip of a vessel (Laubenheimer 1985, 312). Pascual 1 amphorae may also have been produced at Mas d'Aragó (Cervera del Maestrat) where two fragmentary examples have been found (Borras i Querol 1987, 390).

Pascual 1 amphorae were produced in succession to Tarraconense 1 amphorae and rapidly displaced the earlier form. Production began *c.* 50/40-30 BC when the earliest examples of the vessel appear in a silo on Carrer Pujol in Baetulo (Comas i Solà 1985, 17-18; 1987, 162). The form is found associated with a lamp dated *c.* 40-30 BC at Cap Béar 3 (Parker 1992, 97). Production at Platja de Fenals (Lloret de Mar) dates to *c.* 20-15 BC. The form is found in levels dated *c.* 10 BC at Lyon (Desbat 1987, 408). In levels from Baetulo dated *c.* 15 BC Pascual 1 is the most abundant with 85% compared to 13% Tarraconense 1, 1.26% Dr 2-4 and residual local Dr 1. Pascual 1 continues to predominate accounting for 94% of the amphorae from the fill of a well dated to AD 15-20 (Comas i Solà 1998, 223).

The organization of ceramic production is difficult to determine thanks to the fragmentary state of the archaeological record. Many kilns are known only from fortuitous finds and rescue excavations, and many kilns are known only from finds of pottery and ceramic waste. Only on rare occasions have excavations been sufficient to enable the kiln to be viewed within its local and regional archaeological context.

While no Spanish kiln has provided us with sufficient evidence for the manufacturing process to be clear, the process itself is relatively simple. The siting of a kiln was determined by a number of geological and geographical factors: the kiln required access to three primary raw materials: clay deposits, a water source and supplies of combustible material to fire the kiln; also access to communication routes and markets. Clay can be acquired from one of two sources: either from the underlying bedrock or from wind, water or glacial deposits (known as primary and secondary sources respectively) and it seems that the latter was the most common (Orton *et al.* 1993, 114).

Excavation of surface clay deposits would leave little trace in the archaeological record although natural fissures may have been used to supply the kilns at Tricio (La Rioja) (Solovera San Juan 1987, 53). Several pits possibly used for extracting clay have been found to the south of the pottery workshop at Can Jofresa (Terrassa) (Casas *et al.* 1993, 269). Gravel and clay beds in the immediate vicinity of the kiln at L'Aumedina (Tivissa) were exploited by means of small quarries (Revilla Calvo 1993, 17).[2]

The clay would then be broken down and mixed with water. A process of levigation would remove larger inclusions, and waterproof tanks lined with *opus signinum* have been found at a number of kilns. Although wells were used in the northern provinces, Spanish potters seem to have made use of local surface sources. Kilns are typically located in the immediate vicinity of rivers which provided not only water but also communications – for example, the ceramic workshop at Llafranc was situated beside the Ríos Llafranc and Font d'en Xecu (Barti Català *et al.* 1989, 146). The kiln at Can Reverter-Can Perals (Sant Vicenç dels Horts) is situated beside a possible harbour on the Río Llobregat (Revilla Calvo 1995, 196). The harbour at the mouth of the Río Llobregat may have acted as an entrepot receiving amphorae from the surrounding villas: Sant Boi de Llobregat, Can Pedrerol de Baix and Can Tintorer (López Mullor 1998, 237). Pascual 1 amphorae produced at Mas d'Aragó have been found at Piedras de la Barbada at the mouth of the Río Seco (Fernández Izquierdo 1991, 407).

A temper was mixed with the clay and paved areas may have been provided for this use. Although some coarse wares were hand-made, the normal method of forming a vessel was by wheel. The formed vessels would then be dried in the sun or, in larger workshops, in a heated room with a hypocaust. Drying would remove excess water from the clay, helping to prevent breakage or warping during firing.

Although surface kilns may have been used to fire small quantities of coarse pottery, more evidence exists for the use of permanent kilns. Most were up-draught kilns in which the vessels were stacked on a perforated floor with the firing chamber beneath; down-draught and twin-flue kilns may also have been in use but were rare. Both rectangular and circular kilns were used, but the reasons for the selection of one or other shape are not clear.[3]

Several kilns that produced Tarraconense 1 amphorae continued to produce Pascual 1 vessels: La Salut, Torrent de Sistres, El Sot del Camp, Horta Nova, Can Peixau. In addition, there is a marked increase in the number of kilns in the coastal areas of Cataluña as well as along the rivers penetrating further inland. Several kilns have been found associated with villas. In 1928 remains of a substantial villa were discovered at Can Peixau, 1 km to the southwest of Badalona. In 1996 further excavations revealed the *pars rustica* of the villa devoted to the production of amphorae with quantities of ceramic waste and reports of the discovery of a possible kiln during earlier excavations. The amphorae are predominantly Pascual 1 vessels (585 examples), although Tarraconense 1 and Dr 2-4 were also found. The most numerous fine ware pottery was Campanian B, which together with the Pascual 1 amphorae dates the complex to *c.* 30 BC. *Terra sigillata* from the fill of one of the wells on the site dates between 15 BC and AD 15. Residual Attic Black glaze and Campanian A pottery was also found (Padrós 1998, 186-8).

Remains of a substantial villa have been found at Torre Llauder, lying 400 m from the sea to the west of the town of Mataró. Excavations between 1981 and 1985 identified five phases of occupation, the earliest of which consists of a ceramic workshop dating to the end of the first century BC (Prevosti i Monclús 1995, 292-4). The existence of a kiln here has been reported since 1887 and was first excavated by Mariano Ribas (Prevosti i Monclús *et al.* 1987, 199). The kiln seems to have produced primarily amphorae: principally Pascual 1, as well as lesser quantities of Dr 2-4, Dr 6, Dr 9 and Dr 20 amphorae. The kiln appears to have been in use for only a short period as it was covered over by the earliest phase of the villa at some point between 15 BC and the end of the century (Phase 2) (Prevosti i Monclús *et al.* 1987, 200; Prevosti i Monclús 1981, 262; 1995, 295). Mariano Ribas has reported the discovery of a small basin lined with *opus signinum* together with the bases of six *dolia* to the north of the villa (Prevosti i Monclús 1981, 264).

Remains of a possible villa have been found at Can Pedrerol de Baix (Castellbisbal) at the junctions of the Riera de Rubí and the Río Llobregat. Quantities of ceramic waste have also been found, including Pascual 1 and Dr 2-4 amphorae. The site dates between first century BC and the middle of the second century AD (Revilla Calvo 1995, 199). A possible kiln and villa have been found on the Camí del Mig, Riera de Teià (El Masnou). Investigations of the site in 1975 uncovered Pascual 1 and Dr 2-4 amphorae together with ceramic waste (Miró i Canals 1988, 36).

Remains of a villa together with Pascual 1 amphorae and ceramic waste have been found at Torre Martina (Sant Pol de Mar) (Miró i Canals 1988, 36). Excavations at Castellarnau (Sadadell) in 1997-8 uncovered a villa dating from the end of the first century BC. Four pottery kilns were found together with a basin used in wine production (Berni Millet *et al.* 2005, 175-6).

Excavations at Can Ventura de l'Oller (Santa Perpètua de Mogoda) have revealed part of a villa and portico dating from the Augustan period to the end of the first century AD. To the northwest of the villa a ceramic kiln has been excavated that produced Pascual 1 and Dr 2-4 amphorae as well as *tegulae* (Sanmartí Grego *et al.* 1993, 274).

Quantities of ceramic waste indicate the existence of a kiln in the vicinity of the villa at Vilarenc (Calafell). The site first attracted scholarly attention with the discovery in 1883 of the *pars urbana* and baths of a villa (sector 2) dating from the end of the first century to the third century AD (Revilla Calvo 1995, 185; 2003, 294; Pou i

Vallès *et al.* 1996, 105-6; Palet *et al.* 1993, 725-7, 739). Excavations resumed in 1988 with the discovery of an earlier complex located to the northwest of the complex discovered in 1883 (sector 1). The excavations uncovered a rectangular building (800 m^2) arranged around a courtyard. On the western side of the courtyard there is a basin lined with *opus signinum* and an adjacent platform constructed of stones and fragments of *dolia* that has been identified as the base of a press (Revilla Calvo 2003, 287).[4]

The earliest phase of the building dates from the middle of the first century BC and was remodelled between 20 and 10 BC with the construction of baths (Revilla Calvo 2003, 287-90; Pou i Vallès *et al.* 1996, 108; Palet *et al.* 1993, 738-9).[5] At some point in the middle of the first century AD the baths were replaced with a metalworking furnace used to make iron tools and agricultural implements (Revilla Calvo 2003, 294). Ceramic waste including defective pieces and possible remains of a kiln have been found together with local Dr 1, Tarraconense 1, Pascual 1, Dr 2-4, Dr 7-11 and Oberaden 74 amphorae, *dolia* and building materials (Revilla Calvo 1995, 185; 2003, 293; Pou i Vallès *et al.* 1996, 111; Palet *et al.* 1993, 732).[6]

Remains of a villa were reported at Can Madà/Can Bartrina (Argentona) in 1963 and were the subject of limited excavations in 1972 and further excavations in 1979. Two sectors have been excavated: the first consists of a small kiln of uncertain use that was abandoned *c.* 60-40 BC, dated by the presence of Campanian B wares and the lack of either Campanian A or Arretine ware (Pujol i del Horno *et al.* 1996-7, 355-6). Sector 2 lies 90 m to the north. Excavations in 1979 revealed parts of a hypocaust together with remains of two basins constructed from *opus testaceum* (Prevosti i Monclús 1981, 244-6).[7] The lack of stratigraphy makes the dating difficult: the earliest finds are Italian Dr 1 and Dr 21-22 amphorae, although Pascual 1 and Dr 2-4 are more numerous and suggest that the initial construction dates to the Augustan period (Pujol i del Horno *et al.* 1996-7, 356-7). The remains from sector 2 pertain to the *pars urbana* and *pars rustica* of a villa that appears to have been involved in the production of wine or olive oil.[8]

The existence of a villa at Darró (Vilanova i la Geltrú) was first reported in 1789 with systematic excavations first taking place in 1956-7. The first phase of the villa dates between 40/30 BC and the beginning of the second century AD (López Mullor *et al.* 1993, 134; 1995, 302). Contemporary with this first phase are a pair of rectangular kilns associated with Pascual 1 and Dr 7-11 amphorae as well as lesser quantities of Dr 2-4 vessels (López Mullor 1986-9, 68; 1989, 113).

Although the existence of Roman occupation at El Roser (Calella) has long been recognized as a result of surface finds, parts of the *pars rustica* of a villa were first uncovered during road work in 1947 that destroyed part of the villa. Large quantities of amphorae have been recovered from the site, including ceramic waste indicating the existence of an undiscovered kiln. Amphorae seem to have been the principal product: Dr 2-4 were the most numerous (375 examples) followed by Pascual 1 (210) and Tarraconense 1 (10) (López Mullor *et al.* 1985, 172-5).

In addition the kiln also produced coarse wares, *dolia* and building materials such as *tegulae* and *imbrices*. The kiln seems to have functioned to satisfy the demands of an adjoining winery: although the press has not been found, a basin lined with *opus signinum* was found during rescue excavations conducted in 1981-2 (López Mullor *et al.* 1985, 168-9). Although not yet located, the existence of the *pars urbana* is suggested by finds of mosaic *tesserae* throughout the site. Finds of Arretine ware suggest that the villa dates from the final decade of the first century BC and continued to function until the Flavian period (López Mullor *et al.* 1985, 169).

A late Imperial villa has been excavated to the southeast of the town of Sant Boi de Llobregat. In 1958 a rectangular kiln (F2) was excavated underneath the *frigidarium* of the third- to fifth-century AD baths. The kiln was constructed *c.* 30 AD and was abandoned at the end of the first century AD (López Mullor *et al.* 2002, 268-9; 1993, 84). Subsequent excavations revealed an earlier kiln (F1) that preceded F2 and dated from *c.* 30 BC, as well as a third kiln (F3) located north of the later baths that was contemporaneous with the first (López Mullor *et al.* 2002, 286). The kilns primarily produced Pascual 1 and Dr 2-4 amphorae as well as occasional Dr 7-11, coarse wares and building materials. Pascual 1 were the most numerous, accounting for 95.7% of the amphorae from the fill of kiln F1, *c.* AD 20-30 (López Mullor 1998, 233-4).

Excavations at Mas d'Aragó (Cervera del Maestrat) have uncovered remains of a possible villa (sector IV), together with the *piscina* (5.63 x 17 m) of a bath suite (sector I); and four ceramic kilns (sectors III and VI): one ovoid, one circular and two rectangular kilns (Fernández Izquierdo 1990, 212; Borras i Querol 1987, 385-6). The majority of the pottery consists of amphorae, *tegulae* and *imbrices*: the majority of the amphorae are Dr 2-4 with lesser quantities of Dr 7-11 and Dr 28/Oberaden 74. A single stamp has been found on the neck of a Dr 2-4 vessel, reading HERO. The excavator tentatively suggests that this is a contraction of Herennius Optatus (Borras i Querol 1987, 390-3). The stamp may be related LEVHERO, found on Dr 7-11 from the site (Fernández Izquierdo 1990, 212). The presence of two fragmentary Pascual 1 vessels raise the possibility that this form was also produced here (Borras i Querol 1987, 390).[9]

As well as villas, several kilns have been found associated with farms that have yielded no evidence of a villa or *pars urbana*. Roman occupation was first reported at Can Feu (Sant Quirze del Vallés) in 1913. Subsequent excavations have revealed remains of a *villa rustica* and accompanying pottery kilns, but no trace has been found of the *pars urbana* (Carbonell *et al.* 1995, 298). The rectangular *villa rustica* extends over an area of 520 m^2 at the northern end of the site (sector d). The first phase consists of a rectangular building containing silos, a small *dolia* store, a ceramic kiln and a basin for levigation. At some point in the middle of the first century AD the *dolia* store was expanded and a second basin was constructed as well as a basin (9.1 x 3.2 m) used in wine making (Carbonell *et al.* 1995, 297; 1998, 289; Martínez *et al.* 1988, 28-30).[10] Three kilns have been found 35 m to the south (sector b), of which one was excavated in 1987. The kilns are associated with a large pit (measuring 10 x 10 m) used as a dump for amphorae, *dolia* and *tegulae* that were produced on the site. The amphorae are Pascual 1 and Dr 2-4 forms and the stamps CE (or CF?) and H are the most numerous (Carbonell *et al.* 1998, 290). A fourth smaller kiln (e-14) was perhaps used for smaller coarse wares and *pondera* or weights (Martínez *et al.* 1988, 30-2). Elisenda Carbonell and Joaquim Folch (1998, 290) have suggested that the stamp of L.LIC.CHRES that is found on a *dolium* gives the name of the owner of the estate, Lucius Licinius Chres(tus?).

Ceramic waste has been found at Molins Nous (Riudoms) together with two basins lined with *opus signinum* and a possible press. The site dates from the first century BC to the fourth century AD (Revilla Calvo 1995, 178). Six phases of occupation have been identified at Mas Manolo (Caldes de Montbui) dating from the first to the sixth centuries AD.

The site was engaged in agricultural activities with a store of *dolia* and in ceramic production with six kilns (Barrasetas i Dunjó *et al.* 1995, 89). Three kilns date to the first century AD and probably produced Pascual 1 and Dr 2-4 amphorae that have been found among the ceramic waste (Barrasetas i Dunjó *et al.* 1995, 90). The large store of *dolia* was constructed during the second phase at the end of the first century AD (Barrasetas i Dunjó *et al.* 1995, 90). The store included 200 *dolia* – storage on this scale would have exceeded the requirements of the villa. More than 60% of the finds were amphorae (Barrasetas i Dunjó *et al.* 1995, 94).

Quantities of ceramic waste and defective Pascual 1 amphorae have been found at Can Reverter-Can Perals (Sant Vicenç dels Horts). As well as the abundant amphorae, two basins lined with *opus signinum* have been found, together with *tegulae*, *imbrices* and *dolia*. The complex dates from the first century BC to the second century AD (Revilla Calvo 1995, 196). Although much of the site has yet to be excavated, the complex seems to have been engaged in the production and export of wine.

The site of L'Aumedina lies 1 km to the west of Tivissa overlooking the valley of the Lower Ebro. Evidence of Roman occupation was discovered here in 1920 during road widening work. Archaeological excavations have subsequently uncovered remains of a small winery and two or more kilns that extend over an area of 1,500 m^2. In 1978-9 part of a winery was excavated consisting of a square room (squares C and D) containing a counter-weight in the centre of the room and a stone base for the arm of the press against the wall to the west. Beyond the wall were found two basins lined with *opus signinum*.

Unfortunately only a limited area was excavated (90 m^2) making it impossible to say anything about the functioning of the rest of the complex (Miró i Canals *et al.* 1987, 276-8; Revilla Calvo 1993, 46).[11] Two kilns were excavated in 1986, lying 25 m to the northeast of the winery: the *praefurnium* and circular firing chamber of kiln A are preserved, and a second poorly preserved rectangular kiln (B) lies 15 m further to the northeast (Miró i Canals *et al.* 1987, 278-83; Revilla Calvo 1993, 24-37).[12] The dating of the kilns is problematic: the use of Dr 2-4 amphorae in the construction of kiln A would give a *terminus ante quem* of the last decade of the first century BC (Revilla Calvo 1993, 45). The kilns produced a variety of materials (coarse wares, *dolia*, building materials) of which amphorae were the most important: Pascual 1, Dr 2-4, Dr 7-11 and Oberaden 74 (Revilla Calvo 1993, 51-79).

The Roman villa of Mas del Catxorro (Benifallet) was discovered overlooking the Río Ebro in 1902. Excavations carried out between 1987 and 1990 uncovered quantities of Pascual 1 amphorae as well as Dr 2-4, Dr 7-11 and Dr 28/Oberaden 74 forms – two of the Pascual 1 amphorae bore the mark MAL.GAL (Carbonell *et al.* 1993, 66). Several of the vessels excavated in 1988 were defective, indicating the presence of a kiln in the immediate vicinity (Izquierdo i Tugas 1993, 755). The kiln may have functioned as part of a wider estate as three counterweights from presses are reported (Revilla Calvo 1995, 172).

Symptomatic of the growth of ceramic production during the Augustan period is the site of Can Portell (Argentona) where a 117 m^2 area of ceramic waste has been excavated. The dump contains Dr 1 amphorae (7%), Tarraconense 1 (6%), Pascual 1 (11%) and Dr 2-4 (29%) produced from the first half of the first century BC to the beginning of the first century AD (Carreres Vidal *et al.* 1992, 169-71). The dump is perhaps associated with four kilns located in the vicinity – one of which has been excavated, producing Pascual 1 and Dr 2-4 (Olesti i Vilà 1995, 449-50).

As well as an increase in the number of rural sites engaged in the production of amphorae, there is also the appearance of larger potteries that functioned beyond the confines of the villa estates. The lack of accompanying villas suggests that these larger potteries operated as industrial *vici* specializing in the production of pottery. The existence of a Roman occupation at Platja de Fenals (Lloret de Mar) was first reported in 1972; excavations in 1984 uncovered 1,250m^2 of a substantial ceramic workshop consisting of seven rooms arranged around a colonnaded courtyard (àmbit II) (Buxó i Capdevila *et al.* 2002, 59-72).

Two phases of occupation have been identified, dating between 20-15 BC and AD 80-85. A single poorly preserved kiln has been dated to Phase 1 (F1). The remains of two kilns have been dated to the succeeding phase: traces of a large kiln have been found in àmbit IV (F4) and a smaller circular kiln (F2) in the northern part of the courtyard (àmbit II) (Buxó i Capdevila *et al.* 2002, 78-82). Production was concentrated on amphorae which account for 65% of the total pottery produced: the most numerous form being Pascual 1 (1,347 sherds = 54,04% of the amphorae) followed by Dr 2-4 (1,116 sherds = 44,80%). Small quantities of Tarraconense 1 amphorae (17 sherds) as well as a local variant (Tarraconense 2/Fenals 1) (8 sherds) were also found (Buxó i Capdevila *et al.* 2002, 211).

Excavations since 1980-1 have uncovered remains of a ceramic workshop in Llafranc (Palafrugell) dated from the end of the first century BC to the third century AD.[13] Excavations at no. 40 carrer I. Peral uncovered quantities of ceramic waste together with a drying floor upon which *tegulae* had been laid out to dry. Further excavations carried out in 1988-9 at no. 38 carrer I. Peral uncovered three ceramic kilns.

Kiln A is rectangular, measuring 7.80 x 1.95 m; the firing chamber contained considerable quantities of pottery, principally Dr 2-4 amphorae, although Dr 7-11 and coarse wares were also present. Although poorly preserved, kiln B was similar in form to A and was found with fragments of Pascual 1 and Dr 2-4 amphorae and *tegulae*. Kiln C has only been partially excavated and contains building materials. A possible storage area lay to the north containing fine and coarse ware pottery, Pascual 1, Dr 2-4 and Dr 7-11 amphorae (Barti Català *et al.* 1993, 87-90; 1993, 73). Construction work enabled limited soundings to be carried out at no. 31, revealing large quantities of amphorae: Pascual 1, Dr 2-4 and Dr 7-11, although an Oberaden 74 vessel was also found (Barti Català *et al.* 1993, 91-4; 1993, 73).

Several stamps are recorded: .USUL.VEIEN, PRI, QUIETI and S.F.C. (Miró i Canals 1988, 49-50; Nolla i Brufau *et al.* 1984, 133-7; Barti Català *et al.* 1993, 91). The ceramic workshop extends over an area of 7,500 m^2 – the earliest production of Pascual 1 and Dr 7-11 was concentrated around nos 21 and 31, then activities shifted to nos 38 and 40 where Dr 2-4 and Dr 30 predominate. The size of the workshop together with the range of amphorae produced here has prompted the excavators to identify this as an industrial complex devoted to the production of amphorae for export (Barti Català *et al.* 1993, 95).

Rescue excavations conducted in February and March 1987 to the south of the kilns on Carrer Llevant (no. 8) revealed two rooms (estança A-B and C) that may have functioned as housing associated with the ceramic workshop (Barti Català *et al.* 1989, 139-41; 1993, 95).[14]

The workshop at Llafranc seems to have acted as the nexus for several sites in the immediate vicinity: Farena, Ses Artigues, el Golfet and Puig Rodó (Barti Català *et al.* 1989, 146; Nolla i Brufau *et al.* 1984, 137).[15]

Who produced these amphorae? Stamps are increasingly common on Pascual 1 amphorae. Unlike previous forms, no Iberian stamps have been identified and the nomenclature is exclusively Latin. Alberto López Mullor and Javier Fierro Macía have suggested that the ACASTI found at El Roser originated in Northern Italy where the stamp is found on pottery from Aco (1985, 179-85). Ricardo Pascual (1991, 24) has suggested that the name is servile.

Two examples of the stamp C.ANTEST(i) have been found at Badalona dating to the final quarter of the first century BC. The stamp is also found together with that of M. Porcius on a Pascual 1 amphora from Saint Jean de Castets (Gèrs) (Comas i Solà 1997, 22-3; Pascual Guash 1991, 41) and at Can Peixau (Padrós 1998, 187-8). The vessels seem to have been produced at multiple locations: fabric analysis carried out on examples from Can Peixau suggests that they were produced there, however, the fabric is distinct from that of vessels from Badalona (Buxó i Garrigas *et al.* 1998, 203).

The Antesti were Oscan in origin and several late Republican senators are known – the most significant was the suffect consul of 30 BC, C. Antistius Vetus, who was governor of Hispania Citerior in 25 BC. P. Antestius was *duovir* in Calagurris in *c.* 27-5 BC (Curchin 1990, 191). A *mansio* Antistiana which appears on the Vicarello vessels was possibly situated in Penedès (Miró i Canals 1988, 247-8).[16]

IVLI(us) ANICETI(us) has been found on Pascual 1 amphorae produced at Sant Boi de Llobregat (López Mullor 1990, 193; 1998, 235; 2002, 290; Pascual Guash 1991, 75).[17] The cognomen Anicetus indicates an individual of oriental origin who received citizenship under Caesar or Augustus. Eight Iulii Aniceti known from Rome, but the cognomen Anicetus is unknown in Cataluña (Miró i Canals 1988, 249).

A cargo of Pascual 1 amphorae has been recovered from Cap del Vol on the northern side of the Bay of Port de la Selva, dated *c.* 20-15 BC. Although the site has been extensively looted, several stamps have been found: S, H, L, IVLI.THEOPHIL, QFS and M.PORC (Foerster 1980, 245). Stamps of Iulius Theophilus have also been found at Port-la-Nautique, Narbonne, Vieille-Toulouse, Vienne, Lyon, Novaesium and Zaragosa (Beltrán Lloris 1970, n. 198; Pascual Guash 1991, 75-6; Bergé 1990, 153-8). Several stamps from Port la Nautique read O(fficina) IVLI.THEOPHIL (Bouscaras 1984, 110-11).

Theophilus seems to have been of similar origin and status to Anicetus (above). Several Iulii Theophili are found in Rome, but none are known from Cataluña (Miró i Canals 1988, 218).

Titus Valerius Rufus has been found at Vindonissa and Port-la-Nautique (Pascual Guash 1980, 275-5; 1991, 148; Miró i Canals 1988, 222-3; Bouscaras 1984, 126). The *gens* originated in central Italy among the Oscans and is one of the most common in the Peninsula with 400 examples. L. Valerius Rufus is attested at Barcino.[18] Although no connection has been established with T. Valerius Rufus, a number of Valerii appear on amphorae. M. Valerius Felix appears as a *negotiator* engaged in the shipment of fish sauce on a *titulus pictus* on a Beltran IIb amphora from Saint Gervais (Liou *et al.* 1978, 137). The same individual appears on three amphorae from Pompeii and one from Herculaneum (Liou *et al.* 1978, 139). M. Valerius Euphemus appears on a South Spanish amphora from Castro Pretorio and M. Valerius Euphiletus on a Dr 20 amphora from Pompeii (Zevi 1966, 230) – where M. Valerius Heliadis appears on a Dr 7-13 vessel containing *lymphatum* (Zevi 1966, 232-3).

Stamps of Cn. Fulvius Secundus have been found at Empúries, Port-la-Nautique and Coutances (Miró i Canals 1988, 215-17; Pascual Guash 1991, 50; Bergé 1990, 148-9; Bouscaras 1984, 115-17). Members of the *gens* are common in Cataluña (twelve examples from Tarraco, three from Barcino, one from Egara, three from Sant Miquel de Mata and two from Aeso); however, nowhere in the region have the *nomen* and *cognomen* been found together. Pascual (1980, 268) has suggested that the origins of the Catalan *gens* lie with the proconsul A. Fulvius Nobilior who campaigned at Numantia in 153 BC. The stamp may be related to FVL PHIL, which Callender has suggested is Fulvius Phileros. The stamp has been found at Port-la-Nautique, Perpignan and Le Cayla de Mailhac (Bergé 1990, 152-3; Callender 1965, 137). These stamps may be related to QFS, which has been found on Pascual 1 amphora from Baetulo, Port-la-Nautique and Cap del Vol (Comas i Solà 1997, 46; Foerster 1980, 245; Miró i Canals 1988, 124-5).

A stamp of (C) MVSSIDI.NEP(otis) has been recovered from Illes Columbretes off the coast of Castellón (Fernández Izquierdo 1982, 117). Examples of the stamp from Haltern date between 5 BC and AD 9, and from La Longarina between AD 1 and 12 (Hesnard 1980, 145; Izquierdo i Tugas 1993, 761-2; Callender 1965, 107). The *gens* is an obscure one known only during the Augustan period (Miró i Canals 1988, 250-1; 1988, 218-19). The *gens* was Central Italian in origin, being found in Campania, Samnium and Latium.

BL, LICIN and (S)EMPR(ONI) have been found on Pascual 1 amphorae from Cap Béar 3 (Liou *et al.* 1985, 547-51; Colls 1986, 204; Parker 1992, 97-8; Miró i Canals 1988, 125-6). The stamp EGN(nati) has been found on an undated Pascual 1 amphora from Baetulo. The stamp has also been found at Empúries and Laumet. Pascual refers to an amphora bearing the name Q. Egnatius Pompeianus (*CIL* 2.4975; Comas i Solà 1997, 25). Nine examples of the stamp VAS have been found on Pascual 1 amphorae at Baetulo (Comas i Solà 1997, 46-8). Examples from Cap del Vol date to *c.* 20-15 BC (Foerster 1980, 245).

Mariano Ribas (1966, 30-5) reported the find of defective amphorae bearing the stamps of L. HER. OPT from Torre Llauder. Unfortunately the vessels were subsequently lost and the stamp has not been recovered since. The stamp has also been found on *tegulae* dated to the second or third century AD (Pascual Guash 1980, 269).[19] Carlos Borras i Querol (1987, 392) has tentatively suggested that the HERO found on Dr 2-4 amphorae from Mas d'Aragó is related to this individual. The name is particularly well-attested on *tegulae* found at a number of sites in Valencia and Cataluña: Elche, Valencia, Alicante, Tossal de Manises, Saguntum, Tarraco, Barcino, Empúries, as well as locally at San Ginés de Vilassar, Can Torradeta, Can Rafart, Pollentia and Torre Llauder itself (Rico 1995, 197-215). Outside the Peninsula the stamps have been found at Ventimiglia, Frejus and Rome (Tchernia 1971, 62; Pascual Guash 1980, 269).[20]

A number of other Herennii are known: a T. Heren(nius) is found on a Pascual 1 amphora from Empúries (Almagro 1952, n. 207); and *tegulae* bearing stamps of L.HERENN and L.HERENNI/HERENNI have been found at Baetulo, Tarraco, L'Alcudia (Elche), Bocairent, Frejus and Ventimiglia (Rico 1995, 202). The *nomen* Herennius is common in Cataluña: in 107 AD Caius Herennius Optatus erected an inscription in honour of the third consulship of L. Licinius Sura (Pascual Guash 1980, 270). A second-century AD tombstone from Barcino records M. Herennius Severus and his sister Herennia Optata. Severus was *aedile*, *duovir*, *flamen* and *augur* (or *flamen augusti*) in Barcelona (Pascual Guash 1980, 270; Curchin 1990, 183-4). An inscription from Valencia records a dedication to Serapis by P. Herennius Severus (Pereira Menaut 1979, n. 7).[21]

The kiln at Torre Llauder is particularly striking for the variety of stamps that have been found there. Of 29 stamps recovered, eight appear to have been produced on the site (Prevosti i Monclús *et al.* 1987, 201-2; Pascual Guash 1977, 64; Miró i Canals 1988, 38-9): AS, B, VERD, AR (?), CLV, AT, BP and SEC.

M.ANTO has been found on Pascual 1 amphorae from Roda de Berà and Port-la-Nautique (Pascual Guash 1991, 87; Bergé 1990, 161). The stamp is found on both Tarraconense 1 and Pascual 1 from Blanes (Nolla i Brufau *et al.* 1984, 131). The *nomen* is common in Barcelona: for example, M. Antonius Antullus and M. Antonius Crysogonus. Marcus Antonius is recorded as having held the office of *quattuorvir* in Clunia during the reign of Tiberius (Curchin 1990, 199).

In 1961 quantities of Pascual 1 amphorae were found at no. 26 carrer I. Peral, Llafranc. Two vessels carried the stamp SVL.VEIEN. Although originally read as Sulpicius Veiento, further examples were found on Pascual 1 amphorae in 1988-9, reading ..]SVL.VEIENT, and in 1991 the full *tria nomina* were found on *tegulae* from the site reading P(ublius).VSVL(enus).VEIENT(o) (Barti Català *et al.* 1993, fig. 5 and 11).

The family originated in central Italy – Etruria, Samnium or Picenum – and the *cognomen* refers to Veii (Tremoleda i Trilla 2000, 210).[22] Usuleni have been found in Rome, Barcino and Narbonne, where a number of members of the family have been found (*CIL* 12.4426, 4479, 4542, 4892, 5263, 5264, 5265, 5266, 5370; Tremoleda i Trilla 2000, 209-12). The same *nomen* and *cognomen* occur on an inscription from Narbonne (*CIL* 12.4426) that records P. Usulenus Veiento as *duovir quinquennalis* and *flamen*. This is perhaps related to the freedman Publius Usulenus Veiento, who is listed as a *magister pagi* responsible for the restoration of a sanctuary dedicated to Larraso on an inscription discovered in Moux to the west of Narbonne in 1850 (*CIL* 12.5370).

The stamps of CN.LENTUL/…RIS have been found on Pascual 1 amphorae from Empúries, Port-la-Nautique and Auterive (Beltrán Lloris 1970, 135; Miró i Canals 1988, 218; Pascual Guash 1991, 50; Bergé 1990, 150; Bouscaras 1984, 107). The *cognomen* Lentulus is most commonly associated with the *gens* Cornelia, and Piero Gianfrotta (1982) has suggested that the stamps refer to the senator Cn. Cornelius Lentulus Augur. Lentulus was consul in 14 BC and governor of Asia in 2-1 BC. Seneca (*De Beneficiis* 11.27) describes him as *divitarum maximum exemplum* – 'the most conspicuous example of wealth', who owed everything to Augustus – *cum omnia incrementa sua divo augusto deberet*. It was perhaps at this time that he acquired the estates that produced the Pascual 1 amphorae.[23]

The stamps of M.PORCI(us) are particularly common on Pascual 1 amphorae from Badalona, where 77 examples have been found (Comas i Solà 1997, 28-45). The stamp has been widely found through Southern France and Cataluña, as well as at Pompeii and Torralba d'En Salord (Menorca) (Comas i Solà 1987, 171; 1997, 28-9; de Nicolás 1987, 239; Pascual Guash 1980, 271-2; 1991, 90-4; Bergé 1990, 162-6;

Bouscaras 1984, 120-1). Examples from Vieille-Toulouse date to 30-10 and 10-0 BC respectively (Pascual Guash 1980, 271). At Perigús the stamp is dated to between 15 and 10 BC. Examples from Vic-Fesenzac date to the Augustan period. At Saintes and Saint Jean de Castets the stamp dates to the last decade of the first century BC and at Badalona to the first half of the first century AD (Comas i Solà 1997, 29). Examples of the stamp from the wreck of Cap del Vol (Gerona) date from *c.* 20-15 BC (Foerster 1980, 245).

The *gens* Porcia is a common one and there have been a number of attempts to associate the wine producer with a specific individual (Roman 1982, 81-3; Pena 1999, 77-83). The first connection between the family and the Spanish provinces came in 195 BC with the campaigns of Cato the Elder. The focus of Cato's operations lay in the vicinity of Empúries where he campaigned on behalf of the Ilergetes (Livy 34.11-16; Appian *Iberike* 161) before moving south to support P. Manlius in Turdetania (Livy 34.19). Upon his return to the north Cato received the submission of the Sedetani, Ausetani and Suessestani and forced the Lacetani to surrender (Livy 34.11). Cato would renew his connections with the Peninsula in 149 BC when he accused Servius Sulpicius Galba of atrocities committed during his governorship of Hispania Ulterior in 151-150 BC (Cicero *Brutus* 23; Plutarch *Cato Maior* 15.4). These connections were renewed by the exile of Caius Porcius Cato (consul of 114 BC and grandson of Cato the Elder) to Tarraco in 109 BC. Cato was condemned by the commission established by the tribune C. Manilius to investigate the mishandling of the war with Jugurtha (Cicero *Brutus* 34; *Pro Balbo* 11). Although the date of the stamps precludes a direct connection, they may reflect the activities of a descendant of the *clientela* established at this time.

M. Porcii are found in inscriptions from several towns in the region: at Gerona, Barcino and Tarraco (Pascual Guash 1980, 274; Tchernia 1971, 50-1). Robert Étienne and Fausto Zevi have suggested that he was a Pompeian who held a variety of civic offices after the establishment of the Sullan colony. He is recorded as *quattuorvir* on the altar of the temple of Apollo (*CIL* 12.800), as *duovir* responsible for the dedication of the theatre (*CIL* 12.844) and for the amphitheatre (*CIL* 12.852), both with C. Quinctius Valgus. Maria José Pena (1999, 80-3) has suggested that the Pompeian was a member of the family of the Porcii Catones – perhaps the senator M. Porcius Cato (Nepos), suffect consul in AD 36 who is attested on an inscription from Narbonne (*CIL* 12.4407). The recognition of Pascual 1 amphorae as Catalan vessels, however, precludes any direct connection with the Pompeian family, and we would be better viewing Marcus Porcius as a Tarraconensian landowner.

The family was of some importance at Tarraco where Porcius Felix is attested as *VIvir Augustalis* (*RIT* 423). M. Porcius Apro[? served in the East as *Praefectus fabrum* and military tribune of Legio VI Ferrata, *Procurator Augusti ab alimentis* and finally *Flamen [Divorum Augustorum] (per) provinciae Hispaniae Citerioris* (*RIT* 300).[24]

Particularly interesting is the stamp TIBISI, first found at L'Aumedina (Tivissa) in 1856. The stamp has been found at L'Aumedina on Pascual 1, Dr 2-4 and Dr 7-11. In view of the similarity of the name to modern Tivissa, it would appear to be the Latin toponym, although it has also been suggested that it is the genitive form of a Latinized Iberian name Tibisus (Miró i Canals *et al.* 1987, 285-6).[25] The stamp has been found at various locations along the coast extending from Cataluña to Italy: Empúries, Port-la-Nautique, Fos, Vieux-Port de Marseilles, Saint Cyr sur Mer, Pompeii and Carthage (Revilla Calvo 1993, 79-80; 1995, 166; Bouscaras 1984, 119).

While a number of the individuals attested on Tarraconense 1 amphorae continue to appear on Pascual 1 vessels – M. ANTO, Mevius and L. Volteilius – the stamps on Pascual 1 amphorae reflect a number of important innovations with respect to the previous vessels. Iberian stamps disappear, reflecting the Romanization of the native elite. While *duo nomina* continue to appear, *tria nomina* are found in increasing numbers: Q.F.S., C. Mussidius Nepos, Cn. Fulvius Secundus, P. Usulenius Veiento, Cn. Lentulus Augur, L. Herennius Optatus, T. Valerius Rufus. In contrast to the earlier producers the individuals attested appear to have been of a higher social status, being members of the municipal or senatorial elites. Usulenius Veiento was a member of the *curia* of Narbonne, Lentulus Augur was the consul of 14 BC. Members of the civic elite in Tarraco, Barcino and elsewhere in Cataluña are also attested. In addition to the elites themselves, freedmen now appear on amphora stamps, for example Iulius Anicetus and Iulius Theophilus, suggesting an increasingly complex process of producing amphorae that goes hand in hand with the appearance of 'industrial' *vici* at Fenals, Darró and Llafranc.

In Cataluña the norm appears to have been for kilns to be associated with villas, as at Torre Llauder, Riera de Teià, Torre Martina, Can Pedrerol de Baix, Vilarenc, Castellarnau, Madà/Can Bartrina, La Salut, Mas d'Aragó, Darró and El Roser. Several sites, however, have kilns associated with agricultural activities but have not yielded evidence of a villa: Molins Nous (Riudoms), Mas Manolo, Can Feu, L'Aumedina and Mas del Catxorro. The lack of evidence for the *pars rustica*, however, may be due to the lack of wider archaeological excavations.

A striking difference from the preceding period is the appearance of multiple kilns in the same location, although not necessarily contemporaneous. Two kilns have been found at Darró and Ventura d'Oller; a total of three kilns at Sant Boi de Llobregat and at Platja de Fenals; three kilns at Llafranc; three kilns at Can Feu; perhaps as many as four kilns at L'Aumedina and four kilns at Can Portell, Mas de Aragó, Castellarnau and La Salut; six kilns at Mas Manolo. At several sites it is impossible to determine the number of kilns as the evidence is confined to quantities of ceramic waste: El Roser, Riera de Teià, Torre Martina, Vilarrenc and Mas del Catxorro. The largest ceramic workshop appears to be that of Llafranc, extending over an area of 7,500 m^2; however, the limited extent of excavations at many of these sites precludes any certainty about the functioning of the ceramic workshops as a whole.

The presence of multiple kilns suggests large-scale production to supply several estates in the vicinity. Several kilns are associated with multiple amphora stamps; for example, the following stamps have been found at Can Feu: CE, CE or CF, AXUT, CAT, BLAD, PIND, SEVE, SNE, LES, H, HE, IM, NI and N (Carbonell *et al.* 1998, 290). Marta Prevosti has suggested that the villa at Torre Llauder supplied a cultivated area of approximately 7 km^2, or 2800 *iugera* of which 30% (840 *iugera*) would have been devoted to vine cultivation.[26] This in turn would have required 14,076 amphorae p.a. The kiln at Torre Llauder would have had a maximum capacity of 220 amphorae, which if fired every two weeks would have produced 5,720 amphorae p.a. On this basis three kilns would have been required to meet the demands of the estate (Prevosti i Monclús *et al.* 1987, 200-1; Prevosti i Monclús 1981, 535-6).

Characteristic of the kilns in Cataluña is the diversity of products: amphorae, coarse ware pottery, *dolia*, building materials, *tegulae* and *imbrices*. This diversity accords with the prescriptions of the agricultural writers that villas should be able to supply all their domestic and commercial needs.

As well as an increase in the density of villas in Cataluña, the Guadalquivir valley also saw the spread of villas during the Augustan period. Remains of a villa have been found at La Canaleja, 4 km to the north of Montilla. Although only limited rescue excavations were possible, parts of the *pars urbana* and bath suite were uncovered, dating from the final quarter of the first century BC to the end of the first century or beginning of the second century AD (Ruiz Nieto 1991, 191-5).

Remains of a possible villa and bath complex have been uncovered at El Ringo Rango (Los Barrios, Cádiz). The villa, which dates from the reign of Augustus, was remodelled in the middle of the first century AD and abandoned at the end of the first century or beginning of the second century. After a period of abandonment the site was reoccupied in the fourth century for a more utilitarian purpose with the construction of a kiln producing Almagro 51c amphorae (Bernal Casasola *et al.* 1996, 193-206; 1998, 1311-12).

The survey of sites in the vicinity of Montellano carried out by Oria Segura *et al.* has identified several sites as originating during the Augustan period. The site of El Alhorín I (Montellano) seems to have been at its most extensive in the Augustan and early Imperial periods, to judge from the presence of South Gaulish *terra sigillata* (Oria Segura *et al.* 1990, 42). A small rural farm has been discovered at Rancho Estrella at the foot of the Sierra de Montellano. Finds of *terra sigillata hispanica* and *africana clara A* give a date from the first century to the third century AD (Oria Segura *et al.* 1990, 63-4).[27]

The valley of the Guadalquivir provided excellent agricultural land for cereal and olive cultivation. A substantial grain storage area extending over an area of 10,000 m^2 has been excavated at Cortijo de Las Cuevas. The structures consist of semi-subterranean barrel-vaulted rectangular cellars built of *opus caementicum* – the largest of which is 9.5 m long and 4.3 m wide. As well as the cellars there is a large cryptoporticus 32.5 m long. The structures date between the end of the first century BC and the middle of the first century AD. The complex stored grain either gathered from the lessees of *ager publicus* or purchased by the *annona* (Haley 2003, 39). In the summer of 1997 rescue excavations at San Blas (Carmona) uncovered a *horreum* or granary dating to the middle of the first century AD (Román Rodríguez 2001, 249). The granary covers an area of 34 m^2 with five rows of blocks supporting the floor to allow the circulation of air and help prevent spoilage of the grain (Román Rodríguez 2001, 237-8). Several sites in the vicinity of Palma del Río have yielded evidence of cereal cultivation: a *catillus* 60 cm in diameter has been found at Cerro de los Pesebres and *metae* have been found at La Saetilla, San Sebastián and Remolino (Haley 2003, 39).

The most striking example of economic expansion during the reign of Augustus is the production and exportation of olive oil from the Guadalquivir valley. The earliest amphorae associated with the export of olive oil from the Guadalquivir valley are Oberaden 83 vessels. They are ovoid in shape, with an upright rim and a more prominent base than their better known successor, Dr 20. Carlos Fabião (1989, 73-4) has identified several amphorae from Lomba do Canho (Arganil) as Oberaden 83/Dr 25 oil amphorae. The site lies 2 km to the northeast of Vila de Arganil and dates from the late 60s to 27-25 BC (Fabião 1989, 48-9), which would make these the earliest examples of this amphora form (Haley 2003, 25-6). They are derived from late Republican oil amphorae from Brindisi and are found along the Rhine *c.* 15 BC: at Oberaden, Haltern, Aislingen, Augst, etc. Oberaden 83 were produced at Pinguele

(Bonares, Huelva) in the first half of the first century AD. Haltern 70, Dr 7-11, Beltrán II A and B, building materials and coarse wares were also produced. Juan Aurelio Pérez Macías and Aquilino Delgado Domínguez (2007, 70) have suggested that the intensification of agricultural activities in the province of Huelva was prompted by the need to supply the mines of the Río Tinto.

Mines and mining

Particularly notable is the increase in mining activity during the reign of Augustus. The increasing financial requirements of the Roman state were met by the revenues acquired by the annexation of Egypt and the expansion of mining operations in Spain. In the absence of technological advances the principal method of increasing productivity was to open up new mineral resources. The focus of Roman efforts was the mineral resources of Asturias and Galicia, whose importance helps to explain Augustus' personal involvement in the conquest of Cantabria.

The gold mines of Asturias and Galicia were the most important in the Roman world. Primary deposits of gold-bearing quartz are found extending from the Tras os Montes in Portugal through eastern Galicia to the west of Asturias and León. Secondary deposits are found in riverbeds and Miocene alluvia. Although the dating of mining activity is notoriously difficult, the impetus seems to have come from the Romans.[28] There is no evidence of large-scale mining before the Roman conquest, and literary sources refer only to alluvial sources (Bird 1984, 342; Sánchez Palencia *et al.* 1994, 164-5).[29] Strabo's description (3.2.9) of women scraping up gold, silver and tin from riverbeds implies that the scale of operations were small and ancillary to the domestic economy. According to Florus it was only by exploiting their mines for others did the Asturians discover the riches of their lands (2.33.60).

The Roman conquest prompted a dramatic increase in the exploitation of gold sources: Pliny states that the mines of Asturia, Callaecia and Lusitania yielded 20,000 lb of gold p.a. (*Natural History* 33.21.78). This is equivalent to 83.5 million sesterces, between 5.5 and 7% of the total revenue of the Roman state (calculated by Tenney Frank at between 1.2 and 1.5 million sesterces). Pliny also refers to alluvial gold from the river Tagus (*Natural History* 33.21.66).

The fullest account of Roman gold mining techniques comes from Pliny's *Natural History* (33.21.67-78). The detailed nature of Pliny's account suggests that it was based on first-hand experience from his time as a Procurator in Hispania Tarraconensis in AD 72-74.[30] Pliny describes the exploitation of both primary and secondary deposits: auriferous veins and rocks that could be extracted either by open-cast working or gallery mining, and alluvial deposits in river sands or gravels.

The bulk of Pliny's discussion is concerned with a technique of mining called *arrugiae* or *ruina montium*. Tanks were placed at the head of the mineworking from which the water could be directed to the face as required. Pliny's description of the force of the torrent of water released – 'ut repleto stagno excussis opturamentis erumpat torrens tanta vi ut saxa provolvat' – makes clear that this is a process called 'hushing' in which the force of the water washed away debris (Bird 1984, 348; Lewis *et al.* 1970, 183-4). Multiple channels running down from an aqueduct at the head of the slope enabled a process of 'multiple hushing' in which a continuous flow of water exposed a large area of land. Domergue (1974, 513) has suggested that the force of

Fig. 10. Water channels supplying the mines at Las Médulas.

the outflow was sufficient not only to wash away debris but also to expose the gold-bearing rocks beneath. Béatrice Cauvet, however, has argued that hushing would have been ineffective on hard rock deposits (cf. Burnham 2004, 329-30). The water was supplied by aqueducts constructed at a high level in order to provide a sufficient flow of water.

Water was also used to undermine the rock face – 'collapsing' or *ruina montium*, in which water was led through tunnels until erosion caused the face to collapse. A continuous flow of water, the process of ground sluicing, washed the debris down the slope to channels in which the ore was washed in order to separate the gold from the debris. Pliny describes both the use of stepped washing tables – preferably stone-cut – and wooden tables. The tables were lined with gorse to trap the particles of gold (*Natural History* 33.21.76).[31]

Pliny gives two accounts of the refining of gold (*Natural History* 33.69 and 84). The second account is more specific, describing a process of cupellation by which the gold was heated with salt and copper pyrite and then with salt and alum to remove impurities (Healy 1978, 14).

The most important example of Roman gold workings was at Las Médulas in the valley of the Río Sil, and this perhaps best fits Pliny's account of mining operations

(Bird 1984, 352). The gold is found in alluvial deposits eroded from the Montes Aquilianos to the east during the Miocene period (Sánchez Palencia 2000, 147-50). All three of the techniques described by Pliny appear to have been employed: channels at La Frisga, La Furnia and El Couso enabled water to be channelled to wash away surface debris exposing the gold bearing ore beneath. Traces of ground sluicing survive at La Frisga where it was used to expose the final 4 or 5 m of the face at Santalla. The most striking workings are the *ruina montium* at Las Valiñas, as well as at Gallegos and Reirigo (Sánchez Palencia 2000, 178-84).

The size of Roman operations is difficult to determine. The earliest workings lay to the southwest in the vicinity of Carucedo, covering an area of 820,000 m^2. Sector II covered 570,000 m^2 to the east between El Cabuerdo de Valdelobos and Orellán and the largest workings (sector III) extend from Las Valiñas to Chaos de Mourán, an area of 4,000,000 m^2 (Sánchez Palencia 2000, 174-5). F. Javier Sánchez Palencia and Luis Carlos Pérez García have suggested that 93,550,000 m^3 of alluvial soil was excavated yielding 4,677,500 kg of gold (Sánchez Palencia 2000, 155-7).[32]

In order to supply the mines, canals (*canales* or *corrugi*) brought water from Río Oza (La Valdueza) and Ríos Cabrera and Eria to the south (Sánchez Palencia 2000, 189; *Las Médulas* 2002, 132). Traces of the canal network survive at various locations in the vicinity of Las Médulas: the best-preserved stretch of more than 1 km is at Llamas de Cabrera (Benuza). During the final phase of operations the canals from La Valdueza and La Cabrera drained into a basin at Campo de Braña. The tank is situated to the southwest of the mine and supplies the work-faces at Las Valiñas and La Furnia-El Couso to the north and El Barreiro and El Souto to the west. The technique of *ruina montium* was employed at Las Valiñas – a tank holding between 16,000 and 18,000 m^3 of water stands at the head of the face and drains into the galleries at Orellán that extend for 650 m (Sánchez Palencia 2000, 204; *Las Médulas* 2002, 136).[33] The alluvial deposits were then washed to extract the gold from the waste debris (*gangue*), and washing channels are visible at La Llagua de Yeres. Quantities of waste material are visible at various locations: La Brea, Chao de Maseiros, La Balouta, Valdebría, Yeres-Rebordelo and Valdamola, giving a volume of 78,972,179 m^3 of waste material remaining (Sánchez Palencia 2000, 217-23).

R.F.J. Jones and D.G. Bird have studied the mine at Los Castellones in the Duerna valley (1972, 62-70). Three rectangular hushing-tanks are placed at the head of the opencast workings. Two dams situated to the west of the mine ensured a continuous flow of water for ground sluicing (Bird 1972, 52).

The most complete example of an opencast mine is found at Braña la Folgueirosa at the watershed of the Río Arganza and the Río del Coto (Bird 1972, 38-44). The mine was supplied with water from two aqueducts draining into tank B at the top of the opencast workings. The tank measures 61 x 10 m with a capacity of *c.* 1,300,000 litres. The height of the tank would have ensured sufficient force of water when the sluice was opened. The tank also supplied several leats (2, 3, 4) used for washing the ore, and the stepped gully (7) that runs downhill to the west echoes the stepped washing tables described by Pliny (*Natural History* 33.21.76).

Although research has concentrated on the mines of the northwest, important gold mining took place in the Tagus valley where major sites have been found Plasenzuela and Nava de Ricomalillo. At the end of the nineteenth century 3,000 mine shafts were

Fig. 11. Workshops at Orellán.

visible at the former site, however, the evidence is too exiguous for us to quantify the scale of mining operations (Edmondson 1987, 35).

The population remained essentially unchanged from the pre-Roman period: the number of immigrants to the northwest was small and largely confined to capitals and areas with a strong military or administrative presence. This continuity is reflected in the survival of indigenous castros and material culture. The earliest phase of occupation at Orellán dates to the second third of the first century BC and is characterized by the use of indigenous building styles and material culture: indigenous pottery accounts for 59.6% of the total pottery from the site. The primary activity was metalworking, with several smelting furnaces in the upper part of the village, and slag has been found throughout the settlement; however, the discovery of a grain silo indicates that agricultural activities also took place (Orejas *et al.* 2002, 591; Sánchez Palencia *et al.* 1999, 113; Sánchez Palencia 2000, 263). The castro of El Castrelín lies to the northwest of San Juan de Paluezas. Several circular and rectangular houses have been excavated, dating between the third and first centuries BC. These similarities should not, however, obscure the profound transformations that took place and are reflected in the internal organization of the castros and the appearance of Roman structural elements and imports.

In order to explore this further we need to examine the relationship between individual sites in terms of territorial distribution, function and hierarchy. Particularly notable is the increase in the number of settlements during the Roman period: more than 50 archaeological sites dated to the first and second centuries AD have been identified in the area of Las Médulas, compared to only two sites dated to before the Roman conquest (Sánchez Palencia 2000, 253). In contrast to the larger castro communities of the pre-Roman period, Roman sites are smaller with the population being predominately rural and dispersed. Individual sites seem to have been associated with specific functions. There are concentrations of sites in the fertile areas of the Campaña and Borrenes that may have been devoted to agricultural activities. Other sites seem to have been engaged in metallurgical activities. The site of Chaos de Mouran lies near the workings of El Soutín. The site of Orellán was established to exploit the iron workings of El Veneiro with furnaces and quantities of slag on the crest of the hill overlooking the site as well as on the northern slopes.

The growth of mining activities necessitated developments in other areas of the economy as well. Storeroom B at Orellán contained 70 kg of wheat, millet, barley and broad beans – exceeding the requirements of a family unit (*Las Médulas* 2002, 122). Some sites seem to have been situated to maintain the canal network, for example Las Portelas (Voces) and el Castro de la Peña de Saceda. The new distribution of settlements reflects the need to intensify economic activity. The survival of indigenous elements does not, therefore, reflect the survival of pre-Roman communities, rather the appearance of a new settlement pattern reflects the rapid assimilation of the native population to meet the demands of the Romans. The process of assimilation was not uniform: while some sites rapidly evidence a Roman material culture, smaller rural sites continue to display native cultural assemblages.

The Romanized native elite acted as intermediaries in this process, organizing the exploitation of the resources of the region on behalf of the Roman state. Several sites are more 'Roman' in character and perhaps housed Romans or Romanized natives responsible for the operation of the mines. In 1930 a villa was discovered at Santa Colomba de Somoza, dating from between the reign of Tiberius and the third century AD. The villa was organized around a small peristyle and *impluvium* and has yielded pavements of *opus signinum*, wall paintings and fragments of hypocaust from a possible bath suite (Gorges 1979, 276-7). Domergue has suggested that this was the residence of a procurator – perhaps of the nearby mines of Corona de Quintanillas, which were operated between AD 15/20 and 60/70. An Italianate *domus* has been excavated at Las Pedreiras – El Outeiro. The site lies close to the Via Nova linking the mines to the Río Sil (*Las Médulas* 2002, 117-19).

Initially mines were controlled by the Senate and leased out to individuals or *societates*. The best known was the *Societas Sisaponensis*. A first-century inscription from Corduba may refer to a *societas aerar(iarum fodinarum <Cordubensium>* that operated mines to the north of the city (Domergue 1990, 270). The *S(ocietas) C(astulonesis)* operated in the eastern Sierra Morena (Domergue 1990, 261-3). Domergue (1990, 257, 259-60) has suggested that the *Soc(ietas) Vesc( )* attested on an ingot from the Cabrera 4 wreck dating to the first quarter of the first century AD was engaged in lead-silver mining in Baetica. Mines could also be leased to towns – ingots refer to *Colonia Claritas Iulia Ucubi* (Espejo), *Nova Carthago* and *Colonia Augusta Firma Astigi* (Écija). The latter was granted colonial status during the reign of Augustus (Domergue 1990, 236; Pérez Macías *et al.* 2007, 135).

Particularly useful for the mechanics of the exploitation of mineral resources are the names that appear on lead ingots. Domergue has suggested that the ingots were initially stamped by the producers and then by merchants who shipped them down the Guadalquivir, and finally counter-stamped and inscribed with their weight by the merchants who shipped them to Rome and Italy.[34] More simple models may also be possible. Ingots from the Cabrera 4 wreck bear two names: Anteros Eros, L. Iunii Duo, T. L. Osca and Soc. Vesc, and are counter-stamped with the name L. Licinius M.f. // Ausua, suggesting that the ingots were stamped by the *mercator* at their point of production who then handed them to the shipper who would carry them overseas.[35] Ingots from the Sud-Lavezzi B wreck suggest a third possibility: all the ingots from the wreck are stamped with the name of the producer, MINVCIORVM, and are counter-stamped with the name of Ap. Iunius // Zethus, who also appears on a lead anchor stock from the ship. It seems, therefore, that the same individual served as both *mercator* and *navicularius*, purchasing the ingots and shipping them overseas (Domergue 1998, 206-8).[36]

Q. Aelius Satullus may have operated mines in the vicinity of Munigua and appears on an ingot from the Cabrera 5 wreck. He may be connected with the Aelii engaged in the production of olive oil (Chic Garcia 1992, 2-3). Haley (2003, 67) has noted that many of the individuals attested on inscriptions from the mining areas of Río Tinto and the Sierra Morena were immigrants from elsewhere in the Peninsula. Survey work from the vicinity of Munigua shows that during the first and second centuries AD iron smelting was associated with smaller rural dwellings rather than villas (Haley 2003, 67-8).

During the first century AD mines were transferred from private control into that of the state.[37] The best known example of this is the case of Sextus Marius in AD 33. According to the historian Tacitus (*Annals* 6.19.1), Marius was accused of having committed incest with his daughter and was thrown from the Tarpeian rock. Tacitus then notes that the real reason was to confiscate Marius' gold and copper mines.[38] An inscription from Seville dated to AD 97 refers to an imperial freedman, T. Flavius Polychrysus, as Procurator Montis Mariani (*CIL* 2.1179); a second is attested in Ostia (*CIL* 14.52). Marius' mines were probably in the vicinity of Córdoba, where the tombstone of Corinthus, a slave of Sextus Marius, has been found (*CIL* 2.2269) (Domergue 1990, 235).[39]

Two bronze tablets were discovered at Vipasca (Aljustrel) in 1876 and 1906. The mines were owned by the emperor and administered by a *procurator metallorum*. The procurator leased out contracts to work the mines and regulated the maintenance of the mining facilities (Edmondson 1987, 250-4). The procurator also sold contracts to supply the community with various goods: auctioneering, baths, shoemaking, barbers, fullers, teachers (Edmondson 1987, 244-9). Ingots from the tin mines of Albuquerque are stamped with the name of the imperial freedman L. Valerius. Most of the stamps were stamped with a second name: L. Corne(lius) Veg(etus), L. Aur(elius), Antul(lius, or Antuleius or Antullus) and Carinat(ius). The identity of these individuals is unclear: the ingots may have been stamped by the imperial freedman at the time of smelting, alternatively the first stamp may be that of the imperial administrator who sold it to the second individual on the ingot. Some ingots were overstamped with the initials M.T.S. which may indicate that the tin was sold to a private shipper who transported the metal to its market (Edmondson 1987, 38). Twelve tin ingots from the wreck of Port Vendres B bear the stamp L(ucius) VAL(erius) AUG(ustae) L(ibertus) A

COM(mentariis) (Parker 1992, 330-1). Lead ingots from the wreck of Ses Salines (Colònia de Sant Jordi) bear stamps of both private individuals together with imperial stamps: IMP.CAES or VESP.AVG, suggesting that the mines were worked by private individuals and the metals were then sold to the state (Parker 1992, 378-9; Edmondson 1987, 39).

In 1776 three inscribed podia were found at Bº de la Serreta (Mazarrón) (Ramallo Asensio *et al.* 1994, 111-12). The *dispensator* Albanus erected three inscriptions. Many *dispensatores* were of servile status: Pliny (*Natural History* 33.52.145) refers to a slave Claudius Drusilianus who was *dispensator Hispaniae Citerioris* and administered imperial property. The inscriptions are traditionally dated to the Flavian period and it seems likely that Albanus' position related to the mines in the vicinity.

After the conclusion of the Cantabrian wars, three legions remained in the Peninsula: IIII Macedonica at Herrera de Pisuerga (Palencia), VI Victrix in Léon and X Gemina at Rosinos de Vidreales (Zamora). The placing of the legionary bases in Cantabria and Asturias ensured control of the mineral resources of the area as well as providing technical expertise.

During the Augustan period the mines of the Río Tinto were converted into a militarized zone. The mines were administered by a prefect similar to the gold mines of the northwest. Pérez Macías and Delgado Domínguez (2007, 112-22) have suggested that the site of Cerro del Moro was the *castra* for the military garrison and controlled the route from the mines to Corduba via Italica and Seville. Forts have been discovered at Pico Teja (Riotinto) and Sierra de San Cristóbal (Nerva) – the latter dates to the first century AD. The mines were linked to Huelva, Beja, Tejada la Nueva and Mérida by a road network along which a number of forts have been identified dating to the Augustan period: Cerro del Drago and Castejón de Naja (Berrocal), Castrejón del Campo de Tejada (near Tejada la Nueva), Pico Teja and Sierra del Colmenar (near Santa Eulalia) and at the junction of the road to Mérida and the Río Odiel (Pérez Macías *et al.* 2007, 125-7).

A military presence can also be seen in the mines of the Bajo and Alto Alentejo where Rua Mataloto (2002) has identified a series of small forts dating to the late Republic and Augustan periods. Several are situated in the proximity of mines and have yielded evidence of metallurgical activities. Quantities of slag have been found at Caladinho-Castelo da Defesinha (Mataloto 2002, 180) and in the water channels at the base of the northern slope of Outeiro Pintado (Mataloto 2002, 175). Two channels found to the north of Monte do Gato 2 (Mataloto 2002, 190) may have been used in the processing of ore (Mataloto 2002, 195). The fort of Castelinhos do Rosário-Outeiro do Castelinho may also have been engaged in similar activities: the site is near the mine at Mocissos, and four cisterns lined with *opus signinum* have been located to the northwest of the site (Mataloto 2002, 184-6; Pérez Macías *et al.* 2007, 128).

The centre of operations in Río Tinto was the site of Cerro del Moro (Nerva), which dates to the reigns of Augustus and Tiberius. Quantities of slag have been found on the eastern slope of the hill (sector D) indicating that metallurgical activity took place, although not on an industrial scale (Pérez Macías *et al.* 2007, 56-7). Analysis indicates a high iron content as well as lead, suggesting that silver was being extracted from jarosite or iron sulphide (Pérez Macías *et al.* 2007, 82-4). Subsequent excavations of this area in 1984 revealed a small building with a courtyard, *atrium* or peristyle that may have functioned as a workshop (Pérez Macías *et al.* 2007, 58).

Analysis of lead isotopes from Greenland has shown that between 150 BC and AD 50 70% of the lead came from the Río Tinto region (Rosman *et al.* 1997, 3413). Analysis of the metal content of copper coins has shown that from the reign of Tiberius the copper came from southwestern Spain and principally Río Tinto (Chic García 1997, 26). Pérez Macías and Delgado Domínguez (2007, 134-5) have suggested that the expansion of operations in the Río Tinto region may have been prompted by the cessation of mining in the vicinity of Castulo caused by the disruption of the civil wars.

The impetus for mining operations may have come directly from Rome as M. Vipsanius Agrippa may have been involved in mining operations around Cartagena – hence his patronage of the town. In 1981, 102 lead ingots were recovered from the Commachio wreck at the mouth of the river Po. The wreck dates from between 19 and 12 BC. Lead isotope analysis has shown that the ingots originated in the district of Cartagena-Mazarrón (Domergue *et al.* 2005, 4-5). AGRIP is found on 92 ingots, generally accepted as referring to M. Vipsanius Agrippa.

Claude Domergue (*et al.* 2007) has identified the others as members of the municipal elite of Cartagena: FVRI attested on ingots from Fos-sur-Mer; VTI on ingots from Cartagena; PLR may refer to Pl(anius) R(ussinus) – several of whom are attested on ingots; IVNI may be related to the Iunii Paeti – C. Iunius Paetus is attested on an ingot from Magdalensburg (2005, 6-7). In other cases a direct connection cannot be drawn: neither Geme(llus) nor Mat(ius) are attested on inscriptions from the town. A connection between L. Cae(cilius) Bat( ) and Agrippa via his first wife Caecilia Attica has been suggested, although a connection with the local elite seems more likely: several Cae(sii) are attested from the town during the reign of Augustus and a Cae(dius) was *duovir quinquennalis* and moneyer in 42/41 BC. The *cognomen* may be Lusitanian in origin (Domergue *et al.* 2005, 8-9).

However, not all mines were under imperial control; the mines at Vispasca were part of an imperial estate. According to Justinian's *Digest* the landowner was free to exploit minerals that were found on his property as long as it did not damage the crops (7.1.13.5). We have already referred to Tacitus' account of the confiscation of the mines of Sex. Marius in Baetica.

The mining towns also acted as stimuli for other forms of economic activity in the region. The most common amphorae at Cerro del Moro are Haltern 70 vessels produced along the Guadalquivir and on the Bay of Cádiz: in Seville, Orippo, Puente Melchor, Venta del Carmen, Puerto de Santa María and Pinguele (Pérez Macías *et al.* 2007, 63-4). Haltern 70 amphorae are also found at Corta del Lago and Tharsis, as well as at the mines of El Soldado, Buitrón and Ajustrel (Pérez Macías *et al.* 2007, 66-7).

In 1984 and 1985 eight inscribed stone plaques were found at Cerro del Moro and Las Marismillas. Although poorly preserved, they appear to have been receipts for transactions, although the recipient is not stated. Inscription B records the exchange of 19 *modii* (approximately 200 litres) of barley: 'accepi hordei/m(odios) XIX' (Gimeno Pascual *et al.* 2007, 187).[40] The poor quality of Dr 4 lamps at Cerro del Morro may indicate local production although no kilns have yet been found (Pérez Macías *et al.* 2007, 73).[41]

The exploitation of marine resources during the Augustan period

The fishing industry in Cádiz seems to have continued to flourish. A fishery has been partially excavated on Calle Juan Ramón Jiménez. The factory is organized around a central courtyard of *opus barbaricum* and has yielded numerous remains of tunny as well as fishing implements. The complex was built at the end of the first century BC and abandoned in the second half of the second century AD. The site was used as a necropolis during the third and fourth centuries AD (Saenz Gómez 1993, 13-15; Lagóstena Barrios 2001, 108).

The continued growth of the industry is most clearly visible in the appearance of new amphora forms. Four principal types of fish sauce amphorae have been identified: Dr 7-11, Dr 38-39, Dr 12-13 and Dr 14 – subsequently classified as Beltrán I, II, III and IV. The most important of these were the Dr 7-11 vessels that were widely produced across the Western Mediterranean from the late first century BC to the first century AD. Generally they are characterized by an ovoid body (perhaps denoting a Punic prototype),[42] a pronounced lip and ridged handles. There is little uniformity in the shape of the lips or the bases. Dr 7 and 8 vessels are difficult to distinguish. They possess an ovoid body, short neck, thin or moulded lip and pronounced point. They are up to 1 m in height with a narrow mouth. The handles are elliptical and are parallel to the neck. The base is high, cylindrical and clearly separated from the body of the vessel. Dr 9, 10 and 11 are more easily distinguishable with a piriform body that is bulbous towards a less distinct base. They are bag-shaped with a short, wide neck and a broad vertical rim. In view of the widespread production of this form there are a wide number of variants both in form (particularly rims and bases) and fabric.

Although Dr 7-11 vessels seem to have been the most common form associated with the transport of salted fish products, several other forms were also used. Dr 38 (Pelichet 46) vessels are typologically similar to Dr 7-8 with a similar profile but with a broader neck and mouth. Dr 39 are similar in profile but with a narrower neck and mouth. A *titulus pictus* on a Dr 39 from the Castro Pretorio in Rome records its contents as having been 'g(ari) f(los)/AA ATINIS/DOM...' (*CIL* 15.469b). They may have been produced on the Bay of Cádiz as early as the reign of Claudius (Peacock 1974, 236). They are found in deposits dating to between AD 70 and 160 in London (Sealey 1985, 84), and a substantial deposit was found in the wreck at Chiessi dating between AD 60 and 85 (Parker 1992, 140). They have been found alongside Dr 7-11, Dr 12 and Haltern 70 amphorae on the wreck of Tour Sainte Marie A off the coast of Corsica, dated between AD 30 and 53 (Parker 1992, 432).

Dr 12-13 amphorae are characterized by a long, slender neck with a long cylindrical body tapering to a solid point. Examples of the form have been found at the wreck of San Ferreol off Cabo de Palos (Cartagena) (Mas García 1985, 205). Dr 14 amphorae have a piriform cylindrical body, with a thick rim and long vertical handles. Examples have been found at Pudrimel Norte and Bajo de la Campana II (Mas García 1985, 164), El Saler (Martín *et al.* 1966, 166) and at Riells-La Clota (Nieto Prieto *et al.* 1985, 150). An example from Saint-Gervais bears the *titulus*: 'Liq(uamen)/exc(ellens)/Sabini et Aviti' (Edmondson 1987, 162).

Ovoid Lomba do Canho 67 amphorae were produced at Laguna Salada (Puerto de Santa María) and Cerro del Mar, as well as at Sala in North Africa. They seem to have carried both fish sauce and wine; however an example from Punta de la Nao (Cádiz) contained grapes. They date from the second half of the first century BC and first quarter of the first century AD (Pérez Macías *et al.* 2007, 71).

Several of the Republican kilns identified by Lázaro Lagóstena Barrios in the vicinity of El Puerto de Santa María continued to function: Hijuela del Tío Prieto, Vaina, Venta Alta. Several further kilns seem to have begun operating at the end of the first century BC. Lagóstena Barrios has identified several possible kilns in the vicinity of El Puerto de Santa María: Beltrán Ia, c and d and Beltrán IIa amphorae have been found among the ceramic waste at Cantarranas-Los Cipreses (Lagóstena Barrios 1996, 39; Lagóstena Barrios *et al.* 2004, 62). Beltrán Ib and c have been found on the southeastern slope of the Cerro de las Cabezas (Lagóstena Barrios 1996, 46). Ceramic waste containing Mañá C2b, Dr 7-11, Beltrán IIa and possibly Lomba do Canho 67 has been found at Laguna Salada (Lagóstena Barrios *et al.* 2004, 64).

Excavations carried out in 1986 by José Antonio Ruiz Gil on the coast at La China uncovered quantities of ceramic waste consisting primarily of amphorae: Beltrán Ib, as well as Beltrán Ia and c and lesser quantities of Beltrán IIa, Beltrán V and Dr 1 A (Lagóstena Barrios 1996, 43). A possible ceramic workshop with Mañá C2, Beltrán Ic and IIb amphorae has been found at San Ignacio on the southeastern slope of the Sierra de San Cristóbal (Lagóstena Barrios 1996, 61). Ceramic waste containing Mañá C2b and Dr 7 amphorae has been found at Los Sauces (Lagóstena Barrios *et al.* 2004, 66).

Several kilns are associated with other structures – although the lack of evidence means that we cannot be certain of the character of this occupation. *Tegulae*, *imbrices*, worked stone and *opus signinum* have been found at Las Manoteras together with Dr 7-11 and Dr 1C amphorae (Lagóstena Barrios 1996, 53). A possible villa was located at Los Tercios with evidence of ceramic production on the lower slopes consisting of ceramic waste and pottery fragments – predominantly Dr 7-11 (Lagóstena Barrios 1996, 50). A pavement of *opus signinum* has been found together with *tegulae* and *imbrices* at Casa de la Vicuña. Ceramic waste consisting of Dr 1C and Dr 7-11 amphorae has also been found 700 m to the west (Lagóstena Barrios 1996, 57; Lagóstena Barrios *et al.* 2004, 62).

A pair of circular kilns 4.5 m in diameter were excavated at El Palomar-Puerto Nuevo in 1994. The kilns produced Dr 7, 8 and 9, Beltrán II A and II B amphorae and Mañá C2b vessels. Four smaller kilns were also found, which may have been used to produce coarse ware pottery or lids. Several poorly preserved structures were also found including four buried *dolia*, suggesting that the kilns may have been part of a wider estate (Lagóstena Barrios 1996, 47-8; Lagóstena Barrios *et al.* 2004, 64-6).

Several kilns have been associated with salting vats. Vats were found 1 km from Molino Platero where quantities of ceramic waste and Dr 7-11 amphorae were found (Lagóstena Barrios 1996, 37).

There is a dramatic increase in the number of kilns elsewhere on the Bay of Cádiz. Excavations at El Olivar (Chipiona, Cádiz) have revealed two kilns. The kilns produced Dr 7-11, Beltrán IIb and Haltern 70 amphorae dating from the beginning of the first to the beginning of the second century AD. Adjoining the kilns excavations have uncovered the ceramic workshop and housing grouped around a courtyard to the south of which lay a storeroom for amphorae. The excavator has suggested that the kilns functioned as part of a wider villa devoted to farming (Ramos Millán *et al.* 2004, 452-3).

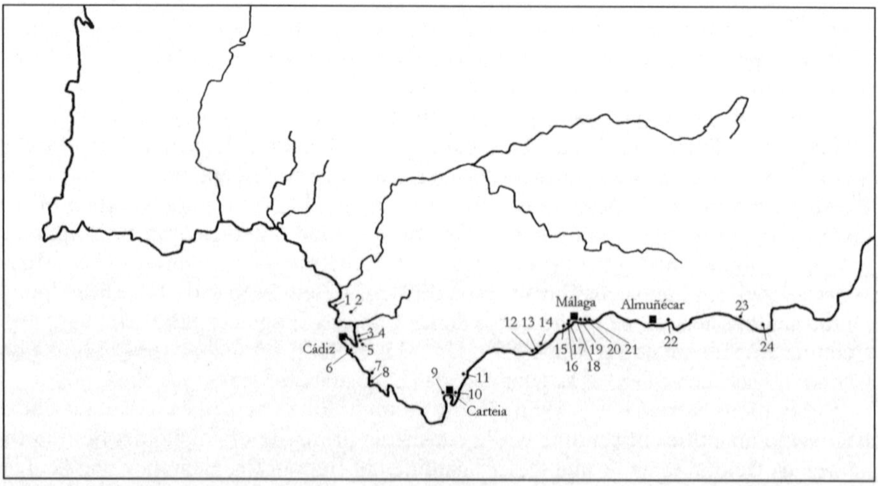

Map 4. Kilns producing fish sauce amphorae in Baetica.

1. El Olivar
2. Jerez
3. El Olivar de los Valencianos
4. Puente Melchor
5. Villanueva
6. Cerro de los Mártires
7. Loma del Puerco
8. Huerta de Luis Santos
9. Guadarranque
10. El Rinconcillo
11. Venta del Carmen
12. Finca el Secretario
13. Benalmádena
14. Huerta del Rincón
15. Colmenares
16. Haza Honda
17. Carranque
18. C/ Carretería
19. El Manganeto
20. Toscanos
21. Cerro del Mar
22. Los Matagallares
23. Calahonda
24. Loma de Ceres

Eighteen kilns have been found in the vicinity of Puerto Real. In 1946 large quantities of amphorae were found at Puente Melchor. Rescue excavations have taken place since 1994 under the direction of María Luisa Lavado Florido. Two large kilns have been excavated: kiln A is circular, 5.75 m in diameter, with a central column 2.90 m in height. Kiln B is similar in design and size. A series of rooms to the southwest of the kilns were devoted to the preparation of the amphorae. In the centre of the workshop there is a circular basin 2.80 m in diameter and 0.60 m deep used for the decantation of the clay. A third smaller piriform kiln is located to the southeast that may have been used for the manufacture of glassware.[43] A wide variety of amphorae were produced here: Dr 7, 8, 9, 10, 12, 17, 20, Haltern 70, Beltrán IIa and IIb during the first century AD; Puerto Real 1 and 2, Dr 12, 14, 20, Keay I, IV, V, XVI and XXIII from the middle of the second century AD; Puerto Real 1 and 2, Dr 12, Keay VI, XXIII and Beltrán 68 vessels during the final phase of activity (Lavado Florido 2004, 473-9; Millán León *et al.* 2000, 215-16). Further kilns were discovered in 1996: the first associated with Puerto Real 1 and 2 and Beltrán IIa and IIb amphorae; a pair of kilns were uncovered to the south (Lavado Florido 2004, 482-4). A number of stamps have been found: HER, OP, APTI, SOC, SOCI, CL.SOC, CON, LVC, BV, FEY and FFR (Millán León *et al.* 2000, 217; Lagóstena Barrios *et al.* 2004, 72).

The site of El Gallinero lies to the west of the town of Puerto Real and has been the subject of archaeological fieldwork since 1991, when a circular kiln (5.40 m in diameter) was discovered. Dr 7, 8 and 10 amphorae have been found dating to the first quarter of the first century AD. A second similar kiln has subsequently been found (Lagóstena Barrios *et al.* 2004, 69-70; García Vargas 1998, 168-71; García Vargas *et al.* 1992, 126).

Two kilns have been found at Olivar de los Valencianos. The first, discovered by Maria Josefa Jiménez Cisneros, is circular, 6 m in diameter with a central pillar and built out of tiles, bricks and fragments of amphorae (Jiménez Cisneros 1971, 146-8). A second kiln 50 m to the west was discovered in 1980 and is perhaps later in date than the first (López de la Orden 1981, 61). The pottery seems to have been in use from the second half of the first century BC to the middle of the second century AD and to have produced Dr 7-11 as well as possibly Dr 12 and Dr 17 amphorae. Several stamps have been identified: C, AQA, A, AL, MAAAT and DAAAT (Campano Lorenzo 1994, 140). The discovery of decorative elements suggests that there was a residential building in the vicinity although the remains are too sparse for the nature of the building to be discerned (Campano Lorenzo 1994, 143; Lagóstena Barrios *et al.* 2004, 70-1).

Quantities of amphorae dating from the end of the first century BC and the first century AD have been found at several locations: El Almendral, La Cabaña 1 and 2, La Cachucha, Las Canteras, El Carpio Chico, El Carvajal, Casines, Cerería, Cerro de los Caracoles, Malas Noches, La Zarza (Lagóstena Barrios *et al.* 2004, 66-74). Several sites have been found in the vicinity of Fábrica Lavalle, where remains have been reported since the end of the nineteenth century. Excavations carried out in 1991 by Silvia Fernández Cacho in the Convento de Franciscanos Descalzos identified the amphorae as Dr 7-11, Beltrán IIa and IIb (Lagóstena Barrios 1996, 78-80; Lagóstena Barrios *et al.* 2004, 69).

Two circular kilns have been found at Cerro de Ceuta associated with Dr 9/10 amphorae (Lagóstena Barrios 1996, 69). Part of the firing chamber of a kiln has been revealed during quarrying at Cantera de Lavalle on the hill of Liaño Alto. Mañá C2b, Dr 1C, Sala I-Lomba do Canho 67, Dr 7 and Dr 9 amphorae have been found in a dump on the northern slope (Lagóstena Barrios *et al.* 2004, 67). A pair of circular kilns have been excavated at Torrealta A associated with Dr 7-11 and Beltrán II amphorae (Lagóstena Barrios *et al.* 2004, 72-3).[44]

Michel Ponsich (1988, 67) reported the discovery of a kiln at Fuente Redonda (Barbate). The kiln is circular with a central pillar associated with Beltrán IIa and Dr 7-11 amphorae dating to the first half of the first century AD (Lagóstena Barrios *et al.* 2004, 50).

Two kilns were excavated in 1996-7 at Venta del Carmen (Los Barrios). They are circular with a central pillar and strikingly similar to those at El Rinconcillo. Kiln H. 102 in Sector D is well preserved with a circular firing chamber 4 m in diameter, a central pillar 1 m in diameter and preserved to a height of 70 cm with the *praefurnium* to the north (Bernal Casasola *et al.* 1998, 87-91).[45] The earliest phase of occupation is dated from the middle of the reign of Augustus by to the presence of Dr 2/4 amphorae, *terra sigillata italica* and Dr 9, Andújar and Loeschke V and VI volute lamps, as well as the absence of Campanian wares and Dr 1 amphorae. The kilns ceased to function during the third quarter of the first century AD – kiln H.101 was demolished during Phase II C and re-used as a lime kiln (Ca. 101) and kiln H.102 was remodelled and perhaps used as a ceramic dump (Bernal Casasola *et al.* 1998, 84-5, 99). The site was covered over *c.* 80 AD (Bernal Casasola *et al.* 1998, 77-9). The kilns seem to have produced primarily Beltrán IIa and Dr 14 amphorae, although small quantities of Haltern 70 and Dr 28 were also found (Bernal Casasola *et al.* 1998, 101).

Several kilns are associated with villas and other agricultural activities. Dr 8, Beltrán IIa and IIb amphorae have been found on the eastern slope of the hill of Liaño Alto. Recently fragments of *opus signinum* with black and white geometric decorations have been found (Lagóstena Barrios *et al.* 2004, 68). Quantities of ceramic waste consisting of Dr 7-11 and Beltrán II amphorae have been found at Santo Domingo. A pavement of *opus spicatum* has also been found (Jiménez Cisneros 1971, 148-9; Lagóstena Barrios 1996, 107-8; Lagóstena Barrios *et al.* 2004, 72).

The concentration of kilns around Cádiz is striking and points to specialized production of amphorae on an industrial scale. Alberto Campano Lorenzo (1994, 144) has likened the concentration of kilns around the Bay of Cádiz to the concentration of kilns along the Ríos Guadalquivir and Genil supplying oil amphorae, and around the Ríos Besós and Arenys for Laietanian wine.

The earliest villas in Lusitania probably date to the reign of Augustus. The foundation of the colony of Emerita Augusta in 25 BC would have been accompanied by an influx of Roman citizens, which may explain the appearance of imported finewares on rural sites in the vicinity. Antonio Aguilar Sáenz and Pascal Guichard (1995, 57) have noted the fact that remains of the earliest phases of villas in the area have been obscured by levels dating to the third and fourth centuries AD, making the dating of the initial phase extremely difficult.

The villa at Doña María is located in the valley of the Río Zújar on the right bank of the Río Guadalemar. Excavations have revealed a peristyle villa dating from the beginning of the first century and abandoned at the beginning of the second century AD (Aguilar Sáenz *et al.* 1997, 96-9, 135-42).[46] The fish factory at Cacilhas (Almada) may date from the end of the first century BC. The factory consisted of six vats arranged around a central courtyard (Lagóstena Barrios 2001, 48; Amaro 1990, 79).

The abiding impression of the Augustan period is of economic expansion, culminating in the economic developments that took place during the first century BC. Not only is there an increase in the number of kilns but there is also a dramatic increase in the size of potteries with multiple kilns operating in the same location. In contrast to the Republic, this expansion extends into parts of the Peninsula previously devoid of Roman settlement.

A number of factors were responsible for this economic growth. The influx of settlers after the period of the civil wars and the spread of urbanism promoted by Caesar and Augustus created both demand and the potential for economic growth. While natives appear to have been involved in the mining operations of the northwest elsewhere in the Peninsula the initiative seems to have been either from immigrants or Romanized natives. Genaro Chic García (1985, 277-8) has suggested that the influx of wealth from the incorporation of Ptolemaic Egypt into the Empire stimulated demand.

The establishment of the *annona* and the *annona militaris* would also have created demand. Justin (44.1.5) states that Spain supplied Rome and Italy with grain, wine, honey and oil. Strabo (3.2.6) says that large quantities of grain were exported from Turdetania.[47] By using privately owned shipping to carry its goods the *annona* encouraged private commerce, effectively subsidizing the costs and assuming part of the risks of transporting goods.[48] The shippers could make additional profits by transporting their own goods alongside their official cargoes (Morley 2007, 72; Whittaker 1985, 53-4). The importance of the *annona militaris* is clear from the distribution of Pascual 1 that extends along the axes of the Rhône and Garonne into northwestern Europe.

5

The Roman Economy

The spread of villas and viticulture

In the course of the first century AD villas began to appear in parts of the Peninsula that had not previously seen Roman settlement. Together with the appearance of farms and villas there seems also to have been a shift away from cereal cultivation towards viticulture and oleiculture.

During the first half of the first century AD several kilns appear producing Dr 2-4 along the coast of Valencia. The establishment of these may have been fuelled by the development of Denia during the Augustan and Julio-Claudian periods, exemplified by the construction of the forum on the plain to the north of the castle. In 1975 a ceramic workshop was discovered on Carrer Santíssim and Carrer Ángel del Alcázar in Oliva. Quantities of Dr 2-4 and Dr 26 amphorae were found as well as two fragments of Dr 28 vessels (Gisbert Santonja 1987, 106-7).

In 1957 Roman occupation was discovered at L'Almadrava to the north of the Punta de l'Almadrava in the town of Setla-Mirarosa-Miraflor. The site lies to the north of the mouth of the Río Girona, which may have functioned as a harbour to

Fig. 12. Square kiln, Sector A, Miraflor.

judge by the quantities of amphorae found in the vicinity. A wreck was found at Punta de los Molinas carrying locally produced Dr 2-4 vessels (Fernández Izquierdo *et al.* 1992, 82).

An area of about 2,000 m^2 has been cleared, revealing a ceramic workshop: sector A consists of two square kilns and sector B contains the ceramic dump from the adjoining kilns. Three phases of occupation have been identified. The initial period of use dates to the second third of the first century AD. The second phase dates from the beginning of the second century AD and marks the apogee of activities on the site. Four workshops were built and 80% of the amphorae date to this phase. The final phase dates to the third century AD with the production of Dr 30 amphorae. Of 177 fragments of amphorae that have been recovered, 56% are Dr 2-4 and 40% are Dr 30 vessels (Gisbert Santonja 1987, 108-10).[1] The site was abandoned *c.* 275-285 AD, although residential occupation continued until the fourth century (Abascal Palazón *et al.* 1990, 135-6; Gisbert Santonja 1999, 68-71). A bath complex has been discovered to the east and fifteen burials dating to the second and third centuries AD have been excavated 150 m to the west (Abascal Palazón *et al.* 1990, 134). The stamp PL.CIS found on Dr 2-4 vessels from the site may be related to those reading CAL.CIS.FI found on Dr 30 amphorae. CIS is perhaps the *nomen* with 'fi' the abbreviation for *figlina*. The stamp C.C.V.LM.F.S perhaps records the name of a senator – C.V. may be an abbreviation of 'c(larissimus) v(ir)'. The last two letters refer to a slave: either 'f(ecit) s(ervus)' or related to the stamp from Villajoyosa that reads F(e)LICIO S(ervus) (Gisbert Santonja 1987, 111-12; 1999, 91).

Several other kilns have been discovered in the vicinity of Denia. The site of La Teulera lies 600 m from the town of Jesús Pobre. Two kilns have been found associated with Dr 2-4 (69%) and Dr 30 (30%) amphorae. Two fragments of Dr 20/26 are also present (Gisbert Santonja 1992, 89-96). Quantities of Dr 2-4 and traces of a kiln have been found at Alter de Perdigó (Gisbert Santonja 1992, 96).

The earliest villas in Extremadura date to the first century AD. Three phases of occupation have been identified at the villa of El Pesquero (Badajoz): the first phase dates to the end of the first century AD; the villa was expanded in the second century with the construction of a central peristyle; the polichrome mosaics have been dated to the third phase. The villa was abdandoned at the end of the fourth or beginning of the fifth century AD. A bath complex to the south was constructed at the end of the second century AD (Aguilar Sáenz *et al.* 1995, 19).

The villa of La Cocosa lies 16 km to the south of Badajoz. The villa extends over an area of 10 ha arranged around a rectangular peristyle and dates from the first century to the fourth or fifth century AD (Aguilar Sáenz *et al.* 1995, 20). Remains of a villa dating from the first to the fourth centuries AD have been found at Peñaflor (Esparragosa de Lares) (Aguilar Sáenz *et al.* 1995, 73). Several other sites in the vicinity of Esparragosa de Lares have yielded pottery from the first century AD: Campo Mojardo I and II, La Barca II, Valle de Sevilla, Los Vadillos I and II (Aguilar Sáenz *et al.* 1995, 83-5).

Villas first appear in the province of Navarra in the middle of the first century AD. In 1944 B. Taracena excavated the remains of a villa at Liédena on a terrace overlooking the Río Irati. The villa is arranged around a peristyle and adjoining bath complex. To the southwest of the *pars urbana* is the platform for a wine press and two adjoining basins into which the liquid from the press could drain. A possible *cella*

Fig. 13. Peristyle of the villa at Liédena.

vinaria has been excavated to the north of the peristyle. Although Taracena dated the villa to the late Imperial period, Mezquíriz Irujo has suggested a date from the end of the first century to the middle of the second century AD for the black and white *opus tessellatum* pavement in the peristyle (Mezquíriz Irujo 2004, 138-40; Aguilar Sáenz 1991, 265-6).

A well-preserved winery has been excavated to the south of the town of Arellano where a villa has been discovered in a small valley enclosed to the south and west by the Sierra de Cortabacoy and to the north by the slopes of Montejurra. The existence of mosaics on the site was first reported in 1882 with excavations taking place since 1985 under the direction of M.Á. Mezquíriz Irujo (2003, 23-5). Two phases of occupation have been identified: the first from the middle of the first century to the end of the third century AD, when the villa was destroyed by fire. The second phase dates from the fourth century until the first half of the fifth century AD (Mezquíriz Irujo 2003, 26-7).

The first phase consists of a peristyle villa opening from a possible *atrium* to the east. The peristyle sits on a terrace overlooking a large *cella vinaria* along the western face of the peristyle. The *cella* measures 28.5 x 7.10 m and was found containing quantities of *dolia* (Mezquíriz Irujo 2003, 89-91). To the north and east of the peristyle is the *pars fructuaria* devoted to the preparation of wine. The grapes would be brought into the pressing room from the north. The room contained two square basins, preserved to a depth of 30 to 40 cm, for the basket of grapes and the press respectively. Both basins were raised above the level of the surrounding floor to facilitate the draining away of the liquid. The press was possibly a screw-press. The base for the counterweight remains in the adjoining rectangular area (7.8 x 4.1 m). After pressing the liquid would be transferred to the two basins preserved on either side of the press before being decanted into *dolia* for fermentation (Mezquíriz Irujo 2003, 68-9; 2004, 135). In 1996 a porticoed *cortinale* was discovered containing a hearth used to heat the must, reducing it to produce either *defrutum* or *sapa*. To the northeast lay an open storage area or *fumarium* where the wine could be aged in the heat and sun (Mezquíriz Irujo 2003, 74-5).[2] A building to the north has been identified as a *granarium*, and there is a possible *horreum* to the south of the villa. The *pars rustica* lies to the east but its original design is largely obscured by its remodelling in the fourth century AD. The find of a *dolium* to the east suggests the presence of a *cella vinaria* (Mezquíriz Irujo 2003, 32-3).

The villa of San Esteban (Falces) lies on a terrace overlooking the Río Arga. Excavations between 1969 and 1977 revealed remains of a small winery in two phases dating to the first and second centuries and the fourth century AD. A single basin measuring 3.88 x 1.90 m and 1.10 m in depth has been excavated abutting the platform of a wine press (9 m long by 3.20 m wide). The *torcularium* was probably located in the room to the east of the platform. In 1972 a subterranean cellar containing three large *dolia* was excavated underneath the west wing of the villa (Mezquíriz Irujo 2004, 141).

In 1982-3 a villa was excavated at Los Villares, 2 km from San Esteban on the opposite side of the Río Arago. The northern part of the villa has been excavated,

Fig. 14. *Torcularium* and adjoining basin, San Esteban.

consisting of the *pars fructuaria* devoted to the production of wine. Two basins and two platforms have been excavated with the *torcularium* to the south. Three counter-weights were found here – Mezquíriz Irujo believes that two were used for the processing of grapes and the third for olives (Mezquíriz Irujo 2004, 143-4).

While *dolia* are commonplace, the absence of the amphora from these sites is striking. Only three fragments of Dr 2-4 amphorae have been found at Arellano (Mezquíriz Irujo 2003, 90-1). Mezquíriz Irujo has suggested that the owner of the villa where the wine was produced was not involved in the production of amphorae (2004, 148). The small scale of production is striking – particularly at Sant Esteban where the capacity of the *cella vinaria* was only 1,650 litres (Mezquíriz Irujo 2004, 143). The surviving basin (*lacus vinarius*) at Arellano measures 1.90 x 1.50 m and is 1.50 m deep giving a capacity of 4,000 litres (Mezquíriz Irujo 2003, 69).[3] Perhaps the wine was produced purely to meet local demand, or alternative types of container were used to transport the wine. No kilns have yet been found in the vicinity.

The largest of the wineries was excavated in 1959 by J. de Navascués at Funes dating to the end of the first century and first half of the second century AD. Although only 300 m^2 of the site has been excavated, four basins have been uncovered as well as areas devoted to the pressing of the grapes. Although no traces of the pressing facilities survive, the volume of the basins and the quality of their construction suggest that the site was primarily devoted to wine production perhaps even on a sufficient scale for commerce (Mezquíriz Irujo 2004, 144-7).[4]

These villas seem to have been particularly associated with the production of wine. The scale of viticulture in the Peninsula is reflected in the appearance of a new vessel – Dr 2-4 – that gradually supersedes Pascual 1 amphorae during the reign of Tiberius (AD 14-37). Dr 2-4 vessels are modelled on wine amphorae from the island of Cos. They are cylindrical in shape with long bifid handles that are parallel to the neck and have a small moulded lip. The diameter of the mouth varies between 12 and 14 cm. They vary in height between 100 and 110 cm. The earliest examples of the form appear at the end of the first century BC. Dr 2-4 amphorae have been found alongside Pascual 1 vessels on the Sud-Lavezzi 3 wreck dated *c.* 15 BC. At La Longarina Pascual 1 and Dr 2-4 have been found dating to the first twelve years of the first century AD (Hesnard 1980, 145-6).

Unfortunately the details of the transition from Pascual 1 to Dr 2-4 are difficult to determine as a result of the lack of quantified and precisely dated samples and the continued production of Pascual 1 during the first century AD. It is striking to note that Pascual 1 amphorae continue to be more common than Dr at 2-4 Baetulo. In the first half of the first century AD Pascual 1 account for 74% compared to 3% Dr 2-4; in the second half of the first century 41% are Pascual 1 compared to 27% Dr 2-4. In deposits dated to the reign of Claudius, Pascual 1 continued to be in use, accounting for 37% and 54% (in both deposits residual material is minimal (3% and 8% respectively) (Comas i Solà 1998, 219-20). Monserrat Comas (1998, 219) has suggested that the large quantities of amphorae found in Baetulo result from the storage of stocks of amphorae in the town. Pascual 1 amphorae are found in levels dated 20-30 AD at Sant Boi de Llobregat, and at Can Feu production of the form continued until the middle of the first century AD. Pascual 1 are found in Zaragoza between 30-40 and 50 AD, and an example from the beginning of the Flavian period has the stamp SENTRO. The form is found at Celsa at the end of the Claudian period. The wreck at Na Guardis

(Mallorca), dated to the reign of Claudius or Nero, has a cargo of Pascual 1, Dr 2-4, Dr 7-11 and PE 25 amphorae.

Level G from Sant Boi de Llobregat, dated *c.* AD 50 when both kilns 2 and 3 were functioning, contained a predominance of Dr 2-4 (70.3%) compared to Pascual 1 (29.7%). The pivot of one of the Dr 2-4 amphorae bears the stamp SOS. Level H at the end of the first century AD contains 44.6% Pascual 1, 54.8% Dr 2-4 and 0.5% Dr 7-11. The following marks are found on the Dr 2-4 amphorae: AN-T, QVA, QV-A and THEOP (López Mullor 1998, 234).

The number of kilns that produced Pascual 1 and continued to produce Dr 2-4 is striking: La Salut, Forn de Morer, Can Portell, Riera de Teià, Can Ventura de l'Oller, Sant Miquel de Martres, Mas Manolo, Vilarenc, Ca l'Oller, L'Aumedina, Mas del Catxorro, Sant Boi de Llobregat, Mas d'Aragó, Can Tintorer, Platja de Fenals, Llafranc.

A ceramic kiln was excavated at Sant Miquel dels Martres between 1949 and 1956. Quantities of Pascual 1 and Dr 2-4 were found, together with the following stamps: C.MC ANT; LLQ and LL.Q; ...LQ; P; PATIC or PTAIC; SLL. According to Pascual the frequency of the marks LLQ and SLL indicate that they were produced here (Miró i Canals 1988, 23-4). Pascual 1 and Dr 2-4 amphorae were also produced at Can Cabot with the marks CAQ, L.CP, L.C...R...ER; MO; SLL, ...QIO (Miró i Canals 1988, 25-6).

Construction of a parking garage on the Avinguda Francesc Cambó in Barcelona in 1984 uncovered quantities of Dr 2-4 and Pascual 1 amphorae related to the villa discovered in 1954 in the Plaza de Antoni Maura (Miró i Canals 1988, 30-1; Granados *et al.* 1987, 128).

A ceramic workshop has been excavated at Calle Guillem de Palafolls 40-42 in Malgrat de Mar dated to the second half of the first century BC (Burjachs *et al.* 1993, 156). The pottery and ceramic waste consists of Dr 2-4 amphorae, as well as Pascual 1 vessels, *tegulae*, *imbrices*, *lateres* and *pondera*. The most common stamps are LMO and AMET, together with less commonly R., R.I, R.L and DO. The workshop may have functioned as part of the villa situated at the foot of Turó de Santa Rita, 100 m to the southeast. Pascual 1, Dr 2-4 and Dr 20 (?) amphorae were found at Montjuïc in 1929 (Miró i Canals 1988, 30; Granados *et al.* 1987, 129). A villa and kiln was discovered in 1928 at El Morrell (San Andreu de Llavaneres) producing Dr 2-4 and Pascual 1 amphorae. The stamp CLV probably originated here being found on two dozen amphorae as well as *tegulae* (Miró i Canals 1988, 41).

Remains of a villa have been excavated at Can Pedrerol de Baix (Castellbisbal) dated to the first and second centuries AD. The majority of the amphorae found were Dr 2-4, together with a smaller number of Pascual 1. The large number of stamps is striking: AD, ALB, ALBA, ALEX, AM, ANT, ATT, CE, CELS and CELSI, EL, GRAE, IV, LYA, MA, NI or IN, NYS, POT, PROTI, SAT, SOSIBIA, TPIM and VIC (Miró i Canals 1988, 17-18). Remains of a villa and a kiln have been found at Can Tintorer dating to the first and second centuries AD. The kiln produced Dr 2-4 as well as lesser quantities of Pascual 1 and Dr 7-11 amphorae (Miró i Canals 1988, 18-20; Revilla Calvo 1995, 203).

A villa and a kiln were excavated in 1980 on the shore at El Roser (Calella de la Costa). The kiln produced *tegulae*, coarse wares and Dr 2-4 amphorae, although two lip fragments from Pascual 1 vessels have also been found. The following stamps were found: ACASTI; CIBA; FAMULI or AEMULI; HILARI; MAX; ADIE (?); IDI or ITDI (?); IRB (?); ISSI or CISSI; .RH (?); ...ANDI; ...NI. The villa dates from the second decade of the first century BC to 60-70 AD (López Mullor 1982, 1983; Miró i Canals 1988, 44-5).

As well as the production of Dr 2-4 amphorae in kilns that had earlier produced Pascual 1 vessels, there seems to have been an increase in the number of kilns with several sites established in the middle of the first century AD. Quantities of Dr 2-4 amphorae have been found at Cararach (Caldes de Montbui) together with the stamp L.M.O.S.A. (Miró i Canals 1988, 23). A poorly preserved kiln was discovered in the nineteenth century at Buada (Reus). Dr 2-4 and Dr 7-11 amphorae have been found with the stamps IR, CR and SVA (Massó Carballido 1998, 283). Excavations in 1997 and 1998 uncovered a ceramic workshop and kilns at Roquís (Reus) (also known as Mas de l'Antoni Corts). Local Dr 2-4 amphorae were found including the stamp GALLIC that is also found at Mas de Gomandí (Massó Carballido 1998, 283). A ceramic workshop was discovered at Mas de Gomandí in the middle of the nineteenth century. Quantities of Dr 2-4 and Dr 7-11 were found with the stamps [S]ILVAN, GALLIC and P (Massó Carballido 1998, 284). A possible kiln producing Dr 2-4 amphorae was located in the vicinity of El Morè (Sant Pol de Mar) dated to the mid-first century AD. The following stamps have been found: AC, AGI (?), A..., CHR (or BR), CIY (?) and RV (?) (Miró i Canals 1988, 43-4).

The site of Tomoví (Albinyana) lies 4 km to the north of Vendrell (Baix Penedès). Finds of architectural elements (especially *tegulae*) and pavements of *opus signinum* indicate the existence of a villa dating to the first and second centuries AD. A second area lies to the west, closer to the riera de la Bisbal, has yielded remains of two kilns together with quantities of ceramic waste, building materials and amphorae. The kilns produced primarily Dr 2-4 amphorae as well as coarse wares, *dolia* and building materials (Revilla Calvo 1994, 114-15; 1995, 187).

Three kilns dating from the Augustan to the Flavian periods have been found at Can Jofresa (Terrassa) (Casas *et al.* 1993, 269; Revilla Calvo 1995, 209). The kilns produced Dr 2-4 amphorae, *tegulae*, *imbrices*, *latera* as well as coarse ware pottery. In 1984 a basin for preparing clay was discovered at Palamós together with quantities of ceramic waste including Dr 2-4 amphorae, *tegulae* and *dolia* (Martín 1993, 75; Tremoleda i Trilla 1987, 210-15).

Excavations at Urbanització Ríncon del César (Creixell) have uncovered walls, basins and large quantities of Dr 2-4 amphorae, including defective examples that suggest that this was a ceramic workshop. Remains of two kilns have been found in the vicinity of Barranc de la Pedrera, perhaps associated with a villa in the neighbourhood. Dr 2-4, Dr 7-11, *tegulae*, *imbrices*, bricks and *dolia* were found (Revilla Calvo 1995, 180; Bermúdez Medel *et al.* 1984).

Two kilns have been found at Els Antigons (Reus). A series of rooms of the *pars urbana* of a villa have also been excavated dated between the first and fourth centuries AD (Revilla Calvo 1995, 183). Dr 2-4 and Dr 7-11 were found (Massó Carballido 1998, 284). Ceramic waste indicates the existence of a kiln producing Dr 2-4 in the vicinity of Burguet (Alcover) (Massó Carballido 1998, 284). Ceramic waste of Dr 2-4 and Dr 7-11 has been found at Canaleta (Vilaseca) (Massó Carballido 1998, 284). In 1945 a kiln was discovered at Brugar (Reus) producing Dr 2-4 (Massó Carballido 1998, 285). Quantities of Dr 2-4 have been found at Timba (Riudoms). The stamp

EVPRA has been found as well as LCM (an import) (Massó Carballido 1998, 285). In 1905 a kiln was discovered at Vilar (Reus) (Massó Cabballido 1998, 285).

Several kilns have been identified in Southern France. At Corneilham (where Pascual 1 were also produced) 54 poorly preserved necks of Dr 2-4 amphorae have been found, one with the stamp TPA.RODANI. At Plaine du Levrau (Velaux) 57 lips or necks and seventeen handles have been found, one with the stamp SENECA on the neck, and at Moulin du Pont (Velaux) 67 lips or necks, 118 handles and 24 points have been found (Laubenheimer 1985, 316-18).

Some of the producers of Pascual 1 amphorae continue to appear: L.CP or L.C.P has been found on both Pascual 1 and Dr 2-4 amphorae from Can Cabot (Pascual 1991, 78). The stamp TIBISI from L'Aumedina (Tivissa) has been found on Pascual 1, Dr 2-4 and Dr 7-11 amphorae. OPTATI has been found on Dr 2-4 at Cavallo 1. The stamp may be related to the OPT that appears with PATI at La Chrétienne H and CIAS at Carthage (Pascual Guash 1991, 104-5). The stamp may be related to those of L. Herennius Optatus that were produced at Torre Llauder.

M.P.M has been found on the handle of a Dr 2-4 from Vilarenc (Revilla Calvo 1995, 186). Five examples of M.P.M. have been found on Dr 2-4 from Grau Vell. The identification of the individual is unclear. A veteran, C. Petronius Maternus, erected a dedication to Mars at Añavieja (Soria) during the Flavian period. Q. Petronius Maternus was a *duovir* in Beja between AD 139 and 161 (Abascal Palazón 1984, 234). L. Porcius Maternus is recorded as a *duovir* on an inscription from Fuente Tójar (Córdoba) dating to the second half of the first century AD (Abascal Palazón 1984, 235). …B.C, …C.S. and RE (last two on the same vessel) have also been found on Dr 2-4 amphorae from Grau Vell (Aranegui Gasco 1978, 310). A Dr 2-4 from Saguntum has the mark L.A. (Mantilla Collantes 1987, 387).

L.M.O.S.A appears on a Dr 2-4 from Can Carerac (Caldes de Montbui) (Revilla Calvo 1995, 222). AMAND has been found at Fos-sur-Mer, Petit Congloué and Ile Rousse – in the case of the latter two on Dr 2-4 amphorae (Pascual Guash 1991, 27). CLAR, ACA and FIR have been found on Dr 2-4 amphorae from the wreck of La Chrétienne H. CLAR is also found on Dr 28 amphorae from Vendres, Nimes and Vaison. The stamps were perhaps produced at Can Tintorer where they are found associated with FIR (Pascual Guash 1991, 47-8). HILARI has been found on Dr 2-4 at El Mujal, Strasbourg, Perduto 1, Diano Marino and London (Pascual Guash 1991, 71-2). The Greek *cognomen* LEAN(dros) has been found on Dr 2-4 amphorae from the wreck of La Chrétienne H, as well as at Can Tintorer (Pascual Guash 1991, 79).

The mark SEX.DOMITI has been found on the neck of Oberaden 74 amphorae from L'Aumedina. The same stamp has been found at various locations in Gaul and along the Rhine frontier: Cébezan, Vivios, Enserune, Vaison, Carpentras, Saint-Paulien, Rodez, Héry, Lyon, Limoges, Périgueux, Basel, Nyon, Lugano, Dangstetten, Neuss and Oberaden. The same stamp is found on a Dr 12 amphora preserved in the museum at Périgueux (Berthault 1995, 270-1). An example from Limoges also bears the stamp SATURIO (Revilla Calvo 1995, 166; Pascual Guash 1991, 137-9).

The identity of Sextus Domitius is unknown. Pascual Guash (1980, 167) has suggested that he may owe his citizenship to the proconsul C. Domitius Calvinus, who campaigned against the Ceretani in 39-37 BC. The Domitii were an important family in the region: C. Domitius Montanus was a member of the *ordo* of Barcino during the third century AD (*CIL* 2.6153). Cn. Domitius Felicio is named on *tituli picti* on Dr 6 and Dr 7-8 carrying 'muria exce(llens) flos' and 'mur(iae) ar(gutae) excel(lentis) f(los)' from Castro Pretorio in Rome and from Bonn (Beltrán Lloris 1970, 234).

As well as *dua* and *tria nomina* there are increasing numbers of single names: Hilarus, Sosibia, Alexander, Leandros, Amandus, Acastus and Eupra[. These are perhaps the slaves responsible for manufacturing the amphorae. Several of the names are Greek in origin and some, such as Felicio, are accompanied by the verb 'facere' meaning 'to make' or 'to do'. Occasionally a second individual is named in a bilinear stamp, perhaps giving the name of the slave. In addition to the stamps of Sextus Domitius and Saturio, C.MC/ANT has been found at Sant Miquel dels Martres (Caldes de Montbui). Q.A.F?/PAR was found in excavations in Barcino in 1944-50. A stamp from Empúries reads ..]M? LOR?[… / MARCEL.AVG? (Berni Millet *et al.* 1998, 116). Stamps of Q. Cor(nelius) Ner( ) are associated with the Eros or Fuscus – slaves who were responsible for producing the amphorae (Berni Millet *et al.* 1998, 115). EROS/Q.C.NER was found in excavations of the Saló del Tinell in Barcino in 1952-3. An identical stamp was found at La Torre (Sax) and is preserved in the Villena museum. The stamp Q.CORNE/FUSCUS was found at Vall de Porcs (Ribaroja, Ribera d'Ebre) in 1988 and from the wreck of Marina di Fiori in a cargo of Tarraconensian Dr 2-4 with the marks EVP, HAM and FLAVI. Dr 7-11 and a Haltern 70 were also present in the wreck, dated to the Flavian period.

This association of landowner and slave is relatively common in South Italy and on the Adriatic coast in the first centuries BC and AD (Berni Millet *et al.* 1998, 119). Associations of individuals may also appear: for example, the stamp M.S.PVP on Dr 2-4 from Planier 1 which Corsi and Liou (1985) have read as Marci and Spuri Pupiorum (Pascual Guash 1991, 94).

The growth of oleiculture

The first century AD also sees the spread of villas along the Guadalquivir valley. The initiative for this expansion comes from a dramatic increase in olive oil production during the Julio-Claudian period. Both Martial (12.63) and Pliny (*Natural History* 15.8) praise olive oil from the Guadalquivir valley as equal in quality to Istrian and Venafrum. The goal of this trade seems to have been Ostia, where an important deposit of amphorae has been studied at La Longarina, and from there to Rome, where a dump of amphorae is located at Monte Testaccio.

The amphora dump of Monte Testaccio lies at the foot of the Aventine Hill behind the store buildings that line the banks of the River Tiber. The mound rises to a height of more than 40 m and consists of at least 24,750,000 olive oil amphorae – 80% of which come from Baetica. The earliest amphorae date to the reign of Augustus and the last vessels were dumped during the reign of Gallienus. This represents 1,732,500,000 kg of olive oil or 7,000,000 kg per annum for the 250 years that the dump was in use (Remesal Rodríguez 1998, 193-7).

Imperial involvement in the supply of olive oil to the *annona* and *annona militaris* appears to have been established between AD 41 and 71 – perhaps by Vespasian. The first *procurator frumenti comparandi*, M. Arruntius Claudianus, dates to the reign of Domitian (Blázquez Martínez 1992, 177). An inscription from Seville dated to the reigns of Marcus Aurelius and Lucius Verus records Ulpius Saturninus Possessor, a *praefectus annonae ad oleum afrum et hispanum recensendum* – prefect of the annona for the purpose of reviewing the African and Spanish oil (*CIL* 2.1180). Possessor would appear to have been involved in the provision of Spanish and African oil to the *annona* in Rome. A further inscription from Seville, found at the base of the tower of the Giralda, records the *diffusor olei ad annonam* – distributor of oil for the annona, M. Iulius Hermesianus (Blázquez Martínez 2007, 182-3).

Evidence of oleiculture comes from the vicinities of the newly established colonies of Hispalis (Seville), Corduba (Córdoba) and Astigi (Écija). Faunal analysis from Celti (Peñaflor) reflects a shift from cereal cultivation to oleiculture. Naked wheat (*Triticum aestivum/durum*) and barley (*Hordeum vulgare*) predominate in Iberian levels compared to olives in levels dating to the Neronian/Flavian periods and later (Phases 7 and 8) (Keay *et al.* 2001, 123).

The production of olive oil entailed three processes: crushing, pressing and settling.[5] According to Varro (*De Re Rustica* 1.55.4-6) olives were either consumed or processed to produce oil. The olives would be piled up and allowed to turn mushy and then transported to a *trapetum* where they would be milled to break their skins. Columella provides more detail: olives could be milled using either a rotary mill (*mola*) or *trapetum* (*De Re Rustica* 12.52.6-7).[6] According to Columella, the Romans wanted to avoid crushing the pit as this would spoil the oil.[7] Once the oil had been crushed, the olives would then be pressed to separate the oil from the skins and flesh. Five types of press were used: the lever and weight press, lever and drum press, lever and screw press, direct screw press and wedge press (Curtis 2001, 384-93; Carrillo Díaz-Pinés 1995, 54-9).

Once the olives had been pressed the oil was then separated from the *amurca* or water. According to Cato (*De Agricultura* 66) this was done immediately after pressing, and was achieved by skimming the oil off the surface of the *amurca* with a shell or ladle (Columella *De Re Rustica* 12.52.8-12). Columella recommends separating three different pressings with the best oil being obtained from the first pressing. The oil is allowed to stand and then strained into the second vat and so on, separating the lees from the oil (*De Re Rustica* 12.52.10-11).[8] Columella praises the high yield in return for only limited labour and expense (*De Re Rustica* 5.8).

A well-preserved oilery has been excavated at El Callumbar, 4.5 km to the southwest of Antequera. All three stages in the preparation of the olives are visible: the extraction of water or *amurca* from the olives and their pitting; the pressing; and the decanting and purification through settling into basins and *dolia*. The *cella olearia* lies to the west of the site (trench 2-Y). The room is paved with cobblestones over which lay a deposit of dark grey earth 12 cm thick which the excavators identified as being *amurca*, indicating that the room was used for the initial preparation of the olives. The olives were then transferred to the milling room (trenches 2-C and 1-D). A circular base (9 cm in diameter) in the north of the room has been identified as the base of a *trapetum*. A rectangular tiled area (2 x 1.6 m) in the southwest corner of the room and covered with *amurca* was used to contain the olives immediately before they were transferred to the adjoining pressing room. The pressing room (trench 2-B) was paved with *opus spicatum*. The base (the *ara*) upon which the basket of olives was placed stands in the centre of the room with a channel on all four sides. The bases of the two wooden pillars that support the beam (*prelum*) are situated in the southwest corner. The olives were then settled: two basins and *dolia* have been excavated in trenches 2-A and 2-Y (Romero Pérez 1990, 500-4). The site dates from the second quarter of the first century to the end of the second century AD (Romero Pérez 1990, 500; 1997, 118-27).

Excavations have uncovered the remains of a farm at Cortijo del Canal on the bank of the Río Cubillas (Albolote, Granada). The complex seems to have been devoted to the production of olive oil. Three vats have been excavated in room E and a fourth vat lined with *opus signinum* in room G. Remains of millstones were found in area D and at the entrance of room I. Room C contained quantities of amphorae and *dolia*. The presence of South Gaulish *terra sigilliata* and *terra sigillata hispanica*, thin-walled wares and Gallic *marmorata*, together with the absence of *terra sigillata italica* and Campanian ware, dates the first phase of occupation from the first half of the first century to the second century AD. The second phase continues until the third or fourth century AD (Raya de Cárdenas *et al.* 1990, 225-32).

The villa of Llanos de Plines lies to the northwest of the town of Loja (Granada). Excavations in 1989 uncovered the poorly preserved remains of a villa and farm. The apogee of the site dates from the second to the fourth centuries AD (Gener Basallote *et al.* 1992, 128) although quantities of South Gaulish *terra sigillata* and *terra sigillata hispanica* suggest that occupation dates from the beginning of the first century AD (Gener Basallote *et al.* 1992, 102-5).[9] Carbonized olive pits indicate oleiculture (Gener Basallote *et al.* 1992, 128). Rescue excavations at Cortijo de Miraflores have revealed a storage area of *dolia*. The site seems to have been occupied from the second century BC with the *dolia* store being constructed at the middle of the first century AD. The site was abandoned at the end of the first century or beginning of the second century AD (Haley 2003, 53).

Several sites have been identified in the vicinity of Dos Hermanas: the presence of South Gaulish *terra sigillata*, *terra sigillata hispanica* and African red slip dates the occupation at Hacienda de Doña Ana to the middle of the first century AD. Finds of marble decoration suggest the existence of a villa. *Dolia* have been found together with remains of a grain mill (Haley 2003, 53-4). A substantial oilery has been excavated at Cerro Lucerico (Cerro de las Estacas, Fuente Tójar) dating from the second third of the first century AD. Fragments of at least three presses have been found in a rectangular structure measuring 25 x 5 m paved in *opus spicatum* (Carrillo Díaz-Pinés 1995, 70-4).

In 1989 a substantial villa was discovered at El Ruedo (Almedinilla). The villa was built in the first half of the first century AD and the final phase of occupation dates to the fourth and fifth centuries. The first phase consists of a farm. During the second century the villa was expanded with the construction of a peristyle that was further developed during the third and fourth centuries. Three rooms (30, 32 and 46) contained basins lined with *opus signinum* that were used for either wine or olive oil production, though no traces of a press have yet been found (Carrillo Díaz-Pinés 1995, 78). Excavations uncovered a necroplis to the northwest of the villa, dating from the third to the seventh centuries AD.

Remains of an oilery have been discovered at Cerro del Capitán to the north of the Sierra de Peñarrubia (Málaga). A mill used to separate the flesh of the olive from the pit has been found, together with fragments of *dolia*. Surface finds of *terra sigillata hispanica* date the site to the second century AD (Haley 2003, 72-3).

The importance of olive oil cultivation is reflected in the appearance of the large scale production of a new amphora form – Dr 20 – that dominates the transport of olive oil during the first and second centuries AD.[10] Dr 20 amphorae are large globular vessels derived from the smaller ovoid Oberaden 83 amphora produced during the reign of Augustus. The vessels were produced from the middle of the first century AD and production ceased *c.* 260. Nearly 100 kilns producing Dr 20 amphora are concentrated along the banks of the Guadalquivir and Genil. The rivers provided not only a source of clay and water to manufacture the amphorae but also a route along which the amphorae could be exported. Barges or lighters could carry the oil to Seville where it was offloaded onto larger sea-going vessels for shipment to Rome (Strabo 3.2.1).

The site of El Castillejo (Alcolea del Río) – the ancient Arva – is situated on the north bank of the Guadalquivir. The site was first excavated by George Bonsor at the end of the nineteenth century. Excavations carried out in 1991 have revealed remains of a substantial workshop and three kilns producing primarily Dr 20 amphorae (172 pieces) as well as Dr 23 (three pieces) (Remesal Rodríguez *et al.* 1997, 168).[11] The kilns seem to have been in operation from the middle of the first century to the third century AD. The first is a large circular kiln dating to the end of the first century or early second century AD.[12] The two remaining kilns are both circular (between 5 and 5.20 m in diameter) with a central pillar (*c.* 3 m in diameter) and radial arches supporting the firing chamber above. The kilns post-date the Severan period. The kilns also produced coarse ware pottery and *dolia* (Chic García *et al.* 2004, 283-4; Remesal Rodríguez 2000, 386; Remesal Rodríguez *et al.* 1997, 157-62).

To the east of Alcolea del Río lies the site of El Tejarillo. Erosion has revealed at least five large kilns measuring 5 m in diameter. The kilns were in use from the middle of the second century to the middle of the third century AD, producing Dr 20 and Dr 23 amphorae as well as building material and *dolia* (Remesal Rodríguez *et al.* 1997, 155; Ponsich 1974, 145; Chic García *et al.* 2004, 284-5).[13]

A large circular kiln (4.80 m in diameter) has been found at La Catria together with the remains of a ceramic workshop producing Dr 20 amphorae. The kiln was part of a larger complex extending over an area of 20 ha. The kiln dates from the second half of the first century to the third century AD (Chic García *et al.* 2004, 299).

Michel Ponsich (1974, 99-108) reported the existence of a circular kiln with central pillar at Villar de Brenes. The kiln produced Dr 20 from the middle of the first century to the first quarter of the third century AD. The most numerous stamps are variants of the name VIRGIN and perhaps give the name of the *figlina* Virginensia (Chic García *et al.* 2004, 286). Several variants of the stamp PORTPAH have been found, also found at Cruz Verde on the other side of the Guadalquivir where Ponsich has reported the existence of three kilns (1974, 108; Chic García *et al.* 2004, 286). Erosion has revealed the existence of three kilns at Casilla de Tarancón dating to from the middle of the first century to the middle of the second century AD (Chic García *et al.* 2004, 295).

A ceramic workshop producing Dr 20 amphorae as well as *tegulae* and *dolia* has been excavated at Remolino, 3 km northeast of Palma del Río. A pottery workshop associated with a villa has been discovered at Las Delicias dating from *c.* AD 50 to 250. The workshop produced Dr 20 amphorae, building materials and ceramic planting pots (Haley 2003, 95). The kiln at Alcotrista lies 8.5 km from Ecija on the Río Genil. The workshop produced amphorae, bricks, *tegulae* and other pottery, including imitation Campanian ware and Iberian pottery. The site was occupied from

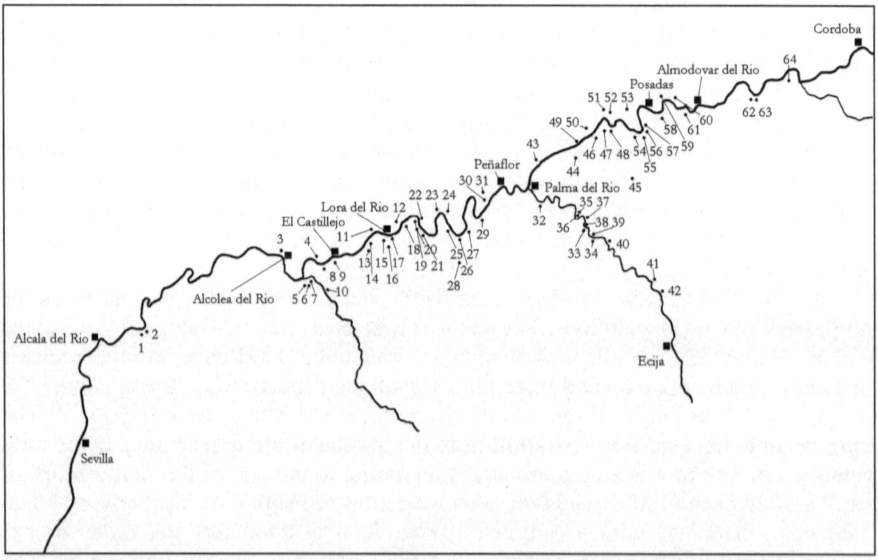

Map 5. Kilns producing Dr 20 amphorae in the Guadalquivir valley (after Ponsich).

1. Cruz Verde
2. Villar de Brenes
3. Huertas de Alcolea
4. El Tejarillo
5. Guadajoz
6. Adelfa
7. Juan Barba
8. Mejia
9. Tostoneras
10. El Tesoro
11. La Estacada de Herrera
12. Huertas del Rio
13. Azanaque-Castillejo
14. Alamo Alto
15. El Judio
16. Cortijo de Mochales
17. La Catria
18. Cortijo del Guerra
19. Haza del Olivo
20. Manuel Nieto
23. La Maria
24. El Berro
25. La Ramblilla
26. Madre Vieja I/II
27. Las Sesenta
28. El Marchante
29. Calonje Bajo
30. La Botica
31. El Tesoro
32. Casas de Picón
33. Cortijo del Judío
34. Tarancón
35. Malpica Sur
36. Tierras del Judío
37. Malpica
38. Cortijo de Villalata
39. Las Valbuenas
40. Isla Grande
41. Alcotrista
42. Las Delicias
45. Cortijo de Bramadero
46. Villacisneros
47. Casa del Encinarejo
48. La Correjidora
49. Isla de la Jurada
50. Cerro de los Vuelos
51. La Umbria de Moratalla
52. Casa del Guarda
53. Haza de los Laticos
54. Soto del Rey
55. Barranco del Picacho
56. La Dehesilla
57. La Estrella
58. Mingoabez
59. Dehesa de Arriba
60. Guadiato
61. Villaseca
62. El Temple
63. El Temple (este)
64. Cortijo de la Reina

the end of the reign of Augustus or beginning of the reign of Tiberius (Haley 2003, 95-6). Surface prospections carried out at Torreón (Burguillos) have revealed a villa together with a bath suite, as well as a kiln producing amphorae and bricks. Counter-weights of a press were also found on the site, which dates from the first to the second or third century AD (Chic García *et al.* 2004, 286).

In 1993 excavations uncovered a ceramic workshop on the estate of El Merino at Azanaque, 6 km to the southwest of the town of Lora del Río. An area of 8,000 m^2 was cleared, revealing two circular kilns with a central column. A tiled drying floor measuring 2.15 x 1.40 m has been excavated to the east of the kilns in square E5.

Abutting the wall of this building is a basin lined with *opus signinum*. Two further basins have been discovered: the first 13 m from the drying floor and a second basin to the southwest of kiln A (Romo Salas *et al.* 2000, 407-9; Romo Salas 1997, 772).[14] The kilns produced a range of ceramic goods, primarily amphorae including Dr 20 and Dr 23 (a single Oberaden 83 vessel has also been found), as well as coarse wares, *dolia* and building materials (*tegulae*, *imbrices* etc.).

As well as the production of pottery, the complex may also have been involved in the processing of olive oil: both kilns contained large quantities of olive pits that were used as fuel for the firing process (Romo Salas *et al.* 2000, 407; Romo Salas 1997, 772). The complex seems to have been in use from the first half of the first century until the second half of the fourth or middle of the fifth century AD (Romo Salas *et al.* 2000, 415). During the final phase of area B/C-2/3, this part of the site seems to have been converted to process olive oil, with the construction of an oil press (Romo Salas *et al.* 2000, 409-10; Romo Salas 1997, 774-6). This site is particularly significant because the excavated area has been sufficiently extensive to enable the archaeologists to explore the relationship of the kiln to other aspects of the rural economy. Further excavations of this type will enable us to determine if the dissociation between kiln and oilery is more apparent than real.

The relationship of the potteries to the estates is unclear – the location of kilns along the banks of the Guadalquivir and Genil away from the oil producing estates implies a disassociation of the pottery producer and the landowner upon whose estate the oil is being produced. The existence of independent ceramic production is in contrast to the production of wine amphorae in Cataluña, where the amphora kilns are associated with estates. Amphorae would have been produced close to the estates on which their contents were made as it would have been unprofitable to transport empty amphorae. Unfortunately, few of these kilns are known by more than surface finds of ceramic waste. Therefore we know very little about their operation. José Remesal Rodríguez laments (2000, 382) that no villa has been systematically excavated ('no se ha producido en Andalucía la excavación sistemática de una *villa* de la región que nos ocupa, tanto de su *pars dominica* como de su *pars rustica*').

Knowledge of the organization of the production of olive oil amphorae comes either from the excavation of the kilns themselves, or from the epigraphy found on the amphorae: the stamps, graffiti and *tituli picti*. There are three main types of stamps: first those that give the names of free individuals – usually in the form of initials of the *tria nomina*, or groups of individuals; secondly the names of the workshop or estate where the amphorae were produced; and thirdly the name of the potter whose name is followed by the verb 'F(ecit)'. In addition components of these three types may be combined in a single stamp, for example, combining the *tria nomina* with the name of the location or even combining all three types in a single stamp. The identity of the individuals named is the subject of debate representing either the proprietor or manager of the kiln in which the amphorae were produced (Mayet 1986, 299); or the owners of the oil (Remesal Rodríguez 1998, 190).

Various stamps have been recovered from Azanaque (Romo Salas *et al.* 2000, 411-14): the stamp CHB may be related to ACHB found nearby at Azanaque-Castillejo, in Adelfa and Guadajoz dating between 140 and 160 AD. They may also be related to the stamp LCHE or FCHE found at Monte Testaccio dating between 218 and 222 AD. CONSFC is also found in the area at Azanaque-Castillejo and El Judío

(Lora del Río). Several variants of the stamp DATZCOL have been found. The stamps may be related to the family of the D. Atici who appear on stamps from Monte Testaccio, dating to the middle of the second century AD, perhaps specifically with D. Aticus Severus dated to 149 and 153 AD. COL may read either C(onductio) OL(earia) or the toponym COL(obraria) (Chic García 2001, 217). FIRMI has also been found at the nearby kiln of Huertas del Río, as well as outside the Peninsula in Rome, Bliesbrück and possibly Nîmes (Chic García 2001, 224-5). EROTI and EROTIZ may be related to the stamp EROTIS that has been found in Rome as well as in Gaul, Germany, Britain and North Africa (Chic García 2001, 224).

Ten variants of the stamp G.AP.F. have been found: the stamp is found at several locations in the northwestern provinces: Caerhun, Caerleon, Corbridge, Wroxeter, Adenau, Saalburg, Vechten, Fins d'Annecy, Citania, Mainz, Banasa, London, Colchester, Loughor, Koenigshoffen, St Ulrich and Bliesbrück. The stamps may be related to those of C. Appius F( ) that are found at Monte Testaccio, *c.* AD 179-180 (Chic García 2001, 219-20; Callender 1965, 87). A stamp reading C AP has been found on a Dr 20 amphora from El Judío (Ponsich 1974, 198). The stamp may be related to that of G.A.F//ROVTO or G.A.F//BOVEQ that has been found Finca de Juan Barba (Alcolea del Río). Genario Chic García (2001, 261) suggests that the second line is perhaps that of a *societas*: 'Bov( ) et Q( )'. Several variants of the stamp G.M.M or G.M.M.F have been found. The stamp is distributed through the northwestern provinces and is found at Monte Testaccio, dated *c.* 179-180 AD (Chic García 2001, 220). MHICA may be related to the MHC and MHICAEC found at Monte Testaccio. The stamp ID.N has beeen found associated with *terra sigillata italica*, coarse wares and a fragment of an Oberaden 83 amphora dating to the first half or middle of the first century AD. VICT and VICTORICI may be related to stamps from El Sotillo (VICTOR) and Almodovar del Río (VICTORINI). Several variations of Q.AE.O.PO have been found: QA.OPCO, Q.AEOPTA, QAEOPTATI, QAEOCO, QAEOPCO, Q AEOPTA, Q.AEOPTATI. Variations of this stamp have been found at several other locations in the region: Q AE.O.POR and QAEOPO have been found at La Catria, Q.AEO.P from the vicinity of La Rambla and Acebuchal, Q AE OPCO from El Judío. Examples from Monte Testaccio date to the first half or middle of the second century AD. The individual named in these stamps has been identified as Q. Aelius Optatus.[15]

Several studies have examined the business interests of the Aelii. The family appears both on stamps and *tituli picti* as being engaged in the production of Dr 20 amphorae and the shipping of olive oil. The earliest member of the family to be preserved is M. Aelius Alexander, who appears on Dr 20 amphorae dating to the middle of the first century AD (Chic García 1992, 1-2): an example from Colchester dates between AD 43 and 61 (Callender 1965, 173). As well as examples from Azanaque, stamps of Q. Aelius Optatus have been found near the kilns at La Catria (Lora del Río). The stamp [Q.A]ELI.OPTATI has been found at Augst, where it is dated between AD 50 and 70 (Martin-Kilcher 1987, 96). Q. Aelius Optatus is attested on an inscription from Peñaflor: an inscription found in the Plaza de España was erected in honour of Quintus by his daugher Aelia Optata and his heir C. Appius Superstes Caninius Montanus (*CIL* 2, 2329; Keay *et al.* 2000, 144).[16] José Remesal Rodríguez has noted that the Aelii give only the names of their father and no earlier generations suggesting that they were only second generation Roman citizens (Keay *et al.* 2000, 145).[17]

Stamps of L. Aelius Optatus have been found at Azanaque-Castillejo and El Castillejo (L.AE OP COL). L. Aelius Optatus appears on several *tituli picti* from Monte Testaccio, one of which gives the date of AD 154 where he is associated with other members of the family: L. Aelius Caesianus, L. Aelius Aelianus and L. Aelius Lupatus (*CIL* 15, 3693-4; Blázquez Martínez *et al.* 1992, 76; Chic García 2001, 218; 1992, 4). L. Aelius Lupatus may have worked at Las Valbuenas where the stamps L.AEL and L.AL have been found, and at Casilla de Tarancón (L.A.L) (Chic García 1992, 7; 1994, 86). Stamps reading L.AL.F, L.A.F have also been found at Las Valbuenas and La Catria (Chic García 1992, 7; 1994, 86). These stamps may rather be related to the L. Aelius Fronto who erected a statue to the deified Vespasian at Munigua.[18]

M. Aelius Severus is attested as a merchant on a Dr 20 amphora dating to AD 145 (Blázquez Martínez *et al.* 2003, 37). C. Aelius Fabianus appears as merchant on *tituli* from Monte Testaccio – one of which gives the date of AD 160 (Blázquez Martínez *et al.* 1992, 76). Caius Aelius seems also to have been engaged in the production of Dr 20 amphorae, a stamp reading CAEL … has been found at Monte Testaccio (Blázquez Martínez *et al.* 1992, 150). C. Aelius Vr( ) appears on a stamp found in La Estación de Palma del Río reading SAX. FER. C AEL VR. Caius Aelius Ursus was *duovir* of the Municipio Flavio Aurigitano (Chic García 1992, 9). A *titulus* dating to AD 145 gives the names of two members of the *gens*: AELI TERTI ET [HERME]TIONIS (Blázquez Martínez *et al.* 2003, 38). P.AEL.OPTATI is found on a Dr 20 amphora from Beusichem (Chic García 2001, 383).

The family seems also to have engaged in shipping, not only of olive oil, but also wine. A Dr 20 amphora from Fos-sur-Mer bears a *titulus* with the name […]/OPTATI (Liou 1987, 62). A Dr 20 amphora from Volubilis bears the stamp MAEVALER (Chic García 2001, 10-11; Mayet 1978, 373). Q. Aelius Minicianus appears on a stamp from Nijmegen (Chic García 1992, 11). The family may have been engaged in the trading of wine as well as olive oil: a Dr 2 amphora from the River Tiber in Rome bears a *titulus* of a merchant Q. Aelius(?) Optatus. The amphora carried wine: 'apianum (vinum) Catiniae Postumae' and the *titulus* lists the consul Cilnius Proculus. The date of Proculus' consulship is unknown, though Chic García (2001, 215; 1992, 3; 1994, 100) has noted C. Cilnius Paetinus, who was a proconsul during the reign of Tiberius (*CIL* 6.1376). C. Aelius Avitus, honoured in Seville by the boatmen of Canania, Oducia and Naeva, may also have been engaged in the shipping of olive oil (*CIL* 2.1182; Chic García 1992, 10). Q. Aelius Satullus is also found on a mould mark on an ingot from the Cabrera E wreck dated *c.* 10 BC to AD 25 (Parker 1992, 82).

Aelii are known from several towns along the Guadalquivir, but their connection to the Aelii engaged in trade is unclear. P. Aelius Fabianus is attested as having assisted the *annona municipalis* at Montemayor during the reign of Tiberius (*CIL* 2.1534). C. Aelius Fabianus was *aedile*, *duovir* and *flamen* at Corduba (Beltrán Lloris 1970, 263). L. Aelius Faustinus was *duovir* in Corduba (*CIL* 2.5524; Curchin 1990, 145). M. Aelius Niger was *aedile* in Cabra in AD 75 (*CIL* 2.1610; Curchin 1990, 148).

L. Aelius Optatus is also associated with the D.D. Caeciliorum on a *titulus* from Monte Testaccio. The D.D. Caeciliorum are also attested on a *titulus* from Pompeii (*CIL* 4.9480; Rodríguez Almeida 1979, 883) and from Fos-sur-Mer (Liou 1987, 57). Thevenot has identified these as D. Caecilius Hospitalis and D. Caecilius Maternus who are attested together on seventeen *tituli picti* from Monte Testaccio (Blázquez

Martínez *et al.* 2003, 45). Caecilius Maternus seems to have been active between AD 140 and 160 (*CIL* 15.3765-8; Blázquez Martínez *et al.* 1992, 77). D. Caecilius Hospitalis also appears with a D. Caecilius Onesimus on a *titulus* from Monte Testaccio (Rodríguez Almeida 1979, 923-4). Onesimus also appears with Maternus on two stamps dating to AD 145 (Blázquez Martínez *et al.* 2003, 47). Either combination of Caecilii may be the individuals associated with L. Aelius Optatus. An inscription from Écija records the dedication of a statue to Pietas in the name Caecilia Trophime and her husband Caecilius Silo by her heirs D. Caecilius Hospitalis, Caecilia Materna and Caecilia Philete (*CIL* 2.1471; Chic García 1994, 120). Hopsitalis erected an inscription in Rome on behalf of the 'negotiatores olearii ex Baetica' in honour of M. Petronius Honoratus, the prefect of the annona in AD 144-146 (*CIL* 15.1625b). D. Caecilius Onesimus also appears on a *titulus* from Monte Testaccio with his daughter [Ch]aritosa (Rodríguez Almeida 1979, 923-4). Caecilius Onesimus is recorded on an inscription from Rome as 'viator apparitor Augustorum, diffusor olearius ex Baetica' (Chic García 1994, 121). Several other Caecilii are known from *tituli picti*: D. Caecilius Montanus, D. Caecilius Callyphitus, D. Caecilius Chrysogonus, Caecilius Victor, T. Caecilius, Caecilii Maternus et Trophim( ), QQ. Caeciliorum (Blázquez Martínez *et al.* 2003, 44-53; Rodríguez Almeida 1979, 886-7). Two merchants, Caecilior(um) Evel(pisti) et Dap(hni) operated in AD 153-154 (*CIL* 15.3756-61; Blázquez Martínez *et al.* 1992, 77-8; Rodríguez Almeida 1991, 258-59).

The stamp M.AEM.RVS has been found at El Castillejo. The stamp is perhaps related to the M.A.R produced at La Catria and Azanaque-Castillejo. Callender (1965, 174) dates the stamp between 80 and 130 AD. Martin-Kilcher (1987, 96-8) dates an example from Augst between 90 and 190 AD. J.M. Blázquez Martínez and J. Remesal Rodríguez (2004, 312) date the stamp *c.* AD 145. M. Aemilius Rusticus appears as a *diffusor* on a *titulus pictus* from Monte Testaccio dated AD 149 (Rodríguez Almeida 1979, 885, 914). M. Aemilius Pastor is attested on *tituli picti* dated AD 145 (Blázquez Martínez *et al.* 2003, 38-9). Stamps reading AEMEVP have been found at Rome and may be related to AEVPH and its variants, which have been found in Rome, Néris-les-Bains and Augst. Chic García has suggested that they may be variants of the stamp M.A.EFPM found at La Catria. The stamp may also pertain to the *diffusor* M. Aemilius Euporio attested at Monte Testaccio in AD 147 and 149 (Chic García 1994, 87-8). M. Aemilius Cutianus appears on Dr 20 amphorae from Monte Testaccio dating to AD 146-147 (Rodríguez Almeida 1979, 911-12).

L. CANTP has been found on stamps from Haza del Olivo and La Catria (Remesal Rodríguez 1977, 104). The stamp has also been found at Monte Testaccio where an example is associated with a *titulus* dating to AD 160 (Blázquez Martínez *et al.* 1999, 35). A Caecilius Anteuplus is attested as a *diffusor* at Monte Testaccio. The stamps Q.C.C. and Q.C.C.F have been found at Las Sesenta and may be related to the Q. Caesius Caesianus who was a *diffusor* in AD 149. He may be related to the stamps Q.C.M that may read Q. Caesius Macrinus. A *titulus* gives the names 'QQ. Caesiorum Caesiani et Macrini' (Callender 1965, 226; Chic García 1994, 90). Alternatively the stamp may be related to those of Q.CAL.MARSI that are found at Besançon, Heidenberg, Lyon, Wiesbaden, Windisch and Vienne (Callender 1965, 221).

The stamp Q.F.C. found at Peñaflor may be related to Q. Fulvius Carisianus. Genaro Chic García has linked the stamp with the Q. Fulvius Carisianus who was honoured as patron and *pontifex* at Arva (*CIL* 2.1064). A *titulus* from Monte Testaccio dated to AD 179-180 may refer to the same individual operating as a merchant with Fulvius Rogatus: FULVIORUM II CHARI/SIANORUM ET ROGATI (*CIL* 15.3876; Chic García 1994, 93-4). Q. Fulvius Rogatus may be the individual attested on several stamps from El Castillejo as having produced amphorae at several different *figlinae*: Maed(iana), Riv(ensis), Sals(ensis) and St(atiana) (Chic García 1994, 94; Remesal Rodríguez 1977, 97-8).

QIM and QIMFN have been found at Casilla de Malpica. The latter stamp has been found in the wrecks of Planier 2 and Saint-Gervais 3. The stamp is perhaps related to the merchant Q. Iuventius M[… attested on a *titulus* from L'Anse Saint-Gervais (Liou *et al.* 1978, 117).[19] The FN perhaps denotes the *figlina*. A *titulus* from Monte Testaccio gives the year AD 149 (Chic García 1994, 95-6). The individual named on amphorae is perhaps a relation of C. Iuventius Albinus who was *aedile*, *duovir* and patron of Axati (Lora del Río) (*CIL* 2.1054; Curchin 1990, 139). A *titulus pictus* from Monte Testaccio reads C IVVENTI ALBINI (Blázquez Martínez *et al.* 2003, 76). Stamps of Albinus have been found on the Saint Gervais 3 wreck and Monte Testaccio (Blázquez Martínez *et al.* 2003, 322). The *tituli picti* indicate that the cargo of Dr 20 amphorae originated in the vicinity of Écija between AD 149 and 154 (Parker 1992, 373-4). The stamp C.I.S from La Catria is perhaps that of the merchant C. Iulius Senex attested at Monte Testaccio (Chic García 1994, 96).

Stamps of C Annius Rufinus have been found at Monte Testaccio *c.* AD 145. The stamps originated from Arva, Azanaque-Castillejo. The stamp may be related to those of P. Annius Ruf(us or inus) that were found at La Catria (Blázquez Martínez *et al.* 2003, 311). QV.R is found on Dr 20 amphorae from Augst dated 50-90 AD (Martin-Kilcher 1987, 140). Stephanie Martin-Kilcher has suggested that the stamp is related to the merchant Q. Vrittius Revocatus who appears on both Dr 20 and Haltern 70 (carrying 'defr(utum) excel(lens)') amphorae from the Port-Vendres II wreck (Colls *et al.* 1977, 62, 73-4).[20]

The stamp VIBIOR.. is found at El Judío. The stamp may be related to the mark VIBIO from Augst that dated to the second century AD (Martin-Kilcher 1987, 142). Several Vibii are recorded as merchants: L. Vibius Hermes (*CIL* 15.3668) and L. Vibius Thes(eus?) (*CIL* 15.4768) from the first century AD; L. Vibius Polyanthus (*CIL* 15.4046), Vibius Restitutus (*CIL* 15.3949-59) and Vibius Viator (*CIL* 15.3949-57). Vibius Phaedimus is recorded as a producer of olive oil in a *titulus pictus* dated AD 153 (*CIL* 15.4286; Chic García 1994, 98).

MANNISATVRNI has been found on a Dr 20 vessel from Augst that dates to the Flavian period (Martin-Kilcher 1987, 96; Chic García 1994, 101). M( ) SATVRNI appears on an amphora from Monte Testaccio (Blázquez Martínez *et al.* 2003, 327). P. ATTO on a Dr 20 from Zugmantel. Possibly P. Att(icus?) O – a D. Aticus Onesimus is recorded as a *diffusor* on a *titulus* from the reign of Antoninus Pius (Chic García 1994, 101). The stamp GAVFL has been found at La Catria (Lora del Río). Examples from Monte Testaccio date between AD 140 and 180. An example from Augst dates from *c.* AD 150-190 (Martin-Kilcher 1987, 100; Chic García 1994, 102). The stamp Q. COR. VIC has been found at La María (Chic García 1994, 102). L.F.SEC has been found on a Dr 20 from Fos-sur-Mer, possibly related to L.F.S found at El Berro and POR.L.F.S at La Catria, both in the vicinity of Lora del Río (Chic García 1994, 103). The stamp DOM/DOMS may have originated in the area of Alcolea del Río where an example of the stamp has been found – dated by *tituli picti* to AD 145, 146 and 154 (Chic García 1994, 104; Blázquez Martínez *et al.* 1999, 41-2; Funari 1996, 388).

The stamp Q.A.GEMELLI was produced at El Judío. Examples have also been found at Arva and Adelfa (Carmona). An example from Arles reads Q.ATT(ius)/GEMELL(us) (Chic García 1994, 106-7). L( ) V( ) TROPHIM(i) is found on a Dr 20 from Augst dating between AD 50 and 70 (Martin-Kilcher 1987, 140). Piero Berni Millet (1998, 221) has suggested a date in the Flavian-Trajanic period for the example from Empúries. T. ATILI ASIATICI is found at several sites: Juan Barba, Adelfa, Tostoneras and Guadajoz (Chic García *et al.* 2004, 289). Stamps of Q. Antonius Quietus were widely distributed in the Peninsula as well as in Britain and along the Rhine (Berni Millet 1998, 201). An example from Carlisle dates to the Flaivian period (Funari 1996, 387).

A number of stamps have been found at Cerro de los Pesebres dating to the end of the second century AD and the early years of the third century. The stamps are variants of L( ) F( ) C( ) C( ) V( ) F( ) SCALE( ) (Remesal Rodríguez 1989, 126-9). The final two words give the name of the *figlina* as 'Scale(nsia)' which is named on other stamps from the site (Remesal Rodríguez 1989, 135). The individual named is of senatorial status – 'c(larissimus) v(ir)' – whom Remesal Rodríguez has identified as Lucius Fabius Cilo Septiminus Acilianus Lepidus Fulcinianus, the consul of 204 AD. Cilo may have acquired estates in the region during the Severan confiscations (Remesal Rodríguez 1989, 144).

Variations of the stamp PORT.PAH have been found at Cruz Verde near Brenes. The stamp may be related to the PAH.SCAR found in Rome and PAH SCAL H found at Chester, Rome and Bonn. Callender (1965, 213) has suggested a date at the end of the first or beginning of the second century AD. It has been suggested that this is P(ublius A(elius) H(adrianus) the father of the emperor Hadrian (Chic García 1994, 115-16; 2001, 12).

The stamps II MV.S.ET.P.R. and II MV.S.E.P.R have been found at Casas del Picón.[21] Genaro Chic García (1994, 107) has suggested that the amphora producer is related to the P. Mussidius Sempronianus named on a circular piece of bronze from Algamitas near Seville that was used to seal amphorae. Several related stamps have been found in Rome and the vicinity of Arva: as well as PMS some of the stamps have a fourth letter (PMSC, PMSA, PMZS) that may indicate either a slave or foreman (Callender 1965, 209). The family may also include the C. Mussidius Nepos found on Pascual 1 amphorae. A stamp from Rouen reads III MVSSIDIOR (Callender 1965, 193).

Stamps of the *societas* III ENNI(orum) IVL(iorum) have been found at Monte Testaccio (Blázquez Martínez *et al.* 2003, 316-17). The same *societas* is found on vessels from Britain: London, Corbridge, Holt, Brecon, York, Brecongaer, Richborough, Shorden Brae, Silchester, Wroxeter, Chester and Piddington villa in Northampton. The stamps originated at Huertas del Río that also produced stamps giving the name of the *figlina* as Saenianensis (Funari 1994, 227).

Other *societates* are attested on *tituli picti* from Monte Testaccio. Eleven examples of II Canuleiorum have been found in Rome (Blázquez Martínez *et al.* 2003, 54-8). Two *tituli* record the name 'Claudiorum et [...]' which may be related to the stamps of M. Claudius Senecio (Blázquez Martínez *et al.* 2003, 59-61).

Several stamps refer to *figlinae*. From the middle of the second century AD stamps begin to give the name of the *figlina* or workshop in which the amphorae were produced. FIG(lina) BAR(ba) is found on several *tituli* from Monte Testaccio between AD 146 and 210 (*CIL* 15.2563b; Blázquez Martínez *et al.* 1992, 151; Chic García 2001, 332). The *figlina* may have been based at El Sotillo (Almodóvar del Río) (Chic García 1992, 13). A stamp from Strasbourg reads [C]OLEARIFBARBA (Callender 1965, 80; Chic García 2001, 321). The *figlina* was operated by the Aurelii Heraclae, who may have been freedmen of Marcus Aurelius; a stamp from Rome reads II AVRHERACLE//PATEFILFBAR (Chic García 2001, 304). An example from Augst reads IIAVRHERACLE/PATETFILBAR (Martin-Kilcher 1987, 142). The same *societas* also worked elsewhere: two stamps from El Portillo refer to a figlina Cepar( ): II AVR HERACLAE // PAT ET FIL F CEPAR (Chic García 2001, 135). A Dr 20 amphora from Rome and Angers reads II AVRHERACLE//PATEFILFGRVM, which Genaro Chic García (2001, 161) suggests was the pottery of La María near Lora del Río where Bonsor found a stamp reading FGRVMESE.A//GGG.NNN C.[E]. The same *figlina* appears on stamps of the *societas* COL.SIC.ET.ASI.

A stamp from Monte Testaccio reads FIG(lina) EDOP[P] P( ) AE(li) F(usciani) (*CIL* 15.2604; Blázquez Martínez *et al.* 1992, 153). The same *figlina* also appears on stamps of P( ) M( ) O( ) C(larissimus) V(ir) FIG(lina) EDO(ppiana) (*CIL* 15, 2605; Blázquez Martínez *et al.* 1992, 161).[22] The same individual also appears in connection with a FIG(lina) PALMA (*CIL* 15.2617; Blázquez Martínez *et al.* 1992, 162). Several stamps refer to the *figlina* Virginensia (*CIL* 15, 2627-30; Blázquez Martínez *et al.* 1999, 45; 2003, 332-3). The *figlina* is also associated with a *tria nomina* Q. V( ) C( ) (*CIL* 15, 3213; Blázquez Martínez *et al.* 1999, 45). FIG(lina) MED(iana), associated with Arva by G. Bonsor (Blázquez Martínez *et al.* 1992, 162-3). Several *tituli* from Monte Testaccio refer to the FVN(di) BEL(lucana) (Blázquez Martínez *et al.* 1999, 38). A Dr 20 from the same site bears the *titulus* FVNDI / PERSEIANI (*CIL* 15, 2618; Blázquez Martínez *et al.* 1999, 38). Stamps giving the name F(iglina) SCIMNIANO have been found at Las Delicias, 4 km from Écija (Chic García *et al.* 2004, 293). Genero Chic García (1994, 78) has suggested that these stamps reflect the increasing industrialization of the ceramic industry.

The sheer number of stamps produced at a single workshop is particularly striking and worth briefly outlining here. Multiple stamps have been found at El Castillejo: ...AXOFFRPF, ...MILI//...LISSI, CAMILI//SILVESTRI, MIM, L.V.TRROPHYMI, C.ANNI.RVFINI, M.F.M.F, L AE OPO COL, G. ST, STLACCI, C.STLACC, DEF, DFF, CLM, CLMAF, LGG, CGR..., GRATI, Q.AG, L.ANNI ANNIA, M.F.C, MFF, MFM, M.F.F.M, P.E.B, MEC.N, M.E.E, M.E.EB, M.E.EF, M.E.EVCO, L.VA.GAL, MAEME, M.AEM.RVS, QFR STS, QFA, Q.FVL.N, MEDIANAF, FIG.MEDQFR.MAED, QFRMED, QF.R RIV, RIVE, FRIVESF, SALS, SALSA, SALSE, L.SS.L.STATI, STATI, ST.P, ST.PF, M.P.F, PERSEI, P.C.ICELI, L.P O, L.PAEOA, PNN, PNNSIS, PNS, PNNAR, NIII, NTIN, FBA, MONTANI, CALISTF, ROMVLI, AVINX, ARVA, ARVA PDVIC, LVAPDVIC, CMIM, CMMCP, Q.M.CALLAIDIS, Q.M.CAL, CALLAIDIS, IIIMINICIOR, MHA, CHR, EYEA, ODV and Q.B. (Chic García *et al.* 2004, 283-4; Remesal Rodríguez 2000, 386).[23]

Multiple stamps have been found from El Tejarillo: MPFF, PVELA, MCLSI, M.M, MMCSAE, MMCSM, MMCSV, MMCSVR, MMCSANTOF, MCS, MCSR, MCSP, CMM, CMMACR, DFM, DEF, D.F.F, F.F, LTIGLLGFIVF? or LTIL.FL.FIIV.F?, FALEXAND, PNN, PNNI, PNNF, II C.L.M, II CCLL MM, II

CCL M, LVPATI, EXOF SPCA, QVA…, ..ELIMFFP (Ponsich 1974, 145; Chic García *et al.* 2004, 284-5). A variety of stamps have been found at Villar de Brenes: PORTPAH, PORPA, POR.P.A.H, PORPAHS, QVC VIR, LFFV, CFSCVFM, CVFC, HERMES, HERMESF, IS HERMF, MILONF, IS MILOF, CAL, CALLISIVS, IS CAL, IS CALLIF, ROMVLVSF, ROMVLF, AVGVSTALF, PQNL, ONE (Chic García *et al.* 2004, 286). Several marks have been recovered from Villar Tesoro on the banks of the Río Corbones: L.G.G., L.M.VE, LQS, F.PAT, LICI.SPEC//FII.P.M, L.SPECVLAE//F.C.P.M, F. ALB. LIC, AFRICANI, LIAFAFRICANI, …VART, GAF, CLMF, LSPBOEQ (Chic García *et al.* 2004, 288).

The following stamps have been found at Las Delicias: LAE, FIGLI, FIGV, CI.CP, C.I.C.P, CEHE, EPHIME, P.S.AVITI, SED.AVITI, P.S.TVSC, P.S.MA, P.S.MAV?, MAR, MEC, GERMA, ROMANI, S.V.M, L.V.IVCV, VIVCVN, IVCVNDI, M.IVC, M.S.IVCV, SYRLI, CAD, ADE, PAIC, ITALI, FELICIS, PROTAE, EROTICIANI, F.SCIM//NIANO, FSCIM..NIANI, L.I.SILVESTRI, SILVESTRI, L.IVNI//MELISSI, II MELISS, II IVN.MELISSI // ET MELISSE, L.IVNI.MELISSI//ET MELISSE, CAMILI SILVESTRI, II CAMILI//MELISSI, LFC.CO (Chic García *et al.* 2004, 293). The following stamps have been found at Alcotrista: P.S.AVIT, P.S.TVSC, CASSI, GAQVIE, ..C.QVIE, .AQVIE, L.AVR.GER, L.AV.GE.BC, L.AV.GER, L.A.C.S LACONF, LA.G.POF, FVSO, M.P.S, M.F.S, CIVENALBEP, MI.C.L, CLLVVASECA, LL.SVA.CE, LFCA.BAB, …LBAB, LFFCA.GAL, LFCA.FID, LFCNFID, LFCAATE, LFCARES, CA.RES, [F]LFBcOLL, FABI, LFC, L.F.C, LFCS, LFC.CN, LCCO, CORBEL, LFCCOLL, FCCO, COL, COLO, LAA, EVCOH, QL.FC, DFCZS, FIG.CEP, RN.FS, PN.FS (Chic García *et al.* 2004, 293).

A wide variety of stamps have been found on Dr 20 amphorae from La Catria: SISEN, EXPEDITI, Q.ANT SAB, POR CIR, BROCODV, L.F.O, POR.LF.S, Q.S.R.P, SEX.I.RV.P, SEX RV P, P ANNIRVF, PANRVF, PNRVF, PANIR, PANRP, RVFIPO, CHRYSAN[TI], CHRYS, L.V.THROPHIMI, LAP.AE, LAR, POR LAR, POR LARC, (PO)RLARV, APCP, PORCPR, PORCSS, POR SS, POR PS, POR P.S.A, POR. P.S.I, PORPSV, [PO]RSEDATI, PPQVLPLI, M.A.R, POR MVN, PQHEHE, POR. QHE.HE, PM.H.POR, P.M.H., P.M.HER, L.SEVILILVPI, L.S.L.P, L.SER.ALB, L.SER.NAEBANI, IIQAEET, Q.AE.O.POR, QAEOPO, AEM OPT PO, M…OPSVR, CR.ROP, CRFAL, PQ FL FL, MMRCI, MMRP, MMPOR, MMRO, SEXN…, SNARP, SNR, SNRP, N.RVFI P, RV.SR, AELFO, L.AL.F, SAL.ALFO, ALFO, POALF, POR ODV, C.E.F.P, CEFPOR, CEFPL, C.E.F.PORTI, CEFH.R, EFDS, LCANTP, Q.C.M, P.Q.A.F, L.A.F, MAMPOR, M.A.EFPM, LCM, GAVFL, M.I.M, C.I.S, L.I.T, LAEPAE, P.Q.S.B, POR.QSB, L.Q.S.P, PM.PP.R, Q.M.S, POR MS, MS PO, MSP, ACIRC, PARVA, FANO, PORTO, POR.PV, POVLI, CAS, LCHE, LVCVMC…, VMFC, V.CLE, CLPV, QVINTP, II QQ.ET CF, II QQ. ET CFS, CQFP, F.P.POR, QQLL, Q.F.F, PPAA, PLAC, CPC, POR QPA, CEN HISPSA, III ENNI IVL, PORENSA, SALS, CRA, ATITAC, MAT DF MAR//SIANESSE (Chic García *et al.* 2004, 299).

Dr 20 amphorae are important also for their *tituli*. Heinrich Dressel's analysis of *tituli picti* dating to the second century AD identified five components classified in Greek: Α, Β, Γ, Δ, Ε: Α painted on the neck gives the weight of the amphora. Β on the shoulder gives the name of the merchant or shipper, the *navicularii*, *negotiatores*, *mercatores* or *diffusores olearii* – sometimes the same individual. Evan Haley (2003,

89) has suggested that these individuals were *honesti viri* of non-decurial status: either from the reign of Trajan or Hadrian *negotiatores* and *navicularii* received exemption from *munera publica* – an exemption for which *decuriones* would have been ineligible. Γ on the lower part of the shoulder records the weight of the oil. Δ is more problematic and does not appear on all of the *tituli*; it includes the name of an agent operating on behalf of the buyer, the name of the proprietor or tenant of the oil producing estate, or the name of the product derived from the name of the estate. It is significant to note that none of the names found on *tituli* have yet been found on the potters' stamps (Chic García 1994, 81). The *titulus* may also include a number (perhaps the number of amphorae from a particular estate) and the name of the individual who weighed the amphora and its contents as well as the location at which this inspection took place and the consular date. E is not found on all *tituli* and may be a control number (Haley 2003, 87-8; Remesal Rodríguez 1998, 191-2; Rodríguez Almeida 1989, 26-30).

The principal source for these *tituli picti* is the amphora dump at Monte Testaccio where numerous merchants are found: T. Gesatius Hermes (Blázquez Martínez *et al.* 2003, 71-3). II IVLIORVUM, IVLI DOM[...](Blázquez Martínez *et al.* 2003, 73-5). QQ Laberiorum Zosimi et [...], [QQ LABE]RIORVM [... ET] PR[O]TOGENIS (Blázquez Martínez *et al.* 2003, 77-8). [II LICINIORVM] CAMPINI ET MATERN(I). Both individuals are also attested separately: C. Licinius Campinus on five *tituli* and M. Licinius Maternus on two *tituli*. Campini et filiorum, together with another member of the family Licinius Cerdonis (Blázquez Martínez *et al.* 2003, 79-83). C.? Crassius Phoenicus is attested on several *tituli* from Monte Testaccio. C. Crassius Latinus is known from *tituli* in Rome (Blázquez Martínez *et al.* 2003, 61-4) and a *titulus* from Fos-sur-Mer reads C CRASSI (Liou 1987, 62).

L. Marius Phoebus is named both individually and on a *titulus* dated to AD 153 with Vibius Viator and Vibius Restitutus (Blázquez Martínez *et al.* 2003, 83). L. Memmius Beryllus (Blázquez Martínez *et al.* 2003, 84-7), also the *societas* Memmiorum et Mu.. (Blázquez Martínez *et al.* 2003, 307). L. Pacuilius Felicio (Blázquez Martínez *et al.* 2003, 89). L. Segolatius Iustus (Blázquez Martínez *et al.* 2003, 90-2) L Segolatius Encolpus is known from a *titulus* with Q. Cornelius Homulus dating between AD 153 and 161, and there is a *societas* of the II Segolatiorum ef F(iliorum) (Blázquez Martínez *et al.* 2003, 307). Sempronius Epagathonis, also found with Ant(oniae) Agathonices (Blázquez Martínez *et al.* 2003, 93-4). M. Servilius Fabianus (Blázquez Martínez *et al.* 2003, 94). C. Sextii Iul[...](Blázquez Martínez *et al.* 2003, 95). Q. Sulpicius Optatus (Blázquez Martínez *et al.* 2003, 95-6). M. Titius Paullinus and P. Magius Maternus (Blázquez Martínez *et al.* 2003, 97). C VIN(ISI) AELI AELIANI [ET] OCRATI MODESTI – T. Ocratius Modestus is already known from Monte Testaccio (Blázquez Martínez *et al.* 2003, 104). C. Vin[...] (Blázquez Martínez *et al.* 2003, 104-5). II Septuminorum (Blázquez Martínez *et al.* 2003, 108-10).

Several members of the Fadii are known from *tituli*: L. Fadius Cilo, Secundus, Anicetus, Paonius and Antiochus, as well as a *societas* FADIORVM or II FADIORVM (Blázquez Martínez *et al.* 2003, 66-70). M FABI FLACCINI and FABI NIPH[...]IS (Blázquez Martínez *et al.* 2003, 64-5).

Several Valerii are known: C. Valerius Alexander, *c.* AD 149 (Blázquez Martínez *et al.* 2003, 98-9) (exported oil from Écija, Corduba, Seville). Q. Valerius Hermetionis (17 examples), may be related to the *societas* of QQ. Valerior(um) Galli et Nigri

(Blázquez Martínez *et al.* 2003, 100-1). C. Valerius Silvanus (Blázquez Martínez *et al.* 2003, 101-2). C. Valerius Paternus and C. Valerius Valerianus are attested on *tituli* from AD 151 and 154. Both Paternus and Valerianus are also found individually (Blázquez Martínez *et al.* 2003, 308). M. Valerius Valens (Blázquez Martínez *et al.* 2003, 102-3) is attested on a number of *tituli picti* from Monte Testaccio together with the stamp DATSCOL. A *titulus* from Barcelona reads M? [VALERI VA]LENTIS (Berni Millet 1998, 231). An inscription from Seville records the dedication of a statue to Minerva by Valeria Qu[.., the daughter of Valerius Valens, in honour of the producers of olive oil (Blázquez Martínez *et al.* 2003, 308 n. 165; Blázquez Martínez 2007, 183).

The scale of operations at El Castillejo (three kilns), El Tejarillo (five kilns), Casilla de Taracón (three kilns), Huertas del Río (two kilns), La Mallena (two kilns) is striking. The pottery at La Catria extends over an area of 20 ha. In addition, the existence of multiple unexcavated kilns is reported at several other sites, for example at Madre Vieja I and II, Manuel Nieto, La María. The proximity of the different groups of kilns is also notable. The kilns at El Merino were probably part of a larger string of sites including Castillo de Azanaque, El Judío and La Catria (Romo Salas *et al.* 2000, 415). The kilns are located away from villas in the immediate vicinity of the Ríos Guadalquivir and Genil that will have enabled the easy shipment of amphorae. The lack of villas in the vicinity together with the abundance of stamps suggests that they were not part of the activities of a wider estate. Instead they seem to have been engaged in the specialized production of Dr 20 amphorae to supply the needs of the *annona* and the city of Rome.

This specialization is evident from the amphora stamps also. Not only are multiple stamps found at individual pottery workshops, but the same individuals are found at multiple locations, for example M.A.R. at La Catria and Azanaque-Castillejo, Q.A.GEMELLI at El Judío, Arva and Adelfa, L.CANTP from Haza del Olivo and La Catria, Q. Aelius Optatus from Azanaque, La Catria, El Judío and the vicinity of La Rambla and Acebuchal.

The individuals named on stamps reflect a variety of different social backgrounds. Several stamps give the names of senators: L. Fabius Cilo, P. Aelius Hadrianus and the P( ) M( ) O( ) named on stamps from *figlina* Edoppiana and *figlina* Palma. Members of the local elite are also attested: C. Iuventius Albinus, Q. Fulvius Carisianus, Q. Aelius Optatus is named on an inscription from Peñaflor, and D. Caecilius Hospitalis erected a statue to Pietas at Écija. Enrique Melchor Gil (1993-4, 335-6) has argued that the profits from oleiculture were channelled by the municipal elites into the urban centres. P. Aelius Fabianus was honoured for assisting the *annona municipalis* of Montemayor, and C. Aelius Avitus was honoured by the river boatmen of Canania, Oducia and Naeva.

Several individuals named in stamps seem also to have been engaged in the transport of olive oil: M. Aemilius Euporio, Q. Aelius Optatus, L. Aelius Optatus, Q. Caesius Caesianus, C. Iulius Senex. Single *nomina* also appear, several of which indicate that they are the names of the potters themselves: Hermes f(ecit), Milo f(ecit), Romulus f(ecit), Calli f(ecit). Workshops produced amphorae for multiple individuals: the *figlina* Palma produced for both P. M. O. and Q. V. C., the Aurelii Heraclae at both the *figlina* Barba, the *figlina* Cepar( ) and the *figlina* Grumese.

Several sites associated with the processing of olive oil have been discovered in

Málaga and Almería. A press has been excavated at the villa of Manguarra and San José (Cartama). Rescue excavations have revealed a villa at Las Viñas (Cuevas del Becerro) beside the Arroyo de las Cuevas. A basin lined with *opus signinum* with a capacity of 10,000 litres has been found adjoining a storage area of *dolia*. Spectographic analysis of three of the *dolia* has shown that they contained olive oil. The site was occupied from the reign of Claudius or Nero until the early fourth century AD (Haley 2003, 58).[24]

Part of a possible oil press has been found at Huerta del Rincón (Baldomera *et al.* 1997, 153). A possible villa was discovered in 1987 at Cortijo Lapuente beside the embalse del Cubillas (Albolote, Granada). Although the site has been the subject of only limited excavations, two basins lined with *opus signinum* have been uncovered. The basins are associated with pottery dating from the end of the first/beginning of the second century to the third century AD when the basins may have been constructed (Raya de Cárdenas *et al.* 1990, 233-5).

Excavations carried out by the German Archaeological Institute in the area of the forum of Munigua (Mulva) have uncovered an oilery and screw press in House number II. The oilery was constructed at the beginning of the second half of the first century and remained in use until the end of the third century AD. The site is particularly interesting in view of the lack of Dr 20 amphorae, instead the oil may have been sold directly from the shops (3, 11 and 12) that form part of the same *insula*. For longer distances barrels may have been used (Teichner 2000, 1344-6).

Several kilns produced Dr 20 amphorae: possibly at Calle Carretería (Málaga); at Huerta del Rincón (Baldomero *et al.* 1997, 153); at Manganeto (Almayate) (Arteaga 1985, 183); El Ejido (Almería) – where the percentage of Dr 20 amphorae is strikingly high, implying an important role in the shipment of olive oil; and at Loma de Cabriles (Baldomero *et al.* 1997, 155). Bartolomé Mora Serrano and Pilar Corrales Aguilar (1997, 32-3) have suggested that local production of olive oil was insufficient to justify the production of Dr 20 amphorae and that the kilns may have supplied estates further inland in the vicinity of Antequera.

Dr 20 amphorae may also have been produced around the Bay of Algeciras. Two oval kilns have been excavated at Los Matagallares to the northwest of the town of Salobreña at the mouth of the Río Guadalfeo. The kilns date to the third century AD and produced primarily fish sauce amphorae: Beltrán IIB, Dr 14, Almagro 51c, Beltrán 72, Keay XVI, XIX and XLI. Limited quantities of Dr 20 amphorae were also produced as well as a variety of wine vessels: imitations of Gauloise 4 amphorae, Dr 30 and local Matagallares I, Majuelo II and Baelo I vessels (Bernal Casasola *et al.* 1998, 1309-10).

BCMATERNI/SAGYNTO has been found on a Dr 20 from Empúries dating to the third century AD. The stamp may be related to the BCMERITIS/SAGYNTO from El Puig and the BC stamps found on Dr 2-4 amphorae from Sagunto (Aranegui Gasco 1981, 531; Berni Millet 1998, 204).

The production of fish sauce

As well as the production of olive oil, the production of fish sauces seems to have expanded at this time. All the 22 fish factories dating to the first century BC studied by Lazaro Lagóstena Barrios in the vicinity of Cádiz continued to operate into the first century AD and nine continued until the beginning of the second century (Lagóstena

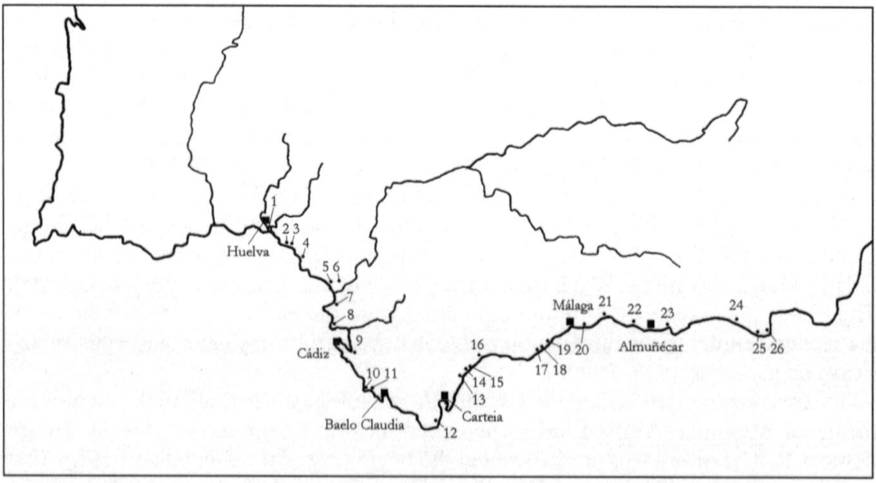

Map 6. Fish salteries in Baetica.

1. El Eucaliptal
2. Torre del Oro
3. Las Naves
4. Cerro del Trigo
5. Algaida
6. Fuenterrabia
7. Rota
8. Las Redes
9. Gallineras
10. Trafalgar
11. Barbate
12. Algeciras
13. Castillo de la Duquesa
14. Villa Sabinillas
15. Arroyo Vaquero
16. Las Bóvedas
17. Finca el Secretario
18. Torreblanca del Sol
19. Benálmadena
20. Loma de Benagalbón
21. Cerro del Mar
22. Torrox
23. Salobreña
24. Adra
25. Guardias Viejas
26. Roquetas de Mar

Barrios 2001, 104). In addition, several factories date to the first century AD. The factory excavated between Calles Ferrocarril and Brunete was in use during the first century AD: fragments of Dr 7-11 amphorae and *terra sigillata hispanica* were found in the fill of vat 4 (Perdigones Moreno *et al.* 1989, 93). Two salting vats have been excavated on Avenida Fernández Ladreda (Lagóstena Barrios 2001, 108). A salting vat has been discovered on Avenida de Andalucía dating to the first century AD (Lagóstena Barrios 2001, 110). Excavations carried out in 1986 on Calle García Quijano (Cádiz) uncovered a small factory. The factory consists of two rectangular tanks lined with *opus signinum* and a well – the excavators have described it as a small family-run installation (Perdigones Moreno *et al.* 1987, 47-8).

As well as the factories in Cádiz, several sites have been identified extending along the coasts of southern Spain. Several fisheries have been discovered in the vicinity of Huelva: a factory dated to the middle of the first century AD has been excavated on Calle Palos (Lagóstena Barrios 2001, 95). A fishery has been excavated extending along the beach at El Eucaliptal (Puente Umbría) at the mouth of the Río Odiel. The most intense occupation dates from the second and third centuries AD although the factory may have been established during the preceding century. A villa may be located in the vicinity thanks to the presence of mosaics and architectural remains. A kiln producing Beltrán I and Beltrán II amphorae has been discovered at La Canaleta (Lagóstena Barrios 2001, 96).[25]

Fig. 15. Factory IV, Baelo Claudia.

In 1977 two fish factories were discovered at Cabo de Trafalgar. The first is partially destroyed by erosion. To the south there are two basins adjoining a room paved with *opus signinum*. A larger basin to the north is only partially excavated. The second factory lies 600 m to the north. A single room has been excavated, subsequently identified as a *columbarium* (Amores Carredano 1978, 441-3; Lagóstena Barrios 2001, 120-1). The finds are primarily of the first century AD and the complex seems to have been constructed during the Augustan period (Amores Carredano 1978, 451). A kiln producing Dr 7-11 amphorae has been found nearby at Huerta de Luis Santos (Lagóstena Barrios 2001, 121).

The fisheries located at Baelo Claudia have attracted considerable scholarly attention. Excavations conducted by Pierre Paris between 1917 and 1921 explored the southern area of the town, where six groups of vats have been excavated. Factory I was a single room structure, 85 m^2 in size, situated to the east of the Street of Columns (cardo 4). The preparation area opens out to the street with six salting vats to the rear. Factory IV consists of a preparation area containing two cisterns used to hold water for the washing and preparation of the fish and seven salting vats. Two large factories (V and VI) adjoin the cardo to the west. Factory V is accessed through room 3 where the fish was washed and dissected. The main preparation room (room 4) lies to the east and covers an area of over 100 m^2 with nine salting vats along the south and east sides of the room. Factory VI lies to the immediate north and is the largest of the factories, covering 250 m^2. The preparation area (room 5) is surrounded on the north, east and south sides by salting vats: six vats have been excavated in the northeast corner with four circular vats in the southeast corner (Sillières 1995, 180-5). Tunny bones were found in the base of one of the vats (Martin Bueno *et al.* 1984, 492).

Michel Ponsich (1988, 198) has suggested that the larger circular vats were used for the salting of larger animals such as whales.

A smaller saltery has been found to the west of the *macellum* on the Decumanus Maximus. The factory was excavated by J-N. Bonneville in 1979. The factory covers an area of 230 m^2 with areas devoted to the preparation of the salted fish and eight salting vats. The fish were prepared in rooms I and II. As well as two small basins, this room also contained a millstone used in preparing the salt and brine. The fish would then be placed in the vats in rooms IX and X for salting. The rooms to the west of the factory may have been shops for the sale of the fish sauce. The factory was constructed during the reigns of Claudius and Nero (Dardaine *et al.* 1980, 386-91; Arévalo González *et al.* 2007, 77-8). In 1983 a small salting vat was discovered to the west of the *macellum* and dated to the reign of Nero (Arévalo González *et al.* 2007, 79).

Several fisheries have been discovered around the Bay of Algeciras. Recent excavations have uncovered a fish factory on Calle San Nicolás.[26] Two installations have been excavated. The first (Conjunto Industrial I) consists of at least 30 vats arranged around a courtyard paved with *opus signinum*. The factory seems to have undergone several modifications during the course of its operation from the first century to the beginning of the sixth century AD. The second factory (Conjunto Industrial II) lies to the west of the first and although only partially excavated consists of fifteen vats with an area for the preparation of the fish. A possible portico has been discovered to the north of factory I fronting on to the street (Bernal Casasola *et al.* 2003, 168-72).

A fish factory has been excavated at La Algaida in Sanlúcar de Barrameda. The factory is organized around a central courtyard with two vats as well as fishing

Fig. 16. Salting vats, Carteia.

implements and fish remains. The factory operated during the first century AD and was abandoned at the beginning of the following century (Lagóstena Barrios 2001, 114).

In his description of the marine resources of the Straits of Gibraltar, Strabo (3.2.8) praises the size of the shellfish and cuttle-fish from Carteia. Pliny recounts a tale of a giant octopus that would consume the fish in the salting vats (*Natural History* 9, 48). In his description of fish sauces Pliny refers to the processing of mackerel in the fisheries at Carteia (*Natural History* 31, 43). The importance of marine resources to the economy of the town is reflected in the appearance of fish, boats and fishermen on the coinage of the town from 130 BC (Roldán Gómez *et al.* 1998, 41; 2006, 29). Excavations conducted under the auspices of the William L. Bryant Foundation in the 1960s uncovered remains of a fish factory in the vicinity of the harbour and the Río Guadarranque to the west of the town (Trench 1). Two basins were excavated in sector 1 that appear to be associated with pottery from the first to the fourth or fifth centuries AD (Woods *et al.* 1967, 11). Lourdes Roldán Gómez and others (Roldán Gómez *et al.* 2006, 451) have recently suggested that the factory dates to the fourth century AD. Remains of an earlier salting vat dating to the first century AD were found in sector 3, another vat in sector 5 and four vats in sector 9 (Woods *et al.* 1967, 16, 22-4; Roldán Gómez *et al.* 2006, 451-2).

A bath complex and villa have been partially excavated at Torreblanca del Sol. Three phases of occupation have been identified, ranging from the first to the seventh centuries AD. The first phase consists of a small bath complex and an unexcavated villa. In the middle of the third century the baths were remodelled to function as a small fish saltery. The factory continued to function perhaps until the sixth century AD, after which the area was used as a necropolis (Puertas Tricas 1986, 145-8). Several fish salting vats have been found together with Beltrán IIa and b amphorae. The fishery may also have produced purple dye as the shell of a *Murex brandaris* has been found on the site (Puertas Tricas 1991, 210).

Excavations at Castillo de la Duquesa on the coast at Manilva have revealed a wealthy villa associated with an extensive fish salting installation dating from the first to the fourth centuries AD. Basins lined with *opus signinum* are arranged on two sides of a courtyard used for the preparation of the fish prior to salting. Abundant *garum* amphorae as well as fishing implements have also been found, and the complex seems to have been at its most active during the first and second centuries AD (Mora Serrano *et al.* 1997, 38). The amphorae may have been supplied by kilns at Barbesula a short distance to the west at the mouth of the Río Guadiaro (Mora Serrano *et al.* 1997, 40; Ponsich 1988, 184).

Three fisheries have been discovered in the vicinity of Benálmadena. In 2002 a fishery was discovered at Los Molinillos on Calle García Lorca. Subsequent excavations in 2005 uncovered baths and a villa decorated with pavements of *opus tesselatum* dating from the first to the fifth century AD. Several basins lined with *opus signinum* have been found together with the base of an oil press. To the east the remains of a kiln were found dating to the third and fourth centuries AD (Pineda *et al.* 2007, 442-6). Campanian C, Dr 1C, Beltrán I or VI, Dr 20 and Beltrán IV/Dr14 amphorae have been found.

Remains of a villa decorated with polichrome mosaics have been found in the cove at Torremuelle (Benálmadena) (Rodríguez Oliva 1982, 9-12; Mora Serrano *et al.* 1997, 41). The villa seems to have been devoted to the production of salted fish: a line of nineteen salting vats has been found aligned north-south with a small building adjoining tank 19. The tanks are lined with *opus signinum* and are uniform in size (2 x 1.8 m in area and 2 m deep) except for tank 10, which is 3.53 m long. Traces of fish sauce were found in tank 12. Beltrán IIa and B, Dr 14/Beltrán IVa and b, Dr 17/Beltrán VI and Dr 18 amphorae have been found (Pineda *et al.* 2007, 440-1) with dates ranging from the first to the fourth century AD (Rodríguez Oliva 1982, 14-19).[27]

The existence of ancient occupation in the vicinity of the Arroyo de la Miel in Benálmadena was first reported in 1903, located 530 m to the west of the fishery of Los Molinillos. Further excavations prompted by the planting of palm trees on the junction of the Carretera Nacional N340 and the Avenida Las Palmeras revealed the remains of a wealthy villa. The villa dates from the end of the first century BC/beginning of the first century AD to the fourth century AD (Rodríguez Oliva 1982, 21-8; Pineda *et al.* 2007, 446-9). Several salting vats lined with *opus signinum* have been excavated together with Dr 7-11, Beltrán IIb, Dr 12, Dr 14, Dr 20 and Dr 17 amphorae (Pineda *et al.* 2007, 449).

As well as increasing evidence for fish sauce production, there is also evidence for the production of fish sauce amphorae. Several kilns have been located in the environs of Cádiz: on the site of Factoría Campsa, at Guadarranque, on the Calle Aurora and at Villa Victoria. A kiln producing Dr 2-4 and Dr 7-11 vessels was discovered at Guadarranque in 1973 (Bernal Casasola *et al.* 2004, 471; Beltrán Lloris 1977, 112-17). A circular kiln approximately 4.5 m in diameter has been excavated at Villa Victoria (Puente Mayorga).[28] The kiln principally produced Dr 7-11, Beltrán IIA and Dr 14 *garum* amphorae as well as lesser quantities of Haltern 70 and Dr 2-4 wine amphorae. Similar forms have been found in Carteia and at Venta del Carmen. Two ceramic dumps have also been excavated together with warehouses for the preparation of the vessels and a number of cremation burials. Fragments of stucco and *opus signinum* have been found in trench 9. Two phases of operation have been identified dated to the end of the first century BC and the second third of the first century AD. The site was abandoned at the end of the first century or beginning of the second century AD (Bernal Casasola *et al.* 2004, 463-71; Roldán Gómez *et al.* 2006, 83-4).

The kilns at Venta del Carmen continued to function until the third quarter of the first century AD when kiln H.101 was demolished and re-used as a lime kiln (Ca. 101) and kiln H.102 was remodelled and perhaps used as a ceramic dump (Bernal Casasola *et al.* 1998, 84-5, 99). Excavations carried out between 1987 and 1989 in the Castillo de la Duquesa in Manilva uncovered remains of a fishery dated between the second century and the fourth century AD together with a residential area, baths and necropolis. One of the vats excavated in 1987 contained *Murex* and purple dye (Villaseca Díaz 1991, 365-9). The final phase of the settlement of El Torreón situated at the mouth of the Río Guadalmansa was devoted to the production of salted fish (Lagóstena Barrios 2001, 138).

Several fisheries have been discovered in the vicinity of Fuengirola. Four vats lined with *opus signinum* have been discovered near the base of the hill upon which the castle now stands (Corrales Aguilar 2001, 348). The site of Finca del Secretario was the subject of rescue excavations in 1991 that revealed a complex of baths, kilns, a fishery and storehouses. A total of five kilns have been excavated: three circular with a central pillar, as well as a smaller kiln. The fifth kiln has not been excavated. The kilns primarily produced amphorae: Dr 30, Keay XXV and vessels similar to Dr 7-11,

Fig. 17. Salting vats, Fuengirola.

Dr 12, Dr 14 and Beltrán IIa (Villaseca Díaz 1997, 261-3). The fish saltery consists of two rooms with eight salting vats. The complex has been dated from the first century AD to the middle of the fourth century AD (Lagóstena Barrios 2001, 142-3; Corrales Aguilar 2001, 349-50). The kilns at Finca del Secretario were located adjoining a fish factory and may also have supplied the fisheries at Torreblanca del Sol, Torremuelle and Benálmadena-Costa.

In 1990 excavations at Huerta del Rincón besides the beach of Carihuela (Torremolinos) revealed a ceramic workshop. Two phases of occupation have been identified dating to the first and second centuries AD and the end of the third century to the fifth century AD. The first phase consisted of a ceramic kiln containing Beltrán IIa and b amphorae, as well as a large rectangular cistern and storage building. In the second half of the first century the workshop was remodelled with the construction of two circular kilns.[29] After a period of abandonment, occupation resumed at the end of the third century and continued until the beginning of the fifth century AD. Beltrán IIa, IIb, Dr 14, 17, 28 and Dr 20 amphorae have been found as well as late imperial forms: Almagro 51a/b, 51c, Dr 23 and Keay XXV (Baldomero *et al.* 1997, 148-60; Lagóstena Barrios 2001, 144-6).

The following stamps have been found at Huerta del Rincón: L(palmeta?)N on a Beltrán IIB and a II/III?; LIC.NIM on an amphora of uncertain type; CLICM on a Beltrán V and CLM on an amphora of uncertain type. L(palmeta?)N is also found on oil amphorae from two *figlinae* in the Guadalquivir valley – perhaps indicating that the same family had business interests in both areas (Baldomero *et al.* 1997, 153-4).

The kilns could have supplied several fisheries that have been found in the vicinity of Torremolinos: sixteen vats have been discovered at Finca el Pilar in the vicinity of

Los Álamos to the northwest of Campamento Benítez; a fish factory is located on the beach at Torremolinos (Gozalbes Cravioto 1986, 313). Excavations carried out in the nineteenth century uncovered a small bath complex decorated with mosaics and adjoining fish vats at San Julián (Mora Serrano *et al.* 1997, 34 n. 18). Kilns have also been discovered at Guadalhorce and Colmenar (producing Beltrán I and II B vessels).

Strabo (3.4.2; 3.1.8) singles out the fish sauces from Almuñécar, Málaga and Cádiz as being particularly good. An inscription from Ostia records a Corpus Negotiantium Malacitanorum whose *quinquennalis*, P. Clodius Athenio, was a fish-sauce merchant (*CIL* 6.9677). Several fisheries have been located in the vicinity of the town: 70 vats from the southern slopes of the hill upon which the Alcazaba is located were published at the beginning of the nineteenth century (Lagóstena Barrios 2001, 147). Late imperial salting vats have been found on Calles Cerrojo, Cañón, Especerías, Sancha de Lara, Afligidos, José Denis Belgrano, and in the gardens of the Iglesia del Sagrario; quantities of amphorae have been found in the Episcopal Palace, on Calle Strachan and on Calle Molina Larios (Lagóstena Barrios 2001, 147-50; Beltrán Fortés *et al.* 1997, 123-7).

The existence of Roman remains at Loma de Benagalbón to the east of Málaga was first reported in 1953. Subsequent excavations revealed a villa with a small four-room bath suite dating from the beginning of the second century to the first quarter of the fifth century AD (Salado Escaño 2005, 355, 357-60). The villa seems to have been engaged in the preparation of salted fish with several salting vats lined with *opus signinum* as well as Beltrán I amphorae (Mora Serrano *et al.* 1997, 41; Lagóstena Barrios 2001, 150).[30]

Several kilns producing fish sauce amphorae have been discovered in the area. Two kilns have been excavated on Calle Carretería (nos 101 and 103) dating from the second half of the first century AD to the second century AD. The kilns appear to have primarily produced amphorae: Beltrán IV and IIA and IIB are the most common forms on the site; Beltrán, Dr 20 and Dr 18 are also present (Rambla Torralvo *et al.* 1997, 61-70). The existence of a kiln at Carranque was reported by López Málax-Echeverría (1971). Dr 7-11, Beltrán II and VI and possibly Mañá C2b amphorae were produced here (Beltrán Fortés *et al.* 1997, 109-10). In 1970 a kiln was discovered (and subsequently destroyed) at Haza Honda – although the finds were transferred to the Museo Arqueológico Malagueño where they have been studied by J. Beltrán Fortés and M.L. Loza Azuaga (1997). The site lies 1.5 km to the southwest of the kiln at Carranque and 4 km from Málaga. The site dates to the Augustan and Julio-Claudian periods. Production appears to have consisted of Dr 7-11, 12 and 14 vessels (Beltrán Fortés *et al.* 1997, 112-15).[31]

Several sites associated with the processing of fish sauce have been identified around the mouth of the Río Vélez. Evidence of fishing has been found at several locations in the vicinity of Cerro del Mar. In 1978 salting vats dating to the Augustan period were found on the southwestern slope (Arteaga 1981, 294). In 1982 a pavement constructed from sand, traces of pottery and lime was excavated, dating to the beginning of the second century AD. The excavators have identified it as preparation area for salted fish (Arteaga 1985, 201-2). Abundant Dr 7-11 have been found in a possible storage area. Three of the vessels were found containing fish sauce, including tunny, anchovies, sardines, mackerel and perch (von den Driesch 1980, 151-4).

Kilns have been discovered on the other side of the estuary of the Río Vélez at Toscanos and Manganeto. Three kilns have been excavated at Manganeto (Almayate Bajo) dating from the second half of the first century to the beginning of the second

Fig. 18. Fish saltery, Torrox.

Fig. 19. Kiln B, Torrox.

century AD. Kiln 1 was associated with Dr 14 amphorae, and Dr 2-4, Dr 17, Dr 20 and Beltrán IIb vessels were found in kiln 3 (Arteaga 1985, 182-3).

Excavations conducted between 1912 and 1915 revealed the remains of a villa, bath complex, fish salting vats and a necropolis in the vicinity of the lighthouse at Torrox. The villa was decorated with polichrome and bichrome geometric mosaics. The existence of a kiln was first reported in 1944 when a circular kiln (B) was discovered 50 m from the shore (Rodríguez Oliva 1997, 273-5). An earlier circular kiln (A) with central pillar was discovered in 1987 underlying the later kiln B (Rodríguez Oliva 1997, 284). The presence of Dr 7-11 and Beltrán IIb amphorae dates the operation of the kiln to the first century AD, particularly the first half of the century (Rodríguez Oliva 1997, 277, 290). The fish factory consists of three vats that were later re-used as part of the late imperial necropolis. Besides the vats several buried *dolia* have been found that may have been used for different types of fish sauce. The principal phase of activity dates to the first and second centuries AD (Mora Serrano *et al.* 1997, 38-9). The stamp .../ICL has been found on the neck of an amphora on the site which Pedro Rodríguez Oliva (1997, 291) suggests gives the name of the *figlina*: (cav)icl(um).

In 1945 poorly preserved salting vats were discovered on the Peñón de San Cristóbal (Almuñécar) (Sotomayor 1971, 148). Sotomayor has excavated a substantial fish factory at El Majuelo (Sotomayor 1971). The factory dates at least from the fourth century BC and continued in use until the fifth century AD.

Fig. 20. Fish factory, El Majuelo.

Several sites have been discovered along the coast of Salobreña. Rescue excavations on the Peñón de Salobreña have revealed a fish factory operating perhaps from the Punic period until the fourth century AD. The *pars rustica* and *pars fructuaria* of a villa has been excavated at Loma de Ceres (Molvízar). Two groups of basins lined with *opus signinum* have been found that were used either for the production of wine or salted fish. The first group consists of three linked basins. The second vat contained a large stone (91 x 81 cm) that functioned as a weight for a press perhaps related to the podium to the west. A second pair of smaller vats (112 x 80 cm and 50 x 45 cm) lies to the northwest. These are lined with *opus signinum* with a small concavity in the base to facilitate cleaning. The design of these vats is strikingly similar to those of fish salteries and has led the excavators to suggest that the two groups served different functions: the first for wine making, the second for fish salting. A storage area containing wine and fish sauce amphorae as well as *dolia* has also been found to the north of the site (Gener *et al.* 1993, 97577).[32]

The villa seems also to have been engaged in the production of pottery: quantities of ceramic waste have been found, including coarse wares and amphorae: Dr 2-4, Dr 7-11, Beltrán IIa and IIb, Dr 14, Dr 18 and Dr 30 amphorae (Gener Basallote *et al.* 1993, 980-1; Lagóstena Barrios 2001, 155; Baldomero *et al.* 1997, 154). To the west of the site a basin constructed out of *tegulae* has been found that seems to have been used to prepare the clay. Several other kilns have been discovered: kilns dating from the third century AD onwards at Los Matagallares, Los Barreros and at Calahonda (Lagóstena Barrios 2001, 156; Bernal Casasola *et al.* 1998, 1309-10).

A factory has been excavated adjoining the hermitage of San Sebastián at the base of the western slope of the Cerro de Montecristo upon which the town of Adra is located. Eleven vats have been uncovered dating from the end of the first century BC to the middle of the second century AD. A second phase of operation dates from the end of the third century to the second half of the fifth century AD (López Medina 1996, 134; Lagóstena Barrios 2001, 158-60). A salting vat found on the southern slope (A) contains two Vegas 3 vessels that are found in Augustan levels at Oberaden. One of the vessels contained remains of fish sauce (Suárez Marquez *et al.* 1987, 19). To the east a factory has been discovered at Guardias Viejas (Ciavieja). Several vats have been located dating to the second and third centuries AD together with *Murex* and *Purpura haemastoma* (Lagóstena Barrios 2001, 163).

Several fisheries have been located along the coast of Almería. A substantial factory has been discovered at Roquetas de Mar. Although unexcavated sixteen vats are visible. The pottery recovered from site dates from the first to the fourth centuries AD and is most numerous between *c.* AD 150 and 250 (Lagóstena Barrios 2001, 164). Rescue excavations have uncovered a factory on Calle Reina in Almería itself. The factory consists of a square building, 36 m^2 in size containing six vats. Pottery has been found from the first to the fifth centuries AD but is most numerous from the end of the first century AD or beginning of the second century until the beginning of the third century AD (Suárez Marquez 1987, 25-7). A fishery dating to the second and third centuries AD has been discovered at Torre García, 15 km east of Almería. The abundance of *Murex brandaris*, *Murex trunculus* and *Purpura haemastoma* suggests that the vats produced purple dye (Martínez Maganto 1994, 211).

Continuing along the coast to the east of Almería, the evidence for fishing installations is scanty although a number of sites have been dated to the late Imperial

Fig. 21. Habitación A, Punta de l'Arenal.

Fig. 22. Free-standing salting vat, Punta de l'Arenal.

period when several sites seem to have operated in the vicinity of Aguilas where a kiln produced fish sauce amphorae (Ramallo Asensio 1985, 436). Several late Imperial fisheries have been discovered in the vicinity of Puerto de Mazarrón: at Rihuete and on Calle Progreso and at Edificio Aquamar in Mazarrón itself (Lagóstena Barrios 2001, 171-2). Six vats have been discovered at El Alamillo associated with a possible villa dating to the early imperial period (Martín Camino *et al.* 1991, 278).

Several fisheries have been located along the Mediterranean from the province of Valencia as far north as Cataluña.[33] The best known of these was excavated by Gabriella Martín in 1963 at Punta de l'Arenal (Xabía). Unfortunately the fragmentary nature of the remains means that an understanding of their function is problematic. Habitación A consists of pavement of rough stone and lime (8 x 7 m) surrounded by a channel 30 cm wide. The structure probably served as a preparation platform for the cleaning and dissection of the fish. The function of Habitación B is unclear as only a single corner remains together with remains of a pavement of *opus signinum* (Martín *et al.* 1970, 43-5).

In addition Gabriella Martín identified ten salting vats on the promontory at Punta de l'Arenal. Both rock-cut (some lined with *opus signinum*) and freestanding basins were found of varying sizes: the largest are basins 7 and 8 measuring 10 x 5 m and 3 m deep (Martín *et al.* 1970, 40-3). Beside several of the vats are smaller circular basins containing fragments of *dolia*. The purpose of these smaller basins is unclear, although the *garum* recipes of Ps.-Rufius Festus and the *Geoponica* both refer to the heating of pots of *garum*. The pottery together with fragments of marble decoration and painted stucco from the vats suggests that the factory was part of a wider villa dating to the first and second centuries AD. The factory may have remained in use until the third century (Martín *et al.* 1970, 18-34; Bolufer Marqués 1987; 1988).

Fig. 23. Fish factory, insula C, Empúries.

Fig. 24. Salting vats, Santa Pola.

Remains of a small fish factory are located in the east of insula C in the Neapolis of Empúries. The factory consists of a square building measuring 15 x 14 m with a typical layout: a central courtyard containing three basins lined with *opus signinum* and a storeroom along the south and east sides. The factory was excavated by E. Gandia between 1917 and 1934 and has never been fully published, making dating difficult. The factory was built either in the first century BC or the first century AD and was abandoned in the second half of the first century or first half of the second century AD (Aquilué i Abadías 2006, 26-8).

Evidence for other factories is more scanty. Three rock-cut basins have been reported on the Punta del Castell at the southern end of the Arenal beach (Martín 1970, 148-9; Martín *et al.* 1970, 91). Figueras Pachero has reported the existence of a no-longer extant factory at Acequia de Noria (1945, 10-11). Remains of a vat lined with *opus signinum* are visible at Tossal de Manises.

Several late Imperial fisheries are known. A small factory has been excavated at Santa Pola consisting of five vats arranged around an area of *opus signinum* pavement (6 x 4 m) (Sánchez Fernández *et al.* 1989, 416-19). A fishery has been excavated to the southeast of the late Imperial complex (area G) at Rosas. The core of the factory seems to have been room G-V that consists of a square area lined with *opus signinum* that was used for the preparation of the fish before the residue was placed in the tanks arranged around the north and east sides. Further basins have been found in rooms G-VII and G-VIII (Nolla i Brufau 1984, 440; Nolla i Brufau *et al.* 1981, 192-4).

The most prominent feature of the fishery at Punta de l'Arenal is a large pool known locally as the Baños de la Reina (Martín *et al.* 1970, 14-18). It consists of a rock-cut basin measuring 28 x 7 m subdivided into three compartments through which

Fig. 25. Baños de la Reina, Punta de l'Arenal.

Fig. 26 Baños de la Reina, Illeta dels Banyets.

Fig. 27. Baños de la Reina, Calpe.

water can circulate by means of a narrow channel cut through the two transverse walls. At the eastern end of the tank are two channels that link it with the sea allowing the inflow of seawater through the larger of the two and outflow through the smaller. Thus by closing the exit it is possible to fill the basin, and the slots for a sluice gate are clearly visible.

The provision of Baños de la Reina is a characteristic of fisheries in Alicante and Valencia that is not found in the larger installations of Southern Spain and North Africa. Three badly preserved fish tanks have been found on the rocky promontory of Punta del Castell (Martín 1970, 148-9; Martín *et al.* 1970, 91; Ponsich 1988, 171-2). One has been found adjoining the Ibero-Roman settlement of Isleta de Campello. The tank measures 12 x 8 m and is subdivided into four compartments of which two survive (Figueras Pachero 1934, 35; Ponsich 1988, 173). A similar rock basin survives at Calpe, which was studied by the eighteenth-century antiquarian Antonio José Cavanilles (Ponsich 1988, 172; Lagóstena Barrios 2001, 185). Rock-cut *piscinae* are a feature of Italy and their presence in Tarraconensis at Javea and Calpe may reflect the presence of Italian immigrants in the coastal *villae* (Bernal Casasola 2007, 96).

The function of these tanks has been the subject of some debate (Figueras Pachero 1934, 35): Adolf Schulten identified those at Calpe as baths (Schulten 1927, 227). Their design, however, recalls the first-century BC description of a salt-water fish tank found in Columella's *De Re Rustica* (8.17.1-4). These tanks served to store live fish – the arrangement of channels and sluice gates enabling the circulation and retention of seawater. In view of the heterogeneous array of marine resources found in the fisheries, and the predominately migratory fish that were exploited, the storage of live fish will have been essential to ensure a regular supply of suitable fish for the salting installations. Although fluctuations in the availability of fish encouraged the storage of fish and the exploitation of a wider variety of marine resources, it is difficult to concur with the view that fish were consumed only in times of famine (Gallant 1985, 43). While seasonal variations meant that fishing was unlikely to have been the primary activity of a large section of the population – Manilius describes the use of migrant fishermen – the summer fishing season fits nicely with the agricultural calendar. The ability to control access to supplies of fish and to provide employment for the agricultural labour force during the summer will have been an important source of patronage for the Roman rural landowner.

Fish factories developed along the coast of Lusitania during the first century AD. According to Strabo (3.2.6) fish salting took place along the coast of the Algarve perhaps dating back to the early first century BC. The importance of the fishing industry is reflected in coins issued by the town of Ossonoba (modern Faro) between 47 and 45 BC (Lagóstena Barrios 2001, 79), and coins from Castro Marim dated to the middle of the first century BC depict tunny (Lagóstena Barrios 2001, 90-1). Unfortunately the archaeological evidence does little to back this up, relying on nineteenth-century surveys by Estacio da Veiga Ferreira and others that paid little attention to the chronology of the site. Edmondson (1987, 107) has suggested that the factories were developed by Phoenico-Punic settlers noting the similarity of the fisheries to those of Cádiz and the presence of Punic amphorae and coins similar to those of Cádiz at Salacia depicting Hercules and tunny fish. The correlation between the locations of the Phoenician settlements and the late fish factories is striking; however, as yet no archaeological evidence has been found to confirm this hypothesis. The earliest archaeological evidence for fisheries dates to the first century AD.

In 1987 remains of *cetariae* and an amphora kiln were published from Sines. The kiln is dated to the third to fifth centuries AD and produced Almagro 51 a/b and c vessels (Lagóstena Barrios 2001, 69-70; Dias Diogo *et al.* 1996, 108-9). A second factory has been discovered at Sines dating from the second half of the first century to the fourth century AD. The factory extends over an area of 74 m^2 and consists of seven vats around a central courtyard (Lagóstena Barrios 2001, 70). Two factories were discovered in 1982 and 1983 on Ilha do Pessegueiro, 15 km to the south of Sines. The first factory dates from the end of the second century or beginning of the third century AD and consists of basins arranged around a central courtyard. The second factory consists of ten basins and dates from the first half of the second century AD until the middle of the fourth century AD (Lagóstena Barrios 2001, 71).

An important fishery has been excavated at Bocca do Rio consisting of fourteen salting vats and a bath complex dating from the first century to the fifth century AD (Lagóstena Barrios 2001, 74; Ponsich 1988, 223). Estacio da Veiga suggested that the salting vats at Salema to the west may be associated with the activities at Bocca do Rio. Two groups of vats have been discovered at Vau at the mouth of the Río Alvor (Mezquita de Figueiredo 1906, 115).

Several fisheries have been discovered in the vicinity of Faro: salting vats dating from the first century BC have been discovered at Quarteira. The nearby factory of Loulé Velho is Imperial in date (Edmondson 1987, 259; Lagóstena Barrios 2001, 82). In the second half of the first century AD a fishery was constructed at Quinta do Lago in Loulé. The fishery consists of five salting vats and extends over an area of 70 m^2. The initial phase dates from the second half of the first century to the third century when the factory was abandoned with production shifting to other vats located in the vicinity.[34] Abundant Almagro 51c amphorae have been found together with lesser quantities of Dr 14 and Almagro 50 vessels indicating that amphorae were also produced in the vicinity although no kilns have yet been found (Arruda *et al.* 1990, 200-2; Lagóstena Barrios 2001, 83).[35]

There is a marked concentration of fisheries at the mouth of the Tagus. Several fisheries have been excavated in Lisbon. Rescue excavations carried out on Rua dos Correeiros between 1991 and 1995 revealed a fish factory consisting of at least 27 vats over an area of 409 m^2 (Bugalhão 2001, 67-79). The factory dates from the beginning of the first century AD and remained in use until the beginning of the fifth century (Bugalhão 2001, 173). In the third century part of the factory was replaced with a bath complex decorated with polichrome geometric mosaics. Excavations revealed houses to the north of the factory built in the third century which the excavators have suggested housed the proprietor of the factory (Bugalhão 2001, 67). A fish factory with four vats has been discovered at Casa dos Bicos. The dating is uncertain although Edmondson (1990, 130) has suggested that production began at the beginning of the first century BC, while the factory was abandoned in the third or fourth centuries AD (Lagóstena Barrios 2001, 44; Amaro 1990, 80).

Further factories were discovered during rescue excavations along the Rua Augusta. An area of 290 m^2 was cleared revealing three of four factories aligned south-east/north-west. Factory 1 consists of seven small vats lined with *opus signinum*. Factory 2 is the largest of the complex containing seven vats arranged around a possible courtyard. To the southwest lies Factory 3 with two vats and a further vat (13) to the southeast may be part of a fourth factory (Amaro *et al.* 1996, 202-4). Almagro 50 and 51 amphorae dating to the third to fifth centuries AD are the most common forms, with Lusitana 9 and Beltrán 72 vessels also present (Amaro *et al.* 1996, 207). The excavators have identified structures dated to the middle or late Iron Age which they suggest were related to fishing activities but offer no further details (Amaro *et al.* 1996, 207-8).

A single vat was discovered during rescue excavations in April 1993 on the corner of Rua dos Fanqueiros and Napoleão.[36] The vat contained pottery dating from the first century to the fifth century AD – the latest forms were *terra sigillata clara D* Hayes 67 plates dating between 360 and 470 AD (Dias Diogo *et al.* 2000, 184-5; Bugalhão 2001, 52). Two vats have been located at Rua dos Franqueiros no. 51-57 and further tanks have been found on Rua dos Douradores (Bugalhão 2001, 52).

To the south of the estuary remains of a fish factory have been found on Rua Alfredo Dinis in Cacilhas (Almada) dating from the end of the first century BC to the middle of the first century AD.[37] The factory consisted of six vats arranged around a central courtyard. Dr 7-11, Dr 14, Beltrán II and Beltrán IVb amphorae have been found. A second factory has been discovered 100 m to the northwest at Rua Carvalho Freirinho (Lagóstena Barrios 2001, 48; Amaro 1990, 79). Two fish traps dated to the first and second centuries AD have been discovered at Espinho to the south of Oporto (Lagóstena Barrios 2001, 42).

As well as the fisheries at the mouth of the Tagus, a second concentration is located at the mouth of the Sado. Strabo (3.3.1) praised the importance of Salacia as a port. The most important of the fisheries is at Tróia where two large factories have been uncovered. Factory I is partially excavated and covers an area of 1,106 m^2 with vats

Fig. 28. Factory I, Tróia (photo courtesy of Betty Jo and George Mayeske).

arranged around a courtyard 514 m^2 in size. Factory II to the north is smaller covering an area of 240 m^2, with vats arranged around at least three sides of the central courtyard. The factories date from the middle of the first century AD (the reign of Claudius or before) and following remodelling in the third and fourth centuries remained in operation until the middle of the fifth century AD (Étienne *et al.* 1994, 30, 39, 82; Lagóstena Barrios 2001, 60-4). A third factory has been excavated under the basilica. This factory is smaller, covering 108 m^2 and consisting of nine basins arranged around a courtyard 21.42 m^2 in size (Étienne *et al.* 1994, 93-4).

As well as the three principal factories, numerous salting vats have been found along the banks of the Sado – perhaps indicating as many as fourteen further factories (Étienne *et al.* 1994, 96-9). The bath-house together with remains of stucco and mosaics from the Rua da Princesa may indicate the existence of a villa in the vicinity of the fisheries at Tróia (Edmondson 1987, 267-8).

Several fisheries have been found in the vicinity of Setúbal: the factory at Praça do Bocage dates from the final quarter of the first century to the end of the second century AD and consists of five square basins (Lagóstena Barrios 2001, 65; Edmondson 1987, 265). A large factory consisting of fourteen salting vats arranged around a courtyard has been discovered at Travessa de Frei Gaspar.[38] Two phases of activity have been identified dating from the first to the fourth century AD and the end of the fourth century and beginning of the fifth century AD (Lagóstena Barrios 2001, 65; Edmondson 1987, 266; Étienne *et al.* 1994, 109).[39] A factory has been excavated at Creiro (Arrábida). The factory covers an area of 65 m^2 containing eleven vats and a courtyard opening to the south. The factory dates to the second half of the first century AD (Lagóstena Barrios 2001, 68; Étienne *et al.* 1994, 109-12). A factory dating from the beginning of the first century to the sixth century AD has been discovered at Comenda overlooking the Ribeira da Ajuda and the Río Sado (Lagóstena Barrios 2001, 66-7).

Several fisheries have been discovered along the northwestern coast of the Peninsula. A fish saltery was excavated at nos 41-43 Calle Marqués de Valladares (Vigo) between 2002 and 2004. The factory extends over an area of 180 m^2. The pottery dates the first phase of the factory to the second half of the first century and the second century AD (Torres *et al.* 2007, 481-2). Five salting vats lined with *opus signinum* were arranged along the north and east sides of a patio 55 m^2 in size (Torres *et al.* 2007, 479-80; Currás 2007, 141). The large quantities of *dolia* that have been found may have been used for the artificial evaporation/heating of the salt and fish (Torres *et al.* 2007, 482). There is no evidence of other occupation on the site (therefore it is not part of villa or of a vicus). The tanks have a capacity of at least 63 m^3 and the absence of other fisheries of this size in Galicia at this time suggests that it may have supplied a large area – perhaps as far as Bracara, Asturica and Lucus (Torres *et al.* 2007, 483). Eight rectangular salting vats have been found at Guétary at the mouth of the Bidasoa. The factory seems to have operated during the first half of the first century AD with Pascual 1, Dr 2-4 and Dr 7-11 amphorae present (Lagóstena Barrios 2001, 35).

Several factories dating to the late Empire have also been found. The best known are the remains of salting vats from a fish factory in the Plaza del Marqués in Gijón, discovered in 1991. The factory dates from the third to the fifth century AD (Fernández Ochoa *et al.* 2003, 114). A fish factory dated to the third and fourth centuries AD is situated on Punta Borralleiro to the east of the beach of O Cocho (Currás 2007, 139-40). Three rectangular vats have been found at O Fiunchal/Alcabre, 500 m to the east of the site of O Cocho. Although only limited excavations have been carried out, the site seems to date between the third and fifth centuries AD (Currás 2007, 140-1).

Edmondson (1987, 135) has suggested that many of the fisheries – especially in the Algarve – were associated with villas. A wealthy villa decorated with bichrome and polichrome mosaics has been discovered at Mexilhoeira Grande (Abicada) dating from the first to the fourth century AD or later. A group of basins has been found together with remains of presses (Gorges 1979, 481-2; Lagóstena Barrios 2001, 76).

A wealthy villa has been discovered at Cerro da Vila situated on the estuary of the Ribeira da Quarteira, 15 km to the east of Faro. The villa is arranged around a peristyle with a bath complex and numerous mosaics. The initial occupation of the villa dates to the first century AD; it was remodelled in the third century. During the late Empire the complex was expanded with the construction of a fishery and harbour facilities (Lagóstena Barrios 2001, 82-3; Gorges 1979, 482-3). A possible villa has been discovered at Cacela decorated with bichrome mosaics (Gorges 1979, 480). Several vats have also been found associated with amphorae and fishing implements. A second factory has been discovered at Quinta do Muro (Lagóstena Barrios 2001, 90). The dating is uncertain but Carlos Fabião (1992, 249) has suggested the first and second centuries AD.

A villa together with a bath complex and an unspecified number of salting vats have been excavated at Las Torres (Estepona) near San Pedro de Alcántara (Gorges 1979, 306). A possible villa has been excavated at Gallineras with a fish factory and two ceramic kilns. The dating is uncertain, though the discovery of bichrome geometric mosaics suggests activity dating to the second century AD (Lagóstena Barrios 2001, 119). Salting vats together with mosaics have been discovered at San Luis de Sabinillas, 6 km north of Fuengirola (Ponsich 1988, 183; Haley 2003, 61).

The villa of la Butibamba lies to the west of Fuengirola on the banks of the Río Cala de Mijas. The *pars urbana* of the villa has been excavated together with a bath suite and dates from the first to the third centuries AD. The *pars rustica* lies to the east and seems to have been engaged in the production of olive oil as well as fishing, with net weights also having been found (Corrales Aguilar 2001, 354).

During the first century AD and continuing through the following century the urban elites sought to garner increasing profits from their rural estates. This investment is reflected in the appearance of agricultural installations in the vicinity of their villas. This is most apparent in the olive oil producing estates of the Guadalquivir valley. An inscription from Gallineras reading ΙΟΥΛΙΟΥ may allude to a *vilicus* operating on behalf of the Iulii in Cádiz (Lagóstena Barrios 2001, 119).

As well as production within the confines of villa estates, several of the factories seem to have been operating on a far larger scale. Together with the remains at nos 1 and 17, the factory excavated at Calle San Nicolás nos 3-5 extends over an area of 87,500 m^2 (Bernal Casasola *et al.* 2003, 171). The only comparable installations are those of Baelo Claudia, El Majuelo and Tróia, as well as at Lixus in Morocco. Sotomayor (1997, 13) has coined the term 'colonies of potters' to describe secondary sites devoted to large-scale ceramic production – like those of Puerto Real, Algeciras and the Dr 20 kilns along the Guadalquivir and Genil.

The scale of operations at Tróia is striking: the capacity of the excavated tanks in Factory I is 465 m^3, Factory II is 141 m^3 and Factory III is 104 m^3. The excavators have suggested that the original capacity of Factory I was 535 m^3 – a capacity that would have required 15,000 amphorae (Étienne *et al.* 1994, 76-9, 94).

Edmondson (1987, 132-4) has drawn attention to the high proportion of freedmen and women attested on inscriptions from Tróia, noting that their presence is consistent with other urban industrial concerns in the Western Empire.[40] A large building associated with salt vats has been excavated on the Rua Infante D. Henrique in Faro. The building was initially identified as a suburban villa, however, it has subsequently been identified as corporation of fishermen. In 1976 a mosaic was discovered depicting the god Oceanus within a geometric medallion. In the two corners there are representations of two winds, the remaining two no longer survive. At the base of the mosaic there is an inscription recording its dedication by four individuals: C. Calpurnius [...]nus, C. Vibius Quintilianus, L. Atti(us) [...]s and M. Verdius Geminus, who it has been suggested were *magistri* of the corporation (Lagóstena Barrios 2001, 80).

The importance of the local fishing industry is reflected in the number of kilns engaged in the production of fish sauce amphorae. Several kilns have been excavated at the mouth of the Tagus. An important ceramic workshop has been discovered at Porto dos Cacos (Herdade de Río Frío). Excavations have revealed three kilns together with workshops. Kiln 1 is piriform in shape, 4.35 m long, with three *suspensurae*; kiln 2 is circular, 3.20 m in diameter (Cordeiro Raposo 1990, 119-21; Cordeiro Raposo *et al.* 1992, 39-40; 1996, 251-2). A third kiln has not been excavated but is probably similar in form to kiln 2 (Cordeiro Raposo 1990, 121; Cordeiro Raposo *et al.* 1996, 251). Two phases of activity have been identified: the first between the first century and the end of the second century AD consisting of the production of Dr 14 amphorae. The second phase continues until the fifth century AD, producing Almago 50, 51c, Dr 30 and Lusitana 9 vessels (Cordeiro Raposo 1990, 125-7; Cordeiro Raposo *et al.* 1992, 38; 1996, 254).

In contrast to the lack of stamps on the Dr 14 vessels, more than 180 stamps have been found from Phase 2. Most common are those referring to Germanus, accounting for more than 130 examples: CERMAN, GERMANI, GERM, GERMAN and CER F, which reads either Ger(manus) F(ecit) or Ger(mani) F(iglina). Amílcar Ribeiro (1996, 276) has noted that there are no direct parallels for these stamps elsewhere. Eleven examples of the stamps T M M or T MAM have been found, seven RVSTICI, seven CLARIANI and a single stamp reading ...AIVNIT or TINVIA... *retro* (Ribeiro Guerra 1996, 274-9). A necropolis consisting of 37 burials (24 of which have been excavated) dating to the third and fourth centuries AD lies 100 m to the northeast (Sabrosa 1996, 283-7; Cordeiro Raposo 1990, 123-4). The lack of any evidence for a villa or urban area in the vicinity of the workshop has led the excavators to suggest that this is an industrial complex.

Three kilns were excavated between 1986 and 1991 at Quinta do Rouxinol. Kiln 1 is piriform, 2.85 m in length, the second kiln is similar, and remains of a third have been located to the northwest. The workshop dates from the second half of the second century to the first half of the fourth century AD, producing Almagro 50 and 51c amphorae (Cordeiro Raposo *et al.* 1992, 41-2; Castanheira Duarte 1990, 101-2; Castanheira Duarte *et al.* 1996, 238-40).[41]

As well as fisheries there is an important concentration of kilns at the mouth of the Sado producing Dr 14, Almagro 50 and Almagro 51c amphorae. In 1988 a pair of kilns were discovered at Largo da Misericórdia in the vicinity of the fishery at Travessa de Frei Gaspar. The kilns are circular (kiln L 11 is 3 m in diameter and J 12 is 3.5 m in diameter) and produced Dr 14 amphorae (Tavares da Silva 1996, 46-7). The kilns are dated to the reigns of Tiberius and Claudius by the presence of *terra sigillata italica* as opposed to the scarcity of South Gaulish *terra sigillata* (Tavares da Silva 1996, 45). Two kilns have been discovered to the east of Setúbal at Quinta da Alegria. These operated from the third quarter of the first century to the middle of the fifth century AD, producing Dr 14, Almagro 50, 51 a/b and 51c and Keay LXXVIII amphorae (Lagóstena Barrios 2001, 65-6).

Two kilns have been found at Herdade da Barrosinha situated beside the Río Sado, 2.5 km from Alcácer do Sal. The kilns operated from the first half of the first century to the beginning of the second century AD, producing Dr 14 amphorae. Thirty-one examples of the stamp T.M.C. have been found together with MA.MV.S (Dias Diogo *et al.* 1987, 85-6). Four circular kilns have been excavated at Monte do Bugio associated with Dr 14 amphorae (Dias Diogo 1980, 149-50). Several kilns have been reported at Echurrasqueira since 1896 associated with Dr 14 and Almagro 51c amphorae (Dias Diogo 1983, 211-12; Lagóstena Barrios 2001, 56-8). 800 m to the east of the kilns at Echurrasqueira a circular kiln has been discovered associated with Dr 14 and Almagro 51c vessels (Dias Diogo 1983, 212-14). A ceramic workshop has been excavated at Pinheiro dating from the first to the fifth centuries AD. Three kilns producing Dr 14 amphorae have been dated to the first phase of operation from the first to the third century, and five kilns produced Almagro 51 a/b, 51c and Keay LXXVIII amphorae (Lagóstena Barrios 2001, 58-60).

The kilns at Largo da Misericórdia date to the first half of the first century AD (the reigns of Tiberius and Claudius) predating the earliest fisheries: Creiro dates from the third quarter of the first century AD; Travessa de Frei Gaspar and Praça de Bocage date to *c.* AD 75 (Tavares da Silva 1996, 49). However, the factory at Comenda dates from the beginning of the first century AD, according to Lagóstena Barrios (2001,

66-7). The discovery of Dr 7-11 with the same fabric as other locally produced amphorae at Alcácer do Sal may indicate that the production of amphorae began earlier at the end of the first century BC (Edmondson 1987, 162-3).

In 1896 Leite de Vasconcellos excavated a kiln and amphora dump at Os Olhos in São Bartolomeu de Castro Marím at the mouth of the Guadiana. Surface exploration carried out in 1986 clarified the types of amphorae that were produced here as Dr 14, Almagro 50 and 51c vessels. On the basis of the amphorae found the kiln was in use from the second half of the first century/beginning of the second century until the fifth century AD (Lagóstena Barrios 2001, 91; Alves *et al.* 1990, 193-6).

In 1960 a mosaic was discovered at Porto do Sabugueiro. Three years later excavations revealed remains of a rectangular kiln initially dated to the late eighteenth or early nineteenth century. Subsequent excavations have corrected this dating revealing quantities of Dr 2-4, Dr 7-11 and Dr 14 amphorae, as well as two small lip fragments from Dr 30 vessels. The presence of the mosaic suggests a villa in the vicinity (Cardoso 1990, 156-8; Lagóstena Barrios 2001, 50). Dr 14 amphorae were produced at Garrocheira. The site lies on the right-bank of the Rio Sorraia where two circular kilns have been discovered, 3.40 m and 1.70 m in diameter respectively (Amaro 1990, 89-90). The kilns produced Dr 14 amphorae dating to the first and second centuries AD (Amaro 1990, 77-8; 1990, 91). The workshop was perhaps associated with the villa at Monte da Parreira (Lagóstena Barrios 2001, 50-1).

In contrast to the abundance of names on Dr 20 amphorae, the names of individuals engaged in the production or shipping of fish sauce are elusive. By analogy with the names attested on the Dr 20 amphorae, the amphorae refer to the proprietors, lessees and potters of the kilns producing amphorae. In addition, some appear to refer to *societates*: SCG at Baelo.

L(ucius) Oc(tavius) Caes(ius) appears on a Dr 9 from Castro Pretorio; C(aius) Fuf(icius) Ant(onius) (or Avitus) on amphorae from Alcalá del Río, Vienne and Geneva (Haley 2003, 202 n. 76). Stefanie Martin-Kilcher (1994, 401-2) has suggested that the P( ) Flac(cus) on a Dr 12 amphora from Augst may be a relative of L. Pomponius Flaccus, the consul of AD 17.[42]

A Dr 8 amphora from the habour of Port-la-Nautique (Aude) reads 'G(ari) F(los)' together with the merchants Q.Q.Caecilii and the producer L.C.F. An example on a Dr 8 vessel from Saint-Romain-en-Gal records the contents of the amphora as the 'flower of garum from the mackerel' ('g(ari) f(los) scombr[r(i)]') (Desbat *et al.* 1987, 164). A *titulus* on a Dr 8 from Rue de la Favorite, Lyon reads QQ CAECILIS (Desbat *et al.* 1987, 156). The Q.Q.Caecilii were engaged in the trading of fish sauce, oil and metals during the reign of Tiberius.

A *societas* of the Auli Atinii is attested at Olivar de los Valencianos. Stamps reading AA.AT.D and AA.AT.M have also been found. As well as producing amphorae, the *societas* was also involved in the trading of olive oil, fish sauces and possibly wine. Several Atinii appear as merchants on *tituli picti*. A *titulus* on a Dr 20 amphora from L'Anse Saint Gervais reads A A Ati[nii] (Liou *et al.* 1978, 112; *CIL* 15.3639-41). The Auli Atinii appear not only to have shipped olive oil but also to have been engaged in the shipping of fish sauce, appearing on Dr 7-13 amphorae. The *titulus* also appears on a Dr 28 amphora from Castro Pretorio (*CIL* 15, 4700; Zevi 1966, 244). Related are the Caii Atinii who appear on fish sauce amphorae from Castro Pretorio in Rome (Desbat *et al.* 1987, 158; Liou *et al.* 1978, 112).

A cargo of South Spanish Dr 7-11 has been recovered from a wreck at Cala Rossano. Several *tituli picti* survive: several give the name C. Annius Senecio, whom Parker identifies as a merchant. One vessel contained *lymphatum* or fish sauce (Parker 1992, 90-1). A Dr 9 amphora from Augst has the name L. Sempronius Fuscus – Martin-Kilcher has suggested that he is related either to the prefect of the Cohors Baetica, M. Sempronius Fuscus, or to the proconsul of Baetica under Vespasian, Sempronius Fuscus (Martin-Kilcher 1994, 406).

The stamp ANTH has been found on several sites in Cataluña, most notably at Empúries. The stamp is almost exclusively found on Dr 8-9 vessels, although a single Dr 2-4 has also been found. No kiln has been associated with the stamp, although the volume of stamps in the vicinity of Empúries has suggested a local origin.[43] Iwona Modrzewska (1993, 172-4) has suggested that the same individual is attested on the stamps ANTHI.FADI and T.ANTHI found on Lamboglia 2/Dr 6 amphorae from Venice. Dr 6 amphorae are generally accepted to have originated in Apulia in the second century BC and were copied a century later in Northern Italy and the Adriatic where they were used for the transport of olive oil, wine and fish sauce (Peacock *et al.* 1986, 98-101). The Spanish origin of the Catalan stamps suggests against any such connection. The stamp may be related to the L. Baebius Anthus attested on a Dr 8 amphora from the Castro Pretorio in Rome (*CIL* 15.4704). M. Baebius Claricus is named on a Dr 10 amphora from the same location (*CIL* 15.4750).

The Baebii were a senatorial family well known in Valencia around Saguntum. Cn. Baebius Geminus is named in an inscription from Saguntum recording his financing of construction work in the forum (*CIL* 2.14/374). The same individual is named on inscriptions from the Plaza de Armas honouring him as pontifex and aedile (*CIL* 2.3854; Alföldy 1977, 12). The aedile Marcus Baebius Sobrinus appears on local coin issues dating to the reign of Tiberius (Alföldy 1977, 31-2). Geza Alföldy (1977, 27) has suggested that the family attained senatorial status during the reign of Vespasian when an inscription from Rome records that Lucius Baebius Avitus was adlected into the senate as a praetor. An inscription from Almago (Ciudad Real) records the construction of a bridge *in honorem domus divinae* by P. Baebius Venustus (Hurtado Aguña 2005, 237).

Several merchants are recorded. A *Corpus Negotiantium Malacitanorum* is recorded from Ostia that was engaged in the trading of salted fish products. The *quinquennalis* P. Clodius Athenio was a *negotians salsarius* (*CIL* 6.9766). A no longer extant inscription from Málaga (*IG* 14.2540) records a corporation of Oriental merchants. Blázquez Martínez (1985, 456) has suggested that the president (?) T. Clodius Iulianus was engaged in the shipping of fish sauce or metals.

M. Numisius Nicer (*CIL* 15.4708) and L. Numisius Silo (*CIL* 15.4709) were members of a *societas* based in Carthago Nova that produced *garum sociorum*. L. Numisius Agathermes was a *negotiator ex Hispania Citeriore* in Ostia. The *gens* is well attested in Tarraco and Cartagena. L. Numisius Laetus was *flamen provincia Hispania Citeriore* during the first half of the second century AD (Ramallo Asensio 1989, 89). An altar dedicated by Sextus Numisius has been found at Rambla de la Boltada. In the seventeenth century an inscription was discovered in the vicinity of the Castillo de Sohail in Fuengirola (*CIL* 15.1944). It is a dedication to Neptune by the *sevir augustalis*, L. Iunius Puteolanus. Evan Haley has suggested that he was a fish sauce merchant from Puteoli who is found on *tituli picti* from Rome reading 'g(arum) sc(ombri) f(los) Puteolani' (*CIL* 15.4687, 4688; Haley 1990, 72-8).[44]

A stamp reading L ME(vius) FAVS(tus) has been found on a Dr 8 amphora from Pinar de Villanueva (Puerto Real, Cádiz). The family may also have operated as merchants: a *titulus* on an oil amphora from Castro Pretorio in Rome gives the name P. Mevius Faustus; L. Mevius Rufus is named as the shipper on a Dr 12 amphora from Saint-Romain-en Gal dated between 15 BC and AD 5 (Chic García 1994, 105).

The apogee of Spanish production seems to have been the middle of the first century AD. This prosperity was prompted by a variety of factors including the promotion of urbanism under the Flavian dynasty and the demand for Spanish goods both from the *annona* and from other sources. Ius Latii was bestowed on communities throughout the Peninsula. The date of the grant is a matter of debate – dating either to AD 70/71 or 73/74 (Fear 1996, 144-6; Haley 2003, 70). Together with this elevation of communities to Latin status the Flavian period also sees a restructuring and monumentalization of urban centres, for example at Celti (Peñaflor) where a public building in the forum area was built in the mid- to late first century AD (Keay *et al.* 2000, 204).[45] It seems also that several of the surviving *oppida* were abandoned at this time or suffered a reduction in size – reflecting a pronounced rural 'drift' (Haley 2003, 74). The distribution of *terra sigillata hispanica* and the earliest African red-slip ware in the middle and upper Guadalquivir and the mountains of the penibético show a dramatic increase in rural settlement at this time.

A recent survey of pottery around Carcabuey (Córdoba) shows that of nineteen rural sites surveyed only one dates to before AD 50; most of the remainder date from the Flavian period. A farm has recently been discovered at La Alcantarilla to the east of Carcabuey. A rectangular kiln has also been found that produced coarse ware pottery as well as *dolia* and building materials.[46] The site was occupied from the Flavian era to the second half of the second century AD. The first phase of the villa at Cercadilla (Córdoba) dates to the end of the first century AD. As well as decorative elements (marble fragments, stucco, *opus sectile*) from the *pars urbana*, the villa seems also to have been devoted to oil processing.

Similarly it is only in the Flavian period that there is a shift from *oppida* to a more dispersed population in lowlying rural farms and villas in northern and western Málaga. In 1988 rescue excavations at Cerro Sánchez in the Sierra de Yeguas revealed remains of a villa decorated with marble fragments and painted stucco. At least one basin was found lined with *opus signinum* containing olive seeds and barley as well as storage and transport vessels. The first phase of the villa of Auta Riogordo in Málaga dates to the end of the first century AD.

The Flavian period saw increased signs of Romanization in the mining areas of the northwest. The villa at Las Pedreiras de Lago dates to the first and second centuries AD. The castro of Chao Samartín lies in the valley of the Río Navia in western Asturias. Excavations have revealed a stretch of fortifications dating from *c.* 800 BC. The site underwent successive transformations during the fourth and second centuries BC with the reconstruction of the fortifications and the appearance of rectangular buildings. An important aspect of the economic activities of the community seems to have been the working of gold, silver and copper to judge by the quantities of slag, cakes, moulds and crucibles that have been found (Villa Valdés 2005, 38).

Although a Roman presence may date as early as the reign of Tiberius, the site underwent profound restructuring during the Flavian period with the abandonment of the fortifications and the construction of paved streets, an open square and rectangular houses – perhaps inspired by the design of military *contubernia* (Villa Valdés 2005, 42-3). Particularly notable is the replacement of individual dwellings with conglomerations of houses, appropriating public areas into larger dwellings that could house all the necessities of the family units. Recent seasons of excavation on the northern slope of the site have revealed an Italianate *domus* organized around a peristyle courtyard and decorated with polichrome wall-paintings. The house was constructed during the first century AD and is a striking example of the adoption of a Roman life-style that has yet to be seen in other castros (Villa Valdés 2005, 115-16).

The decline of Spanish exports

By the end of the first century AD, however, there are signs of recession. As early as the reign of Nero there appears to have been a period of economic decline in the Peninsula. Genaro Chic García (1996, 248) has noted a sharp decrease in the volume of coinage circulating in the mining communities of the Río Tinto – a pattern that is repeated throughout the Peninsula (Haley 2003, 49). John Richardson (1996, 163) has argued that there was a decline in viticulture from the second half of the first century AD. The production of amphorae and wine ceases at Can Feu *c.* 50-80 AD (Carbonell *et al.* 1998, 290). Several other sites ceased operation at this time, for example, Roser (Calella), Darró (Vilanova), Ses Alzines, Mas Carbotí, Mas Font. The press-room at Ses Alzines was remodelled and the press covered over prior to the abandonment of the building during the final quarter of the first century AD (Anglada *et al.* 1998, 440). The absence of Tarraconensian Dr 2-4 amphorae from the deposit at Bas-de-Loyasse (Lyon) is striking, with only three examples suggesting that the export of Spanish wine ceased prior to the creation of the deposit *c.* AD 70 (Dangréaux *et al.* 1987, 117, 147).

The disappearance of Spanish wine amphorae in Gaul is in contrast to their continued presence in Italy: Tarraconensian Dr 2-4 amphorae account for 13.7% of the wine amphorae and 8.7% of the total amphorae found at the Baths of the Swimmer in Ostia (Dangréaux *et al.* 1987, 147).

This decline seems to have affected other areas of the economy. The fishery at Torremuelle (Benálmadena) seems to have been abandoned in the second half of the first century AD, although residual occupation continued on the site for the first three quarters of the second century (Pineda *et al.* 2007, 442). The fishery excavated on Calle San Nicolás (Algeciras) underwent remodelling at the end of the first century AD with the filling in of at least two vats in factory I (Bernal Casasola *et al.* 2003, 177). The kilns at Venta del Carmen (Los Barrios) were abandoned in the late first century AD (Bernal Casasola *et al.* 1998, 78).

Haley (2003, 64) has suggested a period of recession during the reign of Claudius: the kiln at Haza Honda was abandoned in the later Julio-Claudian period, to judge from the absence of *terra sigillata hispanica* (Beltrán Fortés *et al.* 1997, 112).

From the early Flavian period oil imports begin to appear at Ostia from Tripolitania and Tunisia alongside the first *terra sigillata africana A*. By the middle of the second century 45% of the amphorae at Ostia came from Tunisia (Africana I and II and Ostia XXIII), Tripolitania (Tripolitana II and II) and Algeria (Dr 30) (Whittaker 1985, 51).

At Los Molinillos (Benálmadena) there is a shift from olive oil production to the preparation of salted fish at the end of the second century AD or beginning of the third century AD (Pineda *et al.* 2007, 446). Evidence of occupation from the necropolis at

Valdoca dates the decline of mining activity at Vipasca in the second half of the third century AD. Further evidence of decline comes from an inscription erected by the *coloni Metalli Vipascensis* in honour of an imperial *restitutor metallorum*. The dating of the inscription is uncertain, but Edmondson (1987, 46-7) suggests that the disruption caused by Moorish raids would be appropriate for the appointment of a *restitutor* in AD 173.[47]

Traditionally the decline in Spanish exports is attributed to a variety of external factors. As early as the reign of Antoninus Pius there are signs of unrest. A fragment of the *Fasti Ostienses* records the judgement before the senate of Cornelius Priscianus in AD 145: 'De Cornelio Prisciano in sen[atu iudicium]/[cor[am factum quod provinciam Hispaniam hostiliter/[inqu]ietaverit' (Arce 1988, 35). According to the *Scriptores Historiae Augustae* (*SHA*), Cornelius Priscianus committed suicide following an abortive revolt (*Vita Pii* 7.2). Invasions of Mauri disrupted Baetica in AD 171-172 and in 177-178, reaching as far inland as Italica (Arce 1988, 38-46). Mining operations at the Río Tinto were interrupted at this time (Jones 1980, 161-3). An inscription from Vipasca records the procurator Beryllus engaged in restoring the mines, perhaps in AD 173 (Richardson 1996, 232). In AD 186 Herodian (1.10.1-9) records the revolt in Gaul of a deserter, Maternus, who went on to ravage Gaul and Spain. Further dislocation was caused following the defeat of Clodius Albinus in AD 197 when Septimius Severus executed a number of Albinus' Spanish supporters and confiscated their property (*SHA Severus* 12.1-3; Richardson 1996, 238-9). In AD 198-9 Tiberius Claudius Candidus had to campaign in the Peninsula against the governor, L. Nonius Rufus (Blázquez Martínez 1976, 72-3).

The reasons for the decline in Spanish exports may, however, be internal. As we have seen, the Peninsula enjoyed a sustained economic growth from the first century BC onwards that came to embrace large parts of the Peninsula and developed production on a scale that can justly be described as industrial. The evidence of amphora stamps points to a complex social hierarchy and division of labour. Also evident is the involvement of both the local municipal elites as well as senatorial elites. Such was the social and legal stigma attached to commercial activities, enforced by the *lex Claudia* of 219-218 BC and reinstated by Caesar's *lex Iulia de repetundis* of 59 BC which stated that no senator or his son could own a ship of more than 300 jars capacity, that once the local elite had profited from investment in the economy their capital was transferred to land ownership and civic euergetism.

The monumentalization of the towns of the Peninsula in the later first and second centuries AD is testimony to the wealth of the Peninsula but also sounded the death knell of its economy as capital was transferred to the aggrandizement of these same urban centres. Just as the increase in Spanish exports during the reign of Claudius coincides with the appearance of Spanish senators, Whittaker (1985, 67) has noted that the earliest African imports (Ostia LIX oil amphorae and *terra sigillata africana A* pottery) coincide with the first African consuls who took office between AD 74 and 80.

Conclusion

The arguments surrounding modernising and primitive models of the ancient economy have been transformed in recent years by the volume of archaeological discoveries on a scale that go beyond the requirements of mere self-sufficiency. This archaeological evidence is, however, not without problems, creating an imbalance in favour of archaeologically detectable commerce (such as amphorae and other forms of pottery) at the expense of less visible components of the economy (such as textiles or slaves). While archaeology can show that trade took place, it cannot tell us why. The economy, therefore, needs to be viewed within a broader cultural setting – economic activity was as much about displaying cultural values as it was about profit or loss.

Recent discoveries have shown that Phoenician colonization was much more widespread than previously thought: extending along the coast of the Algarve and the Atlantic coast of Portugal – the estuaries of the río Guadiana, the Sado, Tagus and Mondego; and along the east coast at the mouth of the río Segura, at Vinarragell, Torrelló del Boverot d'Almassora and at Aldovesta at the mouth of the río Ebro. Excavations have revealed small farms in the hinterlands of the colonies – in the fertile valleys of the ríos Guadalhorce, Ronda and Guadalteba, which were devoted to the cultivation of wheat, barley and vines. Environmental evidence from Castillo de Doña Blanca shows a dramatic increase in the number of grapes in the later sixth century BC and a winery has been excavated at L'Alt de Benimaquía dating between 625 and 550 BC.

The economic stimuli provided by contact with the Phoenicians and later Greeks enabled the growth of polities that controlled the exploitation of resources to meet this demand.

These demands were intensified with the arrival of Rome. The need to pay taxes and the creation of urban centres fuelled an intensification of agriculture that is reflected in the appearance of the first villas in Cataluña during the second century BC. The appearance of villas coincides with a transition from cereal cultivation to viticulture. Together with the introduction of viticulture, the earliest production of amphorae in the form of imitations of Italian Dr 1 vessels and from the middle of the first century BC Tarraconense 1 amphorae.

Italian immigrants were also attracted to the silver mines of the Sierra de Cartagena. The most valuable indication of this influx are the inscriptions found on lead ingots which Claude Domergue has shown reflects an influx of Italian immigrants in the first century BC, several of whom joined the ranks of the civic elite from the end of the Republic.

Particularly striking are the appearance of large scale fish salteries – at Teatro Andalucía and Plaza de Asdrúbal/ Paseo Marítimo in Cádiz and especially those of

Baelo Claudia that seem to have begun operating at the end of the second century BC. These factories were supplied by several new kilns that have been discovered in Puerto de Santa Maria producing Mañá C2b and local imitations of Dr 1A amphorae.

Although limited in distribution, these early amphora forms reflect an intensification of production that came to fruition at the end of the first century BC. The pacification of the Peninsula, the spread of Roman settlement and urbanism under Caesar and Augustus and the establishment of the *annona* and the *annona militaris* led to an intensification of production and rural settlement. The *annona* would in turn have fostered private commerce – effectively subsiding the costs and assuming part of the risks. Increasing numbers of villas and farms in Cataluña were devoted to viticulture on a sufficient scale to support industrial 'vici' at Fenals, Darró and Llafranc. Unlike earlier stamps on Tarraconense 1 amphorae, the producers named on Pascual 1 vessels seem to have been of higher status including not only Lentulus Augur, the consul of AD 14, but also members of the civic elites of Narbonne, Tarraco, Barcino and elsewhere.

The Augustan period also saw the spread of villas in the Guadalquivir valley and the development of oleiculture with the appearance of Oberaden 83 amphorae and the earliest Dr 20 vessels that came to be ubiquitous during the first century AD. Augustus' conquests brought the gold mines of Asturias and Galicia under Roman control, providing 20,000 lbs of gold a year (Pliny *Natural History* 33.21.78). Legionary garrisons were established at Herrera de Pisuerga, Leon and Rosinos de Vidreales to ensure control.

The early first century AD saw a dramatic increase in the volume of olive oil production, with nearly 100 kilns being discovered along the banks of the ríos Guadalquivir and Genil devoted to the production of Dr 20 amphorae. Testimony to the scale of this trade comes from the dump of Dr 20 amphorae from Monte Testaccio at the foot of the Aventine hill in Rome that includes at least 24,750,000 olive oil amphorae.

In contrast to the close association of villas and wine production in Cataluña, the production of Dr 20 amphorae seems to have been independent of land ownership and instead focused on the industrial production of pottery. Several of the workshops included multiple kilns (three at El Castillejo, five at El Tejarillo, three at Casilla de Taracón, two at Huertas del Río, two at La Mallena) as well as yielding multiple stamps – with several stamps appearing in multiple locations. Seventy-nine stamps have been found at El Castillejo, 31 at El Tejarillo, 22 at Villar de Brenes, 13 at Villar Tesoro, 41 at Las Delicias, 46 at Alcotrista and 125 at La Catria. The individuals names on stamps come from a variety of different backgrounds including senators (L. Fabius Cilo, P. Aelius Hadrianus, P( ) M( ) O( ), members of the local elite (C. Iuventius Albinus, Q. Fulvius Carisianus, Q. Aelius Optatus, D. Caecilius Hospitalis) and individual potters.

During the first century AD the urban elite sought to garner increasing profits from their estates investing in an intensification of agricultural production most clearly seen in the olive oil producing estates of the Guadalquivir valley and the appearance of large-scale fish salting factories at Calle San Nicolás 3-5 (Algeciras), Baelo Claudia, El Majuelo (Almuñécar) and Tróia. This production was supported by the large-scale production of Dr 20 amphorae along the Guadalquivir and Genil, and Dr 7-11, Dr 38-39, Dr 12-13, Dr 14 and Lomba do Canho 67 amphorae in Puerto Real and Algeciras.

By the end of the first century AD and perhaps as early as the reign of Nero there are signs of recession. A number of sites cease operating at this time and Spanish amphorae disappear from Gaul. From the Flavian period onwards Spanish olive oil imports to Ostia are replaced by oil from Tunisia and Tripolitana.

The legal and social stigma attached to commerce meant that rather than reinvesting in continued economic growth, profits were transferred to investment in land ownership and civic euergetism. Profits enabled producers to attain membership first of the civic elite and later entry into the senate in Rome, siphoning capital away from investment in the economy and leading to economic stagnation and decline in the face of the expanding African economy.

Notes

1. Romanization and the Ancient Economy

1. For the historiography of the term 'Romanization', see Freeman 1997.

2. Only one of the parties involved is possibly a Roman citizen: [...]assius Eihar f., who speaks on behalf of the Salluienses, may have had Roman citizenship (Richardson 1983, 38).

3. Note the small size of the Roman bureaucracy; Hopkins (1980, 121) has calculated that for the empire as a whole there was a ratio of one administrator to 350,000-400,000 people.

4. See also Strabo 3.3.5; Polybius 3.167.

5. The volume of publications is too great to list here; see, for example, Belda Navarro 1975, Salinas de Frias 1986, Downs 1996, Hidalgo *et al.* 1998, Hernández Guerra 2002, Abad Casal 2003, Haley 2003, Curchin 2004, Hurtado Aguña 2005.

2. Expanding Horizons

1. On the history of Phoenician archaeology in the Iberian Peninsula, see López Castro 1992.

2. On Posidonius' account of the foundation of Cádiz, see Ribichini 2000.

3. Velleius associates the foundation of Cádiz with the return of the Heraclidae and the fall of the monarchy in Athens. Velleius' dating of the return of the Heraclidae agrees with that of Thucydides (1.12). According to Eratosthenes the Phoenicians founded colonies beyond the Straits of Gibraltar shortly after the end of the Trojan War (i.e. *c.* 1183 BC) (Strabo 1.3.2, see also 3.2.13).

4. Excavations in the vicinity of the island of Erytheia have failed to support its use as the site of the original settlement. Excavations on the Calle Marqués del Real Tesoro have yielded finds of no earlier than the third century BC, though finds from the Teatro Andalucía date back to the seventh century BC, Lavado Florido *et al.* 2000, 870-1.

5. Schubart's chronology has been brought into question by the excavations at Cerro del Villar, see Martín Ruiz 1995, 125. Sixth-century BC plates from Toscanos V with rims of 7.1-8 cm were contemporaneous with rims of 5.6-6.9 cm in diameter from Cerro del Villar – rim sizes that match those of seventh-century BC examples from Toscanos, see Aubet Semmler *et al.* 1999, 160-3.

6. The most famous being the Nora stele that was discovered in Sardinia in 1773 and records in Phoenician the dedication of a temple – although dating most probably to the ninth century BC. Pausanias 10.17.5 attributes the foundation of Nora to Iberians under the leadership of Norax, grandson of Geryon. On the relationship of the Sardinian Bronze Age to Iberia, see Santos Velasco 1997, 161-6. According to Santos Velasco the tale of Norax reflects the fact that in the ninth/ early eighth century BC prior to the arrival of the Phoenicians, the indigenous population controlled shipping in the Western Mediterranean (162).

7. See Karageorghis 2005.

8. Ps.-Scymnos 164 refers to the wealth of tin, gold and bronze to be found in Tartessos.

9. The story of the Phoenicians finding so much silver that they had to make silver anchors is repeated in Ps.-Aristotle *De Mirabilibus Auscultationibus* 135.

10. Native pottery predominates with 2,542 pieces compared to 1,173 sherds of wheel-made pottery; see Pellicer Catalán 1983, 67.

11. The technique of trench mining is repeated at a number of sites that may be of a similarly

early date to the mines at Chinflón: at Cuevas de Masegoso, Minas de Masegoso, Cuevas de Monje, Cuchillares, see Rothenburg *et al.* 1981, 42-4, 49-50, 51-60, 81-2; smelting at Corta Lago, see Rothenburg *et al.* 1981, 101-6.

12. Excavations in Plaza de las Monjas 12 and C/de Méndez Núñez 7-13 in 1997 revealed Attic Mid Geometric II vessels dated *c.* 800-750 BC and subprotogeometric Euboean-Cycladic *skyphoi* (Kearsley type 6) dated *c.* 850-750 BC; see González de Canales Cerisola *et al.* 2004, 184, 196-7.

13. An eighth-century BC date has been suggested for a Phoenician wall excavated on the hill of San Pedro, see Ruiz Mata *et al.* 1981, 256-9.

14. The introduction of coinage at Aegina, Corinth and Athens in the first half of the sixth century BC indicates that there would have been a consistent trade in precious metals by this date; see Chamorro 1987, 203. Unstratified finds from Calles Méndez Núñez, Rafael López and del Puerto have suggested the existence of a permanent Greek enclave at Huelva with the presence of a Greek sanctuary – perhaps dedicated to Demeter and Kore in the vicinity of the harbour; see Garrido *et al.* 1994, 56. Excavations at C/ Méndez Núñez 5-7 yielded pottery dated between 590-570 and 560 BC; see Fernández Jurado *et al.* 1994, 73.

15. Excavations on El Cabezo de la Esperanza have revealed evidence for silverworking and a possible furnace dated to the seventh-sixth centuries BC; see Garrido Roiz 1966, 7. Slag is included among the grave goods in the necropolis at La Joya, see Gómez Ramos 1999, 125-6.

16. Two possible kilns have been found; however, the lack of any evidence for metalworking or ceramic production makes their identification and use unclear: Fernández Jurado 1987, 112-13. The site may have been devoted to mining rather than metallurgy – pre-Roman mines have been identified 1 km to the west at El Carmen and Trinidad, and there is abundant evidence of pre-Roman mining along the Río Corumbel – perhaps centred upon the site at Rozas del Gallego; see Rothenburg *et al.* 1981, 63-6, 234.

17. Analysis of the slag from San Bartolomé reveals a similar composition to that of Los Castrejones, see Hunt Ortiz 1995, 454.

18. Castillo de Doña Blanca was originally thought to have been a native community with a strong Phoenician presence; see Ruiz Mata 1986. Subsequently the excavators have interpreted the settlement as having been Phoenician: Ruiz Mata 2002, 174.

19. Traces of metalworking are reported from the 1995 season at Cerro del Villar; see Gómez Ramos 1999, 122.

20. Particularly interesting is the presence of a Phoenician graffito on an indigenous grey ware carenaded bowl, see Suárez Marquez *et al.* 1987, 17.

21. For a discussion of the literary sources referring to Tartessos, see Blázquez Martínez 1969; de Hoz 1989.

22. Murphy 1977, 59n.291 notes the association of Tartessos with Mons Argentarius is erroneous as the mountain was not located near the Lacus Ligustinus but rather near Castulo. Avienus places an island controlled by the Tartessians in the vicinity of Málaga (428-9).

23. Aubet Semmler 1975, 134 notes that the homogeneity of the pottery fabric suggests a common origin in the vicinity of Setefilla.

24. The rim size varies between 1.6 and 2.4 cm.

25. For a connection with the Straits of Gibraltar, see also dolphin bones in the bichrome cup found in urn 17 under tumulus A, see Maluquer de Motes *et al.* 1981, 88.

26. The identification of cremation burials predating the arrival of the Phoenicians – for example, tumulus 1 at Las Cumbres, Mesas de Asta and elsewhere (Torres Ortiz 2000, 358) throws into doubt the traditional view that the practice of cremation was introduced by the colonists, e.g. Aubet Semmler 2002, 214.

27. The lack of stratigraphy within the structure of the tumuli supports their having been constructed in a single phase, see Maluquer de Motes *et al.* 1981, 61-3; Aubet Semmler 1982, 51.

28. The presence of stelai around tumulus A at Setefilla as well as the discovery of an

engraved stele in 1927 (Aubet Semmler 1975, 160) may reflect the continuation of the earlier Bronze Age social hierarchy into the Orientalizing period. The occupants of the tumuli may have reinforced their status by adopting earlier Bronze Age symbols of status and social differentiation also including the use of inhumation; see Maluquer de Motes *et al.* 1981, 157.

29. The fill of tumulus A contained grave-goods from an earlier burial destroyed by the construction of the tumulus. The orientalizing burial included incised ivories like those from Cruz del Negro, ostrich eggs and amphorae of the seventh/ mid-sixth centuries BC; see del Arco Aguilar 1991, 93.

30. A stone funerary chamber was found underlying tumulus 1 at Huelva but not excavated; see Torres Ortiz 1999, 63. An Ionic cup from the fill of the tumulus gives a *terminus post quem* for the tumulus of 580 BC.

31. Osteological analysis has revealed the presence of horses amongst the ashes associated with a possible *ustrinum* in sector B; see Garrido *et al.* 2000, 1807.

32. Frankenstein 1994 notes that ivory and alabaster were used as symbols of royal status in the Near East and that their appearance in Tartessian tombs points to the creation of 'client kings' by the Phoenicians. However, alabastra and ivories are not confined to wealthy burials and occur in simple cremations lacking other indications of wealth or acculturation, e.g. Cruz del Negro tombs 1, 2, 7, 8, 19 and 28, see Torres 1999, 131; Maier 1999.

33. Torres 1999, 142 has suggested that the closest parallels to the Phoenician exploration of the Iberian Peninsula are to be found in Sicily where the Phoenician settlers at Motya established friendly relations with the native Elymi; see Leighton 1999, 229-30.

34. An Ionian cup similar to those from Huelva and dated to the first half of the sixth century BC has been found at La Bienvenida (Almodóvar del Campo, Ciudad Real), see García Huerta *et al.* 1996, 336.

35. Greek pottery dating to the fifth century BC has been recovered, including the foot of a Castulo cup dating to the second half of the fifth century, see Celestino Pérez 1999, 156-7.

36. The perimeter of the necropoleis of Pajares II and El Cardenillo may have been marked by stones serving a similar function to the perimeter of tumulus A at Setefilla.

37. Three furnaces dated between the third and first century BC have been excavated at Los Castillejos 2; iron slag and a smelting furnace of the third to first century BC has been excavated at El Castrejón de Capote, see Rámos Gomez 1999, 128.

38. The discoveries were made during tin mining operations between 1950 and 1962, making any dating difficult.

39. Arruda 1999, 56 rejects the eighth-century BC date for the site, arguing instead for a date at the end of the sixth century BC.

40. A possible Phoenician colony was located at Quinta do Almaraz at the mouth of the Tagus. The site has yielded a number of orientalizing features: a lack of handmade pottery, red slip wares, an *alabastron*; however, the red slip comes from a single rubbish tip and no other features of the site have been published, see Arruda 1999, 110.

41. The excavators likened Roça do Casal do Meio to Nuraghic sites in Sardinia, see Spindler *et al.* 1973, 150.

42. A ninth-century date was given for the anchor inscribed with Phoenician letters that was found off the coast of Cartagena in 1964, see Martín Camino 1994, 295.

43. On the possibility of an earlier, as yet unidentified, archaic fortification, see González Prats 1999, 21.

44. Quantities of lead, silver and iron have also been found at La Escuera which replaced El Oral in the second half of the fifth century BC, see Abad Casal *et al.* 1993, 201.

45. A vein of galena with a high silver content is located at Moralet (Alicante); copper was found in the Sierras of Orihuela and Crevillente and evidence of copper working has been excavated at Las Peñicas de Santomera (Murcía); tin was found in the vicinity of Cartagena-La Unión, see Herandez Perez 1983, 37.

46. A Chalcolithic settlement with evidence of metal working has also been found, see González Prats 1992, 245.

47. Lesser quantities came from the vicinity of Cádiz-Huelva and elsewhere along the Mediterranean coast.

48. The settlement of Plana Justa (Xàbia) situated on the south-eastern slopes of Montgó has yielded Phoenician and Greek imported pottery of the eighth-fifth centuries BC – Vuillemont R 1, Ebusitanian and Massiliot amphorae and Castulo cups, together with iron ore. Unfortunately the relationship of the ore to the other finds from the site is unknown, see Bolufer Marqués *et al.* 2003, 81.

49. The buckle dates to the seventh century BC and the *thymiaterion* to the first half of the sixth century, see García Gandía 2003, 225-6.

50. Ps.-Aristotle *Politics* 293 says that the Carthaginians dispatched colonists to relieve population pressure.

51. Excavations in the square of San Pablo in Málaga have revealed an indigenous settlement on the west bank of the Río Guadalmedina dating back to the late eighth century BC, see Fernández *et al.* 1997, 228. The site has yielded evidence of metallurgy as well as agricultural activities and may have functioned to trade with the Phoenician settlers before being abandoned at the beginning of the seventh century BC.

52. Further ceramic kilns dated to the eighth-seventh centuries BC were excavated in 1995 in sector 9, see Aubet Semmler *et al.* 1999, 18.

53. Storage-transport vessels account for 47.41% of the pottery found, see Barceló *et al.* 1995, 171.

54. Cereal crops are the most numerous cultivated plants in Cortes 3 and 3/4 accounting for 13.68% of the total sample, see Aubet *et al.* 1999, 310-11.

55. The ratio of adult to juvenile cattle bones bears out the importance of agriculture. Thirty-nine adults compared to five juveniles were identified in Corte 3/4, indicating that the cattle were kept for milk and use as draught animals rather than being killed for meat, see Aubet *et al.* 1999, 316.

56. Ramón type 10.1.1.1 and 10.1.2.1, see Ramón Torres 1995, 82.

57. The excavators have compared Building C with warehouses at Hazor and elsewhere, see Niemeyer 2002, 37.

58. The site of Los Pinares may have served a similar function being located on the periphery of the colonial hinterland, see Martín Cordoba *et al.* 2002, 95-6.

59. Canary grass accounts for 53.6% of the sample from Phase III followed by 19.6% bread wheat and 10.5% barley, see Rosselló and Morales 1994, 27. Cereal crops predominate in eighth- to seventh-century BC levels at La Fonteta (66%), see Pilar Iborra *et al.* 2003, 43.

60. See Columella *De Re Rustica* 12,19,1.

61. Faunal evidence for vines has been recovered from Celtiberia during the sixth century BC, for example at Cabezo de la Cruz de la Muela (Zaragoza); however, the grapes seem to have been consumed as fruit rather than wine, Burillo Mozota *et al.* 2006, 4.

62. A single amphora of Florido IV type – similar to later forms of Vuillemont R1 dating from the first half of the sixth century BC found at the Casa-Palacio del Marqués de Saltillo may have been produced at Cerro Macareno, Belén *et al.* 1997, 84.

63. Luzón 1973, 16-23. The dating of the kiln is disputed: according to Luzón (1973, 25) the kiln dates to the second half of the second century BC, however, the amphorae associated with the kiln conform to Ramón T. 8.1.1.2 and T. 8.2.1.1 that date to the fourth and third centuries BC, Ramón Torres 1995, 222, 225.

64. Four kilns have been excavated at La Casa Guerra (Requena) and a further kiln at La Maralaga dated to the second-first centuries BC, see Duarte Martínez *et al.* 2000, 235-7. 80% of the pottery associated with the four kilns excavated at La Casa Guerra (Requena) consists of storage vessels. The kilns date from the fifth century to the end of the fourth or beginning of the third century BC, Duarte Martínez *et al.* 2000, 235-6.

65. Manuel Cerrillo Millán (2005, 50) has suggested that the sturgeon found at Acinipo (Ronda, Málaga) in levels dated 820 ± 90 BC associated with the earliest wheel-made pottery was imported from the estuaries of the Guadalquivir, Guadiaro or Guadalete.

66. The excavators suggest that four amphorae found with a pitch lining were also used for salted fish products, see González de Canales Cerisola *et al.* 2004, 176.

67. Eupolis fr. 186, Antiphanes fr. 77, see J.M. Edmonds, *The Fragments of Attic Comedy* (Leiden, 1961); see also Curtis 1991, 46 n. 21; Rouillard 1991, 210.

68. Both techniques are described in the eighth-/ ninth-century AD Ms. Lat. 11219 of the Bibliothèque Nationale in Paris, see Curtis 1991, 193.

69. Elsewhere Cato states that one and a half pounds of salt were necessary to produce brine of sea water, *De Agricultura* 106.

70. The earliest evidence for fish sauce production comes from Acinipo (Ronda, Málaga) where an unidentified Phoenician amphora of South Spanish origin containing the remains of *garum* has been found in levels dating to the seventh century BC, see Carrilero Millán 2005, 51. Niveau de Villedary (2007, 419-26) argues that the remains from the Plaza de Asdrúbal are not of a fishery but rather a necropolis.

71. Phoenician Vuillemont R1 amphorae together with fish bones are recorded in seventh-century BC contexts at Teatro de Andalucía, suggesting the possibility of an earlier fish factory on the site, see Muñoz Vicente *et al.* 1999, 204.

72. The presence of Mañá-Pascual A4 amphorae at Teatro Andalucía may indicate the existence of a factory in the vicinity, see Cobos Rodríguez 1999, 30. Hearths have been found on the site dated to the eighth century BC associated with remains of tunny, bream and marine molluscs, see Cobos Rodríguez 1999, 27.

73. A Muñoz E1 amphora was found in the vicinity of vat 1, see Perdigones Moreno *et al.* 1989, 93.

74. *Sparidae* (0.80%) and *Myliobatis aquila* (0.20%) were also found, see Ramón Torres *et al.* 2007, 304.

75. Kiln H4 at Torre Alta may date to the fifth century BC in view of its similarity to the kilns at Camposoto, see Sáez Romero 2004, 707.

76. The quantities involved are small accounting for less that 2% and 1% respectively.

77. The only other Phoenician fish salting installations to have been found are on the island of Sicily at San Vito and Cala Minnola dating from the end of the fourth century BC or beginning of the third century, see Purpura 1982, 53.

78. A Cretan origin has also been suggested on the basis of finds of *Murex* from Middle Minoan II and III levels (*c.* 1900-1700/1650 BC) at Palaikastro, Kouphonisi, Kythera, Knossos and Mallia, see Stieglitz 1994, 49-52, Coldstream *et al.* 1972, 37, Bosanquet 1904, 321.

79. Of these *Murex trunculus* appears to have been the most widely used, see Ziderman 2004, 42.

80. Pliny specifies that one sextarius of salt (approximately 7 lbs) should be added to each 100 lbs of dye, and an amphora (8 gallons) of water was used to dilute 500 lbs of dyestuff, see Ziderman 1990, 99.

81. The silting up of the mouth of the Río Vélez may have been a contributing factor. The harbour was abandoned at the beginning of the sixth century BC and by the Imperial period was completely buried by river sediment, see Arteaga *et al.* 1997, 120.

82. A second Greek colony lay on the northern shore of the Bay of Rosas. According to Strabo (3.4.8; 14.2.10) Rhode was founded by Rhodians before 776 BC. This date is not supported archaeologically as the earliest finds from the site date to the fifth century BC, see Maluquer de Motes 1963, 99-100; Ruiz de Arbulo 1984, 115.

83. Although the ubiquity of Athenian pottery meant that it could be traded by merchants of various nationalities, see Ruiz de Arbulo 1992, 68.

84. Domínguez Monedero 1984, 196-7 has suggested that the silos were cisterns to store

water used to macerate the flax for which Emporion was famous, see Strabo 3.4.9. This identification has since been refuted by Ruiz de Arbulo 1992, 64.

85. Pliny *Natural History* 18.306 describes the use of underground pits for the storage of grain in Spain, Cappadocia, Thrace and North Africa; see also Columella *De Re Rustica* 1.6.15.

86. The *oppidum* controlled a cultivable area of 5600 ha. that included the silos at Garrigàs, Vilafant and Saus-Camallera, see Pons i Brun *et al.* 2001, 148. The identification of silos at Saus is uncertain, see Pujol Puigvehí 1989 vol. 2, 63.

87. Three further silos have been found at Fontudana, see Pons i Brun *et al.* 2001, 153.

88. A further site – Puig de Serra – consisting of a settlement of the second half of the sixth century BC and a necropolis dated between the mid-fifth century and the mid-fourth century BC was discovered in 1982, see Martín Ortega *et al.* 1999, 11-12.

89. Imported pottery accounts for 14.35% of the total between 400 and 375 BC increasing to 79.10% between 375 and 350 BC, see Picazo 1977, ix.

90. Linseed oil is also cultivated from the flax, see Mayerson 1997, 202.

91. The hoard of bronzes discovered in Sant Martí d'Empuries in 1918 points to connections with the Atlantic metal trade during the Late Bronze Age, see Santos Retolaza 2003, 92-3.

92. Copper, argentiferous lead, iron and gold are also found in the hinterland of Rhode, see Ruiz de Arbulo 1984, 125-6.

93. Quantities of iron slag have suggested the presence of an iron workshop dated to the fourth-third centuries BC to the north of the *oppidum* of Puig de Sant Andreu, see Martín Ortega *et al.* 2000, 252.

94. A single piece of lead has also been found, see Martín Ortega *et al.* 1999, 244.

95. Ruiz de Arbulo (1984, 127) cites the existence of quantities of iron, lead and copper from the excavations of the Neapolis between 1908 and 1937. Iron smelting furnaces at Les Coves and adjoining the Hellenistic harbour wall are dated to the second-first centuries BC, see Sanmartí Grego 1995, 163-5.

96. At the time the furnace was identified as a cooking stove.

97. Massiliot amphorae are present in only limited quantities, see Sanmartí Grego *et al.* 1990, 169-70.

98. On the dating of examples from Cerro Macareno, see Sanchez 1992, 330.

99. The fragmentary base of an amphora possibly from Southern Italy or Sicily was found in excavations of the northwest corner of the Temple of Zeus – Serapis in 1986, see Sanmartí Grego *et al.* 1986, 175.

100. Emporion may have been the source of the Punic amphorae found in the 1977 excavations at Rosas that were produced in Tunisia or western Sicily in the fourth-third centuries BC, see Ramón Torres 1995, 36.

101. Identical Mañá-Pascual A4a amphorae have been found at Cartagena, Colmenar and Cueva del Jarro, see Ramón Torres 1985, 384.

102. Examples from Trayamar were lined with resin indicating a use with wine or salted fish products, Miró i Canals 1983, 181.

103. Rhys Carpenter (1925, 117-25) locates the colony at Peñón d'Ifach, Calpe. On the Greek remains on the Peñón, see Aranegui Gascó 1973. Martín (1968, 58-9) argues that Hemeroskopeion does not refer to any single location but to any prominent site suitable for use as a harbour.

104. Carpenter (1925, 54-5) locates Alonis at Javea on the basis of the Iberian hoard discovered there. He notes that the Río Jalon may recall the Greek name and that the Río Gorgos has a strangely ancient ring to it!

105. Amphorae dating to the fifth century BC have been found off shore, see de Juan Fuertes 2002, 123.

106. Further finds were made in the Plaza de Estudiantes by Beltrán Villagrasa, Martí Bonafé 1998, 98.

107. The remains of a temple in the Calle del Sagrario have been associated with the temple of Artemis and dated to the fifth-fourth centuries BC, Almagro-Gorbea *et al.* 1999, 69-74; Moneo 2003, 184-9.

108. Gil-Mascarell and Aranegui Gascó 1977, 198 record the discovery of a kiln at Murta whose existence is unclear, see Martí Bonafé 1998, 135.

109. Quantities of pottery, ash and ceramic waste suggest the presence of a kiln at Barranc del Pla de l'Ajub and a kiln has been located at Mont dels Terrers, Gil-Mascarell *et al.* 1977, 196, 198; Llobregat Conesa 1972, 67; Munzó Nogués 1946, 66.

110. Fragments of mills were found in rooms 2, 4, 5, 6 and 13 as well as in the street.

111. Two further kilns have not been excavated, see García Martín 2003, 30.

112. Bronze Age levels of the site have yielded fish bones and marine molluscs, see Simón García 1997, 125.

113. Parallels are discussed more fully by Llobregat Conesa 1989, 328-9.

114. Almagro Gorbea et al. (1990, 290) have suggested that temple A functioned as a palace. A Phoenician presence is suggested by the altar from temple B, which is similar to examples from Villaricos and Carthage, see Llobregat Conesa 1991, 274-5.

115. The altar is oriental in design paralleling Canaanite, Israelite and Phoenician examples as well as examples from Carthage and Villaricos, see Llobregat Conesa 1984, 274-5. A censer depicting Tanit was recovered from room 30 of the 'Casa del Cura', see Pastor Mira 1999, 446.

116. Earlier excavations revealed pottery of the late fifth to early third centuries BC, see San Martín 1964, 160.

117. The importance of mining to the iron age settlement of the Sierra Morena has recently been disputed by Gutiérrez Soler *et al.* 2000.

118. Dated to the first half of the fourth century BC by Blanco Freijero 1959, 109-12.

119. See Richardson 2000, 151.

3. The Republican Period

1. The few finds reported from the initial excavations confirm the dating of the villa to the end of the second century BC and beginning of the first century: Campanian A (Lamboglia 36), Campanian B (Lamboglia 5/7), Catalan grey ware and Italian coarse ware, Aquilué i Abadías *et al.* 1990, 98; Jàrrega Domínguez 2000, 285.

2. The villa was expanded during the third century AD with an increase in the size of facilities devoted to the agricultural production – either wine or olive oil, and an expansion of the baths originally constructed during the preceding phase, Pardo 1984, 10. Traces of painted stucco survive on the north and west corners of the baths, Garriga Casteblanque 1996, 10.

3. Ribera Lacomba (2006, 81) has suggested that Valentia's support for Sertorius and its destruction by Pompey in 75 BC was due to its Italian roots.

4. Fear (1996, 15) has suggested that these foundations were primarily propaganda gestures that were unlikely to attract long-term interest from their founders and were, therefore, unlikely to act as agents of Romanization amongst the local population.

5. Downs (1996, 56) suggests that Strabo's inclusion of both Romans and natives in the town would have meant that it would not have been a colony. The town probably received its *cognomen* 'Patricia' during the period of Caesar and Augustus and may have been granted colonial status at this time. As Robert Knapp (1983, 11-12) has noted, however, Strabo is explicit that Cordoba was the 'first colony' and therefore did not receive colonial status at a later date.

6. Although these may also have included Romanized natives, see Fear 1996, 41 on Gades.

7. A possible temple dated to the first decades of the second century underlies the later temples at La Encarnación (Caravaca de la Cruz), see Brotons Yagüe *et al.* 1994, 75.

8. The moulding at the base of the podium is like that of the Republican temples at Tivoli and Ostia, see Beltrán Lloris 2002, 449.

9. Silo I contained two Attic Black Glaze *skyphoi* (form Morel 4342) dated to the second half of the fourth century BC, one of which carried graffiti in Greek and Iberian script, Casas i Genover 1989, 39-40.

10. The excavators calculated a population of seven for the site on the basis of a storage capacity of 2,025 kg of grain in the excavated silos, see Bosch *et al.* 1987, 231.

11. In 1984 excavations on the hill of La Muntanyeta to the south of the town of Sant Boi de Llobregat uncovered a basin lined with *opus signinum*; however, the lack of excavations means that the context of the basin is unknown, see Molist i Capella 1993, 79.

12. Attic pottery of the fifth-fourth centuries BC has also been found, see Casas i Genover *et al.* 2003, 15.

13. Two possible storage pits associated with the first phase of occupation have been excavated below the west wall of the complex, see Carreres Vidal 1992, 166.

14. Two *dolia* and a Dr 1 B amphora were found buried in the patio, see Barrasetas i Dunjó *et al.* 1997, 9.

15. The excavators identified this as a tannery. Similar basins have been found at Cabezo de Alcalá, see Beltrán Lloris 2002, 457.

16. Excavations under the Romanesque church of Sant Joan de Bellcaire uncovered remains of a basin lined with *opus signinum* together with Greco-Italic and Italian amphorae, see Codina 2004, 20-1.

17. Faunal analysis indicates an economy based on viticulture, vegetables, cereal cultivation and almonds, see Font Valentí *et al.* 1996, 61.

18. The furnace excavated to the north of the building seems to have been domestic in function, see Font Valentí *et al.* 1996, 96; 1996, 61.

19. In the majority of cases the dating of each is not in precise accord, see Olesti i Vila (1995) 203.

20. 61.07% of the pottery from Casa del Racò was locally produced, see Burch *et al.* 1994, 128.

21. 'Likine' is perhaps an Iberian form of the Latin 'Licinius', see Vicente *et al.* 1993, 752.

22. A *piscina* from a possible bath-suite has been found to the west of the villa, see Palahí Grimal *et al.* 1994, 162.

23. Three Dr 1 B amphorae found on the Carrer Lledó (Badalona) were locally produced, Puerta *et al.* 1987, 188.

24. Lamboglia 2 have been found alongside local Dr 1 elsewhere in Mataró: Plaça de la Peixateria, Barcelona 55-7, García i Roselló *et al.* 1996, 404-6.

25. An example has been found alongside Tarraconense 1 and Pascual 1 amphorae in a cistern dated to the last quarter of the first century BC at Sant Francesc d'Assís 16 (Mataró), García i Rosselló *et al.* 1996, 402-3.

26. While Italian imports predominated in levels dated *c.* 60-50 BC from the harbour area of Baetulo: accounting for 63% (Dr 1B 40%, Dr 1A 28%, Dr 1C 34% and 9% unspecified) compared to 3% from the Adriatic (Lamboglia 2), 19% from Africa (Punic PE 15, 17, 18 and 24; Tripolitanian amphorae and Dr 18); local production: 1% local Dr 1 and 12% Tarraconense 1. By 40-30 BC local production predominates accounting for 44% compared to 27% Italian imports: Tarraconense 1 50%, Pascual 1 42%, local Dr 1 5% and a possible Dr 2-4, Comas i Solà 1998, 222.

27. The name 'Tarraconense 1' is preferred in recognition of the fact they were produced over a wider area than is implied by the use of 'Laietana'.

28. The site may have been occupied at the end of the Iberian period in the third century BC, Olesti i Vila 1995, 482.

29. Pascual (1980, 278) suggests a possible connection with the Etruscan deity Voltumna.

30. Sebastian Ramallo Asensio *et al.* 1994, 88-9, 91 have suggested that the need to control the silver mines of the vicinity contributed to the foundation of Carthago Nova and led to Scipio's rapid capture of the city in 209 BC.

31. A pavement of *opus signinum* has also been found at Fábrica La Pura on the north slope of the hill of Sancti Spiritu together with Campanian A and B pottery. An *opus signinum* pavement has also been uncovered at Faro el Estacio, see Ruiz Valderas 1995, 160.

32. Furnaces have been found at Lomo del Alamillo (Mazarrón) and Los Tinteros (Isla Plana), see Agüera Martínez *et al.* 1993, 528.

33. Domergue and Mas (1982, 907-8) have suggested that this is the same Minucius Pica cited by Varro (*De Re Rustica* 3.2.2).

34. As well as Campanian A vessels, there is an increase in other Campanian products: Calena pottery (3.3%) and Emporitanian D that may have been produced in Pompeii (1.1%), see Ruiz Valderas 1995, 95.

35. The colonnade on the calle Morería Baja dating to the end of the second century BC or beginning of the first century BC may also be part of the development of the harbour at this time, see Noguera Celdrán 2004, 72.

36. Cn. Atellius Cn.f. Bulio attested on ingots may also be pre-Caesarian in date, see Abascal Palazón *et al.* 1997, 249.

37. Five ingots of the same *societas* were found at Cerro del Castillo, see Ramallo Asensio *et al.* 1994, 108.

38. See also Mela 2.85; Strabo 3.4.8.

39. The villa may also have been engaged in cereal cultivation, as a millstone has been recovered from the site, see Leiva Briones *et al.* 1992, 248.

40. Castillo de Doña Blanca was abandoned at the end of the third century BC as was the fishery at Puerto 19 at the end of the third century BC or beginning of the second century BC, cf. Sáez Romero *et al.* 2007, 466.

41. The third-century AD mosaic found in the crypt of the Convento de los Franciscos Descalzos may date to a later phase of the fishery, see Cobos Rodríguez 1999, 20.

42. The function of the basin is unclear: Enrique García Vargas (1998, 159) has suggested that it was used for the decantation of clay. Blanco Jimenez (1990, 79) on the other hand has proposed that it is a salting vat.

43. Remains of fisheries have been found nearby on calle Abarzuza and at La Caleta, see Blanco Jimenez 1991, 78.

44. The amphorae also contained bones of pigs, sheep and goats creating a mixed product, see Arévalo González *et al.* 2007, 83.

45. Beltrán III vessels were also present.

46. Campanian pottery may also have been produced, Niveau de Villedary y Mariñas 2004, 681.

47. Dario Bernal Casasola 1998, 27 has suggested that the Dr 21-22 are in fact Lomba di Canho 67 or Sala I vessels dating to the second half of the first century BC.

48. The predominance of wine amphorae over *garum* vessels has led to the suggestion that the principal export of the region during this period was wine, not fish sauce. Fernández Cacho (1995, 189-90), however, has suggested that the amphorae here would have carried fish sauce. A local Dr 1 A vessel from the fishery at Punta Camarinal – El Anclón contained remains of fish sauce, see Arévalo González *et al.* 2007, 87.

4. Augustan Expansion

1. A second press may have stood in the northeast corner of room V, see Brun 2004, 271.

2. Clay may also have been brought from elsewhere: a number of *negotiatores cretarii* are known, for example the M. Secundinius Silvanus, a *negotiator cretarius britannicus* recorded on an altar from Coljinsplaat, see Hassall 1978, 41-6.

3. David Peacock (1982, 73) has suggested that rectangular kilns were used for brick and tile, while circular kilns – particularly in Baetica – seem to have been used for amphorae.

4. J. Puig i Cadalfach identified area A' of sector 2 as a pressing room, see Revilla Calvo

2003, 294; Pou i Vallès *et al.* 1996, 111; Palet *et al.* 1993, 737. Quantities of *dolia* were also recovered during the 1883 excavations.

5. Pou i Vallès *et al.* 1996, 109 reports the excavation of a kiln in 1994 dating to the second half of the second century BC.

6. Quantities of *dolia* were found in 1967 during the excavation of two cisterns 6-7 m to the east of sector 2, see Palet *et al.* 1993, 736.

7. A third basin lined with *opus testaceum* may have been located to the north of the larger of the two basins, see Prevosti i Monclús 1981, 245.

8. Ribas' initial discoveries in 1963 included amphorae, *dolia*, *tegulae* and *imbrices*, see Pujol i del Horno *et al.* 1996-7, 348.

9. The ovoid kiln similar to the no longer extant kiln at Vall d'Uxó, see Alcina Franch 1949.

10. Carbonized grapes – *Vitis vinifera* – have been recovered from the site, see Brun 2004, 267.

11. Remains of two further basins were excavated in 1986.

12. Possible traces of two further kilns have been found: estructuras D and E, which underlie the later kilns A and B; see Revilla Calvo 1993, 39.

13. Occupation may have begun at the end of the second century or beginning of the first century BC thanks to the presence of Dr 1 amphorae and Campanian B pottery, see Nolla i Brufau *et al.* 1984, 137.

14. A *tegula* recovered from carrer Llevant n. 7 bears the stamp SVL.VEIEN, Barti Català *et al.* 1989, 141. Painted stucco was recovered from level E3 of estança A-B, Barti Català *et al.* 1989, 141.

15. A fragment of a Pascual 1 amphora produced at Llafranc has been recovered from Puig Rodó. The importance of Llafranc as a focus of the surrounding hinterland is reflected in its alignment to the lines of centuriation, see Barti Català *et al.* 1989, 146.

16. Luxsia, the daughter of Aulus Antestius is named on a curse tablet from Carmona, see Stylow 2005, 261.

17. The stamp also occurs on an unspecified amphora from Ensérune, Pascual Guash 1991, 75.

18. A T. Valerius Rufus is attested in Rome, *CIL* 2.28104.

19. For example Miró i Canals 1988, 217 cites the stamp as appearing on *tegulae*.

20. Rico 1995, 203 suggests that the *tegulae* originated in the vicinity of Frejus.

21. Wiseman 1971, 199 refers to M. Herennius Picens as a *negotiator* involved in the amphora trade, perhaps related to the M. Herennius Picens who was suffect consul in 34 BC, proconsul of Asia in 33 BC and father of the suffect consul of AD 1, Wiseman 1971, 235.

22. Callender 1965, 11 lists a *titulus pictus* reading v(inum) veientan(um).

23. Lentulus died in AD 25 at which time Suetonius (*Tiberius* 49.1) tells us that his property was confiscated by the emperor Tiberius. Gianfrotta (1982, 478) suggests that the seizure of Lentulus' estates explains the presence of a stamp from Port-la-Nautique that reads IMP(eratoris) and suggests that Iulius Anicetus and Iulius Theophilus were imperial freedmen – an hypothesis for which I have found no support.

24. M. Porcius Narbonensis pursued an Equestrian military career culminating in the offices of *Praefectus Orae Maritimae* and *Flamen Divorum Augustorum per Provinciae Hispaniae Citerioris*, *RIT* n. 301.

25. Tchernia (1971, 69) has suggested a link with the island of Ebusus – the Catalan Eivissa.

26. Torre Llauder lies between the río Besos and Arenys – an area of 210 km^2 within which ten kilns have been located, see Prevosti i Monclús *et al.* 1987, 200.

27. A Loeschcke IA lamp dating to the reign of Augustus has been found, see Oria Segura *et al.* 1990, 63. The small size of the site and the poverty of the finds suggest that this was a small site with the presence of *dolia* suggesting agricultural activities.

28. Although finds of pre-Roman gold jewellery has been used to explore the distribution of pre-Roman mining activity, many of the finds were no longer *in situ* making their dating and provenance difficult to determine.

29. Domergue has argued that several terms are of pre-Roman origin: *agoga*, *corrugo* and *gandadia* (1990, 484-92). *Arrugia* is an indigenous term used to describe any type of canal.

30. Pliny's description of Astorga (*Natural History* 3.28) is often cited as being first-hand.

31. Lewis and Jones (1970, 184) suggest that Pliny's account is confused, conflating two separate processes. Sánchez Palencia (2000, 213) has pointed out, however, that this interpretation is based on the erroneous relation of the adverb *gradatim* to the excavation of the canal rather than the placing of gorse along the base of the canal.

32. Based on an average yield of 50 mg of gold per m^3.

33. A second gallery, 250 m in length, survives at El Reirigo on the southern side of Las Médulas.

34. Ingots are also marked with graffiti denoting their weight, the amount they exceed a standard weight or symbols of uncertain use, see Domergue 1998, 203.

35. On the ingots from the Cabrera 4 wreck, see Parker 1992, 126. Similarly ingots from the Saint Maries de la Mer 1 wreck bear stamps of L. Flavius Verucla together with IMP.CAES, see Remesal Rodríguez 1998, 207.

36. For the Sud-Lavezzi B wreck, see Liou 1982, 442-7; Parker 1992, 414-15.

37. Domergue has suggested that there was a shift in elite investment in mining to agriculture during the late Republic and early Imperial periods, however, the sources do not record any family or individual whose economic interests shifted from mining to agriculture during this period.

38. Dio 58.22.2 records that Marius fell out of favour with Tiberius because he refused the emperor's advances towards his daughter.

39. The *Antonine Itinerary* (206) refers to a Mons Marianorum in Seville.

40. Wine may also have been supplied: inscription e reads '(v)inum', see Gimeno Pascual *et al.* 2007, 189.

41. A. Morillo Cerdán has associated these lamps with the presence of Roman troops. They have been found at Empúries and at Herrera de Pisuerga where L. Terentius supplied lamps and *terra sigillata* to the Legio IIII Macedonica, see Pérez Macías *et al.* 2007, 74.

42. See González Serrano 1988, 298.

43. A fourth kiln has not been excavated, see Lavado Florido 2004, 478.

44. García Vargas 1998, 186 cites the possible presence of Dr 1C on the site.

45. Kiln H. 101 in Sector C is less well preserved with only part of wall M-105 surviving, however, it seems to have been similar in design to kiln H. 102, see Bernal *et al.* 1998, 81-3.

46. The peristyle (villa B) dates to the second phase from the middle of the first century AD, see Aguilar Sáenz *et al.* 1995, 142.

47. Haley (2003, 44) has suggested that Strabo and Pompeius Trogus (*apud* Justin) may have praised the prosperity of Baetica because the first prefect of the *annona* in AD 8, C. Turranius Gracilis was from Cádiz.

48. For the tax concessions received by merchants, see *Digest* 50.4.5. On concessions to merchants supplying the *annona militaris* see Whittaker 1985, 56.

5. The Roman Economy

1. The remaining 4% have been identified as 'small' Dr 2-4 vessels, see Gisbert Santonja 1987, 109.

2. The excavator has suggested that the villa may also have been engaged in processing of olive oil with a possible small press in square I-9 adjoining the *cortinale*, see Mezquíriz Irujo 2003, 130. The stone base of a *mola olearia* was found against the east wall of the *cella vinaria*, see Mezquíriz Irujo 2004, 138.

3. The *dolia* found in the *cella* at Arellano would have been able to contain 30 amphorae (700-800 litres), see Mezquíriz Irujo 2003, 204.

4. Basin n. 1 measure 5 x 1.7 m and is 1.55 m deep; Basin n. 2 measures 5.80 x 2.00 m and is 1.45 m deep; Basin n. 3 measures 4.80 x 1.20 m and is 1.60 m deep; Basin n. 4 measures 3.40 x 1.80 m and is 1.55 m deep.

5. For the processing of olive oil, see Curtis 2001, 380-94; Brun 2003, 146-64.

6. Columella also refers to the use of a *tudicula* or threshing sledge and to treading the olives, although the *mola* and *trapetum* were more effective. The distinction between a *mola* and *trapetum* is problematic as Cato refers only to the use of a *trapetum* (*De Re Rustica* 64-9) and Varro describes the two as synonymous (*De Re Rustica* 1.64). Frankel (1993, 478) has suggested that the *mola* was the horizontal mill that was found in the Guadalquivir valley.

7. See also Cato *De Agricultura* 66.

8. The lees could also be removed from the oil by overflow or underflow decantation whereby the oil flows from one vat to the next leaving a residue of lees behind, see Curtis 2001, 394.

9. Small quantities of *terra sigillata italica* have also been found. The earliest piece is the rim of a Haltern 7 vessel dated *c.* 25-20 BC, see Gener Basallote *et al.* 1992, 101.

10. A *titulus pictus* on a Dr 20 from Alcester appears to refer to the contents of the amphora as fish sauce: SCO FLOS.SCOM(bri). Fabric analysis shows that it may have originated in the vicinity of the villa at Cortijo de Berro II, see Williams 1994, 122.

11. Geophysical survey identified six kilns, see Chic García *et al.* 2004, 283; Remesal Rodríguez *et al.* 1997, 156.

12. Although not completely excavated the kiln will have had a central pillar supporting the firing chamber, see Remesal Rodríguez *et al.* 1997, 159.

13. Chic García (1985, 89) suggests that the kilns at El Tejarillo were associated with a nearby farm on the site of the Finca de Manuel Recuero.

14. Until the middle of the twentieth century remains of a kiln were visible on the banks of the Guadalquivir. No trace remains, although the kiln may be associated with the pottery from Sector B/B-2/3 and date to the earliest phase of activity in the first half of the first century AD see Romo Salas *et al.* 2000, 407, 415; Romo Salas 1997, 767.

15. Q. Aemilius Optatus has also been suggested, see Chic García 1994, 99; 2001, 188.

16. Several Aelii are known from inscriptions from the town: a tombstone from the vicinity of La Viña is dedicated to Aelia Flaccina, the daughter of Quintus. The lettering of the inscription suggests a date in the second half of the second century AD. An inscription dating to the first half of the second century AD records Q. Aelius Zeno, see Keay *et al.* 2000, 143-5. Aelia Optata is also known from Nescania where a statue is erected in honour of her son, L. Aelius Mela (CIL 2.5492).

17. Perhaps descended from Q. Aelius Zeno, see Keay *et al.* 2000, 171.

18. Chic García (1992, 7; 1994, 86-7) has suggested a connection with the stamps SAL.ALFO, AELFO, ALFO and POALF.

19. Liou and Marichal (1978, 117) have noted a T. Iuventius on an ingot from Castulo (*CIL* 2.6247).

20. The excavators have noted that the *gens* is Gallic in origin, see Colls *et al.* 1977, 74.

21. An example reading II.MV.S.T.PR has been found in Rome, see Callender 1965, 193; *CIL* 15.3032.

22. Callender 1965, 208 has suggested the reconstruction P.MOC(conii) V( ), [ex] FIG(linis) E(t) DO(liariis).

23. Berni Millet 1998, 213 has suggested the the stamp IIIMINICIOR is related to the variant IIMINACRETCAL – the latter individual is perhaps Q. M( ) Callaidis.

24. The villa is perhaps associated with three circular kilns that have been discovered at Cuevas del Becerro.

25. The site may be related to the undated factory on the nearby island of Saltés, see Lagóstena Barrios 2001, 96-7.

26. Further vats and remains of fish factories have been found at calle San Nicolás nos 1 and 7, see Bernal Casasola *et al.* 2003, 165.

27. The mosaic recovered from the site dates to the third century AD, see Corrales Aguilar 2001, 353.

28. A kiln was discovered and subsequently destroyed in the vicinity of Puente Mayorga, see Bernal Casasola *et al.* 2004, 458.

29. A third kiln has been found to the south. The kiln is smaller, 1.20 m in diameter, and may have been used to fire smaller coarse ware vessels, see Baldomero *et al.* 1997, 151.

30. It is not clear if the Dr 2-4 found on the site were imported or locally produced, see Beltrán Fortés *et al.* 1997, 110. A rim of a Dr 18 vessel was also found.

31. Quantities of amphorae have been recovered from the vicinity of Paseo de los Tilos suggesting the existence of a kiln in the area producing Beltrán IIA amphorae, see Beltrán Fortés *et al.* 1997, 111-12.

32. For the association of the villa with wine production, see Haley 2003, 91.

33. García del Toro (1978) refers to several fisheries in the vicinity of Cartagena but provides no further details: Las Mateas (Los Nietos), Castillico, Galifa, Escombreras, El Mojón (Puerto de Mazarrón), El Castellar, Aguilas, La Azohía and Santa Lucia, see also Ramallo Asensio 1989, 136-44.

34. Two small tanks have been discovered 16 m to the north of the factory and a third tank was destroyed, see Arruda *et al.* 1990, 200.

35. Fabric analysis suggests that the amphorae were produced at two different locations, see Arruda *et al.* 1990, 202.

36. Remains of a second vat has been discovered to the west, see Dias Diogo *et al.* 2000, 182.

37. A Dr 1B amphora was recovered, see Barros *et al.* 1984-5, 34.

38. Bones of sardines and tunny have been found, see Edmondson 1987, 266.

39. A third factory has been reported on Rua Antonio Januario da Silva, see Lagóstena Barrios 2001, 65.

40. Edmondson identifies ten freedmen/ women or possible freedmen/women compared to five slaves or possible slaves. The status of six individuals was uncertain, see Edmondson 1989, 132-3.

41. Sherds of Dr 14 vessels have also been found, see Castanheira Duarte 1990, 102.

42. See Suetonius *Tiberius* 42.1.

43. Fabric analysis carried out on a Dr 8 proved inclusive in distinguishing between a Baetican or Catalan origin for the vessel, although the authors decided in favour of the latter on archaeological grounds, see Keay *et al.* 1982, 55.

44. Corrales Aguilar (2001, 347n.15) has pointed out that whilst the inscription dates to the end of the first century AD, the amphorae date from the middle of the century.

45. Direct evidence of a relationship between municipal status and monumentalization is elusive, however, having only been observed at Baelo during the reigns of Claudius and Nero and at Celti and Munigua during the Flavian period. The precise function of the building at Celti is problematic, see Keay *et al.* 2000, 178-80; on the promotion of Celti to municipal status, see Keay *et al.* 2000, 205. For Baelo, see Sillières 1995, 87-128; Munigua, see Hauschild 1986.

46. Traces of a second kiln have also been found.

47. The dating of the inscription depends upon the restitution of the consular name: Cn. Claudius Severus Arabianus (AD 146), Cn. Claudius Severus (AD 173) or Cn. Claudius Severus (AD 235), see Edmondson 1987, 56n.67.

Bibliography

Abad Casal, L., 'En torno a dos mosaicos ilicitanos: el "helenistico" y el de conchas marinas' in *Cuadernos de Prehistoria y Arqueología, Universidad Autónoma de Madrid* 13-14 (1986-7) 97-106.

———, 'Mosaicos romanos de los Banos de la Reina, Calpe, Alicante' in *SPAL* 11 (2002) 341-64.

——— and F. Sala Sellés, 'Reflexiones sobre la metallurgia protohistórica: el poblado ibérico de El Oral (San Fulgencio, Alicante)' in R. Arana Castillo *et al.* (eds), *Metalurgia en la Península Ibérica durante el primer milenio a.C. Estado actual de la investigación* (Universidad de Murcia, 1993) 189-201.

Abascal Palazón, J.M., 'Los cognomina de parentesco en la Península Ibérica: a propósito del influjo romanizador en la onomástica' in *Lucentum* 3 (1984) 219-60.

——— and J.A. Gisbert Santonja, 'Numismatica y evidencia arqueologica en el alfar romano de la Almadrava (Setla-Mirarosa-Miraflor)' in *Lucentum* 9-10 (1990-1) 133-60.

——— and S.F. Ramallo Asensio, *La ciudad de Carthago Nova: la documentación epigráfica*, 2 vols (Universidad de Murcia, 1997).

Adroher, A.M. *et al.*, 'El yacimiento de Mas Castellar de Pontós y el comercio del cereal ibérico en la zona de Emporion y Rhode (ss. IV-II a.C.)' in *Archivo Español de Arqueología* 66 (1993) 31-70.

Aguarod Otal, M.C., 'Un ánfora Tarraconense 1/Layetana 1 con sello ibérico procedente de Salduie' in *Museo de Zaragoza Boletín* 11 (1992) 109-16.

Agüera Martínez, S. *et al.*, 'Carta arqueológica de Mazarrón, resultados de la campaña de 1992-1993' in *Memorias de Arqueología* 8 (1993) 508-22.

——— *et al.*, 'El coto minero de San Cristóbal y Los Perules (Mazarrón). Patrimonio histórico arqueológico e industrial' in *Memorias de Arqueología* 8 (1993) 524-51.

Aguilar, C., 'Denominació d'origen Lauronensis. El vi del Vallès en època romana' in *Lauro* 29 (2005) 5-12.

Aguilar Sáenz, A., 'Dependencias con funcionalidad agrícola en las villas romanas de la Península Ibérica' in *Alimenta: Estudios en homenaje al Dr. Michel Ponsich* (Anejos de Gerión 3, 1991) 261-79.

——— and P. Guichard, *La ciudad antigua de Lacimurga y su entorno rural* (Diputación de Badajoz, 1995).

Alarcón Castellano, F., 'La ocupación de la ensenada de Bolonia en época republicana. Estado de la cuestión' in A. Arévalo González and D. Bernal Casasola (eds), *Las Cetariae de Baelo Claudia. Avance de las investigaciones arqueológicas en el barrio meridional (2000-2004)* (Junta de Andalucía, 2007) 225-35.

Alcina Franch, J., 'El horno romano de Vall de Uxó y su cerámica' in *Saitabi* 31-2 (1949) 12-26.

Aldana Nacher, C., 'Aportaciones al estudio de la toréutica orientalizante en la Península Ibérica' in *Saguntum* 16 (1981) 119-36.

Alföldy, G., *Los Baebii de Saguntum* (Trabajos Varios del Servicio de Investigacíon Prehistorica 56, 1977).

Almagro Basch, M., *Excavaciones en la Palaiápolis de Ampurias* (Excavaciones Arqueologicas en España 27, Servicio de Publicaciones del Ministerio de Educacion y Ciencia, 1964).

Almagro Gorbea, M.J., 'La necrópolis de Medellín (Badajoz). Aportaciones al estudio de la penetración de influjo orientalizante en Extremadura' in *Noticiario Arqueológico Hispánico* 16 (1971) 161-202.

———, 'El periodo orientalizante en Extremadura' in *La Cultura Tartesica y Extremadura* (Cuadernos Emeritenses 2, 1990) 85-125.

———, 'La alimentación de la antigua Baria en época romana y preromana' in *Alimenta: Estudios en homenaje al Dr. Michel Ponsich* (Anejos de Gerión 3, 1991) 119-28.

———, 'La necrópolis de Medellín' in *I Jornadas de Prehistoria y Arqueología en Extremadura (1986-1990)* (Extremadura Arqueológica 2, 1991) 159-73.

———, 'La "precolonización fenicia" en la Península Ibérica' in M.E. Aubet Semmler and M. Barthélemy (eds), *Actas del IV Congreso Internacional de Estudios Fenicios y Púnicos*, vol. 2 (Universidad de Cádiz, 2000) 711-21.

——— and T. Moneo, *Santuarios urbanos en el mundo ibérico* (Real Academia de la Historia, Madrid, 2000).

——— *et al.*, 'Cancho Roano. Un palacio orientalizante en la Península Ibérica' in *Madrider Mitteilüngen* 31 (1990) 251-308.

Alvar, J. and C.G. Wagner, 'La actividad agrícola en la economía fenicia de la Península Ibérica' in *Gerión* 6 (1988) 169-85.

Álvarez García, N., 'El almacén del templo A: aproximación a espacios constructivos especializadas y su significación socio-económica' in M. Olcina Doménech (ed.), *La Illeta dels Banyets (El Campello, Alicante). Estudios de la edad del Bronce y época ibérica* (Museo Arqueológico Provincial de Alicante, 1997) 133-74.

Alves, F.J.S. *et al.*, 'A propósito dos fornos de cerâmica lusitano-romanos de S. Bartolomeu do Mar' in A. Alarcão and F. Mayet (eds), *Les amphores Lusitaniennes: typologie, production, commerce* (Museu Monográfico de Conimbriga/Mission Archéologique Française au Portugal, 1990) 193-8.

Alves Dias, M.M. and L. Coelho, 'Objectos arqueológicos dum túmulo de incineração da necrópole proto-histórica da Herdade da Favela Nova (Ourique)' in *O Arqueólogo Portugués* 4.1 (1983) 197-206.

——— *et al.*, 'Duas necrópoles da idade do ferro no Baixo-Alentejo: Ourique' in *O Arqueólogo Português* 3 (1970) 175-219.

Amaro, C., 'Benavente. Forno romano de fabrico de ânforas' in *Informação Arqueológica* 3 (1983) 12-13.

———, 'Ocupação Romana da margem sul do estuário do Tejo: um (des)alinhar de ideas' in A. Alarcão and F. Mayet (eds), *Les amphores Lusitaniennes: typologie, production, commerce* (Museu Monográfico de Conimbriga/Mission Archéologique Française au Portugal, 1990) 71-85.

———, 'Olaria romana da Garrocheira, Benavente' in A. Alarcão and F. Mayet (eds), *Les amphores Lusitaniennes: typologie, production, commerce* (Museu Monográfico de Conimbriga/Mission Archéologique Française au Portugal, 1990) 87-95.

——— *et al.*, 'Complexo fabril romano na Rua Augusta. Notícia preliminar' in G. Filipe and J.M.C. Raposo (eds), *Ocupação romana dos estuários do Tejo e do Sado* (Actas das primeiras jornadas sobre romanização dos estuários do Tejo e do Sado, Câmara Municipal do Seixal, 1996) 199-214.

Amores Carredano, F., 'Una nueva factoría romana de salazones en Trafalgar (Cádiz)' in *Habis* 9 (1978) 441-53.

Anglada, L. *et al.*, 'L'establiment de Ses Alzines i la producció de vi a la Vall de Tossa' in *El vi a l'antiguitat: economia, producció i comerç al mediterrani occidental* (Actes del II

Colloqui Internacional d'Arqueología Romana, Monografies Badalonines 14, 1998) 438-43.

Antolinos Marín, J.A., 'Estudio preliminar del complejo metalúrgico tardorrepublicano de los Beatos (Cartagena)' in *XXIV Congreso Nacional de Arqueología* (Instituto de Patrimonio Histórico, 1999) 4, 109-18.

Aquilué i Abadías, X., 'La producció de salaons i salses de peix a Empúries' in *Pescadors de l'antiga Empúries* (Museu d'Arqueología de Catalunya, 2006) 26-9.

——— and J. Pardo i Rodríguez, 'La villa romana de Can Martí (Samalús, Vallès Oriental)' in *Cypsela* 8 (1990) 87-100.

Arana Castillo, R., 'El horno romano de fundicion de la Loma de Herrerías (Mazarrón, Murcia). II. Estudio minero-metalurgico' in *XVI Congreso Nacional de Arqueologia* (Universidad de Zaragoza, 1983) 937-45.

Aranegui Gascó, C., 'Materiales arqueologicos del Peñón d'Ifac (Calpe)' in *Papeles del Laboratorio de Arqueologia de Valencia* 9 (1973) 49-69.

———, 'Anotaciones sobre las ánforas del nivel de relleno de Grau Vell (Sagunto, Valencia)' in *Saguntum* 13 (1978) 307-26.

———, 'La produccion de anforas romanas en el Pais Valenciano: estado de la cuestion' in *Archivo de Prehistoria Levantina* 16 (1981) 529-38.

———, *Excavaciones en el Grau Vell (Sagunto, Valencia) (Campañas de 1974 y 1976)* (Servicio de Investigacion Prehistorica, Serie de Trabajos Varios 72, Valencia, 1982).

———, 'De la ciudad ibérica a la ciudad romana: Sagunto' in *La ciutat en el món romà* (Actes del XIV Congrés Internacional d'Arqueologia Clàssica, 1994) 69-78.

———, 'El Círculo del SE y el comercio entre iberos y griegos' in P. Cabrera *et al.* (eds), *Iberos y Griegos: Lecturas desde la diversidad*, vol. 1 (Huelva Arqueologica 13, 1994) 297-318.

——— (ed.), *Els Romans a les terres Valencianes: relació de topònims i jaciments* (Generalitat Valenciana, 1996).

———, *Sagunto: oppidum, emporio y municipio romano* (Bellaterra Arqueología, 2004).

——— and A. Mantilla, 'La produccion de anforas Dr. 2-4 de Sagunto' in *El Vi a l'Antiquitat: Economia, Produccio i Comerc al Mediterrani Occidental* (Actes del I Colloqui d'Arqueología Romana, Monografies Badalonines 9, 1987) 100-4.

Arce, J., *España entre el mundo antiguo y el mundo medieval* (Taurus, 1988).

Arévalo González, A. and D. Bernal Casasola, 'Los orígenes de la industria pesquero-conservera en Baelo Claudia (ss. II-I a.C.)' in L. Lagóstena Barrios *et al.* (eds), *Cetariae 2005. Salsas y Salazones de Pescado en Occidente durante la Antigüedad. Actas del Congreso Internacional (Cádiz, 7-9 de noviembre de 2005)* (BAR Int. Ser. 1686, 2007) 79-91.

——— and D. Bernal Casasola, 'Historia de las investigaciones de la industria pesquero-conservera en Baelo Claudia' in A. Arévalo González and D. Bernal Casasola (eds), *Las Cetariae de Baelo Claudia. Avance de las investigaciones arqueológicas en el barrio meridional (2000-2004)* (Junta de Andalucía, 2007) 71-87.

——— *et al.*, 'La factoría de salazones de Baelo Claudia (Tarifa, Cádiz). Intervenciones arqueológicas' in *Revista de Arqueología* 23 (2002) 22-31.

Arrayás Morales, I., *Morfología histórica del territorio de Tarraco (ss. III-I a.C.)* (Colleció Instrumenta 19, Universitat de Barcelona, 2005).

Arribas, A. *et al.*, *El barco de El Sec (Calvià, Mallorca). Estudio de los materiales* (Ajuntament de Calvià, 1987).

Arruda, A.M., 'O castelo de Castro Marim' in J. de Alarcão (ed.), *De Ulisses a Viriato. O primeiro milénio a.C.* (Museu Nacional de Arqueologia, 1996) 95-100.

———, *Los fenicios en Portugal. Fenicios y mundo indígena en el centro y sur de Portugal (Siglos VIII-VI a.C.)* (Cuadernos de Arqueología Mediterránea 5-6, 1999-2000).

———, 'As cerâmicas de importação do Castelo de Castro Marim: no âmbito do comércio ocidental dos séculos V a III. a. C.' in M.E. Aubet Semmler and M. Barthélemy (eds), *Actas del IV Congreso Internacional de Estudios Fenicios y Púnicos*, vol. 2 (Universidad de Cádiz, 2000) 727-35.

———, 'Importações púnicas no Algarve: cronologia e significado' in *Os Púnicos no Extremo Occidente: Actas do colóquio internacional (Lisboa, 27 e 28 de Outubro de 2000)* (Universidade Aberta, 2001) 69-98.

——— and C. Fabião, 'Ânforas da Quinta do Lago (Loulé)' in A. Alarcão and F. Mayet (eds), *Les amphores Lusitaniennes: typologie, production, commerce* (Museu Monográfico de Conimbriga/Mission Archéologique Française au Portugal, 1990) 199-213.

——— *et al.*, 'Cerâmicas áticas de Mértola' in *Conimbriga* 37 (1998) 121-49.

Arteaga, O., 'Cerro del Mar (Málaga). Campaña de 1978' in *Noticiario Arqueológico Hispánico* 12 (1981) 293-7.

———, 'Los hornos romanos del Manganeto, Almayate Bajo (Malaga): informe preliminar' in *Noticiario Arqueológico Hispánico* 23 (1985) 177-89.

———, 'Excavaciones arqueologicas en el Cerro del Mar (Campaña de 1982). Una aportación preliminar al estudio estratigráfico de las ánforas púnicas y romanas del yacimiento' in *Noticiario Arqueológico Hispánico* 23 (1985) 197-233.

———, 'La crisis del mundo tartesio. Socioeconomía y sociopolítica del iberismo en la alta Andalucía' in *Revista Atlántica Mediterránea de Prehistoria y Arqueología Social* 1 (1997) 181-222.

———, 'Las influencias púnicas. Anotaciones acerca de la dinámica histórica del poblamiento fenicio-púnico en occidente a la luz de las excavaciones arqueológicas en el Cerro del Mar' in M.E. Aubet Semmler (ed.), *Los Fenicios en Málaga* (Universidad de Málaga, 1997) 155-94.

———, 'La emergencia de la "Polis" de el mundo púnico occidental' in M. Almagro Gorbea *et al.*, *Protohistoria de la Península Ibérica* (Editorial Ariel, 2001) 217-81.

——— and H.D. Schulz, 'El puerto fenicio de Toscanos. Investigación geoarqueológica en la costa de la Axarquía (Vélez-Málaga – 1983/83)' in M.E. Aubet Semmler (ed.), *Los Fenicios en Málaga* (Universidad de Málaga, 1997) 87-154.

Aubet Semmler, M.E., 'Materiales punico-tartesios de la necropolis de Setefilla en la coleccion Bonsor' in *Boletin del Seminario de Estudios de Arte y Arqueologia* 39 (1973) 5-30.

———, *La necrópolis de Setefilla en Lora del Río, Sevilla* (Departamento de Prehistoria y Arqueología, 1975).

———, 'Los enterramientos bajo tumulo de Setefilla (Sevilla)' in *Huelva Arqueologia* 6 (1982) *Primeras Jornadas Arqueologicas sobre Colonizaciones Orientales* 49-70.

———, 'La necropolis de Villaricos en el ambito del mundo punico peninsular' in O. Arteaga (ed.), *Homenaje a Luis Siret (1934-1984)* (Consejeria de Cultura de la Junta de Andalucía, 1986) 612-24.

———, 'Notas sobre las colonias del sur de España y su función en el marco territorial: el ejemplo del Cerro del Villar (Málaga)' in *Atti del II Congresso Internazionale di Studi Fenici e Punici. Roma, 9-14 Novembre 1987* (Rome, 1991), vol. 2, 617-26.

———, *The Phoenicians and the West* (Cambridge University Press, 1993).

———, 'Las colonias fenicias de Málaga y su periferia indígena' in *Homenaje a la Dra. Da. Milagro Gil-Mascarell Boscà* (Extremadura Arqueológica 5, 1995) 137-50.

———, 'Aproximación a la estructura social y demográfica tartésica' in *Tartessos. 25 años despues, 1968-1993* (Ayuntamiento de Jerez, 1995) 401-9.

———, 'Un lugar de mercado en el Cerro del Villar' in M.E. Aubet Semmler (ed.), *Los Fenicios en Málaga* (Universidad de Málaga, 1997) 197-213.

———, 'Arquitectura colonial e intercambio' in A. González Prats (ed.), *Fenicios y territorio. Actas del II seminario internacional sobre temas fenicios, Guardamar del Segura, 9-11 de abril de 1999* (Instituto Alicantino de Cultura Juan Gil-Albert, 2000) 13-45.

———, 'Notes on the economy of the Phoenician settlements in Southern Spain' in M.R.

Bierling and S. Gitin (eds), *The Phoenicians in Spain: An Archaeological Review of the Eighth-Sixth Centuries BCE* (Eisenhaus, 2002) 79-95.

———, 'Phoenician trade in the West: balance and perspectives' in M.R. Bierling and S. Gitin (eds), *The Phoenicians in Spain: An Archaeological Review of the Eighth-Sixth Centuries BCE* (Eisenhaus, 2002) 97-112.

———, 'Some questions regarding the Tartessian Orientalizing period' in M.R. Bierling and S. Gitin (eds), *The Phoenicians in Spain: An Archaeological Review of the Eighth-Sixth Centuries BCE* (Eisenhaus, 2002) 199-224.

———, 'The Phoenician impact on Tartessos: spheres of interaction' in M.R. Bierling and S. Gitin (eds), *The Phoenicians in Spain: An Archaeological Review of the Eighth-Sixth Centuries BCE* (Eisenhaus, 2002) 225-40.

——— *et al.*, 'Chorreras. Un establecimiento fenicio al este de la desembocadura del Algarrobo' in *Noticiario Arqueológico Hispánico* 6 (1979) 91-138.

——— *et al.*, *Cerro del Villar – 1. El asentamiento fenicio en la desembocadura del río Guadalhorce y su interacción con el hinterland* (Junta de Andalucía, 1999).

Azuar, R. *et al.*, 'El asentamiento orientalizante e ibérico antiguo de "La Rábita", Guardamar del Segura (Alicante). Avance de las excavaciones 1996-1998' in *Trabajos de Prehistoria* 55 (1998) 111-26.

Badian, E., *Publicans and Sinners* (Cornell University Press, 1972).

Baldomero, A. *et al.*, 'El alfar romano de la Huerta del Rincón: síntesis tipólogica y momentos de producción' in *Figlinae Malacitanae. La producción de cerámica romana en los territorios malacitanos* (Universidad de Málaga, 1997) 147-76.

Barceló, J.A. *et al.*, 'El área de producción alfarera del Cerro del Villar (Guadalhorce, Málaga)' in *Rivista di Studi Fenici* 23 (1995) 147-82.

——— *et al.*, 'Análisis estadistico de la variabilidad de los platos fenicios en el sur de la Península Ibérica' in M.E. Aubet Semmler and M. Barthélemy (eds), *Actas del IV Congreso Internacional de Estudios Fenicios y Púnicos*, vol. 4 (Universidad de Cádiz, 2000) 1459-66.

Barrasetas i Dunjó, E. and A. Monleón, 'Intervenció al jaciment romà del Mas Manolo (Caldes de Montbui, Vallès Oriental)' in *Tribuna d'Arqueologia 1993-1994* (1995) 87-94.

——— *et al.*, 'El jaciment de can Rossell (Llinars del Vallès), segle I a.C.' in *Lauro* 13 (1997) 5-12.

Barrett, J.C., 'Romanization: a critical comment' in D.J. Mattingly (ed.), *Dialogues in Roman Imperialism: Power, Discourse and Discrepant Experience in the Roman Empire* (Journal of Roman Archaeology Suppl. Ser. 23, 1997) 51-64.

Barros, L. and C. Amaro, 'Fábricas de salga de peixe em Cacilhas: achegas para o seu conhecimento' in *Al-Madan* 4-5 (1984-5) 33-4.

Barti Català, A. and R. Plana Mallart, 'Noves aportacions a l'estudi del jaciment romà de Llafranc' in *Cypsela* 7 (1989) 137-46.

——— and R. Plana Mallart, 'La terrisseria d'època romana de Llafranc (Palafrugell, Girona)' in *Cypsela* 10 (1993) 87-99.

——— and R. Plana Mallart, 'Carrer d'Isaac Peral, 38 i 31 de Llafranc' in *Anuari d'intervencions arqueològiques a Catalunya: epoca romana, antiguitat tardana. Campanyes 1982-9* (Generalitat de Catalunya, 1993) 72-3.

Belda Navarro, C., *El proceso de romanización de la provincia de Murcia* (Consejo Superior de Investigaciones Cientificas, 1975).

Belén Deamos, M., 'Ánforas de los siglos VI-IV a.C. en Turdetania' in *Revista de Estudios Ibericos* 4 (2000) 15-51.

——— *et al.*, *Arqueología en Carmona (Sevilla): Excavaciones en la casa-palacio del Marqués de Saltillo* (Junta de Andalucía, 1997).

Beltrán de Heredia Bercero, J., 'La elaboración del vino en el mundo romano: una instalación urbana de producción de vino en Barcino' in *El vi a l'antiguitat: economia, producció i comerç al mediterrani occidental* (Actes del II Colloqui Internacional d'Arqueología Romana, Monografies Badalonines 14, 1998) 277-82.

——— *et al.*, 'Noves aportacions sobre la producció del vi a la Laietània Romana: installacions vinícoles i anàlisis de residus' in *Quarhis: Quaderns d'Arqueologia i Història de la Ciutat de Barcelona* ser. 2, 2 (2006) 92-107.

Beltrán Fortés, J. and M.L. Loza Azuaga, 'Producción anfórica y paisaje costero en el ámbito de la Málaca romana durante el alto imperio' in *Figlinae Malacitanae. La producción de cerámica romana en los territorios malacitanos* (Universidad de Málaga, 1997) 107-46.

Beltrán Lloris, M., *Las ánforas romanas en España* (Institución Fernando el Católico, 1970).

———, *Arqueologia e historia de las ciudades antiguas del Cabezo de Alcalá de Azaila (Teruel)* (Librería General, 1976).

———, 'Roma. República' in *Caesaraugusta* 75 (2002) 427-84.

Bergé, A., 'Les marques sur amphores Pascual 1 de Port-la-Nautique' in *Cahiers d'Archéologie Subaquatique* 9 (1990) 131-201.

Bermúdez Medel, A. and J. Massó i Carballido, 'El horno cerámico del "Barranc de la Premsa Cremada" (Botarell, Tarragona)' in *Butlletí Arqueològic* 5 (1984-5) 63-106.

Bernal Casasola, D., 'La producción anfórica en la Bahía de Algeciras en época romana' in D. Bernal Casasola (ed.), *Excavaciones arqueologicas en el alfar romano de la Venta del Carmen, Los Barrios (Cádiz): Una aproximación a la produccion de anforas en la Bahia de Algeciras en epoca altoimperial* (U.A.M.; Ayuntamiento de la Villa de los Barrios, 1998) 19-42.

———, 'Algo más que garum. Nuevas perspectivas sobre la producción de las cetariae hispanas al hilo de las excavaciones en C/San Nicolás (Algerciras, Cádiz)' in L. Lagóstena Barrios *et al.* (eds), *Cetariae 2005. Salsas y Salazones de Pescado en Occidente durante la Antigüedad. Actas del Congreso Internacional (Cádiz, 7-9 de noviembre de 2005)* (BAR Int. Ser. 1686, 2007) 93-107.

——— and L. Lorenzo Martínez, 'Los Altos del Ringo Rango (Los Barrios, Cádiz): un complejo residencial e industrial de época romana (ss. I-V d.C.) en la Bahía de Algeciras' in *Cuadernos de Prehistoría y Arqueología, Universidad Autónoma de Madrid* 23 (1996) 191-211.

——— and L. Lorenzo Martínez, 'Las excavaciones arqueológicas en el taller alfarero de la Venta del Carmen. Campañas 1996 y 1997' in D. Bernal Casasola (ed.), *Excavaciones arqueologicas en el alfar romano de la Venta del Carmen, Los Barrios (Cádiz): Una aproximación a la produccion de anforas en la Bahia de Algeciras en epoca altoimperial* (UAM; Ayuntamiento de la Villa de los Barrios, 1998) 43-62.

——— and L. Lorenzo Martínez, 'Las cerámicas importadas y la cronología del complejo alfarero' in D. Bernal Casasola (ed.), *Excavaciones arqueologicas en el alfar romano de la Venta del Carmen, Los Barrios (Cádiz): Una aproximación a la produccion de anforas en la Bahia de Algeciras en epoca altoimperial* (UAM; Ayuntamiento de la Villa de los Barrios, 1998) 63-80.

——— and L. Lorenzo Martínez, 'Los hornos y las estructuras asociadas' in D. Bernal Casasola (ed.), *Excavaciones arqueologicas en el alfar romano de la Venta del Carmen, Los Barrios (Cádiz): Una aproximación a la produccion de anforas en la Bahia de Algeciras en epoca altoimperial* (UAM; Ayuntamiento de la Villa de los Barrios, 1998) 81-120.

——— and L. Lorenzo Martínez, 'Excavaciones en alfares romanos de la bahía de Algeciras (La Venta del Carmen y el Ringo Rango en Los Barrios) y la costa de Granada (Los Matagallares, Salobreña). Nuevos elementos para el estudio de la producción anfórica Bética entre Augusto y el s. IV D.C.' in *Congreso Internacional Ex Baetica Amphorae*, vol. 4 (Editorial Gráficas Sol, 2000) 1305-26.

——— *et al.*, 'Las factorías de salazones de "Iulia Traducta". Espectaculares hallazgos arqueológicos en la Calle San Nicolás No 3-5 de Algeciras' in *Almoraima* 29 (2003) 163-83.

——— *et al.*, 'Imitations of Italic amphorae for fish sauce in Baetica: new evidence from the salt-fish factory of Baelo Claudia (Hispania)' in *Rei Cretariae Romanae Fautorum Acta* 38 (2003) 305-13.

——— *et al.* , 'El taller de El Rinconcillo en la Bahía de Algeciras. El factor itálico y la economia de exportación (ss. I. a.C.-I d.C.)' in D. Bernal Casasola and L. Lagóstena Barrios (eds), *Figlinae Baeticae. Talleres alfareros y producciones cerámicas en la Bética romana (ss. II a.C.-VII d.C.)* (BAR Int. Ser. 1266, 2004), vol. 2, 589-606.

——— *et al.*, 'Villa Victoria y el barrio alfarero de Carteia en el s. 1 d.C. Avance de la excavación del año 2003' in D. Bernal Casasola and L. Lagóstena Barrios (eds), *Figlinae Baeticae. Talleres alfareros y producciones cerámicas en la Bética romana (ss. II a.C.-VII d.C.)* (BAR Int. Ser. 1266, 2004), vol. 2, 457-72.

——— *et al.*, 'Los hornos púnicos de praefurnium escalonado (ss. III y II a.C.). Reflexiones a raíz del alfar de la Milagrosa (San Fernando, Cádiz)' in D. Bernal Casasola and L. Lagóstena Barrios (eds), *Figlinae Baeticae. Talleres alfareros y producciones cerámicas en la Bética romana (ss. II a.C.-VII d.C.)* (BAR Int. Ser. 1266, 2004), vol. 2, 607-20.

——— *et al.*, 'Las innovaciones tecnológicas Itálicas en la alfarería Gadirita (s.II a.C.). A propósito del taller anfórico de la Avda. de Portugal' in D. Bernal Casasola and L. Lagóstena Barrios (eds), *Figlinae Baeticae. Talleres alfareros y producciones cerámicas en la Bética romana (ss. II a.C.-VII d.C.)* (BAR Int. Ser. 1266, 2004), vol. 2, 621-32.

——— *et al.*, 'Las Dr. 2/4 Béticas. Primeras evidencias de su manufactura en el Conventus Gaditanus' in D. Bernal Casasola and L. Lagóstena Barrios (eds), *Figlinae Baeticae. Talleres alfareros y producciones cerámicas en la Bética romana (ss. II a.C.-VII d.C.)* (BAR Int. Ser. 1266, 2004), vol. 2, 633-48.

——— et al., 'La topografía del barrio industrial. Baelo Claudia. Paradigma de la industria conservera urbana Hispanorromana' in A. Arévalo González and D. Bernal Casasola (eds), *Las Cetariae de Baelo Claudia. Avance de las investigaciones arqueológicas en el barrio meridional (2000-2004)* (Junta de Andalucía, 2007) 91-221.

——— *et al.*, 'Nuevas evidencias de la occupación en época republicana (ss. II-I a.C.)' in A. Arévalo González and D. Bernal Casasola (eds), *Las Cetariae de Baelo Claudia. Avance de las investigaciones arqueológicas en el barrio meridional (2000-2004)* (Junta de Andalucía, 2007) 237-353.

——— *et al.*, 'Un ejemplo de conservas de pescado Baelonenses en el siglo II A.C.' in A. Arévalo González and D. Bernal Casasola (eds), *Las Cetariae de Baelo Claudia. Avance de las investigaciones arqueológicas en el barrio meridional (2000-2004)* (Junta de Andalucía, 2007) 355-74.

Berni Millet, P., *Las ánforas de aceite de la Bética y su presencia en la Cataluña Romana* (Colleción Instrumenta 4, 1998).

——— *et al.*, 'Sobre dos nuevos Cornelii del vino tarraconense' in *Laietania* 11 (1998) 111-23.

——— *et al.*, 'La *gens licinia* y el nordeste peninsular. Una aproximación al estudio de las formas de propriedad y de gestión de un rico patrimonio familiar' in *Archivo Español de Arqueología* 78 (2005) 167-87.

Berrocal Caparrós, M. del C., 'Aproximación al poblamiento romano de la sierra minera de Cartagena – La Union' in *Actas del XXIII Congreso Nacional de Arqueologia, Elche 1995* (Ajuntament d'Elx, 1997) 111-18.

Berthault, F., 'Une amphore Dressel 12 timbrée SEX DOMITI au Musée du Périgord' in *Aquitania* 13 (1995) 269-72.

Bird, D.G., 'The Roman gold mines of northwest Spain' in *Bonner Jahrbücher* 172 (1972) 36-64.

———, 'Pliny and the gold-mines of northwest Iberia' in T.F.C. Blagg, R.F.J. Jones and S.J. Keay (eds), *Papers in Iberian Archaeology* (BAR Int. Ser. 193, 1984), vol. 1, 341-63.

Blanco Freijeiro, A., 'Cerámica griega de los Castellones de Ceal' in *Archivo Español de Arqueología* 32 (1959) 106-12.

———, 'El ajuar de una tumba de Cástulo' in *Archivo Español de Arqueología* 36 (1963) 40-69.

——— and J.M. Luzón Nogue, 'Pre-Roman silver miners at Rio Tinto' in *Antiquity* 43 (1969) 124-31.

Blanco Jimenez, F.J., 'Excavaciones de urgencia en un solar de la calle Gregorio Marañón. Cádiz' in *Anuario Arqueologico de Andalucía* III, 89 (1991) 78-81.

Blázquez Martínez, J.M., 'Fuentes griegas y romanas referentes a Tartessos' in *V Symposium Internacional de Prehistoria Peninsular* (Barcelona, 1969) 91-110.

———, 'Hispania desde el año 138 al 235 d.C.' in *Hispania* 36 (1976) 5-87.

———, 'Noticia sobre las excavaciones arqueologicas en la mina republicana de La Loba (Fuenteobejuna, Cordoba)' in *Corduba Archaeologica* 12 (1982-3) 29-39.

———, *Fenicios, Griegos y Cartagineses en Occidente* (Cátedra, 1992).

———, 'The latest work on the export of Baetican olive oil to Rome and the Army' in *Greece & Rome* 39 (1992) 173-88.

———, 'Inscripciones de Olearii en Hispalis' in *Acta XII Congressus Internationalis Epigraphiae Graecae et Latinae* (Monografies de la Secció Històrico-Arqueològica 10, 2007) 179-84.

——— and J. Valiente Malla, 'El poblado de La Muela y la fase orientalizante en Cástulo (Jaén)' in H.G. Niemeyer (ed.), *Phönizier im Westen* (Madrider Beiträge 8, 1982) 407-26.

——— and J. Remesal Rodríguez (eds), *Estudios sobre el Monte Testaccio (Roma) I* (Colección Instrumenta 6, 1999).

——— and J. Remesal Rodríguez (eds), *Estudios sobre el Monte Testaccio (Roma) III* (Colección Instrumenta 14, Barcelona 2003).

——— *et al.*, *Excavaciones arqueológicas en el Monte Testaccio (Roma)* (Ministerio de Cultura, 1994).

Bolufer Marqués, J., 'La necropolis del Muntanyar' in *Xàbiga* 1(1986) 109-26.

———, 'Les llanties romanes de la Punta de l'Arenal' in *Xàbiga* 2 (1987) 7-29.

———, 'Ceramiques fines tardanes de la Punta de l'Arenal' in *Xàbiga* 4 (1988) 40-53.

——— and J. Vives-Ferrándiz Sánchez, 'La Plana Justa (Xàbia, Alicante): un nuevo yacimiento con materiales fenicios y del ibérico antiguo' in *Saguntum* 35 (2003) 69-86.

Bonet Rosado, H. and C. Mata Parreño, *El Puntal dels Llops. Un fortín Edetano* (Servicio de Investigacion Prehistorica, Serie de Trabajos Varios 99, 2002).

Boninu, A., 'Un lingotto dei "Plani" della costa orientale della Sardegna' in *VI Congreso internacional de arqueologia submarina* (Museo y Centro Nacionales de Investigaciones Arqueológicas Submarinas, 1985) 451-52.

Borras i Querol, C., 'Avance de las excavaciones en la villa romana del Mas d'Aragó (Cervera del Maestrat)' in *Cuadernos de Prehistoria y Arqueologia Castellonenses* 13 (1987-8) 379-93.

Bosanquet, R.C., 'Some "Late Minoan" vases found in Greece' in *Journal of Hellenic Studies* 24 (1904) 317-29.

Bosch, J. and J. Miret, 'El Bosquet (Sant Pere de Ribes). Una planta per a l'elaboració de vi i la seva distribució' in *El vi a l'antiquitat: economia, produccio i comerç al mediterrani occidental* (Actes del I Colloqui d'Arqueología Romana, Monografies Badalonines 9, 1987) 228-33.

Bouscaras, A., 'Les marques sur amphores de Port la Nautique' in *Cahiers d'Archéologie Subaquatique* 3 (1974) 103-31.

Bouso García, M. *et al.*, 'La producción agrícola y la transfomación y conservación de cereales en Mas Castellar-Pontós' in C. Mata Parreño and G. Pérez Jordà (eds), *IBERS. Agricultors, artesans i comerciants. III Reunió sobre Economia en el Món Ibèric* (Saguntum Extra 3, 2000) 115-23.

Brody, A., 'From the Hills of Adonis through the Pillars of Hercules: recent advances in the archaeology of Canaan and Phoenicia' in *Near Eastern Archaeology* 65 (2002) 69-80.

Brotons Yagüe, F. and S.F. Ramallo Asensio, 'Un santuario suburbano: La Encarnación de Caravaca (Murcia)' in *La ciutat en el món romà* (Actes del XIV Congrés Internacional d'Arqueologia Clàssica, 1994) 74-5.

Brun, J-P., *Le vin et l'huile dans la Méditerranée antique: viticulture, oléiculture et procédés de fabrication* (Éditions Errance, 2003).

———, *Archéologie du vin et de l'huile dans l'empire romaine* (Éditions Errance, 2004).

Brunt, P.A., *Italian Manpower, 225 BC-AD 14* (Oxford University Press, 1971).

Bugalhão, J., *A indústria romana de transformação e conserva de peixe em Olisipo. Núcleo Arqueológico da Rua does Correeiros* (Trabalhos de Arqueologia 15, 2001).

Burch, J. *et al.*, 'Excavacions a la variant-est de Girona: la sitja romana de Fornells' in *Quaderns de la Selva* 5 (1992) 21-9.

——— *et al.*, 'La villa romana de la Casa del Racó' in *Annals de l'Institut d'Estudis Gironins* 23 (1994) 123-38.

——— *et al.*, 'L'establiment vitivinícola de Ses Alzines (Tossa de Mar)' in *Quaderns de la Selva* 10 (1998) 21-30.

Burés i Vilaseca, L. and A. Marquès i Sinca, 'La villa romana de Cal Ros de les Cabres (El Masnou, El Maresme). Notícia de les darreres campanyes d'excavació' in *Laietania* 6 (1991) 115-18.

Burillo Mozota, F., 'Segeda and Rome: the development of a Celtiberian city-state' in L. Abad *et al.* (eds), *Early Roman Towns in Hispania Tarraconensis* (Journal of Roman Archaeology Suppl. Ser. 62, 2006) 159-71.

——— and A. Alzola Romero, 'Food, drink and "the Other" in the Celtiberian city-state of Segeda I (Zaragoza, Spain)' in *Archaeological Review from Cambridge* 20.2 (2006), online at http://www.segeda.net/bibliografia/pdf/arch_review_of_cam_burillo_alzola.pdf

Burjachs, F. *et al.*, 'Un centre Laietà productor d'envasos de vi a Malgrat (Maresme)' in *El vi a l'antiquitat: economia, producció i comerç al mediterrani occidental* (Actes del I Colloqui d'Arqueología Romana, Monografies Badalonines 9, 1987) 224-8.

Burnham, B. and H., *Dolaucothi-Pumsaint: Survey and Excavations at a Roman Gold-mining Complex 1987-1999* (Oxbow, 2004).

Bustamente Álvarez, M. and D. Martín-Arroyo Sánchez, 'La producción de ánforas greco-itálicas de imitación y su evolución en la bahía gaditana durante en siglo II a.C.: los contextos de la Avenida Pery Junquera en San Fernando (Cádiz)' in D. Bernal Casasola and L. Lagóstena Barrios (eds), *Figlinae Baeticae. Talleres alfareros y producciones cerámicas en la Bética romana (ss. II a.C.-VII d.C.)* (BAR Int. Ser. 1266, 2004), vol. 2, 441-6.

Buxeda i Garrigós, J. *et al.*, 'Caracterización arqueométrica de la cerámica ática del palacio-santuario de Cancho Roano (Zalamea de la Serena, Badajoz)' in *Trabajos de Prehistoria* 56 (1999) 157-68.

Buxó i Capdevila, R. and J. Tremoleda i Trilla, *Platja de Fenals (Lloret de Mar, La Selva): una indústria terrissera d'època Romana a la Costa Brava* (Ajuntament de Lloret de Mar, 2002).

Cabrera Bonet, P., 'Comercio internacional mediterráneo en el siglo VIII a.C.' in *Archivo Español de Arqueología* 67 (1994) 15-30.

———, 'Cádiz y el comercio de productos griegos en Andalucía Occidental durante los siglos V y IV a.C.' in *Trabajos de Prehistoría* 51 (1994) 89-101.

———, 'Importaciones arcaicas del Cerro del Villar (Guadalhorce, Málaga)' in P. Cabrera *et al.* (eds), *Iberos y Griegos: lecturas desde la diversidad,* vol. 1 (Huelva Arqueologica 13, 1994) 97-126.

———, 'Greek trade in Iberia: the extent of interaction' in *Oxford Journal of Archaeology* 17 (1998) 191-206.

———, 'Cerámicas griegas y comercio fenicio en el mediterraneo occidental' in B. Costa and J.H. Fernández (eds), *Contactos en el extremo de la oikuméne. Los griegos en occidente y sus relaciones con los fenicios* (XVII Jornadas de Arqueología Fenicio-Púnica, 2003) 61-86.

Callender, M.H., *Roman Amphorae* (Oxford University Press, 1965).

Campano Lorenzo, A., 'De la producción de ánforas de salazón en la Bahía de Cádiz. Materiales del alfar de "El Olivar de los Valencianos", Puerto Real' in *Archivo Español de Arqueología* 67 (1994) 135-46.

Canal i Barcala, D., 'Dieta vegetal y explotación agraria en el mundo Ibérico a través del análisis de semillas y frutos: el Mas Castellar de Pontós' in C. Mata Parreño and G. Pérez Jordà (eds), *IBERS. Agricultors, artesans i comerciants. III Reunió sobre Economia en el Món Ibèric* (Saguntum Extra 3, 2000) 125-31.

Cantarell, I. and J. Estrada, 'La villa romanorepublicana de Can Massot (Montmeló) i el seu camp de sitges' in M. Mayer *et al.* (eds), *De les estructures indígenes a l'organització provincial de la Hispània Citerior. Homenatge a Josep Estrada i Garriga* (Actes de les Jornades Internacionals d'Arqueologia Romana, Granollers 1987) (Societat Catalana d'Estudis Clàssics, 1998) 137-42.

Carbonell, E. and J. Folch 'La producció de vi i d'àmfores a la villa de Can Feu' in *El vi a l'antiguitat: economia, producció i comerç al mediterrani occidental* (Actes del II Colloqui Internacional d'Arqueología Romana, Monografies Badalonines 14, 1998) 289-93.

——— *et al.*, 'Can Feu (Sant Quirze del Vallès)' in *Anuari d'intervencions arqueològiques a Catalunya: epoca romana, antiguitat tardana. Campanyes 1982-9* (Generalitat de Catalunya, 1993) 279.

——— *et al.*, 'La villa de Can Feu (Sant Quirze del Vallès, Barcelona)' in *Journal of Roman Archaeology* 8 (1995) 297-300.

Carbonell, M. and E. Carbonell, 'Mas del Catxorro, Benifallet' in *Anuari d'intervencions arqueològiques a Catalunya: epoca romana, antiguitat tardana. Campanyes 1982-9* (Generalitat de Catalunya, 1993) 66.

Cardoso, G., 'O forno de ânforas de Muge' in A. Alarcão and F. Mayet (eds), *Les amphores Lusitaniennes: typologie, production, commerce* (Museu Monográfico de Conimbriga/Mission Archéologique Française au Portugal, 1990) 153-66.

——— and S. Rodrigues, 'O contexto oleiro de Muge na produção romana do médio e baixo Tejo' in G. Filipe and J.M.C. Raposo (eds), *Ocupação romana dos estuários do Tejo e do Sado* (Actas das Primeiras Jornadas sobre Romanização dos Estuários do Tejo e do Sado, Câmara Municipal do Seixal, 1996) 167-78.

Cardoso, J.L., 'Fenícios e indígenas em Rocha Branca, Abul, Alcácer do Sal, Almaraz e Santarém. Estudo comparado dos mamíferos' in M.E. Aubet Semmler and M. Barthélemy (eds), *Actas del IV Congreso Internacional de Estudios Fenicios y Púnicos*, vol. 1 (Universidad de Cádiz, 2000) 319-27.

Carme Rovira, M., 'Estudi arqueometallúrgic de l'Illa d'en Reixac-Ullastret (Baix Empordà)' in *Revista d'Arqueologia de Ponent* 3 (1993) 65-149.

Carmona González, P., 'El tómbolo de Tiro, el delta del Guadalhorce y la Bahía de Lixus. Geomorfología y geoarqueología de litorales fenicios' in C. Gómez Bellard, *Ecohistoria del Paisaje agrario. La agricultura fenicio-púnica en el mediterráneo* (Universitat de València, 2003) 11-32.

Carpenter, R., *The Greeks in Spain* (Bryn Mawr College, 1925).

Carreres Vidal, N. *et al.*, 'Excavacions a l'autopista A-19, variante de Mataro. Tres exemples del poblament del Maresme: de l'Ibèric ple a la romanització' in *Laietania* 7 (1992) 155-89.

Carretero Poblete, P.A., 'Las producciones cerámica de ánforas tipo "Campamentos Numantinos" y su origen en San Fernando (Cádiz): los hornos de Pery Junquera' in D. Bernal Casasola and L. Lagóstena Barrios (eds), *Figlinae Baeticae. Talleres alfareros y producciones cerámicas en la Bética romana (ss. II a.C.-VII d.C.)* (BAR Int. Ser. 1266, 2004), vol. 2, 427-40.

———, 'Difusión de ánforas tipo "Tiñosa" en Algarve (Portugal) y la comercialización de productos agrícolas púnico-turdetanos entre los siglos V y III a.C.' in *II Encontro de Arqueologia do Algarve (Silves, Portugal 2004)*, online at http://www.ucm.es/info/antigua/cefyp/Biblioteca/Carretero2.pdf.

———, 'Las villas agrícolas púnico-turdetanas de la campiña gaditana (Cádiz-España)' in *III Coloquio del CEFYP (Adra, Almería 2004)*, online at http://www.ucm.es/info/antigua/cefyp/Biblioteca/Carretero3.pdf.

———, *Agricultura y comercio púnico-turdetano en el Bajo Guadalquivir. El inicio de las explotaciones oleícolas Peninsulares (siglos IV-II a.C.)* (BAR Int. Ser. 1703, 2007).

Carrilero Millán, C., 'Sal y comercio costa interior en la prehistoria reciente y protohistoria de la alta Andalucia' in J. Molina Vidal and M.J. Sánchez Fernández (eds), *III Congreso Internacional de Estudios Históricos. El Mediterráneo: la cultura del mar y la sal* (Ajuntamiento de Santa Pola, 2005) 37-55.

Carrillo Díaz-Pinés, J.R., 'Testimonios sobre la producción de aceite en época romana en la Subbética Cordobesa' in *Antiquitas* 5 (1995) 53-91.

Casas i Genover, J., 'Exploracions i excavacions a la villa romana del Mas Gusó (Albons-Bellcaire, Baix Empordà)' in *Annals de l'Institut d'Estudis Gironins* 30 (1988) 9-35.

———, *L'Olivet d'en Pujol i els Tolegassos: dos establiments agrícoles d'època romana a Viladamat (Campanyes de 1982 a 1988)* (Centre d'Investigacions Arqueològiques de Girona, 1989).

———, 'Els Tolegassos, Viladamat' in *Anuari d'intervencions arqueològiques a Catalunya: epoca romana, antiguitat tardana. Campanyes 1982-9* (Generalitat de Catalunya, 1993) 24.

———, 'L'Olivet d'en Pujol, Viladamat' in *Anuari d'intervencions arqueològiques a Catalunya: epoca romana, antiguitat tardana. Campanyes 1982-9* (Generalitat de Catalunya, 1993) 25.

———, 'La villa de Tolegassos (Viladamat, Girona)' in *Journal of Roman Archaeology* 8 (1995) 278-83.

——— and J.M. Nolla i Brufau, *L'abocador oriental de la villa de Tolegassos (Viladamat, Alt Empordà)* (Estudis Arqueològics 1, 1993).

——— and V. Soler i Fusté, *La Villa de Tolegassos. Una explotación agrícola de época romana en el territorio de Ampurias* (BAR Int. Ser. 1101, 2003).

——— *et al.*, *El món rural d'època romana a Catalunya (L'exemple del nord-est)* (Centre d'Investigacions Arqueològiques de Girona, Sèrie Monogràfica 15, 1995).

——— *et al.*, 'Les sitges de Tolegassos. Aspectes de la fase republicana del jaciment' in *Cypsela* 11 (1996) 67-97.

Castanheira Duarte, A.L., 'Quinta do Rouxinol. A produção de ânforas no Vale do Tejo' in A. Alarcão and F. Mayet (eds), *Les amphores Lusitaniennes: typologie, production, commerce* (Museu Monográfico de Conimbriga/Mission Archéologique Française au Portugal, 1990) 97-115.

——— and J.M. Cordeiro Raposo, 'Elementos para a caracterização das produções anfóricas da Quinta do Rouxinol (Corroios, Seixal)' in G. Filipe and J.M.C. Raposo (eds), *Ocupação romana dos estuários do Tejo e do Sado* (Actas das Primeiras Jornadas sobre Romanização dos Estuários do Tejo e do Sado, Câmara Municipal do Seixal, 1996) 237-47.

Castellanos Roca, M. del M., 'Les importacions etrusques del segle V a.C. al nord-est peninsular i el comerç mediterrani' in *Pyrenae* 27 (1996) 83-102.

Cavaleiro Paixão, A., 'Uma nova sepultura com escaravelho da necrópole proto-histórica do Senhor dos Mártires' in *O Arqueólogo Portugues* 4 (1983) 273-6.

Celestino Pérez, S., 'El periodo orientalizante en Extremadura' in *Extremadura Arqueológica* 4 (1995) 67-89.

——— (ed.), *El yacimiento protohistórico de Pajares, Villanueva de la Vera, Cáceres 1. Las necrópolis y el tesoro aureo* (Memorias de Arqueología Extremeña 3, 1999).

——— and J. Jiménez Ávila, 'El conjunto orientalizante de Talavera la Vieja (Cáceres)' [abstract] in *I Symposium internacional sobre tecnología del oro antiguo: Europa y América* (Madrid, 2002) 50.

Chamorro, J.G., 'Survey of archaeological research on Tartessos' in *American Journal of Archaeology* 91 (1987) 197-232.

Chapa, T. *et al.*, 'Análisis económico y territorial de los Castellones de Ceal (Jaén)' in *Arqueologia Espacial* 4 (1984) 223-35.

Chic García, G., 'Los Aelii en la produccion y difusion del aceite Betico' in *Münstersche Beiträge zu antiken Handelsgeschichte* 11 (1992) 1-22.

———, G., 'Economía y sociedad en la Bética altoimperial. El testimonio de la epigrafía anfórica. Algunas notas' in C. González Román (ed.), *La sociedad de la Bética. Contribuciones para su estudio* (Universidad de Granada, 1994) 75-122.

———, 'Un factor importante en la economia de la Betica: el aceite' in *Hispania Antigua* 19 (1995) 95-128.

———, *Historia económica de la Bética en el época de Augusto* (Padilla Libros Editores & Libreros, 1997).

———, *Datos para un estudio socioeconómico de la Bética*, 2 vols (Editorial Gráficas Sol, 2001).

———, 'Comercio y comerciantes en la Málaga republicana y alto-imperial' in F. Wulff Alonso *et al.* (eds), *Comercio y comerciantes en la historia antigua de Málaga (Siglos VIII a.C.-año 711 d.C)* (II Congreso de Historia Antigua de Málaga, Centro de Ediciones de la Diputación de Málaga, 2001) 351-84.

———, 'La zona minera del suroeste de Hispania en época Julio-Claudia' in J.A. Pérez Macías and A. Delgado Domínguez (eds), *Las minas de Riotinto en época Julio-Claudia* (Universidad de Huelva, 2007) 11-34.

——— and E. García Vargas, 'Alfares y producciones cerámicas en la provincia de Sevilla. Balance y perspectivas' in D. Bernal Casasola and L. Lagóstena Barrios (eds), *Figlinae Baeticae. Talleres alfareros y producciones cerámicas en la Bética romana (ss. II a.C.-VII d.C.)* (BAR Int. Ser. 1266, 2004), vol. 1, 279-348.

Cisneros Fraile, F., 'El vino en el hinterland del Portus de Saguntum (ss. I a.C.-I d.C.)' in *Saguntum* 34 (2002) 127-36.

Clausell Cantavella, G., 'La incidencia fenicia en el asentamiento del Torrello de Boverot d'Almassora (Castellón)' in M.E. Aubet Semmler and M. Barthélemy (eds), *Actas del IV Congreso Internacional de Estudios Fenicios y Púnicos*, vol. 4 (Universidad de Cádiz, 2000) 1771-80.

Cobos Rodríguez, L.M., 'Intervención arqueológica en el solar del Teatro Andalucía (Cádiz)' in *Anuario Arqueologico de Andalucía* III, 95 (1999) 19-31.

Codina, F., 'Una premsa de vi romanorepublicana a Bellcaire d'Empordà' in *Estudis del Baix Empordà* 23 (2004) 5-24.

Coldstream, J.N. and G. Huxley, *Kythera* (London, 1972).

Colls, D., 'Les amphores léétaniennes de l'épave Cap Béar III' in *Revue des Etudes Anciennes* 88 (1986) 201-13.

——— *et al.*, *L'épave Port-Vendres II et le commerce de la Bétique a l'époque de Claude* (Archaeonautica 1, 1977).

Comas i Solà, M., *Baetulo les àmphores* (Monografies Badalonines 8, 1985).

———, 'Importació i exportació de vi a Baetulo: l'estudi de les àmfores' in *El vi a l'antiquitat:*

economia, producció i comerç al mediterrani occidental (Actes del I Colloqui d'Arqueología Romana, Monografies Badalonines 9, 1987) 161-73.

———, *Baetulo les marques d'àmfora* (Institut d'Estudis Catalans/Museu de Badalona, 1997).

———, 'La producció i el comerç del vi a Baetulo. Estat de la qüestió' in *El vi a l'antiguitat: economia, producció i comerç al mediterrani occidental* (Actes del II Colloqui Internacional d'Arqueología Romana, Monografies Badalonines 14, 1998) 219-32.

——— *et al.*, 'Un tipus d'àmfora Dressel 1 de producció laietana' in M. Mayer *et al.* (eds), *De les estructures indígenes a l'organització provincial de la Hispània Citerior. Homenatge a Josep Estrada i Garriga* (Actes de les Jornades Internacionals d'Arqueologia Romana, Granollers 1987) (Societat Catalana d'Estudis Clàssics, 1998) 149-61.

Contreras, F. *et al.*, 'Un horno de alfarero protohistorico en el Cerro del los Infantes (Pinos Puente, Granada)' in *XVI Congreso Nacional de Arqueología* (Universidad de Zaragoza, 1983) 533-5.

Contreras de la Paz, R., *Historia biográfica de la antigua Cástulo* (*Cádiz* (Publicaciones Obra Social y Cultural CajaSur, 1999).

Cordeiro Raposo, J.M., 'Porto dos Cacos: uma oficina de produção de ânforas romanas no Vale do Tejo' in A. Alarcão and F. Mayet (eds), *Les amphores Lusitaniennes: typologie, production, commerce* (Museu Monográfico de Conimbriga/Mission Archéologique Française au Portugal, 1990) 117-51.

——— and A.L. Castanheira Duarte, 'Anforas lusitanas. Los alfares del Tajo' in *Revista de Arqueología* 134 (1992) 36-45.

——— and A.L. Castanheira Duarte, 'O forno 2 do Porto dos Cacos (Alcochete)' in G. Filipe and J.M.C. Raposo (eds), *Ocupação romana dos estuários do Tejo e do Sado* (Actas das Primeiras Jornadas sobre Romanização dos Estuários do Tejo e do Sado, Câmara Municipal do Seixal, 1996) 249-65.

——— *et al.*, 'A olaria de Porto dos Cachos, Alcochete' in *Portugal Romano. A exploração dos recursos naturais* (Museu Nacional de Arqueologia, 1997) 60-1.

Córdoba, I. and D. Ruiz Mata, 'Sobre las construcción de la estructura tumular del túmulo de Las Cumbres (Castillo de Doña Blanca)' in M.E. Aubet Semmler and M. Barthélemy (eds), *Actas del IV Congreso Internacional de Estudios Fenicios y Púnicos*, vol. 2 (Universidad de Cádiz, 2000) 759-770.

Corrales Aguilar, P., 'El poblamiento romano del *ager* de *Suel*: zonas costeras de los términos municipales de Benalmádena, Fuengirola y Mijas (Málaga)' in *Baetica. Estudios de arte, geografía e historia* 23 (2001) 343-56.

Costas Ribas, B. *et al.*, 'Ibiza fenicia: La primera fase de la colonización de la isla (siglos VII y VI a.C.)' in *Atti del II Congresso Internazionale di Studi Fenici e Punici. Roma, 9-14 Novembre 1987* (Rome, 1991), vol. 3, 759-95.

Cruz Pérez, M.L., *Necropolis iberica de Los Nietos (Cartagena, Murcia)* (Excavaciones Arqueologicas en España, 1990).

Cuesta, F. and F.X. Ramada, 'Ermita de la Mare de Déu del Bon Viatge' in *Anuari d'intervencions arqueològiques a Catalunya: epoca romana, antiguitat tardana. Campanyes 1982-9* (Generalitat de Catalunya, 1993) 91.

——— *et al.*, 'Avance de los resultados obtenidos en los silos ibericos de la Calle Elisenda (Sant Cugat del Valles)' in *Estudios de la Antigüedad* 2 (1985) 231-62.

Cunliffe, B., 'Diversity in the landscape: the geographical background to urbanism in Iberia' in B. Cunliffe and S.J. Keay (eds), *Social Complexity and the Development of Towns in Iberia* (Proceedings of the British Academy 86, 1995) 5-28.

Cura-Morera, M. and J. Sanmartí, 'Les importacions d'àmfores i ceràmiques comunes del Poblat Ibèric del Molí d'Espígol (Tornabous, Urgell)' in *Empúries* 48-50 (1986-9) 270-9.

Curià, E. *et al.*, 'La organización de la producción de cerámica en un centro colonial fenicio: El taller alfarero del siglo VI a.n.e. del Cerro del Villar (Málaga)' in M.E. Aubet Semmler and M. Barthélemy (eds), *Actas del IV Congreso Internacional de Estudios Fenicios y Púnicos*, vol. 4 (Universidad de Cádiz, 2000) 1475-85.

Curchin, L.A., *The Local Magistrates of Roman Spain* (University of Toronto Press, 1990).

———, *The Romanization of Central Spain: Complexity, Diversity and Change in a Provincial Hinterland* (Routledge, 2004).

Currás, B., 'Aportación al conocimiento de la industria de salazón en las Rías Baixas Gallegas' in L. Lagóstena Barrios *et al.* (eds), *Cetariae 2005. Salsas y Salazones de Pescado en Occidente durante la Antigüedad. Actas del Congreso Internacional (Cádiz, 7-9 de noviembre de 2005)* (BAR Int. Ser. 1686, 2007) 135-49.

Curtis, R.I., *Garum and Salsamenta: Production and Commerce in Materia Medica* (Brill, 1991).

———, *Ancient Food Technology* (Brill, 2001).

da Costa, J.M., 'O tesouro fenicio ou cartaginês do Gaio (Sines)' in *Ethnos: revista do Instituto Portugues de Arqueologia, Historia e Etnografia* (1966) 529-37.

Dangréaux, B. and A. Desbat, 'Les amphores du dépotoir Flavien du Bas-de-Loyasse à Lyon' in *Gallia* 45 (1987-1988) 115-53.

Dardaine, S. and J-N. Bonneville, 'La campagne de fouilles d'Octobre 1979 a Belo' in *Mélanges de la Casa de Velázquez* 16 (1980) 375-419.

da Veiga Ferreira, O., 'Algumas considerações sobre as fábricas de conservas de peixe da antiguidade emcontradas em Portugal' in *Arquivo de Beja* 23-24 (1966-7) 123-34.

de Frutos Reyes, G. and A. Muñoz Vicente, 'Hornos púnicos de Torre Alta (San Fernando, Cádiz)' in J.M. Campos *et al.* (eds), *Arqueología en el entorno del Bajo Guadiana. Actas del Encuentro Internacional de Arqueología* (Huelva, 1994) 393-414.

——— *et al.*, 'Las anforas de la factoria prerromana de salazones de "Las Redes" (Puerto de Santa Maria, Cádiz)' in G. Pereira Menaut (ed.), *Actas del Primer Congreso Peninsular de Historia Antigua* (Santiago de Compostela, 1988) 295-306.

de Hoz, J., 'Las fuentes escritas sobre Tartessos' in M.E. Aubet Semmler (ed.), *Tartessos. Arqueología Protohistórica del Bajo Guadalquivir* (Editorial AUSA, 1989) 25-43.

———, 'Griegos e Íberos: testimonios epigráficos de una cooperación mercantil' in P. Cabrera *et al.* (eds), *Iberos y Griegos: lecturas desde la diversidad*, vol. 1 (Huelva Arqueologica 13, 1994) 245-71.

de Juan Fuertes, C., 'Primera aproximación a la infraestructura portuaria saguntina' in *Saguntum* 34 (2002) 115-26.

del Arco Aguilar, M. del C., 'La necrópolis tumular de Huerta de Cabello (Carmona, Sevilla)' in *Tabona* 7 (1991) 85-124.

de Nicolás, J.C., 'Vi de la Laietània i vi de la Campània a Menorca (Illes Baleares)' in *El vi a l'antiquitat: economia, producció i comerç al mediterrani occidental* (Actes del I Colloqui d'Arqueología Romana, Monografies Badalonines 9, 1987) 237-45.

Desbat, A., 'Les importations d'amphores vinaires à Lyon et Vienne au debut de l'Empire' in *El vi a l'antiquitat: economia, producció i comerç al mediterrani occidental* (Actes del I Colloqui d'Arqueología Romana, Monografies Badalonines 9, 1987) 407-16.

——— *et al.*, 'Inscriptions peintes sur amphores: Lyon et Saint-Romain-en-Gal' in *Archeonautica* 7 (1987) 141-66.

Dias Diogo, A.M., 'Fornos de ânforas do Monte do Bugio. Notícia preliminar' in *Conimbriga* 19 (1980) 147-50.

———, 'Fornos de ânforas do Monte da Enchurraqueira e do Vale da Cepa. Notícia preliminar' in *Conimbriga* 22 (1983) 209-15.

——— and J.M. Costa, 'Elementos sobre a produção de ânforas e a transformação piscícola em Sines durante a época romana' in G. Filipe and J.M.C. Raposo (eds), *Ocupação romana dos estuários do Tejo e do Sado* (Actas das Primeiras Jornadas sobre Romanização dos Estuários do Tejo e do Sado, Câmara Municipal do Seixal, 1996) 107-10.

——— and L. Trindade, 'Vestígios de uma unidade de transformação do pescado descobertos na Rua dos Fanqueiros em Lisboa' in *Revista Portuguesa de Arqueologia* 3 (2000) 181-96.

——— *et al.*, 'Fornos de ânforas de Alcácer do Sal' in *Conimbriga* 26 (1987) 77-111.

Doménech Morante, C., 'Nota sobre los posibles indicios metálicos presentes en las zonas cercanas a los poblados ibéricos del SE. de la provincia de Alicante' in R. Arana Castillo, A.M. Muñoz Amilibia, S. Ramallo Asensio and M.M. Ros Sala, (eds), *Metalurgia en la Península Ibérica durante el primer milenio a.C. Estado actual de la investigación* (Universidad de Murcia, 1993) 202-3.

Domergue, C., 'Les Planii et leur activité industrielle en Espagne sous la République' in *Mélanges de la Casa de Velázquez* 1 (1965) 9-27.

———, 'Les lingots de plomb romains du Musée Archeologique de Carthagène et du Musée Naval de Madrid' in *Archivo Español de Arqueología* 39 (1966) 41-72.

———, *Catalogue des mines et des fonderies antiques de la Péninsule Ibérique*, 2 vols (Publications de la Casa de Velazquez, 1987).

———, *Les mines de la Péninsule Ibérique dans l'antiquité Romaine* (Collection de l'École Française de Rome 127, 1990).

———, 'A view of Baetica's external commerce in the 1st c. AD based on its trade in metals' in S. Keay (ed.), *The Archaeology of Early Roman Baetica* (Journal of Roman Archaeology Suppl. Ser. 29, 1998) 201-15.

——— *et al.* 'Retour sur les lingots de plomb de Comacchio (Ferrara, Italie) en passant par l'archéométrie et l'épigraphie' (2005)
online at http://arxiv.org/ftp/physics/papers/0605/060544.pdf.

Domínguez Monedero, A.J., 'La función económica de la ciudad griega de Emporion' in *Protohistoria Catalana: 6é Colloqui Internacional d'Arqueologia de Puigcerdà, 7-9 de desembre de 1984* (Puigcerdà, 1984) 193-9.

———, 'Los griegos de Occidente y sus diferentes modos de contacto con las poblaciones indígenas. I. Los contactos en los momentos precoloniales (previos a la fundación de las colonias, o en ausencia de los mismos)' in P. Cabrera *et al.* (eds), *Iberos y Griegos: lecturas desde la diversidad*, vol. 1 (Huelva Arqueologica 13, 1994) 19-48.

———, 'Libios, libiofenicios, blastofenicios: elementos púnicos y africanos en la Iberia Bárquida y sus supervivencias' in *Gerión* 13 (1995) 223-39.

——— *et al.*, *Greek Pottery from the Iberian Peninsula* (Brill, 2001).

Downs, M.E., *'Romanization' in Southern Spain: A Regional Study of Iberian and Roman Settlement in the Guadalquivir Valley* (PhD, Indiana University, 1996).

Duarte Martínez, F. *et al.*, 'Tres centres de producció terrissera al territori de Kelin' in C. Mata Parreño and G. Pérez Jordà (eds), *IBERS. Agricultors, artesans i comerciants. III Reunió sobre Economia en el Món Ibèric* (Saguntum Extra 3, 2000) 231-9.

Edmondson, J.C., *Two Industries in Roman Lusitania: Mining and Garum Production* (BAR Int. Ser. 362, 1987).

———, 'Le garum en Lusitanie urbaine et rurale: hiérarchies de demande et de production' in J.G. Gorges (ed.), *Les villes de Lusitanie romaine* (Centre National de la Recherche Scientifique, 1990) 123-47.

———, 'Creating a provincial landscape: Roman imperialism and rural change in Lusitania' in J.G. Gorges and M. Salinas de Frias (eds), *Actas de la Mesa Redonda Internacional El Medio Rural en Lusitania Romana, Formas de Habitat y Ocupacion del Suelo* (Studia Historica, Historia Antigua 10-11, 1992-3) 13-30.

Enríquez Navascués, J.J. and C. Domínguez de la Concha, 'Restos de una necrópolis orientalizante en la desembocadura del río Aljucén (Mérida, Badajoz)' in *Saguntum* 24 (1991) 35-52.

Étienne, R. and F. Mayet, 'À propos de l'amphore Dressel 1C de Belo (Cadix)' in *Mélanges de la Casa de Velázquez* 30 (1994) 131-8.

——— *et al.*, *Un grand complexe industriele a Tróia (Portugal)* (E. de Boccard, 1994).
Fabião, C., *Sobre as ânforas do acampamento romano da Lomba do Canho (Arganil)* (Cadernos da Uniarq 1, 1989).
———, 'Importações de origem mediterrânea no interior de sudoeste peninsular na segunda metade do I milénio A.C.: materiais de Cabeça de Vaiamonte, Montforte' in *Os Púnicos no Extremo Occidente: Actas do colóquio internacional (Lisboa, 27 e 28 de Outubro de 2000)* (Universidade Aberta, 2001) 197-227.
Fear, A.T., *Rome and Baetica: Urbanization in Southern Spain, c. 50 BC-AD 150* (Oxford University Press, 1996).
Fernández, L.E. *et al.*, 'Una poblado indígena del siglo VIII a.C. en la Bahía de Málaga. La intervención de urgencia en la Plaza de San Pablo' in M.E. Aubet Semmler (ed.), *Los Fenicios en Málaga* (Universidad de Málaga, 1997) 215-51.
Fernández Cacho, S., 'Excavaciones arqueologicas en "El Rinconcillo" (Algeciras, Cádiz)' in *Anuario Arqueológico de Andalucía* 92, III (1992) 70-7.
———, 'Las industrias derivadas de la pesca en la provincia romana de la Bética: la alfarería de 'El Rinconcillo' (Algeciras, Cádiz)' in *SPAL* 4 (1995) 173-214.
Fernández Castro, M.C., *Villas romanas en España* (Ministerio de Cultura, Dirección General de Bellas Artes, Archivos y Bibliotecas, 1982).
Fernández de Avilés, A., 'El poblado minero, iberromano, del Cabezo Agudo, en la Union' in *Archivo Español de Arqueología* 15 (1942) 136-52.
Fernández Izquierdo, A., *Las ánforas romanas de Valentia y de su entorno marítimo* (Ayuntamiento de Valencia, 1982).
———, 'El yacimiento submarino de "Piedras de la Barbada" (Benicarlo-Castellon). Campaña 1989' in *Cuadernos de Prehistoria y Arqueologia Castellonenses* 15 (1990-1) 401-17.
———, A. and J.A. Gisbert Santonja, 'Investigaciones arqueológicas subacuáticas en las costas de Denia. 1985-1989' in *III Congrés d'Estudis de la Marina Alta* (Institut d'Estudis Comarcals de la Marina Alta, 1992) 79-88.
Fernández Jurado, J., *Tejada la Vieja: una ciudad protohistorica* (Huelva Arqueologica 9, 1987).
———, 'The Tartessian economy: mining and metallurgy' in M.R. Bierling and S. Gitin (eds), *The Phoenicians in Spain: An Archaeological Review of the Eighth-Sixth Centuries BCE* (Eisenhaus, 2002) 241-62.
——— and P. Cabrera Bonet, 'Comercio griego en Huelva a fines del siglo V a.C.' in P. Rouillard and M-C. Villanueva-Puig (eds), *Grecs et Ibères au IVe siècle avant Jésus-Christ: commerce et iconographie* (Publications du Centre Pierre Paris 19, 1989) 149-59.
——— *et al.*, 'Cerámicas griegas del solar nº 5 de la C/Méndez Nuñez de Huelva' in P. Cabrera, R. Olmos and E. Sanmartí (eds), *Iberos y Griegos: lecturas desde la diversidad*, vol. 1 (Huelva Arqueologica 13, 1994) 67-96.
Fernández Ochoa, C. *et al.*, 'Gijón, enclave marítimo en la ruta comercial Canábrica. Evidencias arqueológicas e hipótesis sobre el puerto romano y los embarcaderos antiguos' in C. Fernández Ochoa (ed.), *Gijón Puerto Romano. Navegación y Comercio en el Cantábrico durante la Antigüedad* (Autoridad Portuaria de Gijón, 2003) 97-117.
Fernández Rodríguez, M. and C. García Bueno, 'La minería romana de época republicana en Sierra Morena: el poblado de Valderrepisa (Fuencaliente, Ciudad Real)' in *Mélanges de la Casa de Velázquez* 29 (1993) 25-50.
Ferrer Albelda, E. and E. García Vargas, 'Producción y comercio de salazones y salsas saladas de pescado de la costa malagueña en épocas púnica y romana republicana' in F. Wulff Alonso *et al.* (eds), *Comercio y comerciantes en la historia antigua de Málaga (Siglos VIII a.C.- año 711 d.C.* (II Congreso de Historia Antigua de Málaga, Centro de Ediciones de la Diputación de Málaga, 2001) 547-71.

Figueras Pachero, F., *Excavaciones en la Isla del Campello (Alicante 1931-1933)* (Memorias de la Junta Superior de Excavaciones y Antigüedades 132, 1934).

———, 'Panorama arqueologico de Javea y sus cercanias' in *Archivo Español de Arqueología* 18 (1945) 1-33.

———, 'La Isleta del Campello del litoral de Alicante. Un yacimiento síntesis de las antiguas culturas del Mediterráneo' in *Archivo Español de Arqueología* 23 (1950) 13-37.

Finley, M., *The Ancient Economy* (Chatto & Windus, 1973).

Foerster, F., 'A Roman wreck off Cap del Vol, Gerona, Spain' in *International Journal of Nautical Archaeology* 9 (1980) 244-53.

——— *et al.*, *El pecio romano de Palamós* (Centro de Recuperación e Investigaciones Submarinas, 1987).

Font Valentí, G. *et al.*, 'El mas ibèric de Can Pons (Arbúcies)' in *Tribuna d'Arqueologia 1994-1995* (1996) 93-103.

——— *et al.* 'Can Pons, la tipificación de un habitat ibérico disperso' in *Revista de Arqueología* 179 (1996) 58-61.

——— et al., 'El jaciment ibèric i la torre d l'alta edat mitjana del turó de la Torre de la Mora (Sant Feliu de Buixalleu). Resultats preliminars' in *III i IV Trobades d'Estudiosos del Montseny* (Monografies 31, 2000) 249-52.

——— *et al.*, 'El mas ibèric de Can Pons (Arbúcies)' in *III i IV Trobades d'Estudiosos del Montseny* (Monografies 31, 2000) 253-7.

Fortó Garcia, A., Martínez Rodríguez, P. and V. Muñoz Rufo, 'El jaciment arqueològic de Ca l'Estrada (Canovelles)' in *Lauro* 28 (2005) 5-16.

Frankel, R., 'The *Trapetum* and the *Mola Olearia*' in M.-C. Amouretti and J.-P. Brun (eds), *La production du vin et de l'huile en Méditerranée* (Bulletin de Correspondance Hellénique Supplément 26, 1993) 477-81.

Frankenstein, S., 'Regional development in the first millennium BC: the Phoenicians in Iberia' in K. Kristiansen and J. Jensen (eds), *Europe in the First Millennium BC* (Sheffield Archaeological Monographs 6, 1994) 41-4.

Freeman, P.W.M., 'Mommsen through to Haverfield: the origins of Romanization studies in late 19th-c. Britain' in D.J. Mattingly (ed.), *Dialogues in Roman Imperialism: Power, Discourse and Discrepant Experience in the Roman Empire* (Journal of Roman Archaeology Suppl. Ser. 23, 1997) 27-50.

Funari, P.P.A., 'Two Dressel 20 stamps from Piddington Villa, Northampton, UK' in *Revista do Museu de Arqueologia e Etnologia* 4 (1994) 227.

———, 'Dressel 20 stamps found at the Annetwell Street excavations in Carlisle, UK' in *Revista do Museu de Arqueologia e Etnologia* 6 (1996) 387-8.

Gago Vidal, M.H. *et al.*, 'El complejo industrial de salazones gaditano de Camposoto, San Fernando (Cádiz): studio preliminar' in *Habis* 31 (2000) 37-61.

Gallant, T.W., *A Fisherman's Tale* (Miscellanea Graeca 7, 1985).

Galve Izquierdo, M.P., *Los antecedentes de Caesaraugusta. Estructuras domésticas de Salduie (Calle Don Juan de Aragón, 9. Zaragoza)* (Institución Fernando el Católico, 1996).

García Alfonso, E., 'Los Castillejos de Teba (Málaga). Excavaciones de 1993. Estratigrafía de los siglos VIII-VI a.C.' in *Mainake* 15-16 (1993-4) 45-83.

———, 'La colonización fenicia arcaica y el mundo indígena de la Andalucía Mediterránea y su traspaís. Una propuesta de análisis' in M.E. Aubet Semmler and M. Barthélemy (eds), *Actas del IV Congreso Internacional de Estudios Fenicios y Púnicos,* vol. 4 (Universidad de Cádiz, 2000) 1799-804.

García Cano, C., 'El departmento B de la Loma del Escorial (Los Nietos, Cartagena)' in *Verdolay* 7 (1995) 259-69.

———, 'El poblado ibérico de la Loma del Escorial, Los Nietos (Cartagena). Informe preliminar de las campañas de 1992 y 1995' in *Memorias de Arqueología* 2001, 182-99.

——— and E. Ruiz Valderas, 'El poblado ibérico de la Loma del Escorial (Los Nietos) durante el s. III a.C.' in *Anales de Prehistoria y Arqueología* 11-12 (1995-6) 129-49.

——— and V. Page del Pozo, 'Panorama actual de las cerámicas griegas en Murcia (1982-91)' in P. Cabrera, R. Olmos and E. Sanmartí (eds), *Iberos y Griegos: lecturas desde la diversidad*, vol. 1 (Huelva Arqueologica 13, 1994) 217-40.

García del Toro, J.R., 'Garum Sociorum: la industria de salazones en la Edad Antigua en Cartagena' in *Anales de la Universidad de Murcia* 36 (1978) 27-57.

García Gandía, J.R., 'La tumba 17 de la necrópolis de Les Casetes (Villajoyosa, Alicante)' in *Saguntum* 35 (2003) 219-28.

García García, G., 'The Río Tinto mines, Huelva, Spain' in *Mineralogical Record* 27 (1996) 275-85.

García Huerta, R. and F.J. Morales Hervás, 'La cerámica griega en la meseta sudoccidental' in R. de Balbín Berhmann and P. Bueno Ramírez (eds), *II Congreso de Arqueología Peninsular* (Alcalá, 1996), vol. 3, 335-45.

García Martín, J.M., 'Les ceràmiques gregues' in M. Olcina Doménech (ed.), *La Illeta dels Banyets (El Campello, Alicante). Estudios de la edad del Bronce y época ibérica* (Museo Arqueológico Provincial de Alicante, 1997) 175-206.

———, *La distribución de cerámica griega en la Contestania ibérica: el puerto comercial de La Illeta dels Banyets* (Instituto Alicantino de Cultura Juan Gil-Albert, 2003).

García Menárguez, A., 'El Cabezo Pequeño del Estaño, Guardamar del Segura. Un poblado protohistórico en el tramo final del Río Segura' in A. González Blanco *et al.* (eds), *El mundo púnico. Historia, sociedad y cultura* (Cartagena, 17-19 de noviembre de 1990) (Coloquios de Cartagena 1, 1994) 269-80.

García i Rosselló, J. and E. Gurri i Costa, 'Les imitacions laietanes d'àmfores itàliques a la zona central de la comarca del Maresme en època tardorepublicana' in *Annals de l'Institut d'Estudis Gironins* 36 (1996-7) 397-424.

García Sánchez, M., 'Epigrafía anfórica de Mas Castellar-Pontós: ánforas grecoitálicas y masaliotas' in *Pyrenae* 28 (1997) 257-69.

García Sanz, C. and P. Rufete Tomico, *La ciudad de Tejada la Vieja* (Diputación Provincial de Huelva, 1995).

García Vargas, E., 'La producción anfórica en la Bahía de Cádiz durante la república como índice de romanización' in *Habis* 27 (1996) 49-62.

———, *La produccón de ánforas en la Bahia de Cádiz en época romana* (Editorial Gráficas Sol, 1998).

———, 'La producción de ánforas "romanas" en el sur de Hispania. República y Alto Imperio' in *Congreso Internacional Ex Baetica Amphorae*, vol. 1 (Editorial Gráficas Sol, 2000) 57-174.

——— and E. Ferrer Albelda, '*Salsamenta* y *Liquamina* Malacitanos en época romana. Notas para un estudio histórico y arqueológico' in F. Wulff Alonso *et al.* (eds), *Comercio y comerciantes en la Historia Antigua de Málaga (Siglos VIII a.C.- año 711 d.C.* (II Congreso de Historia Antigua de Málaga, Centro de Ediciones de la Diputación de Málaga, 2001) 573-94.

——— and F. Sibon Olano, 'Intervencion arqueologica de emergencia. 'El Gallinero' (Puerto Real, Cádiz)' in *Anuario Arqueológico de Andalucía* 92, III (1992) 124-8.

Garrido Roiz, J.P., *Excavaciones en Huelva El Cabezo de la Esperanza* (Excavaciones Arqueologicas en España 63, Servicio de Publicaciones del Ministerio de Educacion y Ciencia, 1966).

——— *et al.*, 'Sobre las inhumaciones de la necrópolis orientalizante de la Joya, Huelva: problemática y perspectivas' in M.E. Aubet Semmler and M. Barthélemy (eds), *Actas del IV Congreso Internacional de Estudios Fenicios y Púnicos*, vol. 4 (Universidad de Cádiz, 2000) 1805-10.

Garriga Casteblanque, S., 'La restauració de les restes arqueològiques de Can Terrés' in *Lauro* 12 (1996) 5-10.

Gener Basallote *et al.*, *Loja durante el dominio romano. Metodología, técnicas e interpretación del yacimiento de Plines* (Universidad de Granada, 1992).

Gener Basallote, J.M. *et al.*, 'Loma de Ceres, un centro de producción anfórico' in *II Congresso Peninsular de História Antiga* (Unversidade de Coimbra, 1993) 971-93.

Genera, M., 'Notícia preliminar sobre la troballa d'una premsa a Sant Miquel de Vinebre' in *El Vi a l'Antiquitat: Economia, Produccio i Comerç al Mediterrani Occidental* (Actes del I Colloqui d'Arqueología Romana, Monografies Badalonines 9, 1987) 233-7.

Gianfrotta, P.A., 'Lentulo Augure e le anfore laietane' in *Tituli* 4 (1982) 475-79.

Gil-Mascarell, M. and C. Aranegui Gascó, 'El poblamiento de Bajo Palancia en época ibérica' in *Saguntum* 12 (1977) 191-242.

Gimeno Pascual, H. and A.U. Stylow, 'Pizarras inscritas del Cerro del Moro y de Marismilla' in J.A. Pérez Macias and A. Delgado Domínguez (eds), *Las Minas de Riotinto en Época Julio-Claudia* (Universidad de Huelva, 2007) 185-91.

Giró Romeu, P., 'Una estación ibérica en els Monjos' in *Ampurias* 6 (1944) 330-3.

Gisbert Santonja, J.A., 'La producció de vi al territori de Dianium durant l'alt imperi: el taller d'àmfores de la villa romana de L'Almadrava (Setla – Mirarrosa – Miraflor)' in *El Vi a l'Antiquitat: Economia, Produccio i Comerç al Mediterrani Occidental* (Actes del I Colloqui d'Arqueología Romana, Monografies Badalonines 9, 1987) 104-18.

———, 'Dues terrisseries del territori de Dianium. Els jaciments de Perdigó i de La Teulera de Jesús Pobre (Dénia, Alacant)' in *III Congrés d'Estudis de la Marina Alta* (Institut d'Estudis Comarcals de la Marina Alta, 1992) 89-100.

———, 'El alfar de l'Almadrava (Setla-Mirarosa-Miraflor)-Dianium-. Materiales de construcción cerámicos. Producción y aproximación a su funcionalidad en la arquitectura del complejo artesanal' in M. Bendala Galán *et al.* (eds), *El ladrillo y sus derivados en la época romana* (Monografías de Arquitectura Romana 4, 1999) 65-102.

Gomes, M.V. et al., 'O Cerro da Rocha Branca (Silves) – Resultados preliminares de três campanhas de escavações' in *Actas do 4o Congresso do Algarve,* vol. 1 (1986) 77-83.

Gómez Bellard, C. and P. Guérin, 'Témoignage d'une production de vin dans l'Espagne préromaine' in M.-C. Amouretti and J.-P. Brun (eds), *La production du vin et de l'huile en Méditerranée* (Bulletin de Correspondance Hellénique Suppl. 26, 1993) 379-95.

——— and P. Guerin, 'Testimonios de producción vinícola arcaica en L'Alt de Benimaquía (Denia)' in P. Cabrera *et al.* (eds), *Iberos y Griegos: lecturas desde la diversidad*, vol. 2 (Huelva Arqueologica 13, 1994) 11-31.

——— and P. Guerin, 'Los lagares del Alt de Benimaquía (Denia): en los inicios del vino ibérico' in S. Celestino Pérez (ed.), *Arqueología del Vino: los origenes del vino en occidente* (Jerez de la Frontera, 1995) 243-69.

——— *et al.*, 'El vino en los inicios de la cultura Iberica. Nuevas excavaciones en L'Alt de Benimaquia, Denia' in *Revista de Arqueologia* 142 (1993) 16-27.

Gómez Ramos, P., *Obtención de metales en la Prehistoria de la Península Ibérica* (BAR Int. Ser. 753, 1999).

Gómez Toscano, F., *El final de la edad del Bronce entre el Guadiana y el Guadalquivir* (Universidad de Huelva, 1997).

González Blanco, A., *Urbanismo Romano en la región de Murcia* (Universidad de Murcia, 1996).

Gonzalez Cordero, A. *et al.*, 'Las Joyas Orientalizantes de Villanueva de la Vera (Caceres)' in *Trabajos de Prehistoria* 50 (1993) 249-62.

González de Canales Cerisola, F. *et al.*, *El Emporio Fenicio Precolonial de Huelva (c. 900-770 a.C.)* (Biblioteca Nueva, 2004).

González Navarrete, J. and O. Arteaga, 'La necrópolis de "Cerillo Blanco" y el poblado de "Los Alcores" (Porcuna, Jaén)' in *Noticiario Arqueológico Hispánico* 10 (1980) 183-216.

González Prats, A., 'La Peña Negra IV. Excavaciones en el Sector VII de la ciudad orientalizante 1980-1981' in *Noticiario Arqueológico Hispánico* 13 (1982) 309-418.

———, 'Las importaciones y la presencia fenicias en la Sierra de Crevillente (Alicante)' in *Aula Orientalis* 4 (1986) 279-302.

———, 'La presencia fenicia en el levante peninsular y su influencia en las comunidades indigenas' in *I-IV Jornadas de Arqueología Fenicio-Púnica* (Trabajos del Museo Arqueológico de Ibiza 24, 1991) 109-18.

———, 'Una vivienda metalurgica en la Peña Negra (Crevillente-Alicante). Aportacion al conocimiento del Bronce Atlantico en la Peninsula Iberica' in *Trabajos de Prehistoria* 49 (1992) 243-57.

———, 'Quince años de excavaciones en la ciudad protohistórica de Herna (La Peña Negra, Crevillente, Alicante)' in *Saguntum* 26 (1993) 181-8.

———, 'Fenicios e indígenas en el levante peninsular' in D. Ruiz Mata (ed.), *Fenicios e indígenas en el Mediterráneo y Occidente: modelos e interacción* (Actas de los Encuentro de Primavera de la Universidad de Cádiz en El Puerto de Santa María, 1998) 107-18.

———, 'La Fonteta. El asentamiento fenicio de la desembocadura del Río Segura (Guardamar, Alicante, España). Resultados de las excavaciones de 1996-97' in *Revista di Studi Fenici* 26 (1998) 191-228.

———, *La Fonteta, 1996-1998. El emporio fenicio de la desembocadura del río Segura* (Organización de los Seminarios Internacionales sobre Temas Fenicios. Área de Prehistoria, Universidad de Alicante, 1999).

——— and A. García Menárguez, 'El conjunto fenicio de la desembocadura del río Segura (Guardamar del Segura, Alicante)' in M.E. Aubet Semmler and M. Barthélemy (eds), *Actas del IV Congreso Internacional de Estudios Fenicios y Púnicos,* vol. 4 (Universidad de Cádiz, 2000) 1527-37.

——— and J.A. Pina Gosálbez, 'Ánalisis de las pastas ceramicas de vasos hechos a torno de la fase orientalizante de Peña Negra (675-650/35 a.C.)' in *Lucentum* 2 (1983) 115-45.

——— and E. Ruiz Segura, 'Una zona metalúrgica de la primera mitad del siglo VII en la ciudad fenicia de La Fonteta (Guardamar, Alicante)' in *XXIV Congreso Nacional de Arqueología* (Instituto de Patrimonio Histórico, 1999) 355-7.

——— *et al.*, 'La Fonteta: a Phoenician city in the Far West' in M.R. Bierling and S. Gitin (eds), *The Phoenicians in Spain: An Archaeological Review of the Eighth-Sixth Centuries BCE* (Eisenhaus, 2002) 113-25.

González Ruibal, A., 'Facing two seas: Mediterranean and Atlantic contacts in the northwest of Iberia in the first millennium BC' in *Oxford Journal of Archaeology* 23 (2004) 287-317.

González Serrano, M.P., 'Anforas y salazones' in *Anejos de Gerión* 1 (1988) 285-305.

González Torraya, B. *et al.*, 'Los inicios de la producción anfórica en la Bahía Gaditana en época republicana: la intervención de urgencia en Avda. Pery Junquera (San Fernando, Cádiz)' in *Congreso Internacional Ex Baetica Amphorae*, vol. 1 (Editorial Gráficas Sol, 2000) 175-85.

Gorges, J.-G., *Les villas hispano-romaines* (Publications du Centre Pierre Paris 4, 1979).

Gozalbes Cravioto, E., *Las vías romanas de Málaga* (Colegio de Ingenieros de Caminos, Canales y Puertos, 1986).

Gracia Alonso, F., 'Producción y comercio de cereal en el N.E. de la Península Ibérica entre los siglos VI-II a.C.' in *Pyrenae* 36 (1995) 91-113.

Gran Aymerich, J., 'Sondeos arqueologicos en 'Cerca Niebla', sobre el valle de Río Vélez, provincia de Málaga' in *XII Congreso Nacional de Arqueología* (Universidad de Zaragoza, 1972) 409-24.

———, J., 'Málaga, fenicia y púnica' in *Aula Orientalis* 3 (1985) 127-47.

———, 'Cerámicas griegas y etruscas de Málaga. Excavaciones de 1980 a 1986' in *Archivo Español de Arqueología* 61 (1988) 201-22.

———, 'Ceramiques grecques du Ve et Ive s. av. J.-C. de Malaga (campagnes de fouilles 1980-1986)' in P. Rouillard and M-C. Villanueva-Puig (eds), *Grecs et Ibères au IVe siècle avant Jésus-Christ: commerce et iconographie* (Publications du Centre Pierre Paris 19, 1989) 169-77.

Granados, J.O. and C. Rovira, 'Tres nou centres de producció d'àmfores a l'ager de la colonia Barcino' in *El Vi a l'Antiquitat: Economia, Producció i Comerç al Mediterrani Occidental* (Actes del I Colloqui d'Arqueología Romana, Monografies Badalonines 9, 1987) 126-32.

Grau Mira, I., 'La reorganización del territorio durante la romanización: un caso de estudio en el área central de la Contestania' in L. Abad Casal (ed.), *De Iberia in Hispaniam. La adaptación de las sociedades ibéricas a los modelos romanos* (Universidad de Alicante, 2003) 54-73.

———, 'Settlement dynamics and social organization in Eastern Iberia during the Iron Age (eighth-second centuries BC)' in *Oxford Journal of Archaeology* 22 (2003) 261-79.

Guerrero Ayuso, V.M., *Colonización púnica de Mallorca. La documentación arqueológica y el contexto histórico* (El Tall, 1997).

——— and C. Quintana, 'Comercio y difusión de ánforas ibéricas en Baleares' in *Cuadernos de Prehistoria y Arqueología Castellonenses* 21 (2000) 153-82.

——— *et al.*, 'L'epave de Binisafuller (Minorque), un bateau de commerce punique du IIIe siècle av. J.-C.' in H. Devijver and E. Lipinski (eds), *Studia Phoenicia X. Punic Wars* (Orientalia Lovaniensia Analecta 33, 1989) 115-25.

Guitart i Duran, J., 'Un programa de fundacions urbanes a la Hispania Citerior del principi del segle I A.C.' in *La ciutat en el món romà* (Actes del XIV Congrés Internacional d'Arqueologia Clàssica, 1994) 205-12.

Gutiérrez López, J.M., 'La factoría "Puerto 19" (El Puerto de Santa María, Cádiz) y la producción de salazones de Gadir' in *XVI encuentros de historia y arqueología: las industrias alfareras y conserveras fenicio-púnicas de la Bahía de Cádiz* (Publicaciones Obra Social y Cultural CajaSur, 2004) 237-62.

——— *et al.*, 'El río Guadalete (Cádiz) como vía de communicación en épocas fenicia y púnica en Andalucia Occidental' in M.E. Aubet Semmler and M. Barthélemy (eds), *Actas del IV Congreso Internacional de Estudios Fenicios y Púnicos,* vol. 2 (Universidad de Cádiz, 2000) 795-806.

Gutiérrez Soler, L.M. *et al.*, 'La minería ibérica en la provincia de Jaén. Fuentes escritas y evidencias arqueológicas' in C. Mata Parreño and G. Pérez Jordà (eds), *IBERS. Agricultors, artesans i comerciants. III Reunió sobre Economia en el Món Ibèric* (Saguntum Extra 3, 2000) 257-63.

Haley, E.W., *Baetica Felix: People and Prosperity in Southern Spain from Caesar to Septimius Severus* (University of Texas, 2003).

Hamilton, H.C. and W. Falconer, *The Geography of Strabo* (George Bell & Sons, 1903).

Hassall, M., 'Roman Britain and the Rhine provinces: epigraphic evidence for Roman trade' in J. Du Plat Taylor and H. Cleere (eds), *Roman Shipping and Trade: Britain and the Rhine Provinces* (London, 1978) 41-46.

Healy, J.F., *Mining and Metallurgy in the Greek and Roman World* (Thames & Hudson, 1978).

Hernández García, J. de D., 'El poblamiento rural romano en el área de Águilas (Murcia)' in J.M. Noguera Celdrán (ed.), *Poblamiento Rural Romano en el Sureste de Hispania (Actas de las Jornadas celebradas en Jumilla del 8 al 11 de noviembre de 1993)* (Universidad de Murcia, 1995) 183-201.

———, 'Un taller de púrpura del S. I d.C. localizado en Águilas. Excavación en calle Francisco Rabal, 5 (Águilas, Murcia)' in *Verdolay* 5 (2005) 165-76.

Hernández Guerra, L., *Indigenismo y romanización de la provincia de Valladolid* (Diputación de Valladolid, 2002).

Hernández Perez, M.S., 'La metalurgia prehistorica en el valle medio del Río Vinalopó' in *Lucentum* 2 (1983) 17-42.

Hesnard, A., 'Un depot Augusteen d'amphores a La Longarie, Ostie' in J.H. D'Arms and E.C. Kopff (eds), *The Sea-borne Commerce of Ancient Rome: Studies in Archaeology and History* (Memoires of the American Academy in Rome 36, 1980) 141-56.

Hopkins, K., 'Taxes and trade in the Roman empire (200 BC-AD 400)' in *Journal of Roman Studies* 70 (1980) 101-25.

———, 'Models, ships and staples' in P.D.A. Garnsey and C.R. Whittaker (eds), *Trade and Famine in Classical Antiquity* (Proceedings of the Cambridge Philological Society Suppl. Vol. 8, 1983) 84-109.

Hunt Ortiz, M.A., 'El foco metalúrgico de Aznacóllar, Sevilla. Tecnicas analíticas aplicadas a la arqueometalurgica del suroeste de la Península Ibérica' in *Tartessos: 25 años despues* (Jerez de la Frontera, 1995) 447-73.

Hurtado Aguña, J., *Los territorios septentrionales del Conventus Carthaginensis durante el Imperio romano. Estudio de la romanización de Carpetania* (BAR Int. Ser. 1415, 2005).

———, 'Los movimientos de población en el área septentrional del Conventus Carthaginensis' in *Gerión* 23 (2005) 233-49.

Izquierdo i Tugas, P., 'Un nou centre productor d'àmfores a la vall de l'Ebre: el Mas del Catxorro de Benifallet' in J. Padró *et al.*, (eds), *Homenatge a Miquel Tarradell* (*Estudis Universitaris Catalans* 29, 1993) 753-65.

Jàrrega Domínguez, R., 'Un possible taller i una nova estampilla amforal de la villa romana de Cal Ros de les Cabres (Ocata-El Masnou, Maresme)' in *El vi a l'antiquitat: economia, producció i comerç al Mediterrani Occidental* (Actes del I Colloqui d'Arqueología Romana, Monografies Badalonines 9, 1987) 246-9.

———, 'Les àmfores romanes del Camp de Tarragona i la producció del vi tarraconense' in *Revista d'Arqueologia de Ponent* 5 (1995) 179-94.

———, 'La producció amforal romana del Camp de Tarragona. Estat de la qüestió' in *El vi a l'antiguitat: economia, producció i comerç al mediterrani occidental* (Actes del II Colloqui Internacional d'Arqueología Romana, Monografies Badalonines 14, 1998) 430-7.

———, 'El poblament rural i l'origen de les villae al nord-est d'Hispania durant l'època romana republicana (segles II-I aC)' in *Quarderns de Prehistòria i Arqueologia de Castelló* 21 (2000) 271-301.

Jiménez Cisneros, M. J., *Historia de Cádiz en la antigüedad* (Instituto de Estudios Gaditanos, 1971).

Jones, R.F.J. and D.G. Bird, 'Roman gold-mining in north-west Spain, II: workings on the Rio Duerna' in *Journal of Roman Studies* 62 (1972) 59-74.

Júdice Gamito, T., *Social Complexity in Southwest Iberia 800-300 BC: The Case of Tartessos* (BAR Int. Ser. 439, 1988).

Kampp, A., 'Geography of the fiber-flax industry' in *Economic Geography* 15 (1939) 165-8.

Karageorghis, V., 'The Phoenicians in Cyprus' in S. Celestino Pérez and J. Jiménez Ávila (eds), *El Periodo Orientalizante* (Anejos de Archivo Español de Arqueología 35, 2005), vol. 1, 31-46.

Keay, S.J., 'Romanization and the Hispaniae' in S.J. Keay and N. Terrenato (eds), *Italy and the West: Comparative Issues in Romanization* (Oxbow, 2001) 117-44.

———, 'Recent archaeological work in Roman Iberia (1990-2002)' in *Journal of Roman Studies* 93 (2003) 146-211.

——— and L. Jones, 'Differentiation of early imperial amphora production in Hispania Tarraconensis' in I. Freestone *et al.* (eds) *Current Research in Ceramics: Thin Section Studies* (British Museum Occasional Paper 32, 1982) 45-61.

——— *et al.*, *Celti – Peñaflor: The Archaeology of a Hispano-Roman Town in Baetica* (University of Southampton Department of Archaeology Monograph 2, 2000).

Keesmann, I. and H.G. Niemeyer, 'Un centro primitivo de la elaboración de hierro en la factoría fenicia de Toscanos' in C. Domergue (ed.), *Mineria y metalurgia en las antiguas civilizaciones mediterraneas y europeas* (Ministerio de Cultura, Dirección General de Bellas Artes y Archivos, Instituto de Conservación y Restauración de Bienes Culturales, 1989) vol. 1, 99-108.

Knapp, R.C., 'The origins of provincial prosopography in the West' in *Ancient Society* 9 (1978) 187-222.

———, *Roman Córdoba* (University of California Publications, Classical Studies 30, 1983).

Lacort Navarro, P.J., 'Cereales en Hispania Ulterior: Silos de epoca ibero-romana en la campiña de Córdoba' in *Habis* 16 (1985) 363-86.

Lagóstena Barrios, L., *Alfarería romana en la bahía de Cádiz* (Universidad de Cádiz, 1996).

———, *La producción de salsas y conservas de pescado en la Hispania Romana (II a.C.-VI d.C.)* (Colleció Instrumenta 11, Universitat de Barcelona, 2001).

——— and D. Bernal Casasola, 'Alfares y producciones cerámicas en la provincia de Cádiz. Balance y perspectivas' in D. Bernal Casasola and L. Lagóstena Barrios (eds), *Figlinae Baeticae. Talleres alfareros y producciones cerámicas en la Bética romana (ss. II a.C.-VII d.C.)* (BAR Int. Ser. 1266, 2004), vol. 1, 39-124.

Las Médulas. Patrimonio de la Humanidad (Junta de Castilla y León, 2002).

Laubenheimer, F., *La production des amphores en Gaule Narbonnaise* (Centre de Recherchers d'Histoire Ancienne 66, 1985).

Lavado Florido, M.L., 'El complejo industrial de Puente Melchor. El centro productor, la organización del espacio y su área de influencia' in D. Bernal Casasola and L. Lagóstena Barrios (eds), *Figlinae Baeticae. Talleres alfareros y producciones cerámicas en la Bética romana (ss. II a.C.-VII d.C.)* (BAR Int. Ser. 1266, 2004), vol. 2, 473-88.

——— *et al.*, 'El asentamiento antiguo de Cádiz a través de las últimas excavaciones arqueológicas' in M.E. Aubet Semmler and M. Barthélemy (eds), *Actas del IV Congreso Internacional de Estudios Fenicios y Púnicos*, vol. 2 (Universidad de Cádiz, 2000) 869-79.

Leighton, R., *Sicily before History: An Archaeological Survey from the Palaeolithic to the Iron Age* (Duckworth, 1999).

Leiva Briones, F. and J.V. Madruga Flores, 'La villa romana de "Las Viñas", en Zamoranos' in *Boletín de la Real Academia de Córdoba* 122 (1992) 247-53.

Lewis, P.R. and G.B.D. Jones, 'Roman gold-mining in north-west Spain' in *Journal of Roman Studies* 60 (1970) 169-85.

Liou, B., 'L'exportation du vin de Tarraconaise d'après les épaves' in *El vi a l'antiquitat: economia, producció i comerç al Mediterrani Occidental* (Actes del I Colloqui d'Arqueología Romana, Monografies Badalonines 9, 1987) 271-84.

———, 'Inscriptions peintes sur amphores: Fos (suite), Marseilles, Toulon, Port-la-Nautique, Arles, Saint-Blaise, Saint-Martin-de-Crau, Mâcon, Calvi' in *Archeonautica* 7 (1987) 55-139.

——— and R. Marichal, 'Les inscriptions peintes sur amphores de l'anse Saint-Gervais a Fos-sur-Mer' in *Archaeonautica* 2 (1978) 109-81.

——— and P. Pompey, 'Direction des recherches archéologiques sous-marines' in *Gallia* 43 (1985) 547-76.

Llobregat Conesa, E.A., 'La colección Andrés Monzó Nogués (Materiales para el estudio del poblamiento antiguo de la provincia de Valencia)' in *Archivo de Prehistoria Levantina* 13 (1972) 55-80.

———, 'Un grafito en escritura punica de la Illeta dels Banyets (El Campello, Alicante)' in *ITEM* 1 (1977) 91-5, repr. *Ilucant: un cuarto de siglo de investigación histórico-ar-*

queológica en tierras de Alicante (Instituto Alicantino de Cultura Juan Gil-Albert, 1991) 179-80.

———, 'El templo ibérico de la Illeta dels Banyets' in J.M. Blazquez Martínez, *Religions prerromanes* (Madrid, 1983) appendix 4, repr. *Ilucant: un cuarto de siglo de investigación histórico-arqueológica en tierras de Alicante* (Instituto Alicantino de Cultura Juan Gil-Albert, 1991) 249-53.

———, 'Un altar de perfumes de tipo oriental en el yacimiento de la Illetya dels Banyets (El Campello, Alicante)' in *Boletín de la Asociación Española de Orientalistas* 20 (1984) 301-5c, repr. *Ilucant: un cuarto de siglo de investigación histórico-arqueológica en tierras de Alicante* (Instituto Alicantino de Cultura Juan Gil-Albert, 1991) 273-5.

———, 'Dos temples ibèrics a l'interior del poblet de la Illeta dels Banyets' in *Fonaments* 5 (1985) 103-112, repr. *Ilucant: un cuarto de siglo de investigación histórico-arqueológica en tierras de Alicante* (Instituto Alicantino de Cultura Juan Gil-Albert, 1991) 281-6.

———, 'El conjunto de templos ibéricos de la Illeta dels Banyets (El Campello)' in *Studia historica in honorem V. Martínez Morellá* (Alicante, 1985) 187-205, repr. *Ilucant: un cuarto de siglo de investigación histórico-arqueológica en tierras de Alicante* (Instituto Alicantino de Cultura Juan Gil-Albert, 1991) 297-325.

———, 'Los "graffiti" en escritura grecoibérica y púnica de la Illeta dels Banyets, El Campello (Alicante)' in *Homenaje a D. Domingo Fletcher Valls* (Archivo Prehistoria Levantina 19, 1989) 149-66, repr. *Ilucant: un cuarto de siglo de investigación histórico-arqueológica en tierras de Alicante* (Instituto Alicantino de Cultura Juan Gil-Albert, 1991) 325-32.

———, 'L'Illeta dels Banyets (El Campello, Camp d'Alacant). Fou un *Emporion*?' in M. Olcina Doménech (ed.), *La Illeta dels Banyets (El Campello, Alicante). Estudios de la edad del Bronce y época ibérica* (Museo Arqueológico Provincial de Alicante, 1997) 13-20.

Lloyd Jones, H., *The Geography of Strabo* (Harvard University Press, 1924).

López Castro, J.L., 'El imperialismo cartagines y las ciudades fenicias de la Peninsula Iberica entre los siglos VI-III a.C.' in *Studi di egittologia e di antichità puniche* 9 (1991) 87-107.

———, 'La colonización fenicia en la Península Ibérica: 100 años de investigación' in *La colonización fenicia en el sur de la Península Ibérica. 100 años de investigación* (Instituto de Estudios Almerienses, 1992) 11-79.

———, 'Los Libiofenicios: una colonización agrícola cartaginesa en el sur de la Península Ibérica' in *Revista di Studi Fenici* 20 (1992) 48-65.

———, 'La produccion fenicia occidental de salazón de pescado' in *II Congresso Peninsular de História Antiga* (Unversidade de Coimbra, 1993) 353-62.

———, *Hispania Poena: Los Fenicios en la Hispania Romana (206 a.c.-96 d.c)* (Crítica, 1995).

——— *et al.*, 'La colonización fenicia en Abdera: nuevas aportaciones' in *Atti del II Congresso Internazionale di Studi Fenici e Punici. Roma, 9-14 Novembre 1987* (Rome, 1991), vol. 3, 981-9.

López de la Orden, M.D., 'Hornos ceramicos romanos en el "Olivar del los Valencianos" (Puerto Real, Cádiz)' in *Boletín del Museo de Cádiz* 2 (1981) 59-62.

López Málax-Echeverría, A., 'Malaca Romana (yacimientos inéditos)' in *Mainake* 4 (1971) 49-60.

López Medina, M.J., *El municipio romana de Abdera. Una aproximación histórica* (Universidad de Almería, 1996).

López Mullor, A., 'Los tallers anfóricos de Darró (Vilanova i la Geltrú, Barcelona). Noticia de su hallazgo' in *Empúries* 48-50 (1986-9) 64-76.

———, 'Nota preliminar sobre la produccion anforica de Darró, Vilanova i la Geltru (Barcelona)' in L. Rivet (ed.) *Société Française d'Etude de la Céramique Antique en Gaule, Actes du Congrès de Lezoux* (Société Française d'Etude de la Céramique Antique en Gaule, 1990) 109-121.

———, 'Une nouvelle fouille dans le centre producteur d'amphores de Sant Boi de Llobregat (Barcelone)' in L. Rivet (ed.) *Société Française d'Etude de la Céramique Antique en Gaule, Actes du Congrès de Mandeure-Mathay* (Société Française d'Etude de la Céramique Antique en Gaule, 1990) 187-97.

———, 'Villa del castell, Castelldefels' in *Anuari d'intervencions arqueològiques a Catalunya: epoca romana, antiguitat tardana. Campanyes 1982-9* (Generalitat de Catalunya, 1993) 97-8.

———, 'Els Ametllers, Tossa de Mar' in *Anuari d'intervencions arqueològiques a Catalunya: epoca romana, antiguitat tardana. Campanyes 1982-9* (Generalitat de Catalunya, 1993) 212-13.

———, 'La villa dels Ametllers (Tossa, Gerona)' in *Journal of Roman Archaeology* 8 (1995) 286-92.

———, 'El centre productor d'àmfores de Sant Boi de Llobregat (Barcelona)' in *El vi a l'antiguitat: economia, producció i comerç al mediterrani occidental* (Actes del II Colloqui Internacional d'Arqueología Romana, Monografies Badalonines 14, 1998) 233-45.

——— and I. Estany, 'Termes romanes, Sant Boi de Llobregat' in *Anuari d'intervencions arqueològiques a Catalunya: epoca romana, antiguitat tardana. Campanyes 1982-9* (Generalitat de Catalunya, 1993) 83-4.

——— and J. Fierro Macía, 'Excavaciones en la villa romana del Roser de Calella (El Maresme, Barcelona). Campañas de 1981 y 1982' in *Empúries* 47 (1985) 162-208.

——— and J. Fierro Macía, 'Arró, Darró o Adarró, Vilanova i la Geltrú' *in Anuari d'intervencions arqueològiques a Catalunya: epoca romana, antiguitat tardana. Campanyes 1982-9* (Generalitat de Catalunya, 1993) 133-4.

——— and J. Fierro Macía, 'Mas Carbotí, Tossa de Mar' in *Anuari d'intervencions arqueològiques a Catalunya: epoca romana, antiguitat tardana. Campanyes 1982-9* (Generalitat de Catalunya, 1993) 211.

——— and J. Fierro Macía, 'Un horno con ánforas de tipo púnico-ebusitano hallado en Darró (Vilanova i la Geltrú, Barcelona)' in A. González Blanco, J.L. Cunchillos Ilarri and M. Molina Martos (eds), *El mundo púnico. Historia, sociedad y cultura (Cartagena, 17-19 de noviembre de 1990) (Coloquios de Cartagena 1, 1994)* 443-63.

——— and J. Fierro Macía, 'Villa romana de Darró (Vilanova i la Geltrú, Barcelona' in *Journal of Roman Archaeology* 8 (1995) 301-7.

——— and J. Fierro Macía, 'Les darreres intervencions a les termes romanes de Sant Boi de Llobregat. Datació i tipologia' in *Empúries* 53 (2002) 261-96.

——— *et al.*, 'Resultats de la primer campanya d'excavacions a la villa romana del Mas Carbotí (Tossa, La Selva)' in *Informació Arqueològica* 44 (1985) 38-43.

——— *et al.*, 'Un nou jaciment a l'ager de Tarraco: la villa romana del Castell de Cubelles' in *Annals de l'Institut d'Estudis Gironins* 37 (1996-7) 841-51.

——— *et al., Les excavacions de 1985, 1989 i 1992 a la villa romana dels Ametllers, Tossa (La Selva)* (Ajuntament de Tossa de Mar, 2001).

López Segui, E., 'El alfar ibérico' in M. Olcina Doménech (ed.), *La Illeta dels Banyets (El Campello, Alicante). Estudios de la edad del Bronce y época ibérica* (Museo Arqueológico Provincial de Alicante, 1997) 221-50.

———, 'La alfarería ibérica en Alicante. Los alfares de la Illeta dels Banyets, La Alcudia y el Tossal de Manises' in C. Mata Parreño and G. Pérez Jordà (eds), *IBERS. Agricultors, artesans i comerciants. III Reunió sobre Economia en el Món Ibèric* (Saguntum Extra 3, 2000) 241-8.

Maas-Lindemann, G., 'La primera fase de la colonización fenicia en España según los hallazgos del Morro de Mezquitilla' in M.E. Aubet Semmler (ed.), *Los Fenicios en Málaga* (Universidad de Málaga, 1997) 47-60.

———, 'El yacimiento fenicio del Alarcón y la cuestión de la cerámica gris' in A. González

Prats (ed.), *Fenicios y territorio. Actas del II seminario internacional sobre temas fenicios, Guardamar del Segura, 9-11 de abril de 1999* (Instituto Alicantino de Cultura Juan Gil-Albert, 2000) 151-68.

———, 'Cerámica fenicia en la Metrópolis y el las colonias fenicias del s. VIII según la forma de platos' in M.E. Aubet Semmler and M. Barthélemy (eds), *Actas del IV Congreso Internacional de Estudios Fenicios y Púnicos*, vol. 4 (Universidad de Cádiz, 2000) 1595-600.

Macias Solé, J.M. and J.M. Menchon Bes, *La villa romana dels Hospitals, El Morell, Tarragona. Un assentament de la via De Italia in Hispanias* (Institut Català d'Arqueologia Clàsica, Tarragona, 2007).

Maier, J., 'La necropolis tartesica de Cruz del Negro' in *Madrider Mitteilüngen* 40 (1999) 97-114.

Maluquer de Motes, J., 'La colonia griega de Rhode, localizada' in *Zephyrus* 14 (1963) 99-100.

——— and M.E. Aubet Semmler, *Andalucía y Extremadura* (Departamento de Prehistoria y Arqueología, Barcelona, 1981).

Mansel, K., 'Los hallazgos de metal procedentes del horizonte fenicio más antiguo B1 del Morro de Mezquitilla (Algarrobo, Málaga)' in M.E. Aubet Semmler and M. Barthélemy (eds), *Actas del IV Congreso Internacional de Estudios Fenicios y Púnicos*, vol. 4 (Universidad de Cádiz, 2000) 1601-14.

Maniatis, Y. *et al.*, 'Punic amphoras found at Corinth, Greece: an investigation of the origin and technology' in *Journal of Field Archaeology* 11 (1984) 205-22.

Mantilla Collantes, A., 'Marcas y ánforas romanas encontradas en Saguntum' in *Saguntum* 21 (1988) 379-415.

Martí Bonafé, M.Á., *El área territorial de Arse-Saguntum en época ibérica: una aproximación a su estudio* (Diputació de València, 1998).

Marti Solano, J. 'Informe de la excavacion de urgencia en el pantano del Guadalcacin, Cádiz' in *Anuario Arqueológico de Andalucía* 92, III (1992) 107-11.

Martín, A. and M. Prevosti, 'El taller d'àmfores de Tomoví i la producció amfòrica a la Cossetània oriental' in J. Guitart, J.M. Palet and M. Prevosti (eds), *Territoris antics a la Mediterrània i a la Cossetània oriental. Actes del Simposi Internacional d'Arqueologia del Baix Penedès, El Vendrell, del 8 al 10 de novembre de 2001* (Generalitat de Catalunya, 2003) 231-7.

Martín, G., *La supuesta colonia de Hemeroskopeion: estudio arqueológico de la zona Denia-Javea* (Papeles del Laboratorio de Arqueología de Valencia 3, 1968).

———, 'Las pesquerias romanas de la costa de Alicante' in *Trabajos de Arqueologia dedicados a D. Pio Beltrán* (Papeles del Laboratorio de Arqueología de Valencia 10, 1970) 139-53.

———, *La factoria pesquera de la Punta de l'Arenal y otros restos romanas de Javea (Alicante)* (Trabajos Varios del Servicio de Investigacíon Prehistorica 38, 1970).

——— and J. Saludes, 'Hallazgos arqueologicos submarinas en la zona de El Saler (Valencia)' in *Archivo de Prehistoria Levantina* 11 (1966) 155-69.

Martín, M.A., 'Forn romà de Palamós, Palamós' in *Anuari d'intervencions arqueològiques a Catalunya: epoca romana, antiguitat tardana. Campanyes 1982-9* (Generalitat de Catalunya, 1993) 75.

Martin Bueno, M. *et al.*, 'Baelo Claudia: Sector Sur 1981-1983 (Avance)' in *Mélange de la Casa de Velázquez* 20 (1984) 487-96.

Martín Camino, M., 'Colonización fenicia y presencia púnica en Murcia' in A. González Blanco *et al.*, (eds), *El mundo púnico. Historia, sociedad y cultura (Cartagena, 17-19 de noviembre de 1990)* (Coloquios de Cartagena 1, 1994) 293-324.

——— and B. Roldán Bernal, 'Punicos en Cartagena' in *Revista de Arqueologia* 12 (1991) 18-24.

——— *et al.*, 'Un templo suburbano consagrado a Iuppiter Stator en Carthago-Nova' in *Revista de Arqueología* 188 (1996) 28-35.

Martín Córdoba, E. and Á. Recio Ruiz, 'Los Algarrobeños. Un yacimiento fenicio en la Vega del Vélez' in *Mainake* 15-16 (1993-4) 313-15.

——— and Á. Recio Ruiz, *Los fenicios en la costa de Vélez-Málaga* (Playa Fenicia, 2002).

Martín de la Cruz, J.C., 'Die erste mykenische keramik von der iberischen halbinsel' in *Praehistoriche Zeitschrift* 65 (1990) 49-52.

Martín Ortega, M.A., *Ullastret. Guia de les excavacions i del seu museu* (Ajuntament de Girona, 1978).

——— and R. Plana Mallart, 'El nord-est català en època ibèrica i l'entitat territorial de l'oppidum d'Ullastret' in A. Martín i Ortega and R. Plana Mallart (eds), *Territori Polític i Territori Rural durant l'edat del ferro a la Mediterrània Occidental. Actes de la taula rodona celebrada a Ullastret del 25 al 27 de Maig de 2000* (Monografies d'Ullastret 2, Girona, 2001) 39-52.

——— *et al.*, *Excavacions arqueològiques a l'Illa d'en Reixac (1987-1992)* (Monografies d'Ullastret 1, 1999).

——— *et al.*, 'Les actitivitats artesanals als poblats d'Ullastret (Baix Empordà, Girona) i en el seu territori' in C. Mata Parreño and G. Pérez Jordà (eds), *IBERS. Agricultors, artesans i comerciants. III Reunió sobre Economia en el Món Ibèric* (Saguntum Extra 3, 2000) 249-56.

Martín Ruiz, J A., *Catálogo documental de los fenicios en Andalucía* (Junta de Andalucía, 1995).

———, 'El "influjo" fenicio en las tumbas principescas de período Orientalizante tartésico' in M.E. Aubet Semmler and M. Barthélemy (eds), *Actas del IV Congreso Internacional de Estudios Fenicios y Púnicos*, vol. 4 (Universidad de Cádiz, 2000) 1835-9.

Martin-Kilcher, S., *Die römischen amphoren aus Augst und Kaiseraugst* (Forschungen in Augst 7, 1987).

———, *Die römischen amphoren aus Augst und Kaiseraugst* (Forschungen in Augst 7/2, 1994).

Martínez, J. *et al.*, 'La intervenció arqueològica al jaciment ibèric i romà de Can Feu (1987). Notes preliminars' in *Arraona* 3 (1988) 25-34.

Martínez Valle, A. *et al.*, 'La producción de ánforas en el alfar ibérico de las Casillas del Cura (Venta del Moro, Valencia)' in C. Mata Parreño and G. Pérez Jordà (eds), *IBERS. Agricultors, artesans i comerciants. III Reunió sobre Economia en el Món Ibèric* (Saguntum Extra 3, 2000) 225-9.

Mas García, J., 'El poligono submarino de Cabo de Palos. Sus aportaciones al estudio del trafico maritimo antiguo' in *VI Congreso internacional de arqueologia submarina* (Museo y Centro Nacionales de Investigaciones Arqueológicas Submarinas, 1985) 153-71.

———, 'Excavaciones en el yacimiento submarino de "San Ferreol" (costa de Cartagena)' in *VI Congreso internacional de arqueologia submarina* (Museo y Centro Nacionales de Investigaciones Arqueológicas Submarinas, 1985) 189-223.

———, 'El puerto de Cartagena y su hinterland en la vanguardia de la arqueología submarina española' in *Scombraria: la historia oculta bajo el Mar* (Museo Arqueológico de Murcia, 2004) 48-65.

Mascort, M. *et al.*, 'Aldovesta. Les bases d'un modèle commercial dans le cadre de l'expansion phénicienne au nord-est de la Péninsule Iberique' in *Atti del II Congresso Internazionale di Studi Fenici e Punici. Roma, 9-14 Novembre 1987* (Rome, 1991), vol. 3, 1073-9.

Massó Carballido, J., 'Dades sobre la producció d'àmfores de vi romanes en el sector occidental del Camp de Tarragona' in *El vi a l'antiguitat: economia, producció i comerç al mediterrani occidental* (Actes del II Colloqui Internacional d'Arqueología Romana, Monografies Badalonines 14, 1998) 283-8.

Mataloto, R., 'Fortins e recintos-torre do Alto Alentejo: antecâmara da "romanização" dos campos' in *Revista Portuguesa de Arqueología* 5 (2002) 161-220.

Mayerson, P., 'The role of flax in Roman and Fatimid Egypt' in *Journal of Near Eastern Studies* 56 (1997) 201-7.

Mayet, F. and C. Tavares da Silva, 'Abul: um estabelecimento orientalizante do século VII a.C. no baixo vale do Sado' in *Setubal Arqueológica* 9-10 (1992) 315-33.

——— and C. Tavares da Silva, 'Presença fenícia no baixo Sado' in *Estudos Orientais* 4 (1993) 127-42.

——— and C. Tavares da Silva, 'Abul: um estabelecimento fenício do baixo Sado' in J. de Alarcão (ed.), *De Ulisses a Viriato. O primeiro milénio a.C.* (Museu Nacional de Arqueologia, 1996) 52-9.

——— and C. Tavares da Silva, 'Abul et la présence phénicienne sur l'Atlantique' in M.E. Aubet Semmler and M. Barthélemy (eds), *Actas del IV Congreso Internacional de Estudios Fenicios y Púnicos*, vol. 2 (Universidad de Cádiz, 2000) 849-57.

——— and C. Tavares da Silva, 'O santuário de Abul B – uma presença púnica no baixo Sado' in *Os Púnicos no Extremo Occidente: Actas do colóquio internacional (Lisboa, 27 e 28 de Outubro de 2000)* (Universidade Aberta, 2001) 173-95.

McGovern, P.E. *et al.*, 'Has authentic tekelet been identified?' in *Bulletin of the American Schools of Oriental Research* 269 (1988) 81-90.

Melchor Gil, E., 'Las élites municipales en el alto imperio: un intento de aproximación a sus fuentes de riqueza' in *Florentia Iliberitana* 4-5 (1993-4) 335-49.

Menéndez, X. and J.M. Solias i Arís, 'Santa Maria de Sales, Viladecans' in *Anuari d'intervencions arqueològiques a Catalunya: epoca romana, antiguitat tardana. Campanyes 1982-9* (Generalitat de Catalunya, 1993) 85.

Mezquíriz Irujo, M.Á., 'Pavimento de "opus signinum" con inscripción ibérica en Andelos' in *Trabajos de Arqueología de Navarra* 10 (1991-2) 365-7.

———, *La Villa Romana de Arellano* (Gobierno de Navarra, 2003).

———, 'La producción de vino en época romana a través de los hallazgos en territorio navarro' in *Trabajos de Arqueología de Navarra* 17 (2004) 133-59.

Mezquita de Figueiredo, A., 'Ruines d'antiques établissements a salaisons' in *Bulletin Hispanique* 8 (1906) 109-21.

Millán León, J., *Gades y las navegaciones oceánicas en la antigüedad (1000 a.C.-500 d.C.)* (Editorial Gráficas Sol, 1998).

——— and M.L. Lavado Florido, 'El complejo industrial de Puente Melchor (Puerto Real, Cádiz)' in *Congreso Internacional Ex Baetica Amphorae*, vol. 1 (Editorial Gráficas Sol, 2000) 215-25.

Miró, C. *et al.*, 'El procés de romanització al curs mitjà de la riera de Caldes (Vallès): estat de la qüestió' in M. Mayer *et al.* (eds), *De les estructures indígenes a l'organització provincial de la Hispània Citerior. Homenatge a Josep Estrada i Garriga* (Actes de les Jornades Internacionals d'Arqueologia Romana, Granollers 1987) (Societat Catalana d'Estudis Clàssics, 1998) 381-90.

Miró i Canals, J., 'Algunas consideraciones sobre las ánforas Ibéricas Mañá B3' in *Pyrenae* 19-20 (1983) 157-89.

———, *La producción de ánforas romanas en Catalunya. Un estudio sobre el comercio del vino de la Tarraconense (siglos I a.C.-I d.C.)* (BAR Int. Ser. 473, 1988).

———, 'Les estampilles sobre àmfores catalanes. Una aportació al coneixement del comerç del vi del conventus Tarraconensis a finals de la república i principis de l'imperi' in *Fonaments* 7 (1988) 243-63.

——— *et al.*, 'Una aportacion al conocimiento de la producción anforica romana en Tarragona. El horno de l'Aumedina, Tivissa (Ribera d'Ebre, Tarragona)' in *Cuadernos de Prehistoria y Arqueología Castellonenses* 13 (1987-8) 275-87.

Molina Fajardo, F., 'Almuñécar fenicio-púnica' in *I-IV Jornadas de Arqueología Fenicio-Púnica* (Trabajos del Museo Arqueológico de Ibiza 24, Eivissa, 1991) 13-20.

Molina Vidal, J., *La dinámica comercial romana entre Italia e Hispania Citerior* (Universidad de Alicante, 1997).

Molist i Capella, N., 'La Muntanyeta, Sant Boi de Llobregat' in *Anuari d'intervencions arqueològiques a Catalunya: epoca romana, antiguitat tardana. Campanyes 1982-9* (Generalitat de Catalunya, 1993) 79.

———, 'El camí vell del Llor: el procés de romanització d'un assentament ibèric al pla' in M. Mayer *et al.*, (eds), *De les estructures indígenes a l'organització provincial de la Hispània Citerior. Homenatge a Josep Estrada i Garriga* (Actes de les Jornades Internacionals d'Arqueologia Romana, Granollers 1987) (Societat Catalana d'Estudis Clàssics, 1998) 391-402.

Moneo, T., *Religio iberica: santuarios, ritos y divinidades (Siglos VII-I A.C.)* (Real Academia de la Historia, Madrid, 2003).

Montero Fernández, A.I. et al., 'Innovaciones, transformaciones y pervivencias. Evolución de la alfarería gadirita durante los ss. III-II a.n.e' in D. Bernal Casasola and L. Lagóstena Barrios (eds), *Figlinae Baeticae. Talleres alfareros y producciones cerámicas en la Bética romana (ss. II a.C.-VII d.C.)* (BAR Int. Ser. 1266, 2004), vol. 2, 413-26.

Monzó Nogués, A., 'Notas arqueológico-prehistóricas del agro saguntino' in *Anales del Centro de Cultura Valenciana* 14 (1946) 58-61.

Mora Serrano, B. and P. Corrales Aguilar, 'Establecimientos salsarios y producciones anfóricas en los territorios Malacitanos' in *Figlinae Malacitanae. La producción de cerámica romana en los territorios malacitanos* (Universidad de Málaga, 1997) 27-59.

Morley, N., *Trade in Classical Antiquity* (Cambridge, 2007).

Muñoz Vicente, Á. and G. de Frutos Reyes, 'La industria pesquera y conservera púnico-gaditana: balance de la investigación. Nuevas perspectivas' in R. de Balbín Berhmann and P. Bueno Ramírez (eds), *II Congreso de Arqueología Peninsular* (Universidad de Alcalá, 1999), vol. 3, 201-12.

——— and G. De Frutos Reyes, 'El comercio de las salazones en época fenicio y púnica en la Bahía de Cádiz. Estado actual de las investigaciones: los registros arqueológicos' in *XVI encuentros de historia y arqueología: las industrias alfareras y conserveras fenicio-púnicas de la Bahía de Cádiz* (Publicaciones Obra Social y Cultural CajaSur, 2004) 131-67.

——— and L. Perdigones Moreno, 'Estado actual de la arqueología fenicio-púnica en la ciudad de Cádiz' in M.E. Aubet Semmler and M. Barthélemy (eds), *Actas del IV Congreso Internacional de Estudios Fenicios y Púnicos*, vol. 2 (Universidad de Cádiz, 2000) 881-91.

Muñoz Vicente, Á. *et al.*, 'Contribución a los orígenes y difusión comercial de la industria pesquera y conservera Gaditana a través de las recientes aportaciones de las factorias de salazones de la bahía de Cádiz' in *Congreso Internacional El Estrecho de Gibraltar* (Ceuta, 1987) 487-508.

Murphy, J.P., *Rufius Festus Avienus 'Ora Maritima'* (Ares, 1977).

Niemeyer, H.G., 'Phoenician Toscanos as a settlement model? Its urbanistic character in the context of Phoenician expansion and Iberian acculturation' in B. Cunliffe and S.J. Keay (eds), *Social Complexity and the Development of Towns in Iberia* (Proceedings of the British Academy 86, 1995) 67-88.

———, 'The Phoenician settlement at Toscanos: urbanization and function' in M.R. Bierling and S. Gitin (eds), *The Phoenicians in Spain: An Archaeological Review of the Eighth-Sixth Centuries BCE* (Eisenhaus, 2002) 31-48.

Nieto Prieto, F.J. and J.M. Nolla i Brufau, 'El yacimiento arqueológico submarino de Riells-la Clota y su relación con Ampurias' in *Cypsela* 5 (1985) 143-62.

Niveau de Villedary y Mariñas, A.M., 'Ánforas turdetanas, mediterráneas y púnicas del s. III del Castillo de Doña Blanca (El Puerto de Santa María, Cádiz)' in *XXIV Congreso Nacional de Arqueología* (Instituto de Patrimonio Histórico, 1999) 3, 133-40.

———, 'La producción de barniz púnico-gaditano en el s. II a.C. Nuevos datos aportados por el conjunto alfarero de Pery Junquera (San Fernando, Cádiz)' in D. Bernal Casasola and L. Lagóstena Barrios (eds), *Figlinae Baeticae. Talleres alfareros y producciones cerámicas en la Bética romana (ss. II a.C.-VII d.C.)* (BAR Int. Ser. 1266, 2004), vol. 2, 677-90.

———, 'Salazón y ritual. Una relectura de las factorías de salazones prerromanas de la Isla Gaditana' in L. Lagóstena Barrios et al. (eds), *Cetariae 2005. Salsas y Salazones de Pescado en Occidente durante la Antigüedad. Actas del Congreso Internacional (Cádiz, 7-9 de noviembre de 2005)* (BAR Int. Ser. 1686, 2007) 417-33.

——— and D. Ruiz Mata, 'El poblado de Las Cumbres (Castillo de Doña Blanca): urbanismo y materiales del s. III a.C.' in M.E. Aubet Semmler and M. Barthélemy (eds), *Actas del IV Congreso Internacional de Estudios Fenicios y Púnicos*, vol. 4 (Universidad de Cádiz, 2000) 893-903.

Noguera Celdrán, J.M., 'Lucro mercantil, inversiones y programas edilicios en Carthago Nova entre la republica tardía y el alto imperio' in *Scombraria: la historia oculta bajo el Mar* (Museo Arqueológico de Murcia, 2004) 66-87.

Nolla i Brufau, J.M. and F.J. Nieto Prieto, 'Una factoria de salao de peix a Roses' in *Fonaments* 3 (1981) 187-200.

———, 'Algunes notes entorn de la villa del Pla de l'Horta a Sarrià de Dalt (Girona)' in *Annals de l'Institut d'Estudis Gironins* 26 (1982) 111-30.

———, 'Excavaciones recientes en la ciudadela de Rosas: el edificio bajo-imperial' in S.J. Keay et al. (eds), *Papers in Iberian Archaeology* (BAR Int. Ser. 193, 1984) 430-50.

———, 'Una nova amfora Catalana: La Tarraconense 1' in *El vi a l'antiquitat: economia, producció i comerç al Mediterrani Occidental* (Actes del I Colloqui d'Arqueología Romana, Monografies Badalonines 9, 1987) 217-23.

——— and J. Casas i Genover, *Carta arqueològica de les comarques de Girona: el poblament d'època romana al nord-est de Catalunya* (Centre d'Investigacions Arqueològiques de Girona, 1984).

——— *et al.*, 'L'àmfora Tarraconense 1. Característiques, procedència, àrees de producció, cronologia' in *Butlletí Arqueològic* 5 (1984-5) 107-44.

Olcina Doménech, M. and J.M. García i Martín, 'Síntesi arqueològica' in M. Olcina Doménech (ed.), *La Illeta dels Banyets (El Campello, Alicante). Estudios de la edad del Bronce y época ibérica* (Museo Arqueológico Provincial de Alicante, 1997) 21-45.

——— and E. López Seguí, 'Prospección y excavación de urgencia en los alrededores del alfar ibérico' in M. Olcina Doménech (ed.), *La Illeta dels Banyets (El Campello, Alicante). Estudios de la edad del Bronce y época ibérica* (Museo Arqueológico Provincial de Alicante, 1997) 207-20.

——— and R. Pérez Jiménez, *La ciudad ibero-romana de Lucentum (El Tossal de Manises, Alicante)* (Museo Arqueológico Provincial de Alicante, 2001).

Oldfather, C.H., *Diodorus of Sicily* (Harvard University Press, 1960).

Olesti i Vilà, O., *El territori del Maresme en època republicana (s. III-I a.C.): estudi d'arqueomorfologia i història* (Caixa d'Estalvis Laietana, 1995).

———, 'Primers productors d'àmfores vinícoles al Maresme (s. I a.C.)' in *Annals de l'Institut d'Estudis Gironins* 36 (1996-7) 425-48.

———, 'El origen de las villae romanas en Cataluña' in *Archivo Español de Arqueología* 70 (1997) 71-90.

———, 'Els inicis de la producció vinícola a Catalunya: el paper del món indígena' in *El vi a l'antiguitat: economia, producció i comerç al mediterrani occidental* (Actes del II Colloqui Internacional d'Arqueología Romana, Monografies Badalonines 14, 1998) 246-57.

Oliver Foix, A.J., 'La presencia fenicia y púnica al sur de las bocas del Ebro' in *Atti del II*

Congresso Internazionale di Studi Fenici e Punici. Roma, 9-14 Novembre 1987 (Rome, 1991), vol. 3, 1091-101.

Orejas, A. and F.J. Sánchez Palencia, 'Mines, territorial organization, and social structure in Roman Iberia: Carthago Nova and the Peninsular northwest' in *American Journal of Archaeology* 106 (2002) 581-99.

Oria Segura, M. *et al.*, *El poblamiento antiguo en la sierra sur de Sevilla: zona de Montellano* (Ayuntamiento de Montellano, 1990).

Orri i Rovira, J. and M. Tenas i Busquets, 'Darreres intervencions a la villa romana de Can Terrés (La Garriga, Vallès Oriental)' in *Lauro* 1 (1990) 20-3.

Orton, C. *et al.*, *Pottery in Archaeology* (Cambridge University Press, 1993).

Padial, B. *et al.*, 'Estudios analíticos de un conjunto de ánforas de tipología fenicia occidental del asentamiento protohistórico de Ronda la Vieja (Ronda, Málaga)' in M.E. Aubet Semmler and M. Barthélemy (eds), *Actas del IV Congreso Internacional de Estudios Fenicios y Púnicos*, vol. 4 (Universidad de Cádiz, 2000) 1841-5.

Padró i Parcerisa, J., 'Las importaciones egipcias en Almuñécar y los origines de la colonizacion fenicia en la Peninsula Iberica' in O. Arteaga (ed.), *Homenaje a Luis Siret (1934-1984)* (Consejeria de Cultura de la Junta de Andalucía, 1986) 526-9.

——— and J. Sanmartí-Grego, 'L'ocupació del territori per la polis emporitana i la seva significació económica. Algunes hipòtesis' in *Fonaments* 6 (1987) 23-6.

Padrós, P., 'Can Peixau. Un centre productor d'àmfores al territorium de Baetulo' in *El vi a l'antiguitat: economia, producció i comerç al mediterrani occidental* (Actes del II Colloqui Internacional d'Arqueología Romana, Monografies Badalonines 14, 1998) 185-92.

Palahí Grimal, L. and D. Vivó i Codina, 'Anàlisi estructural de la villa del Pla de l'Horta' in *Annals de l'Institut d'Estudis Gironins* 33 (1994) 157-70.

Palet, J.M. *et al.*, 'La villa del Vilarenc (Calafell) i el poblament romà a l'àrea del Penedes' in J. Padró *et al.* (eds), *Homenatge a Miquel Tarradell* (Estudis Universitaris Catalans 29, 1993) 723-51.

Palou i Miquel, H., 'Vall de Maria, Arenys de Mar' in *Anuari d'intervencions arqueològiques a Catalunya: epoca romana, antiguitat tardana. Campanyes 1982-9* (Generalitat de Catalunya, 1993) 160.

Pàmies, A. and J. Pardo, 'La villa romana de Can Terrés (la Garriga) – Vallès Oriental' in M. Mayer *et al.* (eds), *De les estructures indígenes a l'organització provincial de la Hispània Citerior. Homenatge a Josep Estrada i Garriga* (Actes de les Jornades Internacionals d'Arqueologia Romana, Granollers 1987) (Societat Catalana d'Estudis Clàssics, 1998) 451-9.

Pardo, J., *Excavacions a la villa romana de Can Terrés (La Garriga). Campanya 1983* (Museu de Granollers, 1984).

Parker, A.J., *Ancient Shipwrecks of the Mediterranean and the Roman Provinces* (BAR Int. Ser. 580, 1992).

Pascual Guash, R., 'Centros de produccion y difusión geografica de un tipo de ánfora' in *Actas del VII Congreso Nacional de Arqueología* (Universidad de Zaragoza, 1960) 334-45.

———, 'Las ánforas de la Layetania' in *Méthodes classiques et méthodes formelles dans l'étude des amphores. Actes du colloque de Rome, 27-29 Mai* (Collection de l'Ècole Française de Rome 32, 1977) 47-102.

———, 'Sobre algunas marcas anfóricas Catalanas' in *Rivista di Studi Liguri* 46 (1980) 261-79.

———, 'Exploración submarina entre Llavaneres y Mataró (Barcelona)' in *Ampurias* 43 (1981) 217-51.

———, *Índex d'estampilles sobre àmfores Catalanes* (Cuadernos de Arqueologia 5, Barcelona, 1991).

Pastor Mira, A., 'La "Casa del Cura": un conjunto singular en la Illeta dels Banyets' in *XXV Congreso Nacional de Arqueología* (Diputació de València, 1999) 445-50.

Peacock, D.P.S., 'Amphorae and the Baetican fish industry' in *Antiquaries Journal* 54 (1974) 232-43.

———, *Pottery in the Roman World: An Ethnoarchaeological Approach* (Longman, 1982).

——— and D.F. Williams, *Amphorae and the Roman Economy* (Longman, 1986).

Pellicer Catalán, M., *Excavaciones en la necrópolis púnica "Laurita" del Cerro de San Cristóbal (Almuñécar, Granada)* (Excavaciones Arqueológicas en España 77, Madrid, 1962).

———, 'El yacimiento protohistorico de Quebrantahuesos (Riotinto, Huelva)' in *Noticiario Arqueologico Hispanico* 15 (1983) 61-90.

———, 'Phoenician and punic Sexí' in M.R. Bierling and S. Gitin (eds), *The Phoenicians in Spain: An Archaeological Review of the Eighth-Sixth Centuries BCE* (Eisenhaus, 2002) 49-77.

Pena, M.J., 'Las marcas de M. Porcius sobre ánforas Pascual 1' in *Faventia* 21/2 (1999) 75-83.

——— and A. Barreda, 'Productores de vino del nordeste de la Tarraconense. Estudio de algunos nomina sobre ánforas Laietana 1 (= Tarraconense 1)' in *Faventia* 19/2 (1997) 51-73.

Percival, J., *The Roman Villa* (Batsford, 1976).

Perdigones Moreno, L. and A. Muñoz Vicente, 'Excavaciones de urgencia en un solar de la calle Garcia Quijano (Cádiz)' in *Anuario Arqueológico de Andalucía* 86, III (1987) 47-9.

——— and A. Muñoz Vicente, 'Excavaciones arqueologicas de urgencia en las obras del alcantarillado de extramuros de Cádiz' in *Anuario Arqueológico de Andalucía* 87, III (1989) 91-4.

——— *et al.*, 'Excavaciones de urgencia en un solar de la calle Ciudad de Santander esquina Avda. Andalucia (Cádiz)' in *Anuario Arqueológico de Andalucía* 86, III (1987) 41-4.

Pereira, I., 'Santa Olaia' in J. de Alarcão (ed.), *De Ulisses a Viriato. O primeiro milénio a.C.* (Museu Nacional de Arqueologia, 1996) 60-5.

Pereira Menaut, G., *Inscripciones Romanas de Valentia* (Trabajos Varios del Servicio de Investigacion Prehistorica 64, Valencia, 1979).

Pereira Sieso, J. and E. de Alvaro, 'Aportes Orientalizante en el Valle de Tajo. Una tumba de la transición Bronce-Hierro: El Carpio (Belvís de la Jara, Toledo)' in *Revista de Arqueologia* 62 (1986) 29-39.

Pérez Macías, J.A., *Las minas de Huelva en la antigüedad* (Diputación Provincial de Huelva, 1998).

——— and A. Delgado Domínguez, 'Los metalla de Riotinto en época Julio-Claudia' in J.A. Pérez Macías and A. Delgado Domínguez (eds), *Las minas de Riotinto en época Julio-Claudia* (Universidad de Huelva, 2007) 37-182.

Pérez Suñé, J.M. and V. Revilla Calvo, 'Sellos ibéricos impresos sobre ánfora' in *XXIV Congreso Nacional de Arqueología* (Instituto de Patrimonio Histórico, 1999) 3, 359-66.

Picazo, M., *Las cerámicas áticas de Ullastret* (Universidad de Barcelona, Instituto de Arqueología y Prehistoria, 1977).

Pilar Iborra, M., E. Grau and G. Pérez Jordà, 'Recursos agrícolas y ganaderos en el ámbito fenicio occidental: estado de la cuestión' in C. Gómez Bellard (ed.) *Ecohistoria del paisaje agrario. La agricultura fenicio-púnica en el Mediterráneo* (Universitat de València, 2003) 33-55.

Pineda, G. and J.L. Puerto, 'Producción de salsas y salazones de pescado en Benalmadena-Costa (Málaga)' in L. Lagóstena Barrios *et al.* (eds), *Cetariae 2005. Salsas y Salazones de Pescado en Occidente durante la Antigüedad. Actas del Congreso Internacional (Cádiz, 7-9 de noviembre de 2005)* (BAR Int. Ser. 1686, 2007) 439-51.

Plana i Mallart, R. and A. Martín i Ortega, 'L'organitzacio de l'espai rural entorn de l'oppidum d'Ullastret: formes i dinamica del poblament' in A. Martín i Ortega and R. Plana Mallart (eds), *Territori Polític i Territori Rural durant l'edat del ferro a la Mediterrània Occidental. Actes de la taula rodona celebrada a Ullastret del 25 al 27 de Maig de 2000* (Monografies d'Ullastret 2, 2001) 157-76.

Ponce, F., 'Sobre la ubicación del Cádiz fenicio' in M.E. Aubet Semmler and M. Barthélemy (eds), *Actas del IV Congreso Internacional de Estudios Fenicios y Púnicos*, vol. 2 (Universidad de Cádiz, 2000) 905-14.

Pons i Brun, E., 'L'expansió septentrional del Mon Iber: el jaciment des Mas Castellar-Pontós i les seves especialitzacions' in *Laietania* 8 (1993) 105-28.

——— (ed.), *Mas Castellar de Pontós (Alt Empordà). Un comple arqueològic d'època ibèrica (excavacions 1990-1998)* (Museu d'Arqueologia de Catalunya, 2002).

——— *et al.*, 'Les sitges dels assentaments de Mas Castellar de Pontós i les del territori' in A. Martín i Ortega and R. Plana Mallart (eds), *Territori Polític i Territori Rural durant l'edat del ferro a la Mediterrània Occidental. Actes de la taula rodona celebrada a Ullastret del 25 al 27 de Maig de 2000* (Monografies d'Ullastret 2, 2001) 145-56.

Pons Mellado, E., 'Acerca de unos hornos ibéricos en la Riera de Sant Simó (Mataro)' in *Laietania* 2-3 (1982-1983) 185-200.

Ponsich, M., *Implantation rurale antique sur le Bas-Guadalquivir, I. Séville – Alcalá del Río – Lora del Río – Carmona* (Publications de la Casa de Velazquez, 1974).

———, *Aceite de oliva y salazones de pescado. Factores geo-económicos de Bética y Tingitania* (Universidad Complutense, 1988).

Pou i Vallès, J. and V. Revilla Calvo, 'Villa Romana de Vilarenc (Calafell, Baix Penèdes): Campanyes 1988-1994' in *Tribuna d'Arqueologia 1994-1995* (1996) 105-12.

Poveda Navarro, A.M., 'Primeros datos sobre las influencias fenicio-Púnicas en el corredor del Vinalopó (Alicante)' in A. González Blanco *et al.* (eds), *El mundo púnico. Historia, sociedad y cultura (Cartagena, 17-19 de noviembre de 1990)* (Coloquios de Cartagena 1, 1994) 489-502.

———, A.M., 'Penetracion cultural fenicia en el territorio indígena del valle septentrional del Vinalopó (Alicante)' in M.E. Aubet Semmler and M. Barthélemy (eds), *Actas del IV Congreso Internacional de Estudios Fenicios y Púnicos*, vol. 4 (Universidad de Cádiz, 2000) 1863-74.

Prevosti i Monclús, M., *Cronologia i poblament a l'area rural d'Iluro*, 2 vols (Caixa d'Estalvis Laietana, 1981).

———, 'La villa de Torre Llauder (Mataró, Barcelona)' in *Journal of Roman Archaeology* 8 (1995) 292-7.

——— and J.F. Clariana, 'El taller de anforas de Torre Llauder: nuevas aportaciones' in *El vi a l'antiquitat: economia, producció i comerç al Mediterrani Occidental* (Actes del I Colloqui d'Arqueología Romana, Monografies Badalonines 9, 1987) 199-210.

Puerta, C. and M. Rodriguez, 'Una indústria urbana de producció de vi a Baetulo (Badalona)' in *El vi a l'antiquitat: economia, producció i comerç al Mediterrani Occidental* (Actes del I Colloqui d'Arqueología Romana, Monografies Badalonines 9, 1987) 183-8.

Puertas Tricas, R., 'Los hallazgos arqueologicos de Torreblanca del Sol (Fuengirola)' in *Mainake* 8-9 (1986-7) 145-200.

———, 'Las termas romanas de Torreblanca del Sol (Fuengirola) y su perduración hasta el siglo VIII' in *Mainake* 13-14 (1991-2) 205-49.

Pujol i del Horno, J. et al., 'El yaciment ibero-romà de Madà (Argentona, El Maresme), un possible cas de continuïtat d'assentament al territorium d'Iluro' in *Annals de l'Institut d'Estudis Gironins* 36 (1996-7) 347-76.

Pujol Puigvehí, A., *La población preromana del extremo nordeste peninsular,* 2 vols (Universitat Autònoma de Barcelona, 1989).

Purpura, G., 'Pesca e stabilimenti antichi per la lavorazione del pesce in Sicilia: I. S. Vito (Trapani), Cala Minnola (Levanzo)' in *Sicilia Archeologica* 15 (1982) 45-60.

Ramallo Asensio, S.F., 'El horno romano de fundicion de la Loma de Herrerías (Mazarrón, Murcia). I. Estudio historico-arqueologico' in *XVI Congreso Nacional de Arqueologia* (Universidad de Zaragoza, 1983) 925-936.

———, 'Envases para salazon en el Bajo Imperio (I)' in *VI Congreso internacional de arqueologia submarina* (Museo y Centro Nacionales de Investigaciones Arqueológicas Submarinas, 1985) 435-42.

———, *La ciudad romana de Carthago Nova: la documentación arqueologica* (Universidad de Murcia, 1989).

——— and R. Arana Castillo, 'La minería romana en Mazarrón (Murcia). Aspectos arqueológicos y geológicos' in *Anales de Prehistoria y Arqueología* 1 (1985) 49-67.

——— and M. del C. Berrocal Caparros, 'Mineria punica y romana en el sureste peninsular: el foco de Carthago Nova' in D. Vaquerizo Gil (ed.), *Minería y metalurgía en la España Prerromana y Romana* (Diputación Provincial de Córdoba, 1994) 79-146.

Rambla Torralvo, J.A. and J. Mayorga Mayorga, 'Hornos de época altoimperial en Calle Carretería, Málaga' in *Figlinae Malacitanae. La producción de cerámica romana en los territorios malacitanos* (Universidad de Málaga, 1997) 61-78.

Román Rodríguez, J.M. 'El almacenamiento de grano en Carmona: el horreum de San Blas' in A. Caballos Rufino (ed.), *Carmona Romana* (Actas del II Congreso de Historia de Carmona, 2001) 233-50.

Ramón Torres, J., 'Togomago I: un pecio fenicio del siglo V a.C. en aguas en Ibiza' in *VI Congreso internacional de arqueologia submarina* (Museo y Centro Nacionales de Investigaciones Arqueológicas Submarinas, 1985) 377-91.

———, *Las Ánforas Punicas de Ibiza* (Trabajos del Museo Arqueológico de Ibiza 23, Eivissa, 1991).

———, 'El yacimiento fenicio de Sa Caleta' in *I-IV Jornadas de Arqueología Fenicio-Púnica* (Trabajos del Museo Arqueológico de Ibiza 24, Eivissa, 1991) 177-96.

———, 'El nacimiento de la ciudad fenicia de la bahía de Ibiza' in A. González Blanco *et al.* (eds), *El mundo púnico. Historia, sociedad y cultura (Cartagena, 17-19 de noviembre de 1990)* (Coloquios de Cartagena 1, 1994) 325-67.

———, *Las ánforas fenicio-púnicas del Mediterráneo Central y Occidental* (Colleció Instrumenta 2, Universitat de Barcelona, 1995).

———, 'The ancient colonization of Ibiza: mechanisms and process' in M.R. Bierling and S. Gitin (eds), *The Phoenicians in Spain: An Archaeological Review of the Eighth-Sixth Centuries BCE* (Eisenhaus, 2002) 127-52.

———, 'La producción anfórica gaditana en época fenicio-púnica' in *XVI encuentros de historia y arqueología: las industrias alfareras y conserveras fenicio-púnicas de la Bahía de Cádiz* (Publicaciones Obra Social y Cultural CajaSur, 2004) 63-100.

——— *et al.*, *El taller alfarero tardoarcaico de Camposoto (San Fernando, Cádiz)* (Junta de Andalucía, 2007).

Ramos Millán, A. and E. García Vargas, 'El alfar romano de "El Olivar" (Chipiona, Cádiz). De la investigación arqueológica al contexto histórico' in D. Bernal Casasola and L. Lagóstena Barrios (eds), *Figlinae Baeticae. Talleres alfareros y producciones cerámicas en la Bética romana (ss. II a.C.-VII d.C.)* (BAR Int. Ser. 1266, 2004), vol. 2, 447-55.

Raya de Cárdenas, M. *et al.*, 'Excavaciones de urgencia relativas a la villa romana del Cortijo del Canal' in *Anuario Arqueológico de Andalucía* 87, III (1990) 225-32.

Raya de Cárdenas, M. and I. Toro Moyano, 'Villa romana del Cortijo Lapuente (Albolote, Granada)' in *Anuario Arqueológico de Andalucía* 87, III (1990) 233-8.

Recio Ruiz, A., 'Vestigios materiales cerámicos de ascendencia Fenicio-Púnica en la Provincia de Málaga' in *Madrider Mitteilüngen* 34 (1993) 127-41.

Remesal Rodríguez, J., 'Tres nuevos centros productores de ánforas Dressel 20 y 23. Los sellos de Lucius Fabius Cilo' in *Ariadna* 6 (1989) 121-53.

———, 'Baetican olive oil and the Roman economy' in S. Keay (ed.), *The Archaeology of Early Roman Baetica* (Journal of Roman Archaeology Suppl. Ser. 29, 1998) 183-99.

———, 'Oleum Baeticum. Consideraciones y propuestas para su estudio' in *Congreso Internacional Ex Baetica Amphorae*, vol. 1 (Editorial Gráficas Sol, 2000) 373-92.

——— *et al.*, 'Arva: prospecciones en un centro productor de ánforas Dressel 20 (Alcolea del Río, Sevilla)' in *Pyrenae* 28 (1997) 151-78.

Revilla Calvo, V., *Producción cerámica y economía rural de el bajo Ebro en época romana. El alfar de l'Aumedina, Tivissa (Tarragona)* (Collecció Instrumenta 1, Universitat de Barcelona, 1993).

———, 'El alfar romano de Tomoví. Producción anfórica y agricultura en el área de Tarraco' in *Butlletí Arqueològic* 16 (1994) 111-28.

———, 'Producción artesanal, viticultura y propriedad rural en la Hispania Tarraconense' in *Gerión* 13 (1995) 305-38.

———, *Producción cerámica, viticultura y propriedad rural en Hispania Tarraconensis (siglos I a.C.-III d.C.)* (Cuadernos de Arqueologia 8, 1995).

———, 'Paisaje rural, economía y élites en el territorio de Tarraco: la organización interna de la villa del Vilarenc (Calafell)' in J. Guitart *et al.* (eds), *Territoris antics a la Mediterrània i a la Cossetània oriental. Actes del Simposi Internacional d'Arqueologia del Baix Penedès, El Vendrell, del 8 al 10 de novembre de 2001* (Generalitat de Catalunya, 2003) 285-301.

———, 'El poblamiento rural en el noreste de Hispania entre los siglos II a.C. y I d.C.: Organización y dinámicas culturales y socioeconómicas' in P. Moret and T. Chapa (eds), *Torres, Atalayas y Casas Fortificadas. Explotación y control del territorio en Hispania (S. III a. de C-S. I d. de C.)* (Universidad de Jaen, 2004) 175-202.

———, 'Ánforas y epigrafía anfórica en Hispania Tarraconensis' in J. Remesal Rodriguez (ed.), *Epigrafía Anfórica* (Colección Instrumenta 17, Universitat de Barcelona, 2004) 159-96.

Ribas i Beltrán, M., 'Un taller d'àmfores a Mataró' in *Pyrenae* 19-20 (1983-4) 281-5.

Ribeiro Guerra, A., 'Marcas de ânforas provenientes do Porto dos Cacos (Alcochete)' in G. Filipe and J.M.C. Raposo (eds), *Ocupação Romana dos Estuários do Tejo e do Sado* (Actas das Primeiras Jornadas sobre Romanização dos Estuários do Tejo e do Sado, Câmara Municipal do Seixal, 1996) 267-82.

Ribera Lacomba, A., *Las ánforas prerromanas valencianas (fenicias, ibericas y punicas)* (Servicio de Investigacion Prehistorica, Serie de Trabajos Varios 73, 1982).

———, 'The Roman foundation of Valentia and the town in the 2nd-1st c. B.C.' in L. Abad Casal *et al.* (eds), *Early Roman Towns in Hispania Tarraconensis* (Journal of Roman Archaeology Suppl. Ser. 62, 2006) 75-89.

Ribichini, S., 'Sui miti della fondazione de Cadice' in M.E. Aubet Semmler and M. Barthélemy (eds), *Actas del IV Congreso Internacional de Estudios Fenicios y Púnicos, vol.* 2 (Universidad de Cádiz, 2000) 661-8.

Richardson, J.S., 'The Spanish mines and the development of provincial taxation in the second century BC' in *Journal of Roman Studies* 66 (1976) 139-52.

———, 'The Tabula Contrebiensis: Roman law in Spain in the early first century BC: I' in *Journal of Roman Studies* 73 (1983) 33-41.

———, *The Romans in Spain* (Blackwell, 1996).

——— (ed.), *Appian: The Wars of the Romans in Iberia* (Aris & Phillips, 2000).

Rico, C., 'Índex de les marques epigràfiques sobre tegulae romanes de Catalunya i el país Valencià (antigua Tarraconensis)' in *Saguntum* 28 (1995) 197-215.

Rodríguez Almeida, E., 'Monte Testaccio: I Mercartores dell'olio della Betica' in *Mélanges de l'École Française de Rome: Antiquité* 91 (1979) 873-975.

———, *Los tituli picti de las ánforas olearias de la Bética* (Universidad Complutense, 1989).

———, 'Anforas olearias béticas: cuestiones varias' in *Alimenta: Estudios en homenaje al Dr. Michel Ponsich* (Anejos de Gerión 3, 1991) 243-59.

Rodríguez Díaz, A. and J.-J. Enríquez Navascués, *Extremadura tartésica. Arqueología de un proceso periférico* (Bellaterra Arqueología, 2001).

——— et al., *El Cerro de San Cristobal, Logrosan, Estremadura, Spain: the archaeometallurgical excavation of a Late Bronze tin-mining and metalworking site* (BAR Int. Ser. 922, 2001).

Rodríguez Oliva, P., *La arqueología romana de Benalmadena* (Ayuntamiento de Benalmadena, 1982).

———, 'Los hornos cerámicos del faro de Torrox' in *Figlinae Malacitanae. La producción de cerámica romana en los territorios malacitanos* (Universidad de Málaga, 1997) 271-303.

Rodríguez Rodríguez, I., 'Las area artesanales: los alfares' in A. Caballos Rufino (ed.), *Carmona Romana* (Actas del II Congreso de Historia de Carmona, Carmona, 2001) 311-20.

Roldán Gómez, L. *et al.*, *Carteia* (Junta de Andalucía, 1998).

——— *et al.*, *Estudio histórico-arqueológico de la ciudad de Carteia (San Roque, Cádiz) 1994-1999*, 2 vols (Junta de Andalucía, 2006).

Roman, Y., 'Les amphores de M. Porcius, constat d'une divergence et plaidoyer pour une analyse physique et chimique' in *Actes du 104e Congrès National des Sociétés Savantes* (Bibliothèque Nationale, 1982) 81-5.

Romero Pérez, M., 'El Callumbar: una villa romana dedicada a la producción del aceite' in *Anuario Arqueológico de Andalucía* 87, III (1990) 500-8.

———, 'Algunas reflexiones sobre la producción de aceite en las villae de la comarca de Antequera' in *Mainake* 19-20 (1997-8) 115-41.

Romo Salas, A., 'El conjunto alfarero romano de Azanaque (Lora del Río, Sevilla). Intervención de 1993' in *Anuario Arqueologico de Andalucía* III, 93 (1997) 766-77.

——— and J.M. Vargas Jiménez, 'Azanaque. Evidencias arqueológicas de un centro de producción anfórica' in *Congreso Internacional Ex Baetica Amphorae*, vol. 1 (Editorial Gráficas Sol, 2000) 405-17.

Ros Mateos, A., 'Les sitges ibèriques de La Bassa (Santa Margarida i els Monjos): aproximació al període ibèric tardà a la conca del Foix' in *I Trobada d'Estudiosos del Foix* (Barcelona, 2005) 185-91.

Ros Sala, M.M., 'El trabajo del hierro en el poblado protohistórico de El Castellar (Murcia). 1: Análisis arqueológico' in R. Arana Castillo *et al.* (eds), *Metalurgia en la Península Ibérica durante el primer milenio a.C. Estado actual de la investigación* (Universidad de Murcia, 1993) 71-109.

Rosman, K.J.R. *et al.*, 'Lead from Carthaginian and Roman Spanish mines isotopically identified in Greenland ice dating from 600 BC to AD 300' in *Environmental Science and Technology* 31.12 (1997) 3413-16.

Rosselló, E. and A. Morales (eds), *Castillo de Doña Blanca: archaeo-environmental investigations in the Bay of Cádiz, Spain (750-500 BC)* (BAR Int. Ser. 593, 1994).

Rothenburg, B. and A. Blanco Freijero, *Studies in Ancient Mining and Metallurgy in Southwest Spain* (Institute of Archaeo-Metallurgical Studies, Institute of Archaeology, University of London, 1981).

Rouillard, P., *Les Grecs en la péninsule ibérique du VIIIe au IVe siècle avant Jésus-Christ* (Publications du Centre Pierre Paris 21, 1991).

Rufete Tomico, P., 'Las primeras cerámicas fenicias en los poblados tartésicos de Huelva' in A. González Prats (ed.), *La cerámica fenicia en Occidente: centros de producción y áreas de comercio. Actas del I Seminario Internacional sobre Temas Fenicios, Guardamar del Segura, 21-24 de noviembre de 1997* (Instituto Alicantino de Cultura Juan Gil-Albert, 1999) 215-40.

Ruiz de Arbulo, J., 'Emporion y Rhode. Dos asentamientos portuarios en el golfo de Roses' in *Arqueologia Espacial* 4 (1984) 115-40.

———, 'Soportes y toberas. Los ejemplares de Emporion' in *Archivo Español de Arqueología* 69 (1989) 315-24.

———, 'Emporion. Ciudad y territorio (s. VI-I a.C.). Algunas reflexiones preliminares' in *Revista d'Arqueologia de Ponent* 2 (1992) 59-74.

Ruiz Delgado, M.M., 'Las necrópolis tartésicas: prestigio, poder y jerarquías' in M.E. Aubet Semmler (ed.), *Tartessos. Arqueología Protohistórica del Bajo Guadalquivir* (Editorial AUSA, 1989) 247-86.

Ruiz Gil, J.A., 'Cronología de las factorías de salazones Púnicas de Cádiz' in *Atti del II Congresso Internazionale di Studi Fenici e Punici. Roma, 9-14 Novembre 1987* (Rome, 1991), vol. 3, 1211-14.

Ruiz Mata, D., 'El poblado metalúrgico de época tartésica de San Bartolomé (Almonte, Huelva)' in *Madrider Mitteilüngen* 22 (1981) 150-70.

———, 'Aportacion al analisis de los inicios de la presencia fenicia en Andalucia Sudoccidental, segun las excavaciones del Cabezo de San Pedro (Huelva), S. Bartolomé (Almonte, Huelva), Castillo de Doña Blanca (Puerto de Santa Maria, Cádiz) y El Carambolo (Cavas, Seville)' in O. Arteaga (ed.), *Homenaje a Luis Siret (1934-1984)* (Consejeria de Cultura de la Junta de Andalucía, 1986) 537-56, repr. 'The beginnings of the Phoenician presence in southwestern Andalusia' in M.R. Bierling and S. Gitin (eds), *The Phoenicians in Spain: An Archaeological Review of the Eighth-Sixth Centuries BCE* (Eisenhaus, 2002) 263-98.

———, 'Castillo de Doña Blanca (Puerto de Santa María, Prov. Cádiz): stratigraphische untersuchung einer orientalsierenden andsiedlung' in *Madrider Mitteilüngen* 27 (1986) 87-115.

———, 'Huelva: un foco temprano de actividad metalúrgica durante el Bronze Final' in M.E. Aubet Semmler (ed.), *Tartessos. Arqueología Protohistórica del Bajo Guadalquivir* (Editorial AUSA, 1989) 209-43.

———, 'Los fenicios en la Bahia de Cádiz, segun el Castillo de Doña Blanca' in *I-IV Jornadas de Arqueología Fenicio-Púnica* (Trabajos del Museo Arqueológico de Ibiza 24, 1991) 89-99.

———, 'El túmulo 1 de la necrópolis de Las Cumbres' in *I-IV Jornadas de Arqueología Fenicio-Púnica* (Trabajos del Museo Arqueológico de Ibiza 24, 1991) 207-20.

———, 'Fenicios en el sur peninsular: sucinta reseña historiográfica y propuesta de objetivos de investigación en los albores del año 2000' in *Arbor* 156 (1998) 413-39.

———, 'Fenicios e Indígenas en Andalucía Occidental. Tartessos Como Paradigma' in D. Ruiz Mata (ed.), *Fenicios e Indígenas en el Mediterráneo y Occidente: Modelos e Interacción* (Actas de los Encuentro de Primavera de la Universidad de Cádiz en El Puerto de Santa María, 1998) 9-37.

———, 'Tartessos' in M. Almagro Gorbea *et al.*, *Protohistoria de la Peninsula Ibérica* (Editorial Ariel, 2001) 1-190.

———, 'The ancient Phoenicians of the 8th and 7th centuries BC in the Bay of Cadiz: state of the research' in M.R. Bierling and S. Gitin (eds), *The Phoenicians in Spain: An Archaeological Review of the Eighth-Sixth Centuries BCE* (Eisenhaus, 2002) 155-98.

——— and I. Córdoba Alonso, 'Los hornos turdetanos del Cerro Macareno' in *XXIV Congreso Nacional de Arqueología* (Instituto de Patrimonio Histórico, 1999) 3, 95-105.

——— and C.J. Pérez, 'El túmulo 1 de la necrópolis de "Las Cumbres" (Puerto de Santa María, Cádiz)' in M.E. Aubet Semmler (ed.), *Tartessos. Arqueología Protohistórica del Bajo Guadalquivir* (Editorial AUSA, 1989) 287-95.

——— and A.M. Niveau Villedary y Mariñas, 'La zona industrial de Las Cumbres y la cerámica del s. III a.n.e. (Castillo de Doña Blanca-El Puerto de Santa María, Cádiz) in *XXIV Congreso Nacional de Arqueología* (Instituto de Patrimonio Histórico, 1999) 3, 125-31.

——— *et al.*, 'Excavaciones en el Cabezo de San Pedro (Huelva) Campaña de 1978' in *Huelva Arqueologica* 5 (1981) 149-316.

——— *et al.*, 'Vinos, aceites y salazones en la Turdetana' in C. Aranegui Gascó (ed.), *Los iberos, principes de occidente. Las estructuras de poder en la sociedad ibérica* (Saguntum Extra 1, 1998) 389-97.

Ruiz Nieto, E., 'La villa romana de "La Canaleja": nuevo asentamiento en la campiña Cordobesa' in J. Aranda Doncel (ed.), *II encuentros de historia local: la Campiña* (Diputación Provincial de Córdoba, 1991) 191-200.

Ruiz Rodríguez, A. and M. Molinos, *The Archaeology of the Iberians* (Cambridge University Press, 1998).

Ruiz Valderas, E., 'Poblamiento rural romano en el área oriental de Carthago Nova' in J.M. Noguera Celdrán (ed.), *Poblamiento rural romano en el sureste de Hispania (Actas de las Jornadas celebradas en Jumilla del 8 al 11 de noviembre de 1993)* (Universidad de Murcia, 1995) 153-82.

———, 'Cerámicas campanienses de Cartagena: el registro arqueológico y la dinámica comercial' in *Scombraria: la historia oculta bajo el Mar* (Museo Arqueológico de Murcia, 2004) 88-100.

Sabrosa, A.J., 'Necrópole romana do Porto dos Cacos (Alcochete)' in G. Filipe and J.M.C. Raposo (eds), *Ocupação romana dos estuários do Tejo e do Sado* (Actas das Primeiras Jornadas sobre Romanização dos Estuários do Tejo e do Sado, Câmara Municipal do Seixal, 1996) 283-300.

Saenz Gómez, M.A., 'Informe sobre las excavaciones de urgencia realizadas en el solar no. 5 de la calle Juan Ramón Jiménez, en Cádiz' in *Anuario Arqueológico de Andalucía* 91, I (1993) 11-16.

Sáez Romero, A.M., 'El alfar tardopúnico de Torre Alta. Resultados de las excavaciones de 2002-2003' in D. Bernal Casasola and L. Lagóstena Barrios (eds), *Figlinae Baeticae. Talleres alfareros y producciones cerámicas en la Bética romana (ss. II a.C.-VII d.C.)* (BAR Int. Ser. 1266, 2004), vol. 2, 699-712.

——— and D. Bernal Casasola, 'Acerca del origen púnico-gaditano de las piletas de salazón en el Mediterráneo Occidental: una innovación de la ciudad de Gadir?' in L. Lagóstena Barrios *et al.* (eds), *Cetariae 2005. Salsas y Salazones de Pescado en Occidente durante la Antigüedad. Actas del Congreso Internacional (Cádiz, 7-9 de noviembre de 2005)* (BAR Int. Ser. 1686, 2007) 463-73.

——— *et al.*, 'Acerca de un tipo de ánfora salazonera púnica-gadirita' in *Habis* 35 (2004) 109-33.

Salado Escaño, J.B., 'La villa romana de la Torre de Benagalbón, Málaga. Primera descripción' in *Mainake* 27 (2005) 353-78.

Salinas de Frias, M., *Conquista y romanización de Celtiberia* (Museo Numantino, 1986).

San Martín, P.A., 'Primer informe sobre la excavacion de la Loma del Escorial – Los Nietos (Cartagena)' in *Noticiario Arqueológico Hispánico* 6 (1964) 157-61.

Sánchez Fernández, C., 'Algunas consideraciones sobre el comercio de ceramica atica en Castulo (Linares, Jaen): siglos V y IV a.C.' in P. Rouillard and M-C. Villanueva-Puig (eds), *Grecs et Ibères au IVe siècle avant Jésus-Christ: commerce et iconographie* (Publications du Centre Pierre Paris 19, 1989) 161-8.

———, 'Las copas tipo Castulo en la Peninsula Iberica' in *Trabajos de Prehistoria* 49 (1992) 327-33.

———, 'Los griegos en España en los siglos V y IV a.C. Ibiza y su papel en la distribución de los materiales griegos de occidente' in B. Costa and J.H. Fernández (eds), *Contactos en el extremo de la oikuméne. Los griegos en occidente y sus relaciones con los fenicios* (XVII Jornadas de Arqueología Fenicio-Púnica, 2003) 133-43.

——— *et al.*, 'Descubrimiento de una factoria bajoimperial de salazon de pescado en Santa Pola (Alicante)' in *Saguntum* 22 (1989) 413-41.

Sánchez Palencia, F.J. (ed.), *Las Médulas (León): un paisaje cultural en la Asturia Augusta* (Instituto Leonés de Cultura, 2000).

——— and A. Orejas, 'La minería de oro del noroeste peninsular. Tecnología, organización y poblamiento' in D. Vaquerizo Gil (ed.), *Minería y metalurgía en la España prerromana y romana* (Diputación Provincial de Córdoba, 1994) 147-233.

——— *et al.*, *La zona arqueológica de Las Médulas* (Junta de Castilla y León, 1999).

Sanmartí Grego, E., 'Recent discoveries at the harbour of the Greek city of Emporion (L'Escala, Catalonia, Spain) and its surrounding area (quarries and iron workshops)' in B. Cunliffe and S.J. Keay (eds), *Social Complexity and the Development of Towns in Iberia* (Proceedings of the British Academy 86, 1995) 157-74.

———, 'La "Tumba Cazurro" de la necrópolis emporitana de "El Portitxol" y algunos apuntes acerca de la economia de Emporion en el siglo V a.C.' in *Archivo Español de Arqueologia* 69 (1996) 17-36.

——— and J.M. Nolla i Brufau, *Ampurias* (Diputació de Barcelona, 1988).

——— and R.A. Santiago 'Une lettre grecque sur plomb trouvée à Emporion' in *Zeitschrift für Papyrologie und Epigraphik* 68 (1987) 119-27.

——— *et al.*, 'Les excavacions a l'àrea del Pàrking al sud de la Neàpolis d'Empúries (Informe Preliminar)' in *Empúries* 45-46 (1983-4) 110-53.

——— *et al.*, 'Las estructuras griegas de los siglos V y IV a. de J.C., halladas en el sector sur de la Neapolis de Ampurias (Campaña de excavaciones del año 1986)' in *Cuadernos de Prehistoria y Arqueologia Castellonenses* 12 (1986) 141-84.

——— *et al.*, 'La secuencia histórico-topográfica de las murallas del sector meridional de Emporion' in *Madrider Mitteilüngen* 29 (1988), 191-200.

——— *et al.*, 'Les amphores massaliètes d'Emporion du milieu du VIe au milieu du IVe s. av. J.-C.' in *Etudes Massaliètes* 2 (1990) 165-70.

——— *et al.*, 'Nuevos datos sobre la historia y la topografía de las murallas de Emporion' in *Madrider Mitteilüngen* 33 (1991) 102-12.

——— *et al.*, 'Can Ventura de l'Oller, Santa Perpètua de Mogoda' in *Anuari d'intervencions arqueològiques a Catalunya: epoca romana, antiguitat tardana. Campanyes 1982-9* (Generalitat de Catalunya, 1993) 274.

——— *et al.*, 'Amphores grecques et trafics commerciaux en Méditerranée occidentale au IVe s. av. J.-C.' in *Etudes Massaliètes* 4 (1995) 31-47.

Sanmartí Grego, J., 'El comercia fenicio y punico en Cataluña' in *I-IV Jornadas de Arqueologia fenicio-púnica* (Trabajos del Museo Arqueológico de Ibiza 24, 1991) 119-36.

———, 'La colonización fenicio-púnica en Cataluña, País Valenciano y Murcia (1980-1993)' in *Hispania Antigua* 19 (1995) 455-67.

———, 'La ceràmica grega fina de l'assentament ibèric d'Alorda Park (Calafell, Baix Penedès, Tarragona). Segles VI-IV a.C.' in *Pyrenae* 27 (1996) 117-39.

Santos Retolaza, M., 'Fenicios y griegos en el extremo N.E. Peninsular durante la época arcaica y los orígenes del enclave foceo de Emporion' in B. Costa and J.H. Fernández (eds), *Contactos en el extremo de la oikuméne. Los griegos en occidente y sus relaciones con los fenicios* (XVII Jornadas de Arqueología Fenicio-Púnica, 2003) 87-132.

Santos Velasco, J.A., 'The transition to a society with a state in the south east of the Iberian Peninsula (6th-4th century BC)' in *Oxford Journal of Archaeology* 8 (1989) 213-26.

———, 'The Iberians in Sardinia: a review and update' in M. Balmuth, A. Gilman and L. Prados-Torreira (eds), *Encounters and Transformations: The Archaeology of Iberia in Transition*, Monographs in Mediterranean Archaeology 7 (Sheffield Academic Press, 1997) 161-6.

Schubart, H., 'Westphönische Teller' in *Rivista di Studi Fenici* 4 (1976) 179-96.

———, 'La forja fenicia del hierro en el Morro de Mezquitilla' in A. González Prats (ed.), *La cerámica fenicia en Occidente: centros de producción y áreas de comercio. Actas del I Seminario Internacional sobre Temas Fenicios, Guardamar del Segura, 21-24 de noviembre de 1997* (Instituto Alicantino de Cultura Juan Gil-Albert, 1999) 241-56.

———, 'The Phoenician settlement of the 8th century BC in Morro de Mezquitilla (Algarrobo, Málaga)' in M.R. Bierling and S. Gitin (eds), *The Phoenicians in Spain: An Archaeological Review of the Eighth-Sixth Centuries BCE* (Eisenhaus, 2002) 3-29.

———, *Morro de Mezquitilla. El asentamiento fenicio-púnico en la desembocadura del Río Algarrobo* (Anejos de la Revista Mainake 1, 2006).

——— and O. Arteaga, 'El mundo de las colonias fenicias occidentales' in O. Arteaga (ed.), *Homenaje a Luis Siret (1934-1984)* (Consejeria de Cultura de la Junta de Andalucía, 1986) 499-525.

——— and G. Maas-Lindemann, 'La necrópolis de Jardín' in *Cuadernos de Arqueología Mediterránea* 1 (1995) 57-213.

——— and H.G. Niemeyer, *Trayamar. Los hipogeos fenicios y el asentamiento en la desembocadura del río Algarrobo* (Excavaciones Arqueológicas en España 90, 1976).

——— *et al.*, *Toscanos: La factoría paleopúnica en la desembocadura del río Vélez* (Excavaciones Arqueológicas en España 66, 1969).

Schulten, A., 'Forshungen in Spanien' in *Archäologischer Anzeiger* 2/3 (1927) 197-235.

Sealey, P.R., *Amphorae from the 1970 excavations at Colchester Sheepen* (BAR Brit. Ser. 142, 1985).

Shefton, B.B., 'Greeks and Greek imports in the south of the Iberian península: the archaeological evidence' in H.G. Niemeyer (ed.), *Phönizier im Westen* (Madrider Beiträge 8, 1982) 337-68.

———, 'Massalia and colonization in the north-western Mediterranean' in G.R. Tsetskhladze and F. de Angelis (eds), *The Archaeology of Greek Colonization: Essays Dedicated to Sir John Boardman* (Oxford University Committee for Archaeology, 1994) 61-86.

———, 'Greek imports at the extremities of the Mediterranean, west and east: reflections on the case of Iberia in the fifth century BC' in B. Cunliffe and S.J. Keay (eds), *Social Complexity and the Development of Towns in Iberia* (Proceedings of the British Academy 86, 1995) 127-55.

Sherwin White, A.N., *Roman Citizenship* (Oxford University Press, 1973).

Sillières, P., *Baelo Claudia une cité romaine de Bétique* (Collection de la Casa de Velázquez 51, 1995).

Simón García, J.L., 'La Illeta: asentamiento litoral en el Mediterráneo Occidental de la Edad del Bronce' in M. Olcina Doménech (ed.), *La Illeta dels Banyets (El Campello, Alicante). Estudios de la edad del Bronce y época ibérica* (Museo Arqueológico Provincial de Alicante, 1997) 47-132.

Solias i Arís, J.M., 'Introducció a l'estudi de les activitats econòmiques d'una villa Laietana' in *Pyrenae* 21 (1985) 113-21.

Solovera San Juan, M.E., *Estudios sobre la historia economica de La Rioja romana* (Instituto de Estudios Riojanos 7, 1987).

Sos Baynat, V., 'Los hallazgos prehistoricos de Logrosan (Caceres)' in *Revista de estudios extremeños* 33 (1977) 261-86.

Sotomayor, M., 'Informe sucinto de la exploracion arqueologica realizada en la carretera de "El Rinconcillo", en la Bahia de Algeciras' in *Noticiario Arqueologico Hispanico* 13-14 (1969-70) 52-7.

———, M., 'Nueva factoria de salazones de pescado en Almuñecar (Granada)' in *Noticiario Arqueologico Hispanico* 15 (1971) 147-78.

Spindler, K. *et al.*, 'Le monument à coupole de l'âge du bronze final de la Roça do Casal do

Meio (Calhariz)' in *Comunicações dos Serviços Geológicos de Portugal* 57 (1973-4) 91-153.

Stieglitz, R.R., 'The Minoan origin of Tyrian purple' in *Biblical Archaeologist* 57 (1994) 46-54.

Stylow, A.U., 'Fuentes epigráficas para la historia de la "Hispania Ulterior" en época republicana' in E. Melchor Gil *et al.* (eds), *Julio César y Corduba. Tiempo y espacio en la campaña de Munda (49-45 a.C.)* (Universidad de Córdoba, 2005) 247-65.

Suárez Marquez, A., 'Memoria de la excavación de urgencia realizada en el solar situado en la c/Reina, Parque Nicolás Salmerón (Almería) 1985' in *Anuario Arqueológico de Andalucía* III, 85 (1987) 22-8.

——— *et al.*, 'Memoria de la excavación de urgencia en el Cerro de Montecristo. Adra (Almería)' in *Anuario Arqueologico de Andalucía* III, 86 (1987) 16-19.

Tavares da Silva, C., 'Produção de ânforas na área urbana de Setúbal: a oficina romana do Largo da Misericórdia' in G. Filipe and J.M.C. Raposo (eds), *Ocupação Romana dos Estuários do Tejo e do Sado* (Actas das Primeiras Jornadas sobre Romanização dos Estuários do Tejo e do Sado, Câmara Municipal do Seixal, 1996) 43-54.

Tchernia, A., 'Les amphores vinaires de Tarraconaise et leur exportation au début de l'empire' in *Archivo Espanol de Arqueología* 44 (1971) 38-85.

Teichner, F., 'La casa num. II de Munigua. Un complejo de producción de aceite en Sierra Morena' in *Congreso Internacional Ex Baetica Amphorae*, vol. 4 (Editorial Gráficas Sol, 2000) 1343-8.

Terré, E., 'El Moro, Torredembara' in *Anuari d'intervencions arqueològiques a Catalunya: epoca romana, antiguitat tardana. Campanyes 1982-9* (Generalitat de Catalunya, 1993) 266.

Torres, C. *et al.*, 'La factoría romana de salazón del yacimiento de "O Areal", Vigo (Galicia): un complejo industrial salazonero altoimperial' in L. Lagóstena Barrios *et al.* (eds), *Cetariae 2005. Salsas y Salazones de Pescado en Occidente durante la Antigüedad. Actas del Congreso Internacional (Cádiz, 7-9 de noviembre de 2005)* (BAR Int. Ser. 1686, 2007) 475-85.

Torres Ortiz, M., 'La cronología de los túmulos A y B de Setefilla. El origen del rito de la cremación en la cultura tartésica' in *Complutum* 7 (1996) 147-62.

———, *Sociedad y mundo funerario en Tartessos* (Real Academia de la Historia, Madrid, 1999).

———, *Tartessos* (Real Academia de la Historia, Madrid, 2000).

Tremoleda i Trilla, J., 'La producció del forn de Palamós (Baix Empordà) 1' in *El vi a l'antiquitat: economia, producció i comerç al Mediterrani Occidental* (Actes del I Colloqui d'Arqueología Romana, Monografies Badalonines 9, 1987) 271-83.

———, *Industria y artesanado cerámico de época romana en el nordeste de Cataluña (Época augústea y altoimperial)* (BAR Int. Ser. 835, 2000).

——— *et al.*, 'La Quintana, Cervià de Ter' in *Anuari d'intervencions arqueològiques a Catalunya: epoca romana, antiguitat tardana. Campanyes 1982-9* (Generalitat de Catalunya, 1993) 145.

Vallejo Sánchez, J.I., *et al.*, 'Factorías de salazones en la Bahía Gaditana: economía y organización espacial' in *XXIV Congreso Nacional de Arqueología* (Instituto de Patrimonio Histórico, 1999) 107-14.

Vicente, J.D. *et al.*, 'Las inscripciones de la 'Casa de LIKINE' (Caminreal, Teruel)' in J. Untermann and F. Villar, *Lengua y Cultura en la Hispania Prerromana. Actas del V Coloquio sobre lenguas y culturas prerromanas de la Península Ibérica* (Universidad de Salamanca, 1993) 747-2.

Vidal, M. and J.-P. Magnol, 'Les inscriptions peintes en caractères ibériques de Vieille-Toulouse' in *Revue Archéologique de Narbonnaise* 16 (1983) 1-28.

Vilà i Bota, M. del V., 'Àmfora amb inscripció llatina i grafit ibèric' in *Pyrenae* 27 (1996) 295-9.

Villa Valdés, A., *El Castro de Chao Samartín* (Sociedad Arqueológica Profesional, 2005).

Villanueva Acuña, M., 'Problemas de la implantación agraria romana y la organización del territorio en la Península Ibérica en el Alto Imperio' in *Espacio, Tiempo y Forma* ser. 2, 4 (1991) 319-50.

Villaseca Díaz, F., 'El conjunto arqueologico romano "entorno del Castillo de la Duquesa" Manilva-Malaga (1987-1989)' in *Anuario Arqueologico de Andalucía* III, 1989 (1991) 365-70.

———, 'El yacimiento romano "Finca del Secretario" (Fuengirola-Málaga): avance al estudio de su producción anfórica' in *Figlinae Malacitanae. La producción de cerámica romana en los territorios malacitanos* (Universidad de Málaga, 1997) 261-9.

Wagner, C.G. and J. Alvar, 'Fenicios en occidente: la colonización agrícola' in *Rivista di Studi Fenici* 17 (1989) 61-102.

West, L.C., *Imperial Roman Spain: Objects of Trade* (Blackwell, 1929).

Whittaker, C.R., 'The Western Phoenicians: colonisation and assimilation' in *Proceedings of the Cambridge Philological Society* 10 (1974) 58-79.

———, 'Trade and the aristocracy in the Roman Empire' in *Opus: International Journal for Social and Economic History of Antiquity* 4 (1985) 49-75.

Williams, C.K., 'Corinth, 1978: Forum Southwest' in *Hesperia* 48 (1979) 105-44.

Williams, D.F., 'Roman amphorae' in S. Cracknell and C. Mahany (eds), *Roman Alcester: Southern Extramural Area. 1964-1966 Excavations, Part 2: Finds and Discussion* (CBA Research Report 97, 1994) 120-3.

Wiseman, T.P., *New Men in the Roman Senate 139 BC-AD 14* (Oxford University Press, 1971).

Woods, D.E., F. Collantes de Terán y Delorme and C. Fernández-Chicarro y de Dios, *Carteia* (Excavaciones Arqueologicas en España 58, 1967).

Zevi, F., 'Appunti sulle anfore Romane: I. La tavola tipologia del Dressel' in *Archaeologia Classica* 18 (1966) 208-47.

Ziderman, I.I., 'Seashells and ancient purple dyeing' in *Biblical Archaeologist* 53 (1990) 98-101.

———, 'Purple dyeing in the Mediterranean world: characterisation of Biblical tekhelet' in L. Cleland, K. Stears and G. Davies (eds), *Colour in the Ancient Mediterranean World* (BAR Int. Ser. 1267, 2004) 40-5.

Zucca, R., 'Rinvenimenti archeologici sottomarini prezzo il ΚΟΡΑΚΩΔΗΣ' in *VI Congreso internacional de arqueologia submarina* (Museo y Centro Nacionales de Investigaciones Arqueológicas Submarinas, 1985) 149-51.

Glossary

ager publicus: public land or land owned by the Roman state.
ala: a recess or corridor to the rear of the atrium.
alabastron: a jar used to carry ointment or perfume.
amurca: a watery fluid expelled from the olive during pressing.
annona: the supply of corn and other foodstuffs to the city of Rome, instituted by Augustus; **annona militaris**: the supply of corn and other foodstuffs to the Roman army; **annona municipalis**: the supply of corn and other foodstuffs to local towns.
aryballos: a small spherical flask with a narrow neck.
atrium: the first room to the rear of the entrance in a Roman-style townhouse.
campiña: area of cultivated land or countryside.
capitolium: the principal temple in the Forum of a Roman town, modelled on the Temple of Jupiter, Juno and Minerva on the Capitoline hill in Rome.
castra: a fortified military encampment.
castro: a hill-fort.
catillus: the upper rotating component of a Roman millstone. The catillus is a biconical funnel that rotates on a fixed conical meta (q.v.) crushing the grain between the two.
cella vinaria: wine cellar.
cetaria: a vat for storing or processing fish.
cognomen: a Roman surname.
colonia: a Roman town or colony.
columbarium: either a dovecote containing niches for the birds, or a sepulchre containing niches for funerary urns.
contubernium: a group of eight Roman soldiers who would share the same tent.
decumanus: a street running east-west through a Roman town.
defrutum: a drink made of grape juice that has been boiled to form a syrup.
diffusor: a bottler.
domus: a Roman-style house.
dromos: a forecourt.
dua nomina: the first two names (the praenomen and nomen) of the full Roman tria nomina.
duovir: the two annually elected senior magistrates in a Roman town.
duovir quinquennalis: as the above; however, every fifth year the two magistrates were responsible for drawing up a census of the population. The position of duovir quinquennalis was considered a more honourable office than that of duovir.
emporion: a market.
fibula: a pin, clasp or brooch.
figlina: a workshop.
flamen: a priest devoted to a particular deity.
frigidarium: the cold room in a Roman bath complex.
fumarium: a smoke-room in which wine was stored to mature.
fundus: a country estate.
garum: a salted fish product, similar to hallec, muria and liquamen.
garum sociorum: lit. 'Garum of the Allies', a salted fish product manufactured in Cartagena.

gens: family.
horreum: granary.
imbrex: a semi-cylindrical tile that covers the join between roof-tiles.
impluvium: a square water basin in the centre of an atrium.
iugerum: a unit of land approximately two-thirds of an acre in size.
kalathos: a bowl shaped like a basket.
kantharos: a Greek wine-cup characterised by high handles.
kotyle: a Greek wine-cup similar to a skyphos (q.v.).
krater: a ceramic vase used to mix water and wine.
latifundia: a large estate, normally associated with slave labour.
lymphatum: wine diluted with water.
macellum: a market place.
magister pagi: a magistrate responsible for the administration of a pagus: a small area of land.
mansio: an inn or roadside lodging.
mercator: merchant or trader.
meta: the cone-shaped base of a mill. Surmounted by a catillus (q.v.).
modius: a unit of measurement of 16 sextarii.
mola: a mill or millstone.
munera publica: public shows.
municipium: a self-governing town.
navicularius: a ship-owner.
negotians salsarius: a salted fish trader.
negotiator: a trader or business-man.
oecus: an apartment attached to a house.
oinochoe: a Greek wine jug with a globular body.
olpe: an early form of oinochoe.
oppidum: a town, usually fortified hill-top location.
opus barbaricum: type of construction consisting of pebbles.
opus caementicum: a form of concrete consisting of lime, sand, water and volcanic debris or pozzolana.
opus incertum: type of construction consisting of irregularly placed stones bonded with opus caementicum.
opus scutulatum: consists of larger stones placed randomly into opus incertum.
opus signinum: a form of waterproof pavement consisting of terracotta, gravel and stone bonded with limestone or clay.
opus spicatum: type of construction consisting of bricks laid in a herringbone pattern.
opus tessellatum: type of construction consisting of stones laid out in horizontal lines.
pars fructuaria: the part of a villa used to house agricultural implements, labourers etc.
pars rustica: the part of a villa devoted to the processing of agricultural produce.
pars urbana: the part of a villa used to house the owner or bailiff of the farm.
piscina: a fishpond.
pithos: a large ceramic storage jar.
pondus: a weight.
praefurnium: the entrance to an oven or furnace.
quattuorvir: one of the four chief magistrates of a municipium (q.v.).
restitutor metallorum: lit. 'restorer of the mines'.
sapa: boiled wine.
sevir: member of a board of six. The sevir augustalis was responsible for maintaining the cult of Rome and Augustus.
skyphos: a Greek two-handled wine-cup.
societas: an association or partnership.

tablinum: a room to the rear of the atrium used as the owner's study.
tegula: a roof tile.
terra sigillata: high quality tableware pottery produced principally in Gaul from the first to the third centuries AD.
terra sigillata italica: terra sigillata produced at Arezzo in Italy during the reign of Augustus; also known as Arretine ware.
tessera: a small square block.
tholos: a circular building with a domed or bee hive shaped roof.
titulus: an inscription or inscribed object.
titulus pictus: a painted inscription.
torcularium: a wine or olive press.
trapetum: a rotary mill used to press olives.
tria nomina: the three names of a Roman citizen: the praenomen, nomen and cognomen.
tuyère: a tube or nozzle used to blow air into a furnace.
thymiaterion: a censer or incense burner.
unguentarion: a ceramic or glass bottle for ointment or perfume.
ustrinum: a place used for the cremation of bodies.
vicus: a village or group of dwellings.
vilicus: an overseer responsible for running a farm or estate.

Index

Page numbers in bold indicate illustrations.